Counseling Unmarried Couples

A Guide to Effective Legal Representation

FREDERICK HERTZ

Counseling Unmarried Couples

A Guide to Effective Legal Representation

AMERICAN BAR ASSOCIATION
**Defending Liberty
Pursuing Justice**

Cover design by Elmarie Jara/ABA Publishing.

Printed in the United States of America.
15 14 13 12 11 5 4 3 2 1

Library of Congress Cataloging-in-Publication Data

Hertz, Frederick.
   Counseling unmarried couples : a guide to effective legal representation / by Frederick Hertz.
— 1st ed.
      p. cm.
   Includes bibliographical references and index.
   ISBN 978-1-61438-119-8
1. Unmarried couples--Legal status, laws, etc.--United States. I. Title.
   KF538.H47 2011
   346.7301'6--dc23

                                                        2011037751

FOREWORD

In 1971 I joined my former Legal Aid colleague Ed Sherman in writing and publishing self-help law books under the name Nolo Press. Operating from the kitchen table of a brown shingle house in what can best be described as a hippie enclave in Berkeley, Ed and I handled divorces, bankruptcies, and consumer cases to pay the bills. Fortunately, Nolo's prospects improved when sales of Ed's *How to Do Your Own Divorce in California* took off after the president of the Sacramento County Bar Association called a press conference to warn the citizens of California against using this dangerous book.

The success of the divorce book convinced me that there was a ripe market for self-help law materials. So, along with Toni Ihara and others, I immediately got to work on writing and publishing books on tenants' rights, bill payers' rights, how to change your name, and other consumer topics.

By late 1973 Nolo began getting calls asking if we had any materials to help unmarried couples deal with property concerns. Typically, a worried couple was concerned about buying a house or had questions about rights and responsibilities where one partner was working to put the other through graduate school. And then there were the unmarried partners who planned to have a baby without first taking a walk down the aisle but didn't want their child to be labeled "illegitimate." Knowing almost nothing about the law that applied to these situations (or the lack thereof), I helped couples draft co-ownership agreements similar to those that any business partners would create.

Word spread and more couples called. One was a young mother (I'll call her Lynn) who had just gotten a divorce. Lynn had bought a tumbledown Victorian in Berkeley; and, providentially, before the city got around to condemning the building, Lynn met and fell in love with Mike, an itinerant Australian carpenter. Soon Mike decided to move in, apply for U.S. citizenship, and fix up Lynn's house. All was good for a few weeks until Mike asked Lynn, "Who owns what here? Or, more to the point, what happens if I spend a year or two rehabbing your house, and then we separate?"

Since neither Mike nor Lynn had a clue how to answer these questions, the work stopped and the relationship faced a crisis. My job was to help with the legal part, accomplished after much talk by drafting an ownership agreement linked to a logbook, where Mike would record his out-of-pocket costs for materials and his labor at an agreed-upon hourly rate. Since Lynn had recently bought the house and its value was known, it was easy to draft a co-ownership agreement that provided for Mike's ownership share to gradually grow based on the value of his contributions until he and Lynn were fifty-fifty owners.

But it wasn't just couples calling Nolo that convinced me that a book for unmarried couples was needed. Northern California in the early 1970s exemplified the near-tectonic shift in American social attitudes toward marriage, with the result that hundreds of thousands of couples nationally were choosing to cohabit rather than visit the altar. So in late 1973, I asked Carmen Massey, a former Legal Aid colleague and friend, to coauthor a legal guide for unmarried couples. Our first step was to research state law as it applied to the legal rights of unmarried couples. What we learned was sobering: Most state courts had ruled that contracts between unmarried partners were unenforceable. Since living together itself was in violation of state criminal law against cohabitation, most courts reasoned that any contracts formed between unmarried partners must also be illegal. At this point, I remember Carmen asking, "Do we really want to do a book full of agreements courts may not enforce because they view the people making them to be living in sin?"

It was a great question, and the best reply I could come up with was this: "Just in the Bay Area alone, tens of thousands of unmarried couples are living together. And it's happening all over the country. The counterculture is changing the social reality, and courts will have to recognize it." Carmen asked, "You mean we should do a book about where we think the law is going to be in a few years, not where it is now? I'm still not so sure it's such a great idea to show people how to write what may turn out to be bogus contracts." I replied, "We will be doing much more than that, I hope. After all, isn't the point of written agreements to allow people of good faith to remember what they said during happy times and thus have a framework to avoid going to court if they break up unhappily?" Carmen agreed, "Sure. So I'm okay with going ahead as long as we include full disclosure that some courts may not enforce agreements between unmarried partners. But, hey, if we are going out on a thin legal limb, let's also include agreements for gay and lesbian couples." I concurred, "Good point. If we are going to write an illegal law book, no sense in holding back."

And so Carmen and I made an outline, assigned chapters, and began to write. As lawyers and recent law students, we were used to the routine and sometimes boring task of trying to dovetail yesterday's legal rule with today's fact situation. But here we realized that we were doing the opposite: creating legal structures to help deal with a fast-emerging social issue. We became so excited and energized that we completed *Sex, Living Together, and the Law* in record time. It was published by Nolo in 1974 and sold well, especially in bookstores in college towns.

But then in 1976, two events overtook our success. First, the California Supreme Court decided *Marvin v. Marvin*, a case brought by the movie actor Lee Marvin's former live-in partner of six years, Michelle Triola, in an attempt to enforce what she claimed was a promise of long-term support in case of a breakup. In a huge legal sea change that ratified the approach Carmen and I had taken, the court ruled that, like anyone else, unmarried partners could form contracts as long as they were not based on meretricious (illegal) sexual services. The second—and for me more devastating—event was that Carmen Massey died. Carmen had been a fine lawyer, a caring person, and a great friend; and I was too devastated to face working on our book, even though the *Marvin* decision obviously demanded a major rewrite.

In the next few years, as the number of unmarried couples choosing to live together continued to increase rapidly, so, too, did the demand for legal information on the rights and responsibilities of unmarried partners. A number of states began issuing their own, often somewhat varying, versions of the *Marvin* case and were also following California's lead in decriminalizing the private sexual acts of consenting adults; and *Sex, Living Together, and the Law* had become dangerously out-of-date. To cope with this legal sea change, I recruited my own living-together partner, attorney Toni Ihara, to coauthor an entirely new legal guide for cohabiting couples called *The Living Together Kit*.

When the *Marvin* case went back to trial (Michelle lost), Toni and I were teaching seminars and promoting *The Living Together Kit*, advocating that unmarried couples prepare agreements whenever shared property, a promise to provide support, or children were involved. We cautioned that even couples who planned to keep everything separate would be wise to record their understanding to avoid a battle like that of Lee and Michelle. From *Today Show* to *The Phil Donahue Show* to *Merv Griffin* to morning shows nationwide, we repeatedly preached this message of "better safe than sorry." All of this was worthy and fun, but before long the calls and letters we received from distressed couples suggested that we were at least partially missing the point.

The problem was, of course, that for every couple who took our advice and planned in advance, many others did not. And for them, the *Marvin* case, with its recognition that almost any kind of contract could be legal, was as much a trap as it was a blessing. Instead of the pre-*Marvin* world where unmarried couples operated in a legal limbo in which courts were unlikely to recognize their agreements, now they could try to prove that pillow talk constituted an enforceable oral contract or that the day-to-day circumstances of the relationship implied an agreement to share ownership of a property. And even if an oral or implied contract couldn't be proved, one partner might still claim that the other had unfairly benefited financially, for example, where one partner worked to put the other through school only to have the graduate run off with her professor.

Unfortunately, in many states, almost any fact situation could now give rise to a lawsuit, some no more than attempts at court-sanctioned extortion. Even worse, trial judges with little experience in this arena were often prejudiced against unmarried partners, especially same-sex ones, and made widely divergent and unpredictable decisions. If there ever was a legal lottery, this was it. Against this background, Toni and I were increasingly asked for help, typically by well-meaning people who were trying to separate with dignity, not engage in the legal version of the shoot-out at the O.K. Corral. Unfortunately for our callers, neither of us at this point practiced law or had significant experience counseling couples in personal and legal distress.

Enter Frederick Hertz, a Bay Area lawyer who has built a unique practice counseling unmarried couples, both gay and straight. Fred not only understands the fast-evolving law as it applies to both straight and gay couples, he sees that the psychological issues faced by the members of separating couples are sometimes even more important than the legal ones. Put another way, Fred believes that whether in forming a contract at the beginning of a relationship or helping a couple craft a fair and litigation-free separation agreement, a counselor should first help partners understand and cope with their feelings.

And since Fred could also write in plain English, he joined Toni and me in 1998 as a coauthor of *The Living Together Kit*, adding a much-needed chapter entitled "When Unmarried Couples Separate." He also became a crucial part of the Nolo team as coauthor of our *A Legal Guide for Lesbian and Gay Couples*; more recently, Fred and Emily Doskow authored *Making It Legal: A Guide to Same-Sex Marriage, Domestic Partnerships & Civil Unions*, a book I highly recommend. What Fred brought to Nolo—which he expands on brilliantly here in *Counseling Unmarried Partners: A Guide to Effective Legal Representation*—is the conviction that while knowledge of the complex body of law that applies to unmarried couples of any sexual orientation is essential for anyone practicing in this area, it is rarely enough. Even where the law is clear (and in many areas, such as the taxation of same-sex couples, it still isn't), providing effective legal counsel requires meeting that person's psychological needs. And this is doubly true when, as is so common, the lawyer is advising both members of the separating couple, meaning that the only good solution is one that both parties embrace.

As Fred points out, people choose to live together for all sorts of reasons, some practical and straightforward, as might be the case when two young professionals move in together for a mutually agreed-upon trial marriage. But other living-together arrangements are, of course, far more problematic from the start, as when an older, financially powerful partner all but imposes the terms of the relationship on a less sophisticated younger partner, who, in some instances, is not even fluent in English. And of course, between these extremes lies a huge menu of other living-together scenarios, varying between opposite-sex couples who are free to marry at any stage but may or may not be covered by applicable domestic partner laws, and same-sex couples who, while sometimes covered by domestic partner statutes, are not free to marry in most states.

I particularly admire that Fred takes the time to illustrate the attorney's very different role when couples are forming a relationship and when they are dissolving a relationship. In the first instance, the lawyer can serve clients best by preaching caution and common sense to dampen unreasonable enthusiasm. But when a couple separates and one, at least, is emotionally overwrought, the practitioner's challenge is to know how to toss a blanket of calmness on the volatile situation long enough to help the couple embrace a cooperative process of dispute resolution.

The genius of this wise and upbeat book is that Fred not only explains the surprisingly complex legal and tax issues involved in living-together arrangements, but by using numerous real-life examples he also ably teaches readers how to include a psychological dimension in their practice. This is exciting stuff, even soul-stirring. For the benefit of all of us and our clients, Fred seeks to empower us to be healers, not just advocates.

Ralph "Jake" Warner
Berkeley, CA

CONTENTS

INTRODUCTION

I filed my first nonmarital cohabitation lawsuit in 1988. My client was a nerdy technical consultant in his mid-forties who had co-owned a lovely old bungalow in Berkeley with his live-in girlfriend for more than a decade. Their respective financial contributions to the purchase of their house and pooled savings were far from equal; and now that they were breaking up, he wanted to divvy up the equity and money in a way that he thought was entirely fair. Not surprisingly, he sought to allocate everything in proportion to their respective financial contributions (as his were the greater by far) and disregard the equal ownership presumption of their joint tenancy deed and bank account title.

My second nonmarital client was a vibrant silver-haired older lady who had lived with her high-earning boyfriend (if you can really call a seventy-five-year-old man a "boy") for most of the twenty years of his lucrative late-in-life career. She had dutifully stood by his side, helping him build and sustain his success as a consultant and traveling with him regularly to meetings and conferences. She considered the bounty of his career equally hers even though they had remained unmarried and despite the fact that his earnings were always deposited into his investment account, not theirs.

One insight that became patently clear to me from the very outset of both of these cases was that I was not practicing family law. The pleadings were filed in the civil division of the local superior court, and none of the family law rules establishing a presumed sharing of post-marital assets applied. Shortly after I delved into the substance of each of these disputes, I learned a second fundamental truth of representing unmarried cohabitants: The legal doctrines that apply to these claims were not just vague and ill-defined; they had little connection to how my clients had lived their lives. These folks had nothing in writing to support any of their alleged agreements, and trying to squeeze decades

1

of inconsistent and loosely remembered personal histories into a legal framework built around a doctrine of implied and oral agreements was a nigh impossible task.

Presenting their arguments in equitable terms seemed equally implausible. The equitable doctrines would force me to recast the breakup into a battle over the righteousness of the claim, and thinking that I could win such a fight was as illusory as winning at the game of who was really at fault for the breakup. Of course, I always believed that my client was the righteous one, but I also knew that the relationship was never so one-sided, and so I could never be entirely sure that the judge (or jury) would be on our side. I knew that winning these cases would not be easy since meeting the clear and convincing standards necessary to overcome the presumptions of a joint tenancy deed (which would strongly have imposed a fifty-fifty split in my first case) and the equally powerful presumptions of the bank account (which would lead to everything being owned by the boyfriend in my second case) was not a simple task.

So, too, I had to navigate around the uncertainty as to whether or not these relationships would be considered confidential and fiduciary in nature and how those characterizations affected the burdens of proof in each case. And if my client's partner in the second case had already started his business before they met and she had never been formally employed in and never had made a financial investment in his business, would her claim for a share of his savings fail for lack of consideration?

Eventually I discerned that there were very few clear answers in the disputed matters that I handled over the course of the next twenty years. Not that I didn't try to find them: I dutifully compiled a list of the published California appellate cases that dealt with unmarried co-owners of real property (as of last count, there are fifty-eight such cases, going back to 1890), and I mastered the key holdings of each of these cases. But as I continued to litigate these conflicts, I was continuously astounded at the unpredictability of the outcomes. Most of them settled eventually, but my ability to settle them (even the arguably weak ones) seemed to happen more because of the good faith of an ex-partner or a desire to avoid legal fees and risks as opposed to any doctrinal analysis. I watched as claims that I was sure would prevail sank into defeat under the questioning of an unsympathetic judge, and I tried to delve beneath the surface of the legal doctrines to discern the underlying justifications for each of the outcomes, but rarely did they make a great deal of sense.

Helping meet the immediate legal needs of happy couples certainly was easier than coping with the broken partnerships, but co-ownership and cohabitation agreements for straight couples were often shadowed by the uncertainties of what would happen if they subsequently married, which is what a great many of them did (usually without checking back with me or considering how their new marital status affected the validity of their prior nonmarital agreement). The politics of gay marriage and the resentments over the denial of access to marriage cast my drafting of agreements for my gay clients into a social context that was often strained and frustrating to all. The tax treatment of unmarried couples of either sexual orientation continually led to great uncertainty, especially for high-asset couples; and in the end (and to my growing angst), most of my clients preferred to ignore the tax laws, hoping that they would never be audited.

Even greater uncertainties emerged in the past decade as domestic partnership and equivalent registries became increasingly available. I believe fervently that much of the change is for the good, but the plethora of alternatives was mind-boggling to my clients (and to most attorneys). Some of the new options applied to same-sex couples only and others to straight couples as well, and in some states there were minimum age thresholds for the straight couples. At first it was unclear if these schemes provided many substantive benefits to the registrants or were a mere symbolic government "blessing" of the relationship. Did it matter if my clients registered, and, if so, in what ways? In San Francisco, couples could choose a local government registration that extended local employer-based benefits and city-based taxes (such as real estate transfer taxes), while same-sex couples (and older straight couples) also could elect to register with the state, which only offered limited benefits until 2005, when it became a marriage-equivalent registration. And it wasn't just my clients who had trouble figuring all this stuff out; title companies, lenders, and probate judges were equally confused.

Eventually I was able to sort through these quagmires and make sense of the interlocking appellate doctrines; statutory presumptions; and details of state, local, and private registries. Obtaining certainty regarding the tax ramifications of cohabitation remained elusive, but soon I had sufficient understanding in this arena to be able to guide my clients through the complex and amorphous stages of their romantic and domestic lives.

But all of this confusion is somewhat beside the point. What matters more is that millions of opposite-sex and same-sex couples in this country fall in love; live together; have children; and eventually part ways, either voluntarily or upon the eventual death of one of the partners. And so, despite all of the legal unknowns, over the course of the past twenty years, I have counseled many hundreds of such couples; drafted a great many cohabitation and co-ownership agreements; and advised, represented, or mediated in several hundred such breakups.

Apparently I am not alone in doing this work, and in recognition of these growing demands, the purpose of this book is to equip you to serve the legal needs of this growing segment of society.[1] My goal is to share with you the broad base of legal knowledge I have gleaned over the years and provide the guidance you will need to become the counselor at law that your clients deserve. Sharing the details of the contractual law of your particular state with your clients or knowing how to draft a trust that anticipates the tax consequences for your clients remaining unmarried "until death do they part" are very important tasks, but they are not sufficient. Beyond summing up the legal rules and writing competent agreements, you also will be called upon to integrate and interpret the legal rules for your clients in a realistic, comprehensible, and meaningful manner. Only by doing so can you effectively guide your clients in making wise decisions about their homes, their children, and their assets.

Counseling unmarried partners is not always simple, and you, too, will experience the pangs of "family law envy" that I often felt when I contrasted the messy rules of cohabitation with the comprehensive codes that apply to married couples. Trust me, though: It is a highly satisfying and stimulating area of practice. If you take the time to learn the law and attune your practice to meet the complicated needs of your clients, I am confident that both you and your clients will be well rewarded.

NOTES

1. Nearly 40 percent of those responding to a recent study by the American Academy of Matrimonial Lawyers noted an increase in the demand for nonmarital cohabitation agreements. www.aaml.org/sites/default/files/Associated%20Press-2-14-2011.pdf.

CHAPTER ONE

UNDERSTANDING THE BROADER LEGAL HISTORY AND SOCIAL CONTEXT

"If it feels good, it's probably illegal."

Section heading in *Sex, Living Together and the Law* (Nolo Press 1974)

A. THE RELEVANT HISTORY OF COHABITATION AND ITS LEGAL TREATMENT

The Criminalization of Cohabitation

Even if you have little interest in the social history of family relationships, knowing the basics of cohabitation history is crucial to an effective representation of unmarried couples, as it will enable you and your clients to understand why the rules regulating their legal lives have ended up as they have and thus will help you counsel your clients more wisely. But it's not just about being a better attorney. With so many headlines focused on the evolving legal rights of lesbian and gay couples and the growing angst about the straight divorce rate, it can be fascinating to delve into the past a bit and witness how unmarried couples—whether opposite-sex or same-sex—have fared in earlier times, and why.[1]

Despite the well-publicized quest of this nation's founders to escape religious intolerance, it turns out that colonial legislatures in the mid-1700s were quite eager to impose one particular aspect of religious harmony in their drive to root out social immorality. Adultery (defined as sexual activity between a married person and someone not his or her legal spouse) and fornication (i.e., sex between two unmarried persons) were both criminalized in the pre-Revolutionary colonies as early as 1692, and apparently these laws were quite regularly enforced.[2] Nearly two-thirds of the criminal prosecutions in Massachusetts in the late 1700s involved violations of these laws: How can anyone forget that the "letter" in *The Scarlet Letter* stood for adultery? While the exact language of each colony's (and, later, each state's) laws differed to some degree and the penalties for violations varied widely, both the occasional nonmarital sexual encounter (sometimes referred to as lewd and lascivious conduct) as well as the longer-term version of such immorality (openly living together in the absence of a legal marriage, aka cohabitation) were prohibited throughout the United States.

The prevalence and the harshness of these rules were no accident. Standards of decency were seen as the proper domain of the legislatures and courts, and a blatant violation of a virtuous social order was viewed as detrimental to the morals of the community. There was no notion of a private life, and the manner in which citizens conducted their intimate affairs was seen as affecting the "public morality" of the entire community. Granted, the frequency of prosecutions of these violations diminished over the subsequent decades; but for a very long time, living in sin continued to be seen as a social and legal wrong with broad societal ramifications and thus not worthy of any legal or social ratification or approval. This is not just a matter of ancient history: Social attitudes do not change quickly, and even the 1955 draft of the Model Penal Code included a criminal prohibition on cohabitation—something that did not change until 1962.[3]

Surprising as it may seem nowadays, as of 1970, more than forty states in this country still imposed criminal penalties for one or more of these moral offenses. Adultery was the most popular prohibition still on the books (in twenty-five states), with cohabitation (in twenty-one states) and fornication (in seventeen states) not far behind. Three states were even more refined in their statutes: They specifically criminalized adulterous cohabitation with more severe penalties because one of the partners was still married to someone else. Even though few of the misbehaving couples were prosecuted, research studies from those decades indicate that the illegality of these relationships was used against the participants in seemingly unrelated actions (welfare claims, neighbor disputes, or adjudication of one partner's divorce or custody disputes), both for same-sex and opposite-sex couples. And it's undeniable that the illegality of the relationship was invoked as a justification for denying any contractual rights or public benefits to those whom society had piously labeled as sinners.

The tide of social change finally began to turn in the mid-1970s, but it was not a steady and consistent march to sexual liberation—at least not in the legal arena. Punitive treatment of so-called illegitimate children was ruled unconstitutional by the U.S. Supreme Court in the late 1960s and early 1970s,[4] and the constitutional right to privacy with regard to sexual conduct slowly began to emerge as worthy of legal protection even in the U.S. Supreme Court. However, the early cases only extended that freedom to married couples (for example, the *Griswold v. Connecticut*[5] case involving birth control), while the criminalization of consensual homosexual conduct was upheld on moral grounds by the Court in the *Bowers v. Hardwick* case of 1986.[6]

For straight couples, the path toward social liberalization happened more smoothly in the decades following the 1960s. Consensual sexual activity was decriminalized in California in 1975 and soon thereafter elsewhere across the country, and zoning prohibitions on nonmarital cohabitation were eventually toppled in many states by the early 1980s.[7] But even today marital status still is not uniformly recognized as a protected class, and so it remains legally unclear whether or not the right to religious freedom can be used to justify discrimination against unmarried couples.

But times have definitely changed. The loosening of community standards—and eventually the recognition of that trend even by the more conservative legal establishment—has shifted the social ground dramatically in the past thirty years. Whereas in 1978 nonmarital cohabitation remained criminal in sixteen states and fornication remained illegal in fifteen states, only seven states still had cohabitation prohibition statutes on their books in 2009 (Idaho, Illinois, Massachusetts, Minnesota, South Carolina, Utah, and West Virginia). However, it is most likely that none of these criminal laws is still valid, based upon the Court's

Even though more than thirty-five years have elapsed since the California Supreme Court ruled that contracts between unmarried partners could not be voided on the grounds of the meretricious nature of these relationships, moral issues still play a role in the drama of cohabitation disputes. Fear of discrimination may lead some couples to conceal their relationships in ways that can create legal problems down the road. In many instances, a conservative judge may focus on the economically dependent woman's "choice" to remain unmarried in viewing her legal vulnerability as a righteous punishment for her disavowal of the traditional marriage arrangement. For gay couples who have failed to sign a cohabitation agreement (or now, in some states, declined to state register or marry), the messiness of their legal situation may well be seen as fair treatment for their election to "live on the margins." Legal justifications are likely to be framed more in terms of a claimant not meeting his burden of proof, but the underlying sentiment (perhaps even unconscious on the part of the judge) may well be moral disapproval.

ruling in its 2003 *Lawrence v. Texas* decision.[8] The court ruled there that a state law criminalizing consensual homosexual conduct violated the individual's liberty interest to engage in sexual acts within the privacy of his own home, regardless of any perceived moral judgment by the state legislature. So far, no one has bothered to bring a constitutional challenge in the remaining states that have laws that seek to penalize cohabitation by consenting heterosexual adults. It's safe to say that those laws are generally considered irrelevant nowadays, and thus those statutes would face the same fate as those used to prosecute Mr. Lawrence in the *Lawrence* case.

It's safe to conclude after decades of controversy that living in sin is no longer a criminal act. So, wherever in the country you practice, you can freely choose to specialize in counseling unmarried couples.

The Contradictory History of Common Law Marriage

In the European medieval era, and in many societies worldwide, marriage has not always been such a well-organized or institutionally supervised event as it is nowadays; in fact, marital status was a rather fluid concept. In Protestant and Catholic countries, religious ceremonies were available for those who wished to participate in them, but civil marriage as a legal status was mostly reserved for the propertied classes.

Historians of marriage describe informal marriage as socially recognized cohabitation by a heterosexual couple that lives as if married and is treated as such by the partners' families and the community. Others have described it as "a legal institution that gives the legal effects of formal marriage to qualified couples who, without formally having entered into marriage, are in agreement and live together under marriage-like conditions."[9] The system has its origins in old English ecclesiastical law and medieval canon law, which, in turn, were both influenced by Roman law—so it's a long-honored tradition.

By the late Middle Ages, European churches launched a campaign to stamp out informal marriage, perhaps hoping to gain more of a monopoly on the grant of marital privileges as part of a larger campaign to expand the church's influence on secular society. As early as 1215, the Catholic establishment's Fourth Council of the Lateran began requiring a public wedding ceremony preceded by some form of public notice. At the same time, the civil institutions (justice courts especially) were concerned about the increasing number of parentage and inheritance disputes tied to uncertainties about couples' marital status. As a result of these intertwined trends, most Roman Catholic countries stopped recognizing informal marriages in 1563, and England abolished them in 1753. Indeed, the law at that time imposed fourteen years of service on the royal estates as punishment for a violation of these rules.

The frontier attitudes and social informalities of the United States in subsequent decades led to a different approach, even in such civilized locales as New York State. Legal traditions inherited from the Spanish and Mexican societies reinforced that trend, and, as a result, more than half of the states in the newly organized United States allowed some form of common law marriage in the early nineteenth century. Thus, while the cohabitation and the presumed sexual activity that accompanied the couple's domestic life remained illegal, a straight couple who acted as if married (and thus did not flaunt its immorality) would be treated as married under the eyes of the law. Odd as it seems from a contemporary perspective, the transgressive couple's cohabitation would not be seen as immoral or criminal but, rather, could magically be cleansed by treating the couple as if legally married.

The U.S. Supreme Court upheld state laws that allowed for common law marriages;[10] however, in most areas of the country, these doctrines were not destined to be long-lasting. A push toward a more systematic framework of marital status soon emerged; and over the course of the late nineteenth and early twentieth centuries, the tide began to turn. Twenty-three states abolished common law marriage in the half-century after 1875, citing fears of immorality, legal confusion, and a preoccupation with supposedly frivolous claims made by dissolute girlfriends against their upstanding paramours. Soon thereafter, the growing federalization of society and the resulting need for standardization of marital status—especially when it came to bestowing public benefits such as Social Security or a military widow's pensions—furthered this trend. Moreover, as an increasing number of cohabiting couples no longer saw the social need to maintain any pretense of a marriage, the underlying "holding out" premise of common law marriage became increasingly inapplicable, even in states that recognized common law marriages.

Still, common law marriage persists as a valid legal status in the District of Columbia and eleven states (Alabama, Colorado, Iowa, Kansas, Montana, New Hampshire (for inheritance purposes only), Oklahoma, Rhode Island, South Carolina, Texas, and Utah). The specific definition differs from state to state, but *Black's Law Dictionary* says that common law marriage requires "a positive mutual agreement, permanent and exclusive of all others, to enter into a marriage relationship, [with] cohabitation necessary to warrant a fulfillment of necessary relationship of man and wife, and an assumption of marital duties and obligations."[11] Each state has its own standards; most require cohabitation, but the specific state rules for the other requirements (a monogamous sexual relationship, express versus implied agreements, standards for "holding out" as married, etc.) vary widely.[12] In each of these states, a cohabitant can petition the court to be treated as a married spouse, though this typically occurs only upon dissolution or the death of a partner.

If the jurisdiction's standards are met, the couple is deemed legally married, retroactive to the commencement of cohabitation. In certain instances (such as a probate or personal injury claim), a court first declares that the couple was effectively married under the common law rules of that state and then will extend marital benefits to that couple. On the whole, however, the focus is on the protection of the more vulnerable party; for example, providing intestate or spousal support benefits to a financially dependent wife-equivalent.

If a couple previously met the standards of their former state of residence, a court in another state can declare the couple legally married even if the residency was very short—though it is rare that another state will extend its reach to grant such privileges.[13] And, contrary to the popular misperception, there is no minimum duration of cohabitation, except in New Hampshire, which requires three years of cohabitation.[14] An increasingly small universe of couples has been declared married under common law marriage rules, so lawyers practicing in these states should make sure that their clients are aware of this possibility. Interestingly, so far, none of the states that allow common law marriage has extended that concept to cover same-sex couples; but from a doctrinal perspective, there's no reason that should not eventually occur.

The Evolution of Contract-Based Doctrines

The shift to a contractual approach (as opposed to a status-based system of de facto or common law marriage) was clearly evident by the early 1970s. Nolo Press' 1974 self-help book for unmarried couples (originally titled *Sex, Living Together, and the Law*) was illustrative of that shift: It included a section called "If it feels good, it's probably illegal," and it offered practical tips and sample agreements for co-owning everything from furniture to a house as well as providing basic terms for sharing financial obligations. While a few state courts tossed out contractual claims between unmarried partners as meretricious, most others looked to historic precedents upholding financial and property-based

In the 1974 edition of *Sex, Living Together, and the Law*—still in print with a more restrained title, *Living Together: A Legal Guide for Unmarried Couples*—the outsider status of unmarried cohabitants is quite pronounced. Ten pages are devoted to a detailed chart setting forth each state's criminal penalties for fornication, adultery, and/or cohabitation; an entire chapter is devoted to the problems that cohabitation can cause with regard to a partner's prior divorce or child custody arrangements. The chapter on breaking up is rather short, and the only legal precedent cited to help a dependent partner is the 1973 California case of *In re* Marriage of Cary, 34 Cal. App. 3d 345 (1973). Interestingly, the *Cary* case (which extended marital rights to an unmarried couple as a judicially imposed common law marriage remedy) was overruled by the California Supreme Court just a few years later in the *Marvin* v. *Marvin* decision.

agreements between friends and cohabitants, as long as they focused on a particular asset or property and were not based upon sexual services.

The pre-*Marvin* reasoning behind the legal recognition of property claims was rather straightforward, grounded in well-accepted common law doctrines. While title always imposes a presumption of sole ownership in the name of the titled owner, that presumption could be rebutted by proof of an agreement to the contrary. However, there were two daunting hurdles that needed to be overcome: First, was there any valid consideration for the alleged agreement? Second, had the standard of proof required of the off-title claimant been met?

The consideration challenge in many of the early cases was that sexual services could not serve as consideration, and, moreover, promises of gifts typically were unenforceable. Thus, only where the nonowner had made a significant financial contribution in excess of the free housing usually received, which was considered a benefit conferred on the claimant, could a claim succeed. The doors of the courthouse were not impenetrably locked to unmarried partners, but there were not many victories in the early decades.

The standards of proof varied from state to state. California courts had early on determined that it would not be fair to impose the statute of frauds on claimants who lived in a family-like relationship or where the claimant could prove a confidential or fiduciary relationship.[15] Other states allowed property claims to go forward based upon a good-faith contributor argument or even an adverse possession basis. But still, even in California and in most other states, clear and convincing evidence was required to establish a claim, severely limiting the number of successes. With very few exceptions, claims could not be made for post-separation support in the absence of a legal marriage, and rarely would such claims ever be effective in a probate context.

The turning point in the evolution of the legal treatment of cohabitants was the California Supreme Court's ruling in *Marvin* in 1976. Actor Lee Marvin's girlfriend had changed her surname to his (resulting in decades of confusion amongst law students asking why an unmarried couple's dispute involved people of the same last name); and when they broke up, she sued to enforce an alleged promise by Lee to pay post-separation support. She lost at trial, but on appeal the state supreme court issued a sweeping ruling that opened wide the state court's door for claims by unmarried cohabitants.[16] Rejecting any approach based upon common law or de facto marriage, the California justices winnowed down any concerns for the immoral (meretricious) nature of the relationship.[17] They ruled that any cohabitant could make a claim based upon alleged contractual agreements (based upon an express written or oral agreement or even implied-in-fact or implied-in-law contracts) and even for post-separation support as long as sexual services were not the consideration. Opening the gates even wider, the justices declared that a cohabitant could present *any* equitable claim that was fair and reasonable given the overall circumstances of the relationship. Claims could be based upon constructive trust or resulting trust arguments (based upon an oral promise or monetary contributions), quantum meruit (for work done to improve the value of a partner's assets), or any other general principles of equity.

The notoriety of the case and the broad influence of the California court set the tone for the legal doctrine across the country, and the *Marvin* approach soon became the new norm for unmarried couples when it came to financial and property disputes. Only three states (Minnesota, New Jersey, and Texas) subsequently required that claims be based upon written agreements (by statute); and only three states (Illinois, Georgia, and Louisiana) barred all contract or equitable claims by cohabitants—and even there, claims can be made if they clearly relate to business or property agreements.[18] All other states have effectively adopted the

The Washington State approach is the most creative, and many legal commentators and scholars contend that it is the fairest. Rather than searching for a contract that rarely exists or imposing all the rules of marriage unequivocally on cohabitants in the form of common law marriage, marital rules have been deemed the most appropriate guideline for resolving disputes between unmarried regarding equitable adjudication. As such, the rules will only be applied if the court determines that the relationship meets the standards for a marriage-like relationship and can be disregarded if there was an oral or implied agreement to the contrary. But the power balance definitely shifts to the nontitled or economically dependent partner, as it is the financially dominant partner who has the burden to convince the court not to apply marital law. A similar approach was taken in 2002 by the American Law Institute (ALI) in *Principles of the Law of Family Dissolution: Analysis and Recommendations*.[19]

The term "domestic partnership" first appeared in a 1976 law review article coauthored by Jay Folberg, then a law school professor in Oregon, entitled "Domestic Partnership: A Proposal for Dividing the Property of Unmarried Families" in 12:3 Willamette Law Journal (1976). The article, focusing on the rights of straight unmarried cohabitants, used the term in an effort to avoid the outmoded legal theories based upon "concepts of fault and sin, resulting in inequities when the families dissolve."

Tom Brougham and Barry Warren used the same term (without any knowledge of the Folberg article) as part of a policy initiative in their efforts to obtain benefits for same-sex couples from their employers in Berkeley, California, in 1980. The term was chosen to focus on the domestic aspect of the partnership rather than its sexual connotations, echoing the partnership concepts as enunciated in the recently issued *Marvin* decision. They proposed an affidavit with criteria constituting a "domestic partnership" that included most features of marriage minus the opposite-sex requirement, plus an assertion of mutual financial support congruent with the *Marvin* decision. While initially set up only for a particular employer's use, the concept was later adopted by local governments, allowing the registration to be relied upon by a wide range of employers and insurers, and still later by states.

Marvin rules, except Washington State, which follows a de facto marriage approach that allows cohabitants to make claims based upon a presumption that marital law should apply to cohabitants—rebuttable unless the responding party establishes that the presumption should not apply.[20]

In each of these settings, however, the contractual basis of the legal approach only extends relief in disputes between the cohabitants, with little if any effect on the rights of third parties (such as creditors, government agencies, or other relatives) or access to any government benefits. Except for a very few limited instances (e.g., workers' compensation claims by an economically dependent partner or tort liability in narrowly defined circumstances), unmarried couples remain legal strangers and thus are ineligible to receive any of the government benefits available to married spouses.

The Emergence of Marriage Alternatives

The domestic partnership movement was born in the early 1980s, fueled primarily by a political struggle led by lesbian and gay activists seeking to construct some kind of marriage-equivalent form of relationship recognition. In sharp contrast to the later efforts to extend traditional marriage to include same-sex couples, the early strategy was to demand as many of the rights and benefits of marriage as possible through local and private registrations. This avoided the more conservative state legislatures and the courts and allowed a progressive local jurisdiction (or even a private employer) to bestow a small bundle of rights on its own residents or employees.

The initial push was for health insurance coverage for partners of public and private employees, which later was expanded to include hospital visitation rights. It's no surprise that these were the early goals given the specter of AIDS that hovered over the gay community. Over the course of the next twenty-five years, a growing number of rights and benefits were included in many such registries, but until 2000 none of the registries extended any of the fundamental marital rights and obligations to registrants.

It was only when gay advocates successfully pressed their constitutional claims for access to *all* of the rights of marriage that state legislatures voted to provide marriage-equivalent registrations as a compromise that avoided opening the marital doors to same-sex couples. The Vermont Civil Union registration, enacted under order of the Vermont Supreme Court, modeled its legislation on the *pacte civil de solidarité* (PACS) that had recently been enacted in France, which extended all of the state-granted marital benefits to state-registered civil union partners as a marriage-equivalent registration. Similar marriage-equivalent

One of the most surprising developments in the emergence of these marriage-alternative systems is the prevalence of straight registrants in the French PACS registry. PACS registration bestows most of the desired benefits of marriage (a reduced schedule of post-separation asset sharing, significant tax benefits, limited inheritance benefits, and, most importantly, access to employer-based benefits such as vacation schedules for both partners for the same weeks) without the notoriously complicated property rules and burdensome inheritance limitations and drawn-out divorce procedures that apply to married couples in France. If recent trends continue, more straight couples may be registering with PACS than getting married in France, with the original primary intended beneficiaries of the law (same-sex couples) making up less than 10 percent of the registrants.

registries are now in effect in six states, some open to all couples and others limited to same-sex partners. And over the course of the past thirty years, county and local registries offering limited local benefits and employer-based programs have been established in hundreds of locales.

While the political engine behind these registries was fueled initially by gay activists, many of the resulting registries have been open to opposite-sex couples from the outset.[21] For some, it was a matter of political expediency (i.e., not appearing to be favoring lesbians or gay men and not being vulnerable to a legal claim of discrimination based upon sexual orientation). For others, there was a genuine desire to

In a further discussion of the subtler policy dimensions of the contract versus status debate, Grace Blumberg artfully summarizes the "welfare function" of traditional marriage (i.e., "redistributing" wealth from the higher earner to the lower earner, especially upon death or dissolution).[22] As one of the chief authors of the ALI report mentioned earlier, Blumberg argues that a failure to marry should not be understood to signify that the parties agreed that they should not have any economic obligations to each other. Moreover, even if that was the intent of one of the parties, that does not mean that the law should "side with" that party. Rather, Blumberg's position is that once a couple enters into a marriage-like relationship that is long-lasting and economically intertwined, and especially when the partners are co-parenting children, it is fair for the law to protect the dependent partner from dislocation due to death or dissolution. In other words, there should be a presumptive right to family law–type benefits and obligations, rebutted only when there is evidence of an agreement to the contrary.

Blumberg suggests that the free market tendencies and the emphasis on individual self-determination push the law in a contrary direction, where unmarried partners lack benefits unless they can prove an implied or oral agreement. She also points out that our broader disdain for any sort of welfare state type of prescribed caretaking contributes to this legal approach, weakening any legal doctrine that would impose a duty of financial redistribution to the needier partner.

For those who are not legally able to marry (such as same-sex couples), it certainly cannot be said that their nonmarital status reflects a willful rejection of marital rights and obligations. But is this really true for opposite-sex couples who have consciously chosen to remain unmarried?

provide an alternative to full-scale marriage for straight couples who wished to obtain some of the key benefits but did not wish to sign up for the full panoply of marital obligations. Currently, straight couples in the registries of Washington, DC, and Nevada and older straight couples in California, Washington State, and New Jersey are entitled to the same domestic partnership benefits as same-sex couples there.

Implications for the Legal Practitioner

What does this history mean for the practitioner? A great deal. It explains the basis of the most fundamental factor that defines the non-marital law practice, which is that nonmarital legal rules operate very differently than the doctrines of family law. Family law is a world in which obligations are imposed by law as a matter of legal status regardless of the intent or assent of either party, whereas cohabitation (in the absence of domestic partnership or civil union registration) rarely extends rights to or imposes duties on either partner—or offers any third-party recognition—in the absence of contractual agreement. With few exceptions, partners are "legal strangers" without the right to any property or access to any benefits, intestacy protections, or recognition as a couple by governments or private institutions. Except in those few states that recognize common law marriages or in Washington State, obligations between the partners generally can only be created by private agreement (implied or express), and most third-party benefits can only be obtained by a specific registration with a third-party institution.

This is why counseling unmarried couples requires an emphasis on the intentions and the actions of the parties in ways that rarely arise for family law attorneys. The lawyer meeting with an unmarried partner (or couple) must explain to the client(s) the absence of status-based recognition in the pertinent jurisdiction and then structure an agreement. This is no easy task. Inherent in the nature of romantic relationships is a belief, usually unstated, that mutual generosity and affection will result in good-faith reciprocity. Given these assumptions, asking a partner to put it in writing doesn't just feel uncomfortable—it can seem antithetical to the core values of the relationship.

Lawyers working in this field soon come to understand how inappropriate the emphasis on contracts appears to clients, despite all the

THE BASIC LEGAL FRAMEWORK
FOR UNMARRIED COUPLES

Unmarried couples now have a wide range of options from which to choose depending on their sexual orientation and the state in which they live. Here is a list of the basic array of available choices, on a spectrum from the least protective to the most inclusive. [See Appendix for a detailed chart of states' rights.]

NOTE: This list does not include employer-based registration programs that may be offered to same-sex or opposite-sex couples or both, usually based upon an employer-created declaration of cohabitation; and it does not include city or county registrations, which generally provide limited benefits either as registrations that a local employer can rely upon to grant private benefits to government employees or, in a few instances, as exemptions from local taxes (especially real estate transfer taxes). This list also does not include states that allow for common law marriages or recognize those formed in other states.

No Contractual or Status-Based Rights

Some states offer no registration-based benefits and do not honor private contracts between cohabitants, unless they are clearly business- or property-based.

No Status-Based Rights and Only Limited Contractual Claims Allowed

Some states do not offer any registration as cohabitants but honor express contracts (in some instances, written only; in some, oral as well).

No Status-Based Rights but Broad Contractual Claims Available

Some states do not offer any registration for cohabitants but honor express and implied contractual claims, with varying thresholds for proving such claims.

Contractual Claims Available and Limited Status-Based Rights

Some states have registration systems that provide a narrow range of benefits, both private and public, but do not provide full marriage equivalence to registrants; some include both opposite-sex and same-sex couples, but others are limited to same-sex couples or only allow older straight couples to register.

Allowance of Contractual Claims and Marriage-Equivalent Status-Based Rights

Some states have registration systems that provide a full range of benefits, both private and public, including full marriage equivalence for registrants; some include both opposite-sex and same-sex couples, but some are limited to same-sex couples or only allow older straight couples to register.

Atypical Combinations of Rights and Benefits

Some states offer some rights and benefits, either status-based (Illinois) without honoring contract claims or presumptive status-based without requiring registration (Washington State).

well-intentioned encouragement from the legal community. Indeed, as so well stated in a seminal article on the *Marvin* case, basing a legal doctrine on a contractual approach to romantic relationships is no less than a "fatal flaw" in the applicable legal rules.[23] Family lawyers face many of these same challenges when drafting a prenup, but most couples simply sign on to the state-imposed rules of marriage in a moment of legally unconscious marital bliss; and for married couples, there is an established legal framework that sets parameters on what their agreement must address. The world in which most unmarried couples live is far more nebulous, both socially and legally, but it is the foundation onto which lawyers working in this area must build their practices.

B. The Demographics of Contemporary Nonmarital Cohabitation

At first glance, the dramatic increase in the population of cohabiting couples conveys the impression that the demand for legal services in this arena should likewise be soaring. Yet, while the demand for experts working in this field has indeed increased significantly in the past thirty years, it is important for practitioners to be cognizant of the demographics of this growing segment of our population, as not every cohabiting partner is a potential client for such legal services.

It is not at all easy to find agreement on the extent of the unmarried population in this country. Some surveys indicate that as many as fifty million American adults are living in unmarried relationships, with a variety of family configurations.[24] The most recently available U.S. Census data estimates that approximately fifteen million adults are living with an unmarried partner in the United States, which constitutes just under 10 percent of the adult population. About 20 percent of these couples are in same-sex relationships, though it is hard to be precise about these estimates given the range of legal options available to same-sex couples from state to state and the absence of clear data on married or married-equivalent couples until recently. Some of these same-sex couples, perhaps between one-third and one-half, will eventually marry or enter into a marriage-equivalent registration in states that offer or recognize marriages or equivalent partnerships for lesbians and gay men. Further complicating the demographic estimates, unmarried cohabitation is the only Census data available to same-sex couples who live in nonrecognition states (except for those who travel outside of their home state to make a political statement), even though many of those couples may, in fact, be married.

More than half of the estimated fourteen million unmarried straight couples are under age thirty. Most observers believe that the majority of these couples will either break up relatively early or subsequently marry, and so their nonmarital cohabitation is unlikely to give rise to any substantive asset, property, estate, and benefits issues that require legal assistance. Reinforcing this dynamic, a large percentage of the cohabiting couples of all ages are of lower income than the national norm. The most recent research studies indicate that marriage is increasingly seen as a reward for financial stability rather than a path toward such success, and, as a result, a growing number of low-income and minority couples are deferring marriage.[25]

Most such couples have very simple legal needs. For some, it will be an apartment-sharing agreement or a short consultation with regard to a debt recovery action or qualification for some kind of public benefit. Questions arise regarding shared credit card liability, qualifications for a student loan or other public benefit, or difficulty evicting an ex-lover.

A large percentage (40 percent) of cohabiting couples of all income levels, but especially those of lower income, are raising children in their households.[26] Some of these are the biological children of both cohabitants, but a great many couples are raising children born of a prior relationship of one or both of the partners. These couples are likely to need advice regarding parentage rules and occasional help with a paternity or child support action.

The segment with the greatest importance to lawyers is the higher-asset, long-term couples who make up around one-third to one-half of the straight couples and a somewhat higher percentage of the gay couples.[27] These are the older, economically solvent couples who are choosing to remain unmarried as an alternative to marriage and not as a prelude or who are legally unable to marry or register as a same-sex couple. They are the partners who are more likely to own their homes, co-parent children over an extended time, have jobs with benefits they want to share with their partner, and have estates large enough to warrant planning or probating.

Most of the legal issues facing these couples are similar regardless of their sexual orientation. Contracts need to be drafted, wills or trusts prepared, and benefits and debt liability issues analyzed and dealt with as part of the couples' financial planning. There may be striking political and cultural differences between straight and gay couples, and straight couples have the option of getting married and having their marriages recognized nationally and federally, but the primary tasks for the legal adviser are not substantively different.

In their excellent book on the practical and social aspects of cohabitation titled *Unmarried to Each Other* (Marlow & Co. 2002), Dorian Solot and Marshall Miller identify six basic types of cohabitants: instant, accidental, escapist, evolving, situational, and deliberate. They also chart out the wide range of arrangements between unmarried partners, from "mergers and acquisitions" to "never would've predicted" to the long-term group, those "still not married" after ten years or longer! Knowing where the bulk of your clients sit on this continuum will help you design your approach to meeting their legal needs.

C. Developing Underlying Skills for Effective Client Counseling

Providing competent legal counsel to unmarried couples is not simple as it mandates a diverse assortment of legal knowledge as well as an enlightened understanding of who these folks are and why they have chosen to remain unmarried. You need to know whether theirs is a path that has been foisted upon them, as is the case for same-sex couples in nearly forty states, or if they made this election voluntarily. And if they decided to remain unmarried, what are their reasons? Is this truly the decision of both partners, or is one partner deferring to the other's demands? It's not that every lawyer working in this field must become a marriage and family therapist and interrogate his clients for hours on end with regard to their deeper issues of commitment. Rather, it's a matter of knowing the basic goals and concerns of the clients in order to provide effective counseling.

One anecdote tells it all. Some time ago, I met with a successful mid-fifties civil engineer who had recently emerged from a nasty divorce. He was dating a wonderful woman, a successful marketing executive. They were considering living together, and he was seriously considering asking her to buy a 50 percent interest in the valuable Berkeley house he had recently acquired in his divorce. In part the house buy-in was motivated by a mutual desire to share a residence as equal owners, but my client also was concerned about the debt he had taken on to buy out his ex-wife's interest. I met with this man and his girlfriend to discuss their marital and nonmarital options, and they both expressed a strong preference to "keep their lives simple" and not get married. But a few weeks later, the engineer asked me to review the tax consequences if his girlfriend were to buy a 50 percent interest in his house. I explained to him how much the city and county transfer taxes would be as well as the increase in property taxes they would both be paying and the capital gains taxes he would owe on the sale of the partial interest to his girlfriend, and then I said that all of this could be avoided if they simply got married. His candid response said it all: "Please don't tell my girlfriend about the tax savings of the marital option!" His honest comment revealed to me that there were deeper issues beneath their previously stated mutual election to remain unmarried and made me wonder what my ethical duties were to his girlfriend.

Knowing the *why* behind a couple's decision to remain unmarried is vital. I recently consulted with a woman whose boyfriend was adamant about not signing up for the marriage rules, in terms of both sexual monogamy and financial obligations. She had adopted his point of view because it was also in sync with her basic values, although she seemed unrealistic about the risks she was facing as the lower-earning partner. But before I could advise her, I had to understand the reasons for their decision to remain unmarried. Likewise, when I met with a woman in her early eighties who was newly cohabiting with her younger boyfriend (of age seventy-five), it was crucial that I understood her discomfort around this new form of relationship she had entered into so that I could hear her real reasons (loyalty to her children and a perception by them that a remarriage would be disrespectful to their father) for what was, for her, a very unconventional living situation.

So, too, for gay clients. Lawyers must acknowledge the political and social prejudices that prevent these clients to marry in most states in order to be compassionate to their situation and strategic in their counseling. The clients' legal complexities generally do not arise out of their own decisions but rather because of the bias of others, and that is a vitally important difference. If a straight couple is remaining unmarried just for a short time until a career or business opportunity is fully realized, they will have unique needs and will approach the core issues from a particular angle. Their behavior differs sharply from the needs of the couple that objects to marriage out of social principles or is legally precluded from marriage.

The contract-based focus in nonmarital law also mandates a different way of organizing a legal practice. Palimony cases in many jurisdictions are frequently taken on a contingency basis, something that is unheard of (and generally prohibited) in family law dissolutions. The emphasis on implied and oral agreements mandates a more nuanced approach to the intake interview than may be the case for a marital dissolution, given the need to assess testimony and credibility in valuing the claim of an implied agreement. It's not just a matter of compiling a list of assets; the lawyer needs to hear the full story to know how to advise the client. This is equally true in estate planning situations where the cohabitation status is seen by the clients as temporary, because it can be difficult for them to appreciate the need for an expensive living trust when they believe that a marriage in the near future will resolve any intestacy concerns.

For some attorneys there may also be latent issues of morality, social conventions, and personal styles that get in the way of effective representation. As broad-minded as I think I am, it took some mind expansion on my part when I was called in to advise two members of a bisexual alternative sexuality household, led by a dominant master and consisting of a cluster of subordinate lovers, ex-lovers, siblings, and friends. My legal assignment was rather routine: I was asked to help them sort out a messy co-ownership dispute with a few title inconsistencies and a standard dispute regarding unequal contributions. But feeling at ease with the clients, and making sure they felt okay working with me, took a deeper kind of understanding than any legal treatise could have provided. The same goes for the client with atypical gender behaviors: Clients need to know that their lawyers are there to help them with their legal quandaries, and they need to feel assured that their lawyers are not judging them for who they are or for the situation they have found themselves in.

Bear in mind that for most of your clients, you may well be the only lawyer they meet with, and so you also need to have a breadth of knowledge that to some degree extends beyond the expertise of the particular representation. You may be asked to draft a will for an unmarried partner, but chances are that she will also ask you how to take title to the house she is buying with her boyfriend. You may be called when her insurance company tells her that she and her partner each need to buy their own umbrella coverage policy, and you may be asked how to fill out a credit card application in connection with their shared mortgage loan. While it is wholly appropriate for you to establish a well-defined specialty and limit your substantive work to that area, some basic knowledge of the surrounding legal issues is essential. A necessary aspect of that knowledge, of course, is knowing the limits of your expertise; and that is why it is also essential that you assemble a list of qualified tax advisers, insurance agents, trusts and estates attorneys, and other professionals who can provide the expertise that lies outside of your primary legal terrain.

There is one additional requirement for effective counseling of unmarried partners: an ability to provide useful counsel in an environment of legal and emotional uncertainty for clients who may be utterly confused about their own legal status. Even in California, where there is perhaps more law in this arena than anywhere else, there are great expanses of uncertainty, and explaining this to your clients will never be routine. Neither the state nor the federal tax authorities have determined whether or not post-separation support payments are taxable, for example, and there are no clear rules for reimbursement of a down payment on a house purchased when the couple was unmarried and then subsequently marry. Add to the legal uncertainties the unavoidable personal uncertainties of such clients, and lawyers are plying their craft in a very murky sea.

Nonetheless, clients want to be helped now, not when the law is finally resolved or when they know with more certainty how they want to structure their lives. Relationships often are amorphous and subject to rapid change and financial crises, and parentage opportunities can arise in the most inopportune moments. As a result, it's not just legal knowledge that lawyers need to have handy in order to serve these clients; there is an equal demand for emotional and interpersonal flexibility and sensitivity.

D. Developing a Market for Your Specialty

Even in the larger urban areas that have a greater population of unmarried couples, it is unrealistic to build an entire practice solely around the representation of unmarried couples, even if you include both gay and straight couples. Most of my professional colleagues have done as I have, which is to maintain a diverse practice that features this field but is not exclusively targeted at unmarried couples. I have always maintained a general real estate practice handling purchase and sale and financing transactions, neighbor boundary disputes, and property management questions, with an emphasis on handling real estate disputes between unmarried partners.

Other attorneys combine a nonmarital practice with a more traditional family law practice, which is an approach that serves clients well, especially in states where parentage and other aspects of unmarried couples law are handled by the family courts. For others, handling all varieties of estate planning and probate work with a special emphasis on nonmarital estate planning, especially the complex tax problems of high-net-worth unmarried partners, can be a lucrative approach. Nonmarital law is best seen as an emphasis or a specialization integrated into a broader range of work that is compatible with this focus and recognizable in the marketplace as such.

One of the most frustrating challenges of taking up unmarried couples as an area of legal specialization (or as one of several areas of concentration) is that it is not recognized as a specialty, not even in the San Francisco Bay Area, where these types of cases are especially prevalent. Family law attorneys frequently are unfamiliar with nonmarital law, and they are not always open to including in their professional networks someone who lacks a long-standing connection to traditional marriage and divorce law. Real estate attorneys occasionally take on a partition dispute between unmarried couples, but often they are uncomfortable with the strained emotions of what turns out to be more like an ugly divorce; and general civil litigators may have a disdain toward what they see as the family law orientation of your practice as opposed to their more commercial priorities. The lawyers who serve the lesbian and gay community are likely to have their own

An enterprising pair of lawyers (one of them gay and two straight) opened up a "boutique" firm in San Francisco for unmarried couples, both gay and straight. After a few years, they each moved on to other businesses, but they learned a lot along the way about marketing in this arena. They discovered that there was no single marketing strategy that worked: it was awkward figuring out what terms to use to describe their clientele, especially during a time when same-sex couples were winning marriage rights, and there was no one place to go to market their services to straight unmarried couples. They also learned that the reasons that straight folks remain unmarried are different than those of same-sex couples, and the legal needs also differ. The main strategy that one of the lawyers advocated was reaching out to other professionals who are likely to intersect with couples when they are in the midst of a major life change: real estate agents, mortgage brokers, accountants, and even mainstream estate planners. These are the folks who will understand the need for legal consultation and will be able to steer potential clients to the lawyers best suited for their nonmarital status.

professional organization and community networks, but these are not always the best place for someone who is primarily serving unmarried straight couples. The end result is that there is no well-defined professional niche into which you can fit.

Identifying and reaching out to potential clients is not easy. Unmarried couples rarely self-identify as a distinct culture or community, and they may be surprised to learn that most family law attorneys can't answer their legal questions. Even when they have made contact with you, it is hard to explain to a client with a custody dispute that he needs to hire a separate non-family law attorney to deal with the fight over the family residence. These are the challenges you need to consider when you set up your practice and when you market it. You will want to think through how best to label your cohabitation practice and how to talk about it to other attorneys, perhaps settling on a tag line that summarizes what you do (e.g., nontraditional family law or cohabitation law). In other words, you will need to brand your practice in a user-friendly way and then look to that branding to draft your brochure and your website.

Part of the marketing challenge is that many of the clients, as well as the folks they talk to about their business and financial lives, don't realize they need specialized legal help. Some time ago, I represented a guy who had put down $400,000 on a house he bought with his girlfriend, relying on his mom's assurance that since they weren't married, he didn't need a premarital agreement. In fact, in California he had a weak argument for recouping his investment when they broke up since they took title as joint tenants (which presumes a fifty-fifty ownership); had they been married, this would clearly have been a reimbursable separate property investment. So, instead of spending $1,500 on a simple co-ownership agreement, he ended up spending nearly $30,000 litigating the dispute with his girlfriend and settling for far less than the $400,000 he had invested in the property. Real estate agents, ministers, moms, best friends, and even other lawyers often fail to spot the legal issues and thus fail to make the referrals that will feed the practice of lawyers specializing in unmarried couples.

Given all of these complications, a central facet of your marketing campaign must be educational—that is, teaching your clients and other professionals about the legal needs that you can meet and explaining why they need your assistance. This is especially true for those who believe—often erroneously—that they will soon be getting married or—even more troubling—those with a false belief that after living together for seven years, they are common law spouses. Until your potential clients understand that they need written agreements, powers of attorney, and wills, they won't be drawn to use your services no matter how well you market yourself. Having a website that includes basic educational materials about the legal landscape for unmarried couples in your jurisdiction is extremely beneficial, as it signals that you know your stuff and care about educating your clients as well. Family law attorneys handling traditional divorces don't need to take on these educational tasks, as their clients usually know when they need to hire an attorney.

The other big challenge is figuring out where to target your marketing. My strategy has been to market to key gatekeeper professionals (especially other lawyers), relying on them to steer clients to me when they get an inquiry from an unmarried partner. Unlike a narrowly targeted marketing effort that is focused on gay clients, for example, I found that targeting the straight unmarried crowd directly is too difficult given how diffuse and diverse the population is. My professionals-oriented marketing approach instead relies on educational talks that I present to real estate agents (knowing that they intersect with those who are buying or selling homes), estate planning lawyers (since they won't be handling the property agreements that I write for clients), and family law attorneys (since most of them are reluctant to take on the civil court cases brought by unmarried partners). I write articles, I write books for the public as well as for lawyers, and I present seminars (all of which are offered for free since these are part of my marketing efforts) to any group that offers me the opportunity.

You also will need to be strategic about how you use the Internet and the expanding number of available social networking tools in spreading the word about your practice. It is always useful to be listed in directories published by your local bar association, though most likely they don't have a section for cohabitation or unmarried partners law. Try to be included in both the family law and real estate sections of the listings, even though neither of those categories really is accurate. You should be explicit in stating whether or not you are open to working with same-sex couples as well as straight ones, and you will want to be specific about the sorts of matters you handle (e.g., parentage, dissolution, estate planning, or real estate work only). Make sure you send the right message about your approach to these legal needs. A Facebook page that might work for marketing your services to young unmarried straight folks is not likely to be effective when it comes to reaching older couples who need estate planning.

Building a website for your practice will be essential, and you need to be strategic about how you approach this task. Consider maintaining two websites, one for your general legal practice and another one just for your same-sex legal practice; they can link to each other so nothing is hidden from anyone, but this system allows clients to focus on the topics that are of most importance to them. Be careful about the terms you use in describing your work, perhaps doing some test marketing with couples of various stripes to see how they react to the labels and terms you choose. If you include visual images on your site, make sure the photos are representative of the diversity of couples you wish to serve.

There are two additional marketing strategies that should always be considered: (1) no-cost "counseling" on an informal basis to other professionals; and (2) getting involved with nonprofit legal and social groups, which will put your name in front of potential clients. Each of these approaches has its risks, but they can offer bountiful benefits as well.

Counseling does not mean legal advice; that is something you should only provide to clients. Informational counseling takes many forms: responding to a call from a title officer asking you to explain how an excess down payment is treated for a joint tenancy purchase; engaging in a conversation with a nurse about an older unmarried patient who has children from a prior marriage and a new love interest who doesn't like her kids; or even having a discussion with a local judge about the latest rulings for same-sex domestic partners. The key benefit of these conversations is that you aren't just getting your name out there; you are demonstrating your expertise.

Marketing through involvement with organizations can be particularly complicated, mainly because of the intersecting personal and community agendas. While your primary purpose for joining any civic organization—be it your religious institution, a local bar association section, or political campaign—should be to help that group, you can also leverage your participation in a way that successfully markets your professional skills. Doing community work is a way for others to meet you, learn about what you do, and develop a loyalty and professional connection that can be incredibly valuable as long as you keep your personal goals in perspective and don't overuse the social and community setting for your own personal gain.

Consider the following possibilities:

- Serve on a committee of the local family law, real estate, or trusts and estates section of the bar association; your fellow board members will get to know you, hear about what you do, and add you to their referral network lists.
- Volunteer for a young parents' school committee or neighborhood community social action group, where you will meet young couples (many of whom are unmarried), and they (and their friends) will learn about your area of concentration.
- Join an effort to lobby your city council to provide health insurance or other benefits for unmarried city employees, both straight and gay, where you can show your expertise about the complex benefits and tax rules for unmarried couples.
- Volunteer as an attorney for a local advocacy group or for the local bar association's pro bono panel, so that the staff and board of that group learn about you and develop a loyalty and appreciation for your volunteer activities.

E. A FEW WORDS ABOUT WORDS

It's hard to develop a legal specialization focused on a segment of the population that doesn't have a defined label. What do lawyers counseling unmarried partners call their clients? *Domestic partner* was a socially acceptable term for years, but now that state registration can mean that marital law applies (in California and elsewhere) and the term has so many different meanings in other jurisdictions, the term should perhaps be reserved for those who are state-registered. *Lover* is definitely out of fashion—too informal, too sexual, and too provocative for most folks. *Partner* sometimes works, though in some settings it only creates more confusion (especially around lawyers, who always think that the word refers to someone's law or business partner). *Cohabitant* sounds overly technical and in some contexts can refer to married couples living together, and *fiancé* can be misleading since, legally speaking, the prospect of a future marriage really isn't relevant. *Unmarried partner* has its own drawbacks as it defines the couple in terms of what it is not (i.e., married) as opposed to who the partners are, and acronyms don't feel sufficiently dignified (POSSLQ was the term coined by the Census

Bureau in the 1970s to refer to "persons of opposite sex sharing living quarters," and it didn't catch on, for good reasons). *Nontraditional family law* is often used to refer to both unmarried straight and same-sex partners and their children. Solot and Miller's book lists no less than forty possible labels for an unmarried partner, including *life partner* (sounds like a prison sentence), *mate* (sounds too casual), and *significant other* (way too technical). My favorite term, used by a law firm in San Francisco, is *family law for the twenty-first century.*

My suggestion? Don't feel boxed in to using just one term, but instead use a combination of words and phrases that will resonate with your clients. You can use *cohabitants, co-owners, unmarried partners,* or *nontraditional families* as the context demands. I tend to describe my work as "helping unmarried couples, both gay and straight" (even though many of my gay clients now are married). For this book, I use *unmarried partner* to refer to the individual in a nonmarital relationship and *unmarried couple* to refer to the two of them; from time to time, I refer to the individuals as *cohabitants* where their "living together" status is the most significant aspect of their relationship. I reserve the term *domestic partner* or *civil union partner* for those who are registered under a statewide system that provides some degree of marital benefits to the couple, simply because that is a reminder that marital rules need to be considered when talking about or helping such a couple.

NOTES

1. The magisterial history of "informal" or common law marriage by Goran Lind, Common Law Marriage (Oxford Univ. Press 2010), covers more than 2,000 years of legal history, from Roman times to the present, and includes more than 2,500 citations to legal cases in the United States alone.
2. See, for example, the discussion of the issue in Colonial Williamsburg: http://www.history.org/foundation/journal/spring03/branks.cfm.
3. *See* Cynthia Bowman, Unmarried Couples, Law, and Social Policy (Oxford Univ. Press 2010) (comprehensive social history of cohabitation).
4. Levy v. Louisiana, 391 U.S. 68 (1968); Weber v. Aetna Cas. & Sur. Co., 406 U.S. 164 (1972).
5. 381 U.S. 479 (1965).
6. 478 U.S. 186 (1986).
7. *See, e.g.,* City of Santa Barbara v. Adamson, 27 Cal. 3d 123 (1980).
8. 539 U.S. 558 (2003).
9. Lind, *supra* note 1, at 7.

10. Meister v. Moore, 96 U.S. 76 (1877).

11. Black's Law Dictionary 277 (6th ed. 1990).

12. The best summary is set forth in Lind, *supra* note 1, at 387, 508.

13. Generally speaking, it is the law of the state where the common law marriage allegedly took place that rules, even if the couple's subsequent state of residence does not allow common law marriages to be formed in that state. *See* Lind, *supra* note 1, at 644, 732 (list of detailed state-by-state requirements).

14. N.H. Rev. Stat. Ann. § 457:39.

15. Estrada v. Garcia, 132 Cal. App. 2d 545 (1955).

16. 8 Cal. 3d 660 (1976).

17. Various scholars argued for a marriage-equivalent approach, where a court would have equitable jurisdiction to divide assets acquired during the domestic partnership in the same way that marital assets are divided upon dissolution or death, but this approach was rejected by the court.

18. The appellate history in Illinois has been especially convoluted. The court's decision in Hewitt v. Hewitt, 394 N.E.2d 1204 (Ill. 1979), effectively precluded any legal claims based upon a nonmarital cohabitation; however, subsequent cases have carved out numerous exceptions to this restrictive rule, finding equitable grounds or businesslike contracts that can be enforced legally. *See, e.g.,* Spafford v. Coats, 455 N.E.2d 241 (Ill. App. Ct. 1983).

19. *See also* Grace Blumberg, *Cohabitation Without Marriage: A Different Perspective,* 6 UCLA L. Rev. 28 (1981). Blumberg, who helped draft the American Law Institute (ALI) recommendations, argues that cohabiting couples should be treated as if legally married after two years of cohabitation or if they co-parent a child, in effect reinstating common law marriage but with a set durational requirement.

20. *In re* Pennington, 142 Wash. 2d 592 (2000) (using the term *meretricious* to describe the quasi-marital relationship). In Washington State, the family law matters are heard in the same court as the civil actions, and there is no right to a jury trial for equitable claims; thus, the nonmarital claims for couples who subsequently married can usually be consolidated.

21. The California history is especially interesting. Including straight couples was seen as politically advantageous to some, making the legislation less of a "gay rights" bill; but to others, this was viewed as undermining the primacy of marriage. Reference was often made to the Social Security concerns of older straight couples, but other than those obtaining a marital divorce in order to avoid the combined family limits on total payments, very few straight couples ever achieved any real benefits from state registration.

22. Grace Blumberg, *The Regularization of Nonmarital Cohabitation: Rights and Responsibilities in the American Welfare State,* Notre Dame L. Rev., Oct. 2001, at 1265.

23. Ira Mark Ellman, *Contract Thinking Was Marvin's Fatal Flaw,* Notre Dame L. Rev., Oct. 2001, at 1365. As Ellman points out, contracts are built upon formal negotiations, explicit quid pro quo exchanges, and

stated conditions of exchange—all of which are at odds with the faith, trust, and optimism inherent in romantic relationships.

24. U.S. Census Bureau, "America's Families and Living Arrangements: 2007."

25. ANDREW CHERLIN, THE MARRIAGE-GO-ROUND: THE STATE OF MARRIAGE AND THE FAMILY IN AMERICA TODAY (Knopf 2009).

26. Cherlin, op. cit.

27. Cherlin, op. cit.

CHAPTER TWO

THE FUNDAMENTALS OF REPRESENTING UNMARRIED PARTNERS

A. ESTABLISHING THE SCOPE OF THE REPRESENTATION

The complexity of nonmarital law and the widespread lack of awareness of the intricacies of nonmarital relationships result in some difficult choices when it comes to defining the scope of your representation. Frequently, your phone will ring with a caller asking a narrow question such as how to take title when buying a house with a partner, and it is hard to ascertain how best to respond. Do you simply provide a summary of legal information at no cost, or should you insist that the buyer come in and engage in a discussion on all of the issues of palimony and cohabitation claims? Is there something you can offer in between these extremes?

The absence of legal formalities at both ends (formation and dissolution) of nonmarital relationships further compounds the representation difficulties. For someone who is getting married in a few months and is considering a premarital agreement, there is a defined timeline, both socially and legally, and a well-recognized series of tasks: reviewing marital law presumptions and determining whether an agreement is appropriate and, if so, drafting the agreement and getting it signed. The couple and their friends (and their concerned relatives) know about this process, and they will provide the nagging reminders of what needs to be done. By contrast, two people who have been living together for several years, aren't planning to get married, and already own a house (but without any co-ownership or cohabitation agreement) are not likely to have such a clear timeline. This lack of a set agenda is true, too, regarding parentage questions, which often arise only in connection with a particular problem (e.g., getting a passport) and not on any defined timeline. Requests for assistance arrive in seemingly random fashion: A client may call asking how to handle a credit card debt arising out of charging her boyfriend's car repair on her credit card and then casually mention to you that she is pregnant in the context of a volatile relationship with the boyfriend, with whom she isn't living.

Handling the threshold tasks of establishing your representation calls for the integration of several intertwining concerns:

- What information is needed and what tasks must be undertaken in order for you to answer the presenting question?
- What are the broader consequences that are likely to flow, for better or worse, from the decisions made by the client with regard to the specific action contemplated by the client?
- What are the peripheral issues that surround the central question, and how crucial is it that you address those issues as part of your overall representation?
- What are the limits of your expertise, and what other professionals should be consulted in order to answer the broader questions that you believe should be addressed?
- What are the client's financial and emotional limitations, and how do these constraints affect your ability to provide comprehensive services to that client?

Your assignment is to take a quick snapshot of the client's situation, reflect on the larger issues that he may not be aware of and may not want to handle, and then recommend an approach that is comprehensive but realistic. Your clients always get to choose what tasks to take on, but you need to educate them so that they can make prudent decisions.

The first step is to engage in a meaningful intake conversation. Because of the high degree of confusion about the legal landscape, using a preprinted form in lieu of a personal intake process for nonmarital representation probably will be ineffective and even misleading. At the same time, engaging in protracted conversations with each potential client before you are even retained can be both expensive and risky. Callers might construe casual comments that you might make as legal advice no matter how many disclaimers you repeat. Or, if you labor in the contested minefield of palimony claims, you might inadvertently step into an unintended conflict of interest bind by receiving confidential information from someone who never hires you, only to be precluded from representing the other party when he calls a few months later.

Asking the caller to send you an email describing his situation with a description of what he thinks his legal needs are might seem like a good place to start, but that approach also carries its own risks. A client might fill his email with an excess of confidential information so that once you have opened it (and presumably read it, despite your protestations to the contrary), you will have allowed a potential conflict of interest to arise.

These problems can only be avoided (or at least minimized) by combining a brief telephone conversation with a follow-up email exchange. The conversation is best handled by you, the attorney, but in some instances can be done by a trusted assistant as long as the assistant has some basic knowledge of the legal terrain and can be clear in communicating to the caller that the call does not create an attorney-client relationship and is not considered advice in advance of a retention. It might be preferable for you to handle the calls yourself whenever possible, despite the concerns of a misperceived offering of legal advice, simply because other people might not be able to extract the right information to be able to determine the caller's legal needs. Some lawyers feel strongly about the risks of this approach and only allow an assistant to handle these intake calls. You will have to decide whether your budget, staffing level, personal schedule, and tolerance for risk allow you to do otherwise.

Commence the call by clarifying that you are not able to give any legal advice over the phone, especially not to a nonclient. Explain that the purpose of the call is to briefly discuss the legal situation in general terms to help both of you decide whether you (the lawyer) can be useful in this particular situation. Explain that if it appears appropriate that you serve as the lawyer, you will set up an appointment to meet in person, at which time all of the issues will be discussed and you will be able to give legal advice. Let the potential client know that there is no charge for this initial conversation (avoid calling it a consultation since you are not providing any legal advice or counsel), but always point out that you will charge on an hourly basis—or however it is you charge—once you are retained. Keep a stack of New Client Information forms handy and write down the caller's name, phone number, and email address and the names of any other parties involved before even beginning the intake conversation.

Guide the caller through a set of preliminary questions: Is he married or state-registered? Is he living with someone? What is the gender of everyone involved? (You should not make assumptions based upon first names or voice characteristics.) Ask the caller to summarize the nature of his question and deliberately repeat that you don't want to hear any confidential information or hear "his side" of the story if this is a contested matter. If the caller inadvertently strays into too much personal detail, interrupt and repeat the admonishment (in a friendly tone) that this is not the time to hear this detailed information. Lighthearted reminders (e.g., "I need the two-minute synopsis and not the two-hour dramatic reading.") should help to keep the conversation on the right track and within the allotted fifteen minutes.

Once you have a good grasp of the purpose of the call, head in one of the following four directions:

1. *Decline to Represent.* In some situations, you will conclude that there is no need for your legal services, though occasionally you might offer some general legal information. If the caller has decided that he cannot afford to hire you to draft a co-ownership agreement and mentions that he isn't going to be on the title right away but will be added after the loan is funded, you could note that in Oakland he might avoid an expensive transfer tax when being added to the title (since he isn't entitled to the marital exemption), but only if he is added within six months of the purchase. This is a form of legal information rather than legal advice, and there is no harm in sharing this beneficial information. Similarly, if you're asked about a claim of discrimination because an insurance carrier wouldn't issue the unmarried couple a joint policy, you might mention a recent appellate case on the subject before referring the caller to a local attorney who handles discrimination claims.

   When you decline to represent the caller or the caller elects not to retain you, you typically do not need to follow up with a letter confirming the declination of representation for these simple matters. However, if the conversation is at all protracted and especially if the subject is a palimony or cohabitation contractual claim that has a time-sensitive deadline, you should follow up, typically in an email but sometimes in a letter, confirming that you are not going to be representing the caller and telling the caller about the applicable statute of limitations (two years from separation in most instances). You should retain the filled-in client information form and a copy of your letter or email even if you haven't been hired, for two reasons: Occasionally you might follow up a few months later to see if the client needs something from you, and it's useful to have these forms available if you are ever challenged in a conflict of interest situation or accused of failing to perform legal services. Notes that support your assertion that you did not give any advice or receive any confidential information will help you if you are later faced with a recusal motion or malpractice claim.

2. *Solicit Further Information.* You may discover in the course of the intake that it just isn't clear whether or not it makes sense for the caller to engage you. The desired estate planning task may or may not be beyond your level of expertise, or there may be other parties involved in the situation and you can't accept the representation until you address the conflict of interest questions. The caller's story may be too complicated to digest in a simple conversation, or you may not have time to complete the conversation. This is especially true when there is a risk that a common law marriage had been entered into or even a risk of such a claim being raised. Whenever this picture emerges, you should invite the caller to send you a more detailed email and should propose that you will respond to him in a day or two. You may end up receiving confidential information this way despite your requests to the contrary, and this could preclude you from representing any other party involved in this matter; but this is a risk you should be willing to take in order to gain the client's business, though only if it is a substantial matter. Always follow up after reviewing the more detailed description, either with a phone call (from you or your assistant) and a letter or an email so that it is clear whether or not you are handling the matter.

While these are tasks that every lawyer must incorporate into his operations, the complexities of nonmarital life and the optionality of many of the legal services you offer makes the retention process especially tricky. But there's no way around this aspect of a cohabitation law practice; it comes with the territory.

3. *Represent in a Limited Scope.* In some instances, there is a question that requires more than legal information but probably will take less than an hour to answer. While some lawyers decline to help in this situation because it is not being economically prudent, you should make every effort to do so, for several reasons. There aren't a lot of qualified attorneys in this field, and if you decline to help the caller, she may be lost at sea without anyone to turn to. She also may have waited until the last minute (don't be surprised to get a call from the title company or closing attorney's office asking about a deed that is about to be signed), so sending her on to someone else will not be effective. But even from a blatantly self-interested perspective, you never know: A thirty-minute consult could result in a valuable case if that client (or any close friends or family members) needs a lawyer later on.

In these situations, get all the contact information for the client, including a billing address, and make it clear (and note it on your intake form) that you will be charging for your time. Then put your other tasks to the side and listen to the question. Try to point out the related issues that warrant a further meeting, and perhaps follow up with an email confirming those concerns, but do your best to stick to the question presented and answer it appropriately.

This is frequently what happens with deed-vesting questions. If the parties have contributed equally to the property, they may not need a co-ownership agreement, so their primary question (in California) is whether to take title as joint tenants or tenants in common. Explain the differences between these two designations, ask the client regarding her preferences and concerns, and advise her accordingly. Similar situations arise regarding credit card liability (e.g., whether the partner is a cosigner or simply an authorized user) or whether shared residency requirements for domestic partnership registration can be satisfied if the parties are in a committed relationship.

An easy way to be sure you are paid for this brief consultation is to accept credit cards (though since you won't be spending more than one hour in this informal arrangement, the amounts at stake are small), but it is rare not to be paid. Clients appreciate your taking time out of your busy day to help them, and they realize that they may need your services later, so you will most likely be paid. In these instances, always send a brief note (either by email or included in the bill) that makes it clear that you are not doing any further work for them and inviting them to contact you again if something else is needed.

Again, providing a small dose of legal advice is not just a service to the client; it is likely to be one of your most effective marketing strategies.

4. *Accept the Representation.* If the nature of the work is something that you handle and the client is interested in retaining you and has agreed to pay your hourly rate for the engagement, accept the representation and schedule an appointment. It is fine to have your assistant handle the scheduling task, though it can be useful to take this on yourself. It's a way of getting to know your new client and a chance to learn where he works, what his schedule is, and if he has kids; and for folks who are particularly anxious about retaining a lawyer, engaging in these routine conversations can foster a smoother and more constructive interaction. Remember, you will be the first lawyer to whom many of your clients have spoken, and the underlying issues (the formation, duration, or dissolution of a relationship) can be very emotionally laden for them.

In most instances, you should send out a formal retainer letter after the call even before you meet with the client. This is especially important when the work is significant and a financial retainer is requested; or when you're concerned that the client hasn't really focused on some of your warnings (e.g., that you don't give tax advice or that you no longer provide litigation services). You should also follow up with an email confirming the appointment and setting forth a list of preliminary questions for the client to consider before you meet. Asking the key questions in advance has some real advantages, especially in particularly complicated situations. It engages your clients in the process ahead of time so they are more likely to be prepared and at ease when they come to your office, and it reduces the prospect of having to schedule a second meeting because they've forgotten to bring in some crucial information or documents. And third, assuming they respond prior to the meeting, it helps you get prepared both in terms of understanding their particular legal needs and also, if needed, enabling you to do a bit of research before they show up.

At some point early in the process, either in the initial phone call or in the first in-person meeting, it is essential that you address the issue of the scope of representation. Once you have spoken with your client for an hour or so, you should be able to discern what the broader legal issues are. As described above, it is appropriate for you to limit your assistance to a particular task, but it is crucial that you alert clients to the surrounding legal landscape and let them know what you are *not* going to handle for them. If you are asked to do an estate plan for your clients, make sure you remind them that this document won't determine who gets what if there is a breakup in the relationship. If the couple has significant assets and is coming to you to discuss one partner buying into the residence owned by the other one, make sure to remind the partners that there are significant tax consequences and that they should be consulting with a tax adviser before making any final decisions. If a client mentions that she never completed her divorce from her prior partner (and was legally married to that partner), you should point out to her, in writing, that you are not going to be handling that task—and why you think it's important that she take care of it.

There are three good reasons to be as careful as you can in setting the limits of your representation and documenting that decision. Most importantly, it will shield you from a malpractice claim later on if and when the client's failure to address those peripheral issues haunts him in unforeseen ways. The unfinished divorce, the absence of a co-ownership agreement, the tax audit for failure to report a gift when a partner was added as a joint tenant to a house previously owned solely by the other partner—any of these events can create strong pangs of regret in the client's mind for not taking up your offer of a broader range of legal counseling. Given the vagaries of memories and the fuzzy nature of so many of our conversations, having a written confirmation of the nonrepresentation election can be crucial. Second, it will serve as a reminder to the client to deal with the problem, and that may actually

I represented a woman whose ex-girlfriend was seeking to recover her $250,000 down payment from their joint tenancy house purchase on the grounds that they'd agreed she would be reimbursed before any appreciation was divided up. My client disagreed, claiming that they had agreed to own it fifty-fifty regardless of contributions. When I discovered that their living trust exhibits each referred to their 50 percent interest in the property, I raised that information at trial, and the judge subpoenaed the estate planning lawyer (there was no confidentiality here because they were both his clients). To our delight, his notes confirmed that he had asked them whether they had any agreement for unequal ownership and that they said no, and his retainer letter expressly stated that their characterization of property for estate planning purposes might be binding on them in a dissolution. His careful demarcation of what he was doing for them (estate planning) and not doing for them (drafting a co-ownership agreement) not only assured my client of prevailing in the lawsuit, it also protected him from any malpractice claim by the losing party.

be effective in motivating him to act in the future. And third, it is a way of modeling how you handle your work: with clarity, openness, and consistency.

B. Gaining the Requisite Competence

A dear friend of mine is the author of more than twenty-five cookbooks, and one of the most memorable chapters she ever penned features a checklist of what should be in every cook's pantry, along with some detailed tips on options when the most desired ingredients aren't readily available.[1] Every top-notch bartenders' handbook includes a similar sort of checklist so that you won't find yourself empty-handed and unable to satisfy your cocktail hour guests.

The same goes for practicing law. You don't want to find yourself unable to answer a fundamental legal question when you meet with your clients even if they are the first unmarried couple with whom you meet, and you certainly don't want to "serve" them an inedible (or undrinkable) legal meal when they are paying you hundreds of dollars for the experience! Mind you, no one expects you to be the "Iron Chef" of cohabitation law in your first year of practice, but having a solid grasp on the core skills and a basic understanding of the central legal tenets that apply to your clients is a prerequisite for taking on any assignment. Remember, having a basic competence in the field in which you are practicing is one of the obligations of professional responsibility in every single state, and there is no "cohabitation law is complicated" exemption to this requirement.

Bear in mind that clients with atypical lives will understand and accept that their situation may be unique and not readily comparable to the standard property, estate, or employee benefits situation that lawyers typically encounter. This may make them more tolerant of your need to do some research before advising them. But you want to be in good possession of the key rules so that you can gain the confidence of your clients and be equipped to approach the task of serving them.

However, gaining core competency in the field of nonmarital law is not going to be easy. Here is my list of the necessary ingredients that you need to gather up for your cohabitation law "pantry":

- A thorough understanding of the marriage-alternative registries available in your jurisdiction and, if you live near another state's border or your clients typically work or live in adjacent states, what's available in those cities and states as well. Make sure you know about any local domestic partnership registry.[2] In San Francisco, for example, county registration is open to straight and gay couples alike, enabling a couple to avoid a transfer tax when one of them is being bought out of the other's property. So, too, some local employers will extend health insurance coverage to county-registered partners without requiring them to sign up for the marriage-equivalent state registration. You need to know whether the registries are open to opposite-sex couples and whether there is a shared-residency requirement for registration.
- A detailed understanding of the rules of common law marriage in the state where you practice, as well as in the state where your clients may have previously lived. While the number of such claims is diminishing each year, you want to be attuned to the possibility of raising such a claim or perhaps defending against one made by the other party.
- Basic knowledge of the statutory and appellate law in your state on co-ownership agreements, claims based upon oral and implied

Another frustrating aspect of cohabitation law is that the existing legal research systems are as insensitive to this area of law as many old-fashioned legislators used to be. There is no single category of nonmarital co-ownership in most real estate treatises, and finding appellate cases in your jurisdiction may itself be a significant challenge. Secondary sources often are wildly incorrect. Computerized search engines are likely to do a better job as long as you explore all of the possible topics and word options, including unmarried couples, cohabitation, palimony, or nonmarital relationships.

agreements, and equitable claims as well. Some of this law will be found in the rules for rebutting presumptions of title (i.e., the requirement of clear and convincing evidence and the time frame for when the statute of frauds will preclude any such claims); and in most states, there will be additional doctrines that can only be found in published appellate cases. Be forewarned: In most states, there is very little published law, and you may need to look beyond the narrow scope of cohabitation law (i.e., co-ownership doctrines) to gauge what the options are in your state.

- Some level of familiarity with how the civil courts in your local area are handling these cases, especially if you are going to be taking on litigation. As it turns out, hardly any palimony cases have been successful in the San Francisco Bay Area in the past twenty years, in part because of the steep burden of proof but also because of the attitudes of the local judges. Jurors also tend to be surprisingly unsympathetic to palimony claims, perhaps because they can't imagine that they would ever be so unwise as to rely on vague promises of support from a rich boyfriend!

- Basic knowledge about the arenas closely related to your specialization area. If you are handling parentage and custody matters, most of which are typically handled in family court or its equivalent, you will need to know how the civil court procedures work as that is where the financial disputes between the partners will be handled. One of the most burdensome aspects of a nonmarital dissolution in most states is that the custody and support proceedings are handled in different courts from the civil law contractual claims, and oftentimes the two actions are not even coordinated or consolidated. The same goes for couples, whether gay or straight, who cohabited and later married: Each state has different rules as to whether claims arising out of the nonmarital period can be combined with the marital dissolution. If you don't feel equipped to practice in those different courts, you will have to farm out one or more aspects of the dispute to someone else, but, at a minimum, you should understand how those procedures will play out.

- A general knowledge of the tax problems so that you ask the right questions and point out the higher-priced problems your clients might face. You aren't expected to know the precise tax rules, but you need to know enough to warn them that transfers of major assets are not tax-free and to caution them to get competent advice before they make any major decisions. A review of the most salient tax rules and problems are covered in this book, but you should be cognizant of your state rules as well as any local transfer tax, property tax, or tax liability rules.

- A general awareness of how public and private benefits are applied to unmarried partners. The employer primarily establishes employment-based benefits; however, in some instances a union contract may provide for a greater range of benefits, and in some instances federal law (ERISA and COBRA) limits what an employer can offer. Learn about the restrictions on Social Security survivor benefits as well as pension and retirement account rollover rules. Again, even if you are not planning to specialize in this area, you will want to know enough to warn your clients of the risks of remaining unmarried or, in some instances, the benefits of remaining single.

- Knowledge of how the intestacy rules affect your clients so you can raise these concerns and motivate your clients to do their estate planning with an attorney (either you or someone to whom you send them). Closely related to the probate and trust aspects are the illness and incapacity protocols, and you should have a clear understanding of what is required for a valid medical directive (health care power of attorney) and a financial power of attorney. In many instances, your clients will be filling out these forms on their own, but you need to understand the basic rules so you can answer their questions.

• Some familiarity with the local cultures of unmarried couples, both gay and straight. If you haven't worked with gay couples before and aren't gay yourself, take the time to read some of the books listed in the Resources section of this book and attend a continuing education program on the legal and tax issues facing same-sex couples. Read up on the growing segment of older straight unmarried couples and take the opportunity to talk with some of your older friends and relatives to learn what their primary concerns are. If you sense that your best market for new clients is in a particular subset of the universe of unmarried couples (racial minority, sexual minority, or otherwise), get to know someone who lives (or at least socializes) in that territory so you can display a familiarity with that community when you meet with your clients.

C. Resolving the Actual and Potential Conflicts of Interest

Almost every time a lawyer provides counseling of any kind, a fundamental question will arise: Who is the client? If more than one client is involved, is there an actual or potential conflict of interest; if so, can it be waived? While these questions arise in every type of representation, answering them when it comes to representing unmarried partners can be especially tricky as problematic uncertainties arise with regard to all of these questions.

Who Is the Client?

At a minimum, the client must be the person who is facing the legal issue or question presented. As simplistic as that instruction may seem, identifying that client and confirming the nature of the representation is not always simple. You may be contacted by another lawyer who has a client whom she is trying to help, by a title company officer, or by the parents or siblings or even new partner of the potential client. Recently, a savvy business-oriented guy contacted me; his current fiancée still owned a house with her former boyfriend. It was clear to me that this new boyfriend was eager to see the co-ownership dispute between his girlfriend and her ex resolved, but it was equally apparent that he was not my client. I answered some of his questions over the phone but then clarified that I needed to be contacted by her, not just by him, in order for us to proceed. She promptly contacted me and we made an appointment, and I consented to the new boyfriend's attendance at the meeting, pointing out that she was the client and that the meeting was not confidential since a nonclient was in the room.

Part of the difficulty of advising unmarried partners is that oftentimes they are only moderately interested in learning about and dealing with their legal situation, in comparison to the heightened concerns of others around them. For this reason, you should always make a point of communicating from the start with the one who is really the client so that you can be assured that he truly desires to engage your services. You might be totally comfortable providing some basic legal information to anxious nonclients (like the man in the prior example), but reserve the bestowal of advice for clients only!

The truly dicey question is whether the client is the individual partner or the couple. In some situations, the answer is obvious. If the couple as such is jointly facing discrimination in a rental situation or a denial of insurance coverage as domestic partners, then it is proper that both partners be your client; and most likely there is no conflict of interest as they are both seeking the same remedy. Conversely, if only one of the partners has a legal problem, such as a denial of an individual benefit or a question about how to handle a creditor's claim that does not really affect the other partner, or if only one partner wishes to sign a medical directive, then only one partner needs legal counsel. That certainly is the case when there is a disputed palimony claim brought by one partner against the other partner.[3]

In almost every other situation, however, both partners need legal counsel to some degree and the issues they face are inevitably intertwined, and so in nearly every instance there is some degree of conflict of interest. This is definitely true when the couple is signing a co-ownership or cohabitation agreement and most often the case when the two partners are executing wills, but it also can be true in a liability dispute or a benefits conflict. If one partner is filing bankruptcy (as a single person) but the two of them are joint debtors on a loan or credit card debt, the strategy taken by the bankrupt partner may affect the other partner. Even if a couple is breaking up amicably, the way that one partner characterizes a buyout payment for her interest in their residence on her tax return could have an impact on the buying partner's future tax liability.

Effective Representation and Conflict of Interest Waivers

It's well recognized that whenever more than one person is going to be a client, it is crucial that you obtain a waiver of conflicts of interest, both actual and potential.[4] While lawyers who work with married couples have a well-thought-out protocol for addressing these issues, the task is more complicated when it comes to representing unmarried partners. First, there is not the clear demarcation of "marriage" with well-defined professional rules accompanying such status. For example, there may not be any statutorily imposed fiduciary duties imposed on your unmarried clients, but if they've been together for a while, there may be de facto confidential duties arising out of their co-ownership of property or comanagement of assets. Whereas many states' provisions on premarital agreements expressly state that an agreement waiving spousal support is presumed invalid unless each party has separate counsel, there is no similar bright-line standard for the lawyer's role in negotiating a cohabitation agreement.[5] You also may find a wider range of professional approaches to these situations amongst your fellow lawyers—that is, if you are lucky enough to find another lawyer in your town who handles cohabitation matters.

The strategy for the best way to handle these issues involves a multistage analysis using the following decision pathway:

1. Which person(s) has the primary need for legal counsel as the one who is being asked to take (or decline to undertake) some particular action?
2. Is there someone else (most likely the partner) who will be affected by the decision and action of the primary client?
3. Does the partner have his own decisions to make or opinions that should be taken into account, and will those opinions and/or decisions in turn affect the primary client?
4. Is the nature of the problem such that it will be particularly difficult for either or both parties to hear and understand the anticipated information and advice and proceed with a reasonable decision if they are in the presence of the other partner?
5. Will you be able to provide effective counsel to both parties without curtailing your advice because of your concerns about how it will be interpreted by the other partner?

6. If it is not appropriate for you to represent both parties, is there a workable and affordable way to enable them to obtain the required counsel, or will this leave one partner without any guidance at all?

7. Is either party likely to complain later about the joint representation, and, if so, will a written waiver be sufficient to address that concern?

Having reviewed the situation from these different perspectives, the matters can be divided into three probable clusters:

- those where it is clear that the conflicts of interest are merely potential and are not significant and therefore can readily be waived,
- those where it is clear that the conflicts of interest are either actual and/or are so significant (and so difficult to manage) that you probably don't want to take the chance on joint representation, and
- those where the conflicts of interest are real and could well become significant but can be waived under appropriate circumstances.

A recurring example of the first type is where a couple is buying a house together, with each partner putting in 50 percent of the investment and covering 50 percent of the costs and when there are no tension-producing issues regarding other assets or liabilities. Most likely they want an agreement so that the breakup process will be appropriately structured and fair and to avoid a court-managed partition action. Another example of the first type is where an unmarried couple is attempting to jointly adopt a child and the state is putting up roadblocks out of a prejudice against an unmarried couple jointly adopting a child. Sure, there are potential turns of fate that could result in the parties having different concerns and disputes in the future. In the house situation, one of them may regret having agreed to a forced sale if neither party completes a buyout of the other owner within ninety days; and in the adoption scenario, one of the parties might announce that she wants a breakup before the adoption process is completed. But these are unlikely events, and in the meantime the parties have a unity of interest and purpose, so the advice you give is going to be of fundamentally equal meaning to both of them. You still need a signed waiver of the conflict of interest, but advising both of them is just fine.

An example of the second situation is where one partner is the sole legal parent and is considering allowing his boyfriend to undertake a second-parent adoption of his child; here, it can be tricky to offer your services to both of them as a joint attorney, though that is precisely what many attorneys will do, with the appropriate conflict waivers in place. Similarly, if one partner is the sole owner of a valuable house and wants to make a gift of 50 percent of the equity to her boyfriend, it is only sensible to make sure that just one of the parties is your client. In each of these situations, you could serve as a joint mediator for both parties and could even provide legal information and write up a legal agreement for both of them as their mediator, but representing both parties as their attorney would not be a good idea.

Given the sensitivity of these scenarios and the awkwardness of talking through the legal concerns in the presence of the other party, you probably won't want to go forward as joint counsel even with a signed conflict of interest waiver. Take the "get real" test: If the client in truth cannot listen calmly to the advice you need to give him (such as "Don't consent to an adoption that you may regret the rest of your life" or "Don't give up 50 percent of your house to someone who has already filed bankruptcy or has sued his prior girlfriend") and if you cannot effectively counsel that client (either to proceed with the adoption or gain access to a 50 percent interest in the other's house) without jeopardizing the needs of the other person, then you can't represent both of them, even with a signed conflicts of interest waiver. You need to be free to say to your client, "Don't get into business with that guy!"—even when "that guy" could lose his home of a decade or more if your client accepts your advice. If it is hard to imagine uttering such a warning while both parties are your clients, they need separate counsel.

Many nonmarital retentions, however, fall into the third category: There are significant conflicts of interest, but they can be waived with a thorough waiver. This is always a judgment call. I tend to be a bit more flexible than many lawyers who handle marital matters simply because I know that my clients are concerned about duplicative fees and they may not have access to another qualified attorney in this area. At the same time, I'm not the most flexible lawyer in town because I've seen (and experienced) the problems that can arise from an overly casual approach to this problem.

Obtaining a thorough waiver should never been seen as routine. The issues should be discussed in person with the clients (or, at a minimum, over the phone) *before* any waiver is signed; if not, the written waiver cannot "confirm" that the conflicts have been waived. The discussion and the written waiver should use appropriate and realistic potential conflict scenarios to illustrate the problem. If the subject is a house purchase and the couple is trying to decide how to deal with one partner's excess down payment, you can do some quick calculations to explain how a reimbursement model might result in a different payout as compared with a proportional ownership model. If the subject is whether or not to register as domestic partners with an employer as opposed to a city registration, you can review the termination procedures for each method and describe how they might play out differently for each of them, especially if they should relocate to another city or switch employers.

Make sure that the written waiver is detailed and appropriate to the particular type of representation, using real examples of foreseeable problems so that the letter is meaningful to the clients. I'll never forget the time I received an angry call from a cohabiting partner shortly after the couple had broken up, complaining that she didn't understand that she had waived any right to a reimbursement of her excess contributions to the monthly mortgage payments. I reminded her that we had discussed that issue and how it was clearly stated in the agreement that she had signed, but her response said it all. She acknowledged that I had probably said these words to her but claimed that because of her belief that her relationship would never end, she didn't really "hear" what I had said. The lesson of this caller's words is obvious: You need to point out these potential problems loud and clear for them to be heard!

Whenever possible, insist that the conflicts of interest waiver letter is signed before you do any substantive work—and certainly before you finalize any document. Just to be doubly sure, always insert a paragraph about your representation and the conflicts of interest waiver in the body of any agreement that you are drafting. This has three purposes: It reminds everyone of whom you are representing (and who else might be involved as a reviewing attorney), it serves as a record if the retainer agreement is lost or not signed, and it restates the conflicts waiver (or lack thereof) and reminds the clients where things stand in this regard.

Having the recital in the agreement also means that if one of the parties calls you a decade or so later to ask for advice when things have gone awry in the relationship, you can quickly check your computer files (even if your electronic draft is unsigned) to see if you can answer her questions.

Management of the Multiparty Representation

Once you have figured out who is going to be your client, you need to handle the counseling process in a way that honors that arrangement. If only one party is your client, you need to be attentive regarding with whom you are communicating and when it is okay to include the nonclient in the meeting or communication. In an excess of caution, you should always assume that your client shares the emails that you write with the other partner, and you should temper your words accordingly; but for confidentiality's sake, you should communicate only with your client. If something is particularly sensitive, you may ask the client to come into the office or speak with you on the phone to avoid the potentially destructive email chain of forwarded comments. If your client is about to do something particularly worrisome, you may even send her a postal letter asking her to confirm in writing that she understands your concerns. But be careful about sending a letter that asks for a signed acknowledgement: If you don't get one back, you can't assume that the advice has been heard. Instead, tell your client orally and then confirm that admonishment in a letter that doesn't call for a written response so at least you know that you have proffered the necessary warning.

If you are representing just one party and the other party needs counsel, you should be reluctant to meet with both of the parties together unless the other party's lawyer is present or consents to the meeting in advance. Occasionally you might deviate from this rule, either because the other party's situation is fairly simple and that party has elected to proceed without counsel or because there are preliminary matters that can be discussed jointly. In that event, you should follow up with an email or letter to both of them confirming that you only represent one of them. It is usually best to follow that up with a written confirmation of the representation arrangements. If you are sending out a letter to the two of them, you should typically address the letter just to your client with a "cc" to the partner, again demonstrating in the formality of the correspondence the parameters of the attorney-client relationship.

One situation that comes up on a regular basis is where a lawyer meets with both partners and subsequently realizes that each of them needs independent counsel, most typically in the review of a cohabitation agreement. This can arise because one lawyer has done estate planning work for both partners, and they later decide to have a cohabitation agreement for which separate counsel is advised. In this case, they can agree to release the previously joint attorney to be the lawyer for just one of them and bring in a new counsel for the other party. This also is appropriate where the partners have met jointly with an attorney to deal with an unrelated issue of mutual concern and then need separate counsel to handle the transfer of an asset between themselves. These sorts of arrangements only make sense for a newly formed relationship or an intact couple who does not have active conflicts, and the professional relationships should be well documented in a letter signed by both of the parties, not just by the lawyers.

A parallel set of concerns applies when there is joint representation. It is crucial that both parties receive the same information and advice. You should never assume that telling one partner is the same as telling both of them, especially when it comes to crucial information. Again, email is a wonderful tool. If one partner calls you and asks a critical question about a deed vesting or account titling, you can confirm the telephonic advice with an email to both parties. It is also essential to remember that joint representation means that you owe full and equal duties to both parties, not just to "the relationship." It can be very awkward to sit with a couple and describe how advantageous it might be for one of them to not be legally tied to the other one, especially if the other one has serious alcohol problems or is a known overspender; but if you fail to do this, you have not met the standards of serving each of the clients fully.

Even though you have a duty to both parties, at times it may be necessary to convey particular advice or voice additional concerns to just one of the parties. Oftentimes, this problem arises in the midst of an engagement; for example, you may be drafting a simple co-ownership agreement, and one of the parties reveals to you that he's still married to someone else. You also may discover that one of the partners has made a significant loan to a partner that he now wants to forgive. In these situations, you should send a letter to just one of the parties explaining the particular risks that he is facing because of this matter and inviting him to consult privately with another attorney to deal directly with this problem. It is entirely appropriate to share a copy of this letter with the other party so that the other party also knows that you have given this client-specific warning and advice.[6]

It also is acceptable in most states for one person to pay the other's fees as well as her own or to pay fees for one or both parties out of a joint account as long as there is a written retainer agreement that clarifies who is the client. Absent a written agreement, the one who pays the fees is presumed to be the sole client, so this is something that needs to be cleared up in advance. This is especially true if the services are being paid by just one party but are for the benefit of the other party alone. The one thing never to do is to receive payment solely from one party for services being provided to another party (especially if that party has a conflict of interest with the paying party) without getting something in writing confirming the representation. Similarly, you should always check about whether or not it is okay in your state to be paid out of a joint account when you are helping one partner file a lawsuit against the person who is the co-owner of the joint account.

DOCUMENTS NECESSARY FOR AVOIDING CONFLICTS OF INTEREST

(FORMS FOUND ON INCLUDED CD)

Form 01: Decline to represent client letter
Form 02: Client retention letter with referral for certain issues
Form 03: General retainer letter with waiver of conflicts of interest

NOTES

1. MARTHA SHULMAN, THE VERY BEST RECIPES FOR HEALTH (Rodale Books 2010); MEDITERRANEAN HARVEST (Rodale Books 2007).
2. *See* HUMAN RIGHTS CAMPAIGN, CITY AND COUNTY DOMESTIC PARTNER REGISTRIES, http://www.hrc.org/issues/marriage/domestic_partners/9133 .htm (list of local registries on the Alternatives to Marriage Project website, http://www.unmarried.org).
3. If you have previously represented one partner, you cannot represent the other partner; and if you have represented both of them, you can't

represent either of them. So make sure you thoroughly document the nature of your representation.

4. Each state has its own rules, but the safest strategy is to assume that there is a potential conflict of interest that needs to be waived in writing by all clients.

5. *See* NAT'L CONFERENCE OF COMM'RS ON UNIFORM STATE LAWS, UNIFORM PREMARITAL AGREEMENT ACT, http://www.law.upenn.edu/bll/archives/ulc/fnact99/1980s/upaa83.htm (model premarital agreement code that has been adopted in nearly thirty states so far).

6. Most lawyers drafting wills for both partners require that the clients waive any confidentiality between themselves and expressly authorize counsel to disclose one party's confidential information to the other party.

CHAPTER THREE

LIVING APART, LIVING TOGETHER, AND THE OPTION OF MARRIAGE

"We don't need no piece of paper from the city hall keeping us tied and true."

From Joni Mitchell, "My Old Man" (1971)

A. SPECIAL CONCERNS FOR NONCOHABITING COUPLES

While most of your prospective clients will either be living together already or planning to cohabit soon, not all unmarried couples share a residence, even over the long haul. Some choose to reside in their separate quarters for years on end; some end up camping out in distant states in a long-term, long-distance commuting relationship; and others live primarily in their own homes but spend significant time in each other's residences. Living apart is especially popular for older couples wanting to retain their own homes so that they can maintain their autonomy and the settled-in lives that they have created over decades. In rare instances, one of the partners may be lingering on in a shared household with a former spouse (or with a current spouse), oftentimes to preserve a degree of continuity in an ongoing extended-family relationship.

Cohabitation is a threshold requirement for just about every domestic partnership or civil union registry, both public and private, as well

It is truly ironic that while living together prior to marriage was historically seen as a mortal sin, living together and being in an "intimate relationship" is a requirement under just about every domestic partnership
ordinance. The origin of this nontraditional requirement dates back to
the early 1980s, when many gay men were seeking domestic partnership recognition in order to obtain health insurance for their partners.
Since many of these men were at risk for AIDS, local governments were
concerned about false registrations by friends (or even strangers) of public employees supposedly seeking valuable insurance benefits for their
so-called partners.[1] Since registration did not impose any of the legal
liabilities of marriage (and local agencies could not impose such requirements as they were the terrain of state governments), it was politically
expedient to limit registration to those who lived together in a marriage-
like relationship. Such a requirement made sense given the concerns of
that era, but it can create serious obstacles for those couples who live in
a commuting relationship because of job or other family demands. And
since there are no such requirements for a legal marriage, a strict application of this requirement would force noncohabiting couples to select the
marriage option.

as a prerequisite for most palimony claims, but it is not an absolute
threshold for every possible legal complication or legal concern.[2] For
that reason, you need to have an accurate picture of your clients' living arrangements and be prepared to respond to the inquiries that your
noncohabiting unmarried partner clients will present.

It is unlikely that noncohabiting partners will present serious financial claims or complex legal issues, especially in states where cohabitation is a requirement for filing a palimony claim; but there are some
couples for whom having a simple written agreement—most frequently
one that contains a waiver of financial claims upon termination of the
relationship—may nonetheless be appropriate. These situations include
those where one partner is the primary source of financial support for
the other one over an extended period of time, or where one partner has
relocated or is giving up a lucrative employment situation to live with a
partner, especially if one partner has significant assets.

While it is rare for noncohabiting partners to face such claims, it
is not unheard of. I once handled a case where my wealthy older client
had supported his younger girlfriend for more than a decade; when they
broke up, she filed a palimony suit on the grounds that she had given

up a promising career in order to be his companion. They had never lived together in any formal sense of the term, but she claimed that they cohabited from time to time in various hotels and in her apartment. Eventually the case settled—quite favorably for him—but her complaint survived the demurrer that we filed arguing that she had failed to meet the minimum California requirement of cohabitation.

Apart from the occasional request for an agreement confirming a waiver of palimony claims or a simple financial agreement about relocation costs or housing expenses, legal issues also can arise for noncohabiting couples in the following arenas: parentage, financial affairs, illness and disability, and claims regarding romantic promises.

Parentage. If the biological co-parents of a child are living apart yet are still in an ongoing relationship, it may be prudent to draft a formal parenting agreement to clarify their respective responsibilities, especially regarding future transitions. While agreements regarding children are considered nonbinding from a judicial perspective unless confirmed in a court proceeding, having an understanding between the parents can avoid many a strained dispute. In other situations, it may be wise to obtain a judgment of parentage on the part of the father, and you may be called upon to counsel a semi-absentee father on the issues involved in preserving his parentage rights. In some states, a father's name can be added to the birth certificate even after the birth, and most states have an expedited declaration of parentage form that can be signed. If the biological father refuses to accede to such a request and refuses to pay child support, a formal paternity action may need to be filed by the mother, including a subsequent demand for child support.

The issues for noncohabiting lesbian and gay parents are especially complicated because at least one of the partners is not likely to have a biological connection to the child. Because cohabitation is required for a domestic partnership or civil union registration, a noncohabiting same-sex partner generally can't pursue a stepparent adoption of the other partner's child; and it is rare that a court will grant a second-parent adoption to a noncohabiting co-parent unless it is part of a dissolution of a relationship between previously cohabiting co-parents. Seeking some kind of formal parentage confirmation is not unheard of for couples who have parted ways, regardless of whether or not they previously cohabited and even in some situations where the partners were not both biological parents of the child. Oftentimes there is a mutual desire to establish a parental relationship for purposes of long-term future legal and financial security for the child and the nonlegal parent, and courts in many states have welcomed such requests.

Financial Affairs. Partners living separately may need assistance with various sorts of financial entanglements, perhaps regarding a co-owned car, a joint checking account, or the sharing of some or all of their incomes or expenses. Historically, many gay couples maintained separate residences to preserve their privacy, and some older straight couples wish to stay in their respective separate homes despite their intimate relationship. For most of these couples, it is fine to maintain a joint account, contributing equally to joint expenses (such as vacations) or as they agree from time to time—without the need for any written agreement. But if one partner is providing a significant amount of financial support or has made sizable loans to the other, a simple agreement documenting these arrangements might be useful. Such an agreement is also appropriate where one partner's credit card is being used by his partner, with an express or an implied promise that the one incurring the debts will be responsible for paying the balance on the card. You should create a variety of standard templates for these sorts of simple financial agreements so that you can readily modify them for your clients for a reasonable fee.

While no one can predict the future with any certainty, it is useful to have as clear a sense as possible about whether or not your clients are planning to cohabit or get married sometime soon as those decisions will affect the terms of their agreement. The shift from a noncohabiting relationship to living together by itself rarely creates a need for new legal documents, though the sharing of expenses that is likely to result from cohabiting may change the fundamental terms of the partners' financial interactions. It's important that your clients understand that a subsequent marriage or state registration can invalidate many of the terms of a nonmarital agreement, and you want to be sure that your clients understand how to manage these transitions.

Illness and Disability. Noncohabiting couples may need financial powers of attorney and medical directives to deal with each partner's future illness or disability, and there may be a desire to purchase insurance policies and/or make an agreement for reciprocal wills that provide financial security for each of them in case of death. This is especially true for older couples who do not have former spouses or children to whom they can turn for these important tasks or for those partners who wish to designate their noncohabiting partner as the primary heir.[3]

Claims Regarding Romantic Promises. One arena where the law does not dare to tread is in connection with alleged broken promises of marriage. Most states expressly preclude the filing of such claims, also known as the "anti-heart balm" statutes (as in "don't ask the judge to soothe your broken heart"). Promises of marriage are seen universally as social promises that are made without consideration and are outside of the legal realm and thus not legally enforceable. Despite these limitations, it may be appropriate in some circumstances for a couple to sign a financial agreement covering the costs that one of them is going to incur in relocating or taking time off from paid employment to plan a relocation or marriage. In this context, you are not providing compensation for a potential broken promise to marry per se; rather, you are providing an appropriate reimbursement of expenses incurred for a particular purpose that might be subsequently unrealized.

One further caution: Don't be surprised to find out that some of your clients have been rather casual with regard to the cohabitation rules of a registration or access to certain benefits. There is quite a bit of nonmarital opportunism going on in the world, and many folks have signed up for employer-based insurance benefits, privately funded homeowners or car insurance benefits, or other such "freebies" based upon a misstated declaration of cohabitation. Be familiar with the local or state rules of cohabitation (California's rules, for example, allow partners to retain separate residences or cohabit in a residence owned solely by one of them as long as they primarily live together), and be prepared to kindly inform your potential clients that you are not able to assist them unless they clear up their inappropriately inaccurate cohabitation status.

B. THE OPTION OF MARRIAGE

At some point in the conversation, you may be called upon to counsel your clients on the topic of whether or not they should get married. As a lawyer, your focus will be on the legal consequences of the marriage decision, though you will want to be equally prepared to discuss the interrelated nonlegal issues as well. Express an openness to either option, and do not place a moral thumb on the marriage-decision scale or reinforce any social pressures in favor of marriage—that is something that your clients' mothers and best friends will do in spades! None-theless, even the most routine of legal explanations, such as the joint liability rules of community property, inevitably will touch upon the financial concerns of each of the partners, for better or for worse. So, too, discussing the financial consequences of divorce will no doubt reso-nate differently with each partner, especially if one of them is secretly craving the legal security of marriage and the other one feels differently.

Quite often, these questions arise while the partners are living apart since not all couples live together before getting married. But regardless of their cohabitation status, even when partners elect to remain unmar-ried, at least one of them may be holding onto a loosely formed inten-tion or hope of tying the knot sometime in the future.[4] However, it is not possible for anyone to know with any certainty when (or even if) the couple will get married; therefore, the legal documents that you prepare need to be valid even if they never get married, and the under-lying terms must also be acceptable to both parties even if they never get married. There is an understandable tension between your desire to document the current nonmarital situation (and motivate your clients to do the same) and their resistance to putting energy into what may be perceived by one or both of them as a temporary condition. Nonethe-less, you should not let their reluctance to deal with their current legal status distract you from your present-focused goals.

You will also need to evaluate whether there is any basis for making a claim of a common law marriage, depending on the applicable law of the state that your clients currently live in or previously lived in. Such claims are indeed rare, but not unheard of; and depending on the par-ticular facts of your clients' situation, it may be prudent to explore this option.

Concerns for Same-Sex Couples

You also will need to be prepared to explain the particular marriage-related consequences that are at play for same-sex couples. There are numerous resources for your background education on gay and lesbian marriage law (see Resources section), but here are the basic rules you want to bear in mind when helping your lesbian or gay clients:

- While same-sex couples can register as civil union or domestic partners (California, for example does not require residency as a condition of registration) or can travel to and get legally married in more than a half-dozen states or Canada, their otherwise valid registration or marriage will not be recognized if they live in or move to one of more than thirty nonrecognition states. In some states, their marital status will be ignored; and in other jurisdictions, the legal treatment they will receive is less than certain at this time. Prior to the allowance of same-sex marriage in New York, for example, some but not all of the rights of marriage were extended to same-sex couples, whereas California currently extends all of the "rights and obligations" of marriage to out-of-state married couples "but not its designation." Meanwhile, state domestic partnerships will be recognized as marriage equivalents in dissolution proceedings by some state courts but not all of them, and most likely the couples won't be treated as married for federal tax purposes.

- Even though there is no residency requirement for registration or marriage in any of the fifty United States, every state has residency requirements for a dissolution, primarily to prevent a spouse from fleeing his home state to a state with lesser alimony or property requirements than those in effect in his state of residency. Making matters worse, some extreme nonrecognition state courts (Texas and Oklahoma, for example) have refused to grant a dissolution to their gay and lesbian residents, decreeing that granting a dissolution (even when no property rights are being asserted) is a form of recognition of the out-of-state marriage. As a result, residents of nonrecognition states may have to relocate to a recognition state for the requisite time period in order to obtain a dissolution, leaving them with having to choose between two unfortunate options: a very expensive move or the inability to remarry in the future.

- Until the federal Defense of Marriage Act (DOMA)[5] is repealed by Congress or invalidated by the U.S. Supreme Court, most federal benefits do not apply to same-sex married couples, even if they live in a recognition state. Thus, the partners in same-sex married relationships will file their federal tax returns as single individuals and will not be eligible to share in federal retirement benefits, Social Security survivor benefits, or immigration priorities as spouses.[6]

- Same-sex couples in many states still face serious obstacles establishing parentage for both partners, only some of which are resolved by registering or marrying. In fact, in some situations marrying or state registering can seriously complicate matters. So, while in some instances a marriage can help facilitate a stepparent adoption, in other situations a same-sex marriage is a pronouncement of the partners' homosexuality; and this alone can make it impossible for either partner to adopt a child overseas.

- Because of the high degree of fluidity in the legal treatment of same-sex couples, it is impossible for any lawyer, even the most well-educated one, to provide certainty to same-sex couples regarding their legal futures. Most dramatically, couples who marry thinking that marriage will have no legal consequences may find that their state shifts positions and becomes a recognition state, thereby extending all marital rights and obligations to those couples. Courts and legislatures are changing the rules on a regular basis, and lesbian and gay couples need to understand that they are participating in a social experiment—and with that adventurous status comes a high degree of legal uncertainty.

The Basic Rules of Marriage

Educating clients about the legal consequences of marriage is not a simple task, especially when you may only have an hour or two to do so. The range of your clients' comprehension skills can vary widely, as will the complexity of their personal and financial lives. Add to the mix their likely anxieties and perhaps some emotional turbulence between the two of them (sometimes spoken, sometimes not), and you are facing a daunting challenge.

There are two approaches that you can take when performing this important task. One option is to present an explanation composed of broad conceptual legal principles in the hope that your clients will be able to apply these principles to the important details of their lives. The alternate approach (which seems to be more effective) is to explain the rules within the specific context of the clients' own personal and financial lives. While the second approach may seem overly narrow and hard to organize in an initial session with your clients, oftentimes it is the only approach that hits home with your audience. By all means, you will need to present the explanations in general terms initially and continue to sprinkle in some broader statements about the legal rules as you explain the particulars, but wherever possible you should embed your doctrinal explanations into the factual realities of your clients' lives. If you fail to do this, they probably won't understand your advice, let alone follow it.

A client-focused approach also enables you to tackle one of the more challenging aspects of this sort of discussion, which is to stay on the central path of the counseling track and avoid getting lost in the tangled underbrush of the peripheral details. Most folks want to navigate through this evaluation in a single meeting, but very few nonlawyers can stay focused for more than two hours. Unless you stick with the core concerns, you won't have time to cover even the basics.

With these goals firmly in mind, you will want to spend the first ten to fifteen minutes gathering the basic facts of your clients' lives. If at all possible, you should have your clients send you a summary narrative in advance so that they will be better organized—and you will be as well. If an advance briefing is not possible, you can ask these questions at the outset of the meeting:

- Are you state-registered (either to each other or to someone else), married to someone else, or without any formal marital or partnership status? Did you cohabit in a state that recognizes common law marriage, and, if so, would you be considered married under the legal rules of that state?
- How long have you been a couple, how long (if at all) have you been living together, and are you considering marriage in the future?
- Does either of you have any life-threatening illnesses or disabilities?
- Is either of you the legal parent of a minor child, do any minor children live with either of you, and does either of you have adult children from a prior relationship?
- What is the approximate annual income for each of you, and is this likely to change much in the next year or two?
- What is the approximate net worth of each of you, and what individual debts do you have?
- Does either of you own any real estate, individually or jointly, either with your partner or someone else, and what is the approximate value and estimated mortgage debt for each property?

- Do you have any oral or written agreements about any aspects of your lives, and, if so, what are the basic terms of the agreement(s)?

Armed with this basic information about their lives, you can explain how living under the regime of marital law would change their legal relationship. First explain in general terms the rules of jointly owned property (or whatever the property default rules are in their state of residence), joint debt liability, parentage presumptions, and the central rules of the dissolution process. This generalized "lecture" should be very short: fifteen minutes maximum. Focus on the ways in which the legislature has set up the rules for married couples, providing for an opt-out process by means of an agreement as opposed to the opt-in approach that applies in the unregulated world of nonmarital law. Perhaps the most crucial message that you will convey during this presentation is that marital obligations are imposed on couples without regard to their knowledge of them or assent to them, in contrast to the voluntary nature of nearly all nonmarital obligations.

Most nonlawyers find it hard to grasp these rules as general principles, and so even if you do an excellent teaching job, clients aren't likely to remember many of the details. That is why you should spend the bulk of the discussion presenting the marital rules in the context of the clients' particular situations. Explain how the rules will determine who "owns" each asset and whether there is likely to be any separate property asset that needs to be identified or recharacterized. Use examples of debts that are realistic given their life situation, but hopefully free from any notions of blame. When it comes to talking about troubling possibilities, mention accidents, illness, or involuntary unemployment rather than drug use or criminal behavior in order to avoid any notion of blame in any particular worst-case scenario. It's crucial to convey how paternalistic the marital rules are—and how inflexible they can be when it comes to the decision making of any particular couple.

Focus on the specific areas of the law that are likely to affect them the most, such as the allocation of equity of a house purchased prior to marriage, the loss of any means-tested public benefits based upon the income of the new spouse, termination of public or private benefits such as a pension earned by a now-deceased former spouse or spousal support from a prior marriage, or possible immigration issues. Review the likely exposure arising out of a spouse's business activities or other financial risk taking, focusing on the benefits of remaining unmarried when it comes to avoiding liability. Given current economic times, spend some time discussing debt liability, credit rating issues, and possible bankruptcy implications.

The Concerns of Older Couples

Older couples present unique issues. First, there may be emotional advantages for them in remaining unmarried, especially if either or both partners had a nasty divorce or have children who may be troubled by a perceived "displacement" of the memory of a recently deceased parent. A remarriage also can trigger intense concerns about estate outcomes in the minds of children, especially if they believe that this is part of a plan to shift "their" inheritance to the new spouse. In some states, a spouse is entitled to a minimum share of the estate of a deceased spouse, and thus marrying will trigger these obligations in a way that cohabitation would not. Marriage also can result in one spouse being on the hook financially for a partner's long-term care expenses or reduce the collective Social Security income; and if the remarriage happens before a divorced or widowed spouse turns sixty, it could jeopardize the divorced or widowed spouse's ability to receive Social Security survivor benefits. Remarriage typically cuts off alimony payments from a prior marriage, and it generally terminates survivor annuities for various public pension and even military pensions. When partners combine their lives, this can also result in higher reported incomes, which can jeopardize one partner's child's college financial aid eligibility.

After reviewing the financial and property aspects of marriage, discuss with your clients the illness and disability issues (powers of attorney and medical directives) and the consequences of not having wills or trusts. If there are children in the picture, discuss how marital status might affect parentage rights and obligations (an issue that only arises if one or both of them are not the biological parents of the child). Then, depending on the financial condition of your clients, explain the basic tax consequences of marriage, which generally provides a tax burden for dual-career couples during the course of the relationship but a sizable tax savings upon dissolution or the death of either partner.

Review the couple's particular questions with a goal of empowering the partners to figure out which concerns would impact their choice from among a variety of acceptable options as married or unmarried (such as a property-sharing arrangement) and which issues will be determined entirely based upon their marital or registration status (or registration for same-sex couples) without any option of a private agreement, such as access to Social Security benefits or certain health insurance benefits. Strive to help them identify their top-ranking concerns—which may be philosophical, financial, tax-based, or emotional in nature and not necessarily just legal—so that they can figure out which choice is best for them given their real-life priorities.

In light of all of these concerns, sketch out in holistic terms four viable paths that they could follow: the nonmarital/unregistered status road, with or without a private agreement, or the marital/registration status road, with or without a private agreement. Once you've completed the preliminary mapping of the options, then try to gain a more precise sense of whether or not a modifying agreement is needed under each option. Few nonlawyers understand the concept of fiduciary duty, and this is something that should be discussed with your clients. Simply put, a confidential or fiduciary relationship imposes a duty on each party to put the other's interests on equal footing with his own. It's the legal version of the Golden Rule: Do not treat others differently than the way you would want to be treated. Fiduciary rules apply generally to married couples based upon their marital status; they don't apply to unmarried partners unless they take on those roles through particular actions, such as co-owning a house or having one person handle both partners' finances. While these nuances don't have a great deal of impact on most couples, the rules can make a very real difference at the time of breakup, where an alleged breach of fiduciary duty can greatly expand the scope of claims made by one partner against the other one.

After reviewing how being married is likely to affect your clients' lives while they are living happily together, you should then walk your clients through the dissolution process. Referring to their current financial situation, explain which assets most likely would be marital or community property and which would be separate property and explain how the alimony rules (called *spousal support* in California) would most likely be applied. You can then explain how some of these rules can be modified by a premarital or post-marital agreement and compare those scenarios to what would happen (in the absence of an agreement) if they remained unmarried. Finally, describe how they could implement their financial plans (such as a sharing of assets) either as a married or an unmarried couple, explaining how the legal presumptions work and how they would be different depending on their marital status.

Guided through this multistage analysis, most couples will be able to determine rather quickly that they should follow one of the following four paths:

1. Remain unmarried and unregistered without signing any written agreement but with some adjustments to their financial arrangements (e.g., retitling of accounts or deeds) and the basic disability and death planning documents.
2. Remain unmarried and unregistered but enter into a written co-ownership or financial agreement either waiving or providing for some sharing of assets long-term and addressing any potential claims for post-separation support (especially important for couples living in a common law marriage state) and also make some adjustments to their financial arrangements (e.g., retitling of accounts or deeds) as well as sign the basic disability and death planning documents.
3. Get married or registered (depending on which is recognized in their jurisdiction given their sexual orientation) but also enter into a premarital or post-marital or registration agreement, opting out of some of the marital rules.
4. Get married or registered and not enter into a modifying agreement, simply accepting the statutory marital rules to regulate their life together.

Once you jointly determine which is the best path for them to follow, which sometimes requires a second meeting after some additional research or fact-finding or some emotional soul-searching on their part (usually without you in the room), you can then jointly determine what specific tasks need to be done to implement the agreed-upon plan.

A note about the impact of marriage on the choice of surnames: In most states, a spouse can take the other partner's last name upon marriage or domestic partnership registration as part of the process of obtaining a marriage license, though in some states the rules are still gender-biased and only allow the wife to take the husband's last name. Believe it or not, this discriminatory legal remnant was eliminated in California only a few years ago! Absent a legal marriage or registration, the ordinary name change rules apply: In some states, this can only be done by court order; and in other jurisdictions, a last name can be changed by usage. Your clients should avoid name changes by usage as this practice can create tremendous difficulties, especially in the realm of Homeland Security.[7] Be sure that your clients understand the procedures for changing names; the consequences in terms of credit, titles, passports, and Social Security; and the difficulty of changing their names back in the event of a dissolution.

C. The Indirect Consequences of Cohabitation

One of the myths that many clients have is that cohabitation is so utterly outside of the legal realm that it has few, if any, legal consequences, except perhaps for the very rich or famous. This is not entirely true, and depending on the applicable rules of your jurisdiction and the particulars of the couple's legal and financial lives, there can be unforeseen consequences of nonmarital cohabitation. Some of these issues, as already mentioned, involve exposure to a palimony claim or the imposition of state-mandated partition rules about co-owned property or the nonreimbursable treatment of gifts between partners. Explaining these risks is part of the general education you need to provide to your clients as they consider cohabiting. Some of the lesser-recognized risks of cohabitation include the following:

- loss of means-based government benefits due to imputed income or housing-related benefits from cohabiting, especially if the financially dependent partner is living rent-free in a partner's residence; this can arise for those receiving disability benefits that are means-based or where a reduction in necessary expenses (e.g., housing) can reduce the amount of the benefit;
- loss of child or spousal support due to the application of a state statute or judgment (which usually refers to cohabiting with a person of the opposite sex but could be interpreted to apply to a same-sex cohabitation with a romantic partner);
- negative impacts on existing child custody arrangements, especially if the other parent and the new partner don't get along or if the cohabitation confirms a shift in sexual orientation (either by a formerly lesbian or gay co-parent who is now living with an

Every few years, a client asks me about the option of adopting his partner, as an adult adoption. At first blush, this seems like an attractive option; it can ease inheritance issues and reduce some transfer tax issues, and it is far less likely to be challenged by a suspicious and resentful relative. For same-sex couples who are not allowed to marry or register as civil union or domestic partners, it creates a legal relationship that feels secure to the partners. But I strongly discourage clients from choosing this option. It can create terrible problems in the event of a breakup and just doesn't seem appropriate given the romantic partnership relationship. My favorite "be careful what you wish for" story involved an adult adoption of a woman by her wealthy partner, seeking to make the younger partner a beneficiary of the wealthy woman's father's trust (as a legal grandchild). They later broke up, and the wealthy woman and her family all tried to invalidate the adoption on the grounds that the state in which they truly resided had a minimum age-differentiation requirement between the partners that they did not satisfy. The case eventually settled, but what a legal mess!

opposite-sex partner or a formerly straight co-parent now living with a same-sex partner);

- unintended encouragement of a de facto parental relationship between a nonbiological, nonlegal parent and a minor child (especially a child who doesn't have a second legal parent or, in states that have adopted the intentional parentage doctrine, a child born of one of the partners via an assisted reproduction process); and

- imposition of marital law through a finding of a putative marriage, for couples in common law states or on couples who have participated in some form of formal wedding or marriage ceremony, where a court might find that they have a putative marriage even if either of the partners has a decided preference to not be considered legally married.

NOTES

1. Not surprisingly, the strongest push for domestic partnership coverage occurred in cities with the greatest numbers of gay men concerned about health insurance. While rarely documented in any written reports, I often

encountered these concerns when lobbying for passage of such provisions in San Francisco, Berkeley, and Oakland in the early 1980s.

2. *See, e.g.,* Devaney v. L'Esperance, 949 A.2d 743 (N.J. 2008) (holding that a noncohabiting girlfriend was able to pursue a palimony claim against her boyfriend of twenty years).

3. The shift of allegiances by an older unmarried partner (from his children to the new partner) can be fraught with emotional tensions, especially if the children view the new partner as an outsider. Given these concerns, it is especially important that the lawyer be clear about who is the client and who is giving directions and making the key decisions.

4. Excellent overviews of the powerful influence that marriage has on our social culture can be found in Andrew Cherlin, The Marriage-Go-Round (Random House 2009); E. J. Graff, What Is Marriage For? (Beacon Press 2000); and Stephanie Coontz, Marriage, A History (Viking Press 2005).

5. 1 U.S.C. § 7 and 28 U.S.C. § 1738C.

6. A few federal agencies have found ways to extend spousal rights and burdens to same-sex couples. The Internal Revenue Service recently issued a Chief Counsel Advisory Opinion stating that community property income in California, Nevada, and Washington would be treated as such even though the partners are still legally single, and a bankruptcy court recently ruled that a registered couple would only be entitled to a single residence exception based upon state law treatment of the partners as a married couple. I.R.S. CCA 2010210; *In re* Balas and Morales, U.S. Bankruptcy Court, 2:11-bk-17831 TD.

7. Transportation Security Administration (TSA) rules mandate that boarding passes at airports be in the same name as the government identification, and most airlines insist that the names match the credit card information, so playing loose with surnames can create real problems for travelers.

CHAPTER FOUR

COUNSELING LOW-ASSET COHABITING RENTERS

They don't own a home, they barely have any savings, frequently they are burdened by a weighty load of credit card debt, and they are way too young to turn their attention to estate planning. As it turns out, the majority of cohabiting couples fit this description. If you are going to market yourself as an attorney who provides counseling to unmarried couples, you will need to be equipped to serve the needs of these lower net-worth clients—and be able to do so in an affordable manner.

Some lawyers take the attitude that it isn't worth serving clients who can't afford to pay their regular hourly rate, or those unwilling to work with a lawyer who prefers to meet all of their needs in a comprehensive manner. While this approach may seem fine for some lawyers, especially those with several decades of experience in this area who are turning away full-paying clients on a regular basis, most young lawyers cannot afford to adopt such an attitude. For them, the less affluent clients will be the only ones coming in the door in the early years.

Regardless of your attitude, you should bear in mind that many of those folks go on to save money, buy houses, receive stock options, have children, and sometimes break up, in or outside of a marriage. Many may become high-paying clients one day, and so their calls should not be spurned. Other lawyers may be inclined to lend a hand out of a sense of social duty, assisting a broader range of clients with a wider range of assets and questions. Most lawyers would benefit by serving a full range of clients in an efficient and effective manner; it can be the best form of lawyer advertising available, usually at a lower cost than taking out a display ad in a local newspaper!

A. BEST METHODS OF SERVING LOWER-INCOME CLIENTS

You need to approach these clients with the realization that most of them will not be able to afford three to five hours of your time for a comprehensive co-ownership or cohabitation agreement and may not be able to spend two to three hours in your office talking about the legal consequences of marriage. Thus, in order to be effective and not drain yourself by underbilling for hours of work that your clients can't afford, you will want to develop creative ways of serving these clients.

Here are a few practical suggestions on how to do so:

1. Create a simple one-page summary of your state's key rules for each subarea of your practice (property law, parentage and adoption, estate planning, public benefits, elder law, etc.) and distribute it free of charge to all potential clients. Make sure that you aren't giving any legal advice (add an express disclaimer to that effect at the bottom of the page), and display an attractive logo at the top of the summary sheet or use your letterhead so potential clients know your contact information.

2. Launch a website that contains your summary of legal information as well as links to other resources of interest to unmarried couples, both gay and straight. Again, each page should have contact information for your office and a disclaimer that this information does not constitute legal advice. You may want to provide regular updates on changes in the law that you learn about as a way of providing useful educational information and expanding the marketing value of your blog or website.

3. Distribute a list of published resources (such as the Nolo Press books *Living Together: A Legal Guide for Unmarried Couples* and *A Legal Guide for Lesbian and Gay Couples*) and encourage your clients to read them in advance of meeting with you.

4. Create a series of simplified templates such as those included in this volume, appropriate to the laws of your particular state and your primary areas of emphasis. The time you spend creating these forms is not billable, but doing this ahead of time will make it possible for you to serve your clients more affordably.
5. Consider a flat fee arrangement for certain simple agreements such as a co-ownership agreement—even if that rate is lower than what your hourly fee would be for doing that same amount of work—and treat the additional time you spend on this work as part of your marketing plan.
6. Offer a private "clinic" for unmarried couples on a regular basis, ideally in the evenings, where you provide basic education (not legal advice) on the key issues facing unmarried couples. You can tell prospective clients that if they attend that clinic in advance, the total fees for your work will be lower since you won't have to spend time providing them basic legal information. You can either charge a nominal fee ($25 or $50 per attendee) or, better yet, offer the clinic for free as part of your marketing strategy.
7. Train your legal assistant or paralegal to handle the intake process, and empower your staff to compile the basic financial information on your clients; and in some instances, have them create agreements, powers of attorney, or estate planning documents based upon the templates that you have drafted.

Be warned: Unmarried couples seem particularly reluctant to spend money on lawyers. Part of this has to do with their generally lower incomes compared to married folks, but it's heightened by their view of their status as temporary and thus disconnected from any legal obligations. Because of this resistance, you may hit up against the wall of your own standards of attorney competence and the quality of your work as you plow your way through the thicket of counseling low-asset clients.

There are times when each of us bangs up against limits that must be acknowledged. Even when I strive to tailor my way of working to meet the lower-income clients' needs, I still am told by some callers that they cannot afford to pay my fees or retain me on a limited-scope basis. In part that is because I can't afford to discount my fees dramatically, and sometimes it's because I am reluctant to donate pro bono services to clients that I believe can afford my fees. Thus, from time to time, I simply decline to accept the work—and surely you will have to do the same from time to time as well.

The best way to achieve a balance in these potentially turbulent waters is to develop a three-tiered approach to responding to low-income clients' needs:

- *Full-Service Work.* You bill on an hourly basis in a comprehensive manner, including meeting with clients to evaluate their overall legal situation, preparing detailed agreements that fully meet your legal standards, and sending out summary letters and cautionary advice to address the peripheral issues that are not being handled in your immediate scope of work.
- *Limited-Scope Legal Services.* You agree to perform a limited scope of work (such as drafting a simple co-ownership agreement or reviewing a will that was drafted by your client from a self-help resource) but don't provide any of the broader counseling services and/or perhaps agree to a flat-fee or reduced-fee arrangement as part of your long-term marketing strategy (in this situation, you always should have a signed retainer agreement that delineates the limited scope of your work).
- *Declination of Services.* You provide a packet of informational material and reference books and, if appropriate, an invitation to participate in one of your legal educational clinics (in this situation, you should send out a note or email confirming that you're not providing any legal services to this client).

B. THE RENTERS' CONCERNS

The chief concern of many lower-income couples is how to share their rented home. There are two dimensions to this scenario: (1) the relationship between the unmarried tenants (jointly) and their landlord and (2) the relationship between the unmarried tenants.

Landlord-Tenant Relationship

In most instances there will be a signed lease, and only the party who has signed the lease is directly liable to the landlord—and only that tenant has a presumptive right to occupy the unit. As long as the couple is living together, this won't be a thorny issue, and most landlords won't care if there is an unrelated tenant sharing the unit. Historically, there were landlords who refused to rent to unmarried couples, and only one partner could sign the lease or negotiate with the landlord, but few couples face this sort of discrimination nowadays (and it is probably illegal in most states).[1] But the landlord has the right to know who is living in the unit, and if both partners are sharing the occupancy of the rental unit, they should be up-front about their cohabitation.

Cohabitants should not conceal their cohabitation status or refuse to cosign a lease together. Landlords have good reasons for insisting that every occupant signs the lease. Only where the relationship is transient or where the partner only lives in the unit part-time is there a legitimate reason for both partners declining to sign the lease.

The tougher problems arise if the couple breaks up. If only one of the partners is on the lease, in most jurisdictions the landlord can evict the nonsigning partner at the expiration of the lease or when the legal tenant moves out. The nonsigning partner is, in effect, a guest (an "invitee") or a subtenant, and in either scenario the guest or subtenant also must leave when the legal tenant leaves. If market rent is being paid and the remaining partner has a decent income, the landlord generally will be glad to have him sign a new lease and become the legal tenant. However, if the rent has been unusually low or if the landlord has other plans (e.g., to sell the building or rent to a family member) or if the nonsigning partner has questionable credit or income, the landlord may exercise her right to throw them out. This is the primary reason why it's best to have both parties on the lease.

On the other hand, not being on the lease can come in handy when the lease has been broken or if some of the rent hasn't been paid. In most states, a landlord can "deem" an occupant a tenant and seek rent for the period of time that he is living there or else evict him. But if both parties have vacated and back rent is due, chances are that the landlord will only be able to pursue the one who signed the lease. This is especially true when there is an attorney fees clause in the lease as that would only be binding on the one who signed the lease, especially where the occupancy status of the partner is a bit gray or if the details of the occupancy are unknown to the landlord.

The handling of security deposits can be tricky for unmarried tenants. Usually, the landlord will treat the one who signed the lease as the

If you have clients who live in one of the few remaining cities with rent control (such as San Francisco or New York City), the legal status of their relationship can have a great impact on the rent that can be charged to the one who stays behind if the couple breaks up, and even on the determination of whether or not the partner can remain in the unit. In some cities, there is a process by which a partner must be accepted as a legal tenant (generally by notifying the landlord of the relationship during the occupancy of the legal tenant), and subsequently that tenant can benefit from the reduced rent and security of tenancy even if the original tenant moves out or dies. Some cities recognize domestic partnership or civil union partners, and in some instances de facto cohabitation is sufficient for survivability of a rent control benefit—but you should be on top of the rules for your particular city when advising unmarried tenants.[2]

"owner" of the security deposit even if the partner contributed to it. If a tenant who legally paid the deposit leaves, then that is the one who gets the deposit back. An ex who wants to stay in the apartment has to pony up a fresh deposit, and if that person contributed to the other's deposit, the landlord will leave it to the tenants to battle over its distribution.

Shared-Tenant Relationships

Sometimes there are no conflicts with the landlord but rather a dispute between the partners at the time of a breakup. Some disputes are rather straightforward, where one partner claims that they had an agreement to share rental expenses and is seeking reimbursement from the one who didn't pay his share. This claim will be handled as any other nonmarital dispute and may or may not be enforceable in the absence of a written agreement. Most clients are best served by pursuing a small claims action on their own, with your services limited to advising and coaching them on their presentation in court.

The more difficult conflict arises where the couple is breaking up, and both of the partners want to keep the unit, especially if the rent is particularly low. Unless the partners have a written agreement that covers that issue, the one on the lease has the first right to stay; and if both of them are on the lease (or if there is no written lease), neither of them has a legal primary right that can be enforced in court. Rather, it's an issue best delegated to mediation, where the broader issues of need, financial ability, and the history of the occupancy of the apartment can

Not every couple sharing an apartment needs a written agreement. However, you should recommend an agreement whenever any of the following situations exists:

- The rent is exceptionally high (over $2,500 a month), and one partner is paying all or nearly all of it.
- The rent is significantly below market rate, either with or without rent control protections, such that having to move would be onerous for the relocating partner.
- There is a personal connection between one of the partners and the rental unit, either a family connection with the owner or a workplace or child-care proximity, such that relocating would be especially hard on one of the partners.
- One of the partners resided there for some time before the other one moved in, and so it would be unfair to force the original occupant to relocate upon a breakup.

be taken into consideration. Given the typically small amount of money at issue, it usually makes most sense for your clients to work with a local community mediation board, and you can limit your services to a brief consultation where you explain the lack of legal options to your client. You might consider suggesting that the one leaving should be paid something by the one who gets to stay behind so that there is a sharing of the financial benefits of the lower-cost housing.

C. Co-Ownership of a Particular Asset

While owning a car or a computer may not compare to a major corporate transaction for most lawyers, the proper handling of these assets can be of great significance for low-income clients, both because of the utility value of these items and because they often represent their only asset. Helping the couple document its arrangements and working out the specifics of its co-ownership is a valuable service that you should offer.

There are several key issues that come up in each of these situations: ownership, title, purchase contributions, payment of ongoing expenses, debts connected to the asset, use of the asset, insurance coverage, breakup, and pets.

Ownership

In most instances one of the partners is the sole legal owner of the asset, and in other situations (such as a car) the partners are co-owners. You need to state clearly who the legal owner is and be sure you (or the client) inspects the legal title (if there is one) to confirm that it is consistent with their understanding. For a car or boat (or even a mobile home), the partners will need to decide whether this is an "and" or an "or" ownership, because in many states either of the owners can unilaterally transfer title (to a third party or to himself) if it is an "or" co-ownership.

Title

If for any reason the title is not in sync with the partners' agreement, they need a written contract to address the equitable ownership rights of the nontitled owner. Bear in mind that if there is a fraudulent purpose for keeping someone off title, the agreement may not be legally enforceable. And even if the arrangement is totally legitimate, there can be problems if the titled owner makes off with the proceeds of an unauthorized sale because the other partner may be unable to recoup her losses. Given these concerns, it is always preferable to have the documented title match the agreed-upon terms.

Purchase Contributions

The agreement should recite who contributed what amounts to the purchase of the asset; and if the contributions are inconsistent with the ownership (either because one investor was off the title or because one co-owner contributed more than 50 percent), the agreement should state whether the excess contribution is a gift, a loan, or an investment that results in one partner owning a greater percentage of the asset. Bear in mind that many of these items have very little resale value, and so if one partner is entitled to a reimbursement of an excess contribution (as opposed to a greater share of the proceeds), there may be nothing left over for the other partner.

Payment of Ongoing Expenses

Frequently, there are ongoing expenses associated with the ownership of an asset, such as car payments or repairs or monthly subscription fees for an electronic device. As with the purchase price, the allocation of these costs should be detailed in the agreement along with a provision that covers the consequences of one person paying less than his fair share.

Debts Connected to the Asset

Whenever something is purchased with a credit card or if there is a loan associated with the asset, the partners need to figure out who carries the burden of the loan. This is especially true where only one partner is listed on the loan as the borrower as that is who will be stuck legally if the debt doesn't get paid. At a minimum, there should be an indemnification agreement so that a partner who pays more has a right of recovery from his partner (most likely becoming an ex-partner rather soon). As with all other debts, the partners must bear in mind that a legal right to collect something doesn't guarantee payment if the debtor turns out to be a deadbeat.

Use of the Asset

The use of most shared things is best handled informally, but in some instances (especially if it's a car) there can be a provision for divvying up the use of the resource. Sometimes it's simply a matter of reciting that the use will be shared "equitably," but occasionally there should be specific times and dates of preferred access for each partner, for instance, if the primary purpose of the vehicle is for one partner's job.

Insurance Coverage

If the asset in question has significant value or could cause injury to someone (e.g., an automobile), the insurance issues must be addressed. Every effort should be made to make sure that both partners are covered by the insurance, and the extent of coverage and the payment of the premiums should also be addressed. Bear in mind that if one partner is the sole owner of a home, her unmarried partner's personal belongings are not going to be covered by the homeowners policy. And unless there is a joint renters policy (which may not always be available for unmarried partners), each partner will have to obtain a separate renters policy.

Breakup

The relationship may not outlast the working life of the asset, and so the issue of who gets to keep it (and under what terms) will need to be covered. It is questionable to have the partners share an asset post-dissolution—at least that should not be a requirement of the agreement. Instead, one partner should be entitled to keep the asset with some form of compensation (or trading of another asset) to the other partner. If the couple's relationship is such that a shared use is possible post-dissolution, then that is something that should be worked out at the time and not set up as an obligation in advance. If selecting the lucky recipient of a special asset can't be dealt with in advance, then you should set up a selection system (a coin toss works fine) with the terms of reimbursement to the losing party set up in advance. The hardest challenge is figuring out what is a fair payment, especially where the resale value may be much less than what it would cost to actually replace the item. Finding a good-quality used car may be possible at a decent price, but finding a reliable used computer is rarely so easy. One way to deal with this is to set up reciprocal trades that leave each partner with a bundle of items with a total value that is roughly equivalent; if that's not possible, pick a midway point between resale and replacement cost for the buyout value (e.g., one-third of the spread between the two extremes).

Pets

Disputes over pets can be devastating whether the couple is married or not, and sometimes they can be as heated and passionate as child custody disputes. Oftentimes, the partners have a powerful emotional connection to a pet as well as a genuine devotion to its care and well-being. If a pet has been in the family for some time and is in poor medical condition at the time of the breakup, the feelings can be intense both because of the financial burden of the veterinary care and because of the uncertainties surrounding long-term care. Making matters worse, legal ownership of a pet is often ambiguous; usually one partner is the only one on the documents, but that may simply be the result of who happened to pick up the pet or whose credit card was used for the purchase or licensing. A pet may have been a gift from one partner to the other or may have started out as one partner's pet and then become a member of the family. Moving can create difficulties, especially if one of the partners is moving to a home or apartment that doesn't accept pets.

While each pet-custody drama has its own resolution, it is best to urge your clients to designate one partner as the primary owner with the first right to keep the pet upon a breakup. As with other assets, if they can't agree on this designation in advance, they should agree on a fair resolution process to follow at that time. Unless a fair amount of money was spent on acquiring the pet (over $100 would be a reasonable threshold), don't recommend any financial settlement. Rather, encourage folks to consider an informal "visitation" policy or, better yet, a trade-off for some other valuable asset (even a nonliving asset like a work of art). The pain of the loss should be recognized with some gesture of acknowledgement that is commensurate with the loss. Ongoing shared custody of a pet is simply too difficult for the pet, let alone for the owners long-term.

D. Shared Accounts, Credit Cards, and Joint Liability

Shared Debts

Just like owning an American Express card, being in a same-sex unmarried relationship has some advantages, or, to adapt a modified version of their marketing slogan, "Oppression has its privileges." In other words, there are certain areas of the law, such as joint liability for debts, where being unmarried has some definite benefits. This is true for unmarried couples of any sexual orientation, and while high-net-worth couples and even homeowners can encounter messy struggles in the territory of debt, it is often the lower-asset partners who most frequently need this help.

The problems generally arise out of the following scenarios: Either one partner has bad credit and thus can't get a loan or a credit card, or the couple (either individually or jointly) has sufficient financial problems that the partners take on too much debt without adequately addressing which debts are whose. Married couples often are jointly liable for all debts simply because the lender or credit card issuer insists on treating the partners as a single borrower or because the partners' credit ratings are so intertwined that neither of them can access credit independently or on better terms than the spouse. And even when married spouses are not directly liable jointly, there are preset rules for reimbursements and indemnification if one of them has to shoulder a debt that is legally considered joint. Unmarried partners can apply for loans or credit cards as single individuals and have their own credit history and aren't linked legally to their partner, but they still can find themselves in sticky messes when they could have avoided the problems by keeping their accounts and loans separate.

Your emphasis should be on keeping your clients free of these predicaments, as you may not be able to help after the problems have arisen. The following is a survey of the problems that most typically arise.

Your Debt Is My Debt. If one partner elects to help out a partner by authorizing him as a user of the credit card or if one partner takes out a loan (student or car or personal credit line) and uses the proceeds to pay for something that solely benefits the nonborrower, there is going to be a serious problem if the beneficiary of this generosity never repays the borrower. The lender is not going to care how the funds were used, and if the partner is an authorized user of the card, there hasn't been any illegality or impropriety so the borrower can't seek to escape the debt. The only escape is bankruptcy or just being so poor that the lender gives up trying to recover any payment, neither of which is very attractive to most clients.

A variant of this situation can arise when both parties are on the card or loan, but the proceeds only benefit one of the parties. The creditor typically has the right to pursue either or both parties, including the one who didn't benefit from the loan. There is no legal defense that the nonbenefiting party can raise in response to this claim, and the one stuck paying the bill only has a private right to pursue the other partner for reimbursement.

Even when your client believes that she has been defrauded, the credit card issuer might contend otherwise. A client of mine once discovered that her ex-partner had "borrowed" her identity and obtained a second credit card and then took out a major cash advance against my client's balance. The ex felt that this was only fair given that the borrower had dumped her unceremoniously. My client claimed that this was a fraudulent charge that should be reversed, but the creditor took a very pro-relationship position (in its own self-interest), claiming that since the girlfriend had access to the account information and theirs was a marriage-like relationship, it wasn't fraud and so my client was liable for the debt.

Having a written agreement confirming the obligation is a good thing, and small claims court is the best route for your clients to take. But remember—receiving a winning judgment won't produce the funds if the obligated party is broke.

Our Debt Is My Debt. The reverse situation arises where the debts were incurred for a joint expense either on a joint credit card or loan or as one partner's debt where one of the partners doesn't pay his share of the bill. This can arise in a breakup situation, an intact relationship where one partner simply doesn't have the funds to make a fair contribution, or even where both partners have the funds but where one has a grudge or claim on an unrelated matter and feels entitled to withhold payment on an otherwise valid debt.

In a marital divorce, the paying party often can obtain an offset against some other debt or obligation or obtain a judgment that can haunt the debtor for decades. For unmarried partners, unfortunately, the only remedy is a civil lawsuit, most typically in small claims court. Such claims rarely are successful since, in the absence of a written agreement for repayment, the judge may conclude that the excess contributor was making a gift or there was some other form of exchange. As with the other debts, having a written contract is a good thing, and you should always encourage your clients to get one signed—but they should not be naïve about the likelihood of recovery.

The Bottom Line. The results in court for shared liability claims by unmarried couples are woefully unpredictable in the absence of a written contract, and lenders are going to pursue the one whose name is on the dotted line without regard to any private arrangements. They aren't going to be concerned about the stories of breached obligations and no-good ex-partners; and unless there is a valid written agreement, chances are that most judges aren't going to be sympathetic to a claim for reimbursement launched against a former lover. Add to these problems the slim chances of actually recovering on a court judgment, and there really is only one way to approach these situations. A partner should only "lend" (or take on liability) for the benefit of the other partner if the lending partner is willing to have those funds retroactively converted into a gift. The outcome is not going to be a pleasant one, especially where the recipient shows little or no appreciation (and may already have left the client or left town or both), but there's little other guidance that a lawyer should provide.

Shared Savings

Every state has its own rules about who "owns" a depository account, but generally the rules are quite simple: the named owner owns the funds in the account. Adding someone as a "payable on death" (POD) party doesn't make that person an owner of the assets as long as the titled owner is alive, and if the account includes savings from a nonowner, that partner won't be able to make a claim against the financial institution but has to pursue the other partner to get the rightful share.

Having said this, though, it's not always clear who owns the funds in a joint account. If it's a joint tenancy account, which is most common, then presumptively each party owns 50 percent regardless of his contributions. If one partner has put in more than half of the investment, she can make a claim for reimbursement in some states, but proving a legal right to some of the money back will be nearly impossible. In most instances funds were put in and taken out over years, and so it isn't possible to claim that any one portion of the account "belongs" to one of the parties. Once again, in the absence of a written agreement, the partners should assume they own the account fifty-fifty. However, they need to be careful: In some states a joint tenancy account is deemed to be owned "equally and fully" by both parties, and so either party can withdraw the entirety of the funds without any duty of reimbursement to the other party.[3]

If the account is held as tenants in common and there is demonstrable proof that one partner put in all or most of the investment funds, courts in most states can allocate the funds in proportion to each party's contribution. But this rarely happens. In most instances this is because the evidentiary trail is just too fuzzy to meet the legal standards for proving an agreement or an equitable basis for a reimbursement or unequal distribution; or the funds are already depleted, so spending money to pursue such a claim is just another example of good money chasing after bad.

In many jurisdictions, there is another overriding cause for concern: Whether or not the judge contends that this is a marriage-like relationship where everything is shared, for better or worse, or is disdainful of the claimant for being so ill-advised as to enter into a nonmarital relationship, there may well be a lack of sympathy—and sometimes even some not-so-hidden contempt—for the claimant. In either event, the judge probably isn't going to reach out and help the plaintiff; and so, just as with the shared debts, the one who put more into the account is likely to be disappointed.

There are all sorts of "dumb" reasons why folks put their money in other people's accounts. Sometimes this happens for entirely legitimate reasons; for example, one partner is traveling overseas for a few months and there is a payment in cash that is received after he is out of town. Other times, the partners are working on a joint venture or are selling a joint asset such as a car, and it is just simpler to deposit the funds into one account. In some cases, a client might felt that the partner's investment adviser is doing a fabulous job and doesn't want to be bothered setting up her own account. In each of these situations, the partners were acting as trustful friends in a marriage-like situation, and the one whose name was on the account was clearly acting as a fiduciary or constructive trustee. In other situations, your client might add a partner as a joint tenant with rights of survivorship in lieu of a will, where the client doesn't realize that a POD designation would achieve the same result without jeopardizing the ownership of the account during her lifetime. If the facts can be proven, the off-title contributor will win a judgment recovering the investment, but that doesn't bring the money back if the titled owner has already taken off with the funds.

The trickier situations arise when the motivations for the shifting of funds were less than honorable. There are many varieties of messy situations: "lenders" who turn out to be drug dealers hiding the profits of

Early on in my career, I agreed to represent a guy who had a signed promissory note from his partner, so I figured it wouldn't be hard to win at trial. I was only hired a few weeks before trial, and there wasn't time or funds for discovery, but the case seemed pretty straightforward. Unfortunately, when my client was being questioned on the stand by his ex-lover (who was sufficiently savvy as to go to trial without an attorney) as to where he thought the funds for repayment were going to come from, my client burst out with the true answer: "I knew you had used my money to invest in a drug deal, so I expected to get my fair share of the profits." Telling the truth didn't help here at all: The judge promptly banged the gavel on his desk and said, "Case dismissed," strongly suggesting that if we didn't all leave the courtroom quickly, he would have the bailiff send my client and his ex over to the district attorney's office for questioning.

their trade, welfare recipients who didn't want to have to report under-the-table earned income, partners who were trying to conceal their full income from their ex-spouses (thus hoping to avoid having to pay child support), and those whose debts to others were sufficiently great to motivate them to hide money in their partner's name for years on end. In these situations, the legal advice is short and brutal: If the underlying purpose of the agreement is illegal, no court is going to grant recovery even if the result is a windfall for the one who ended up with the funds.

E. Allocation and Record of the Shared Living Expenses

One of the luxuries of marital law is that the rules for sharing of living expenses are fairly well defined. Spouses have a legal duty to take care of each other's basic needs. If they pool their incomes or share their expenses, or even if one spouse covers joint expenses with separately owned funds to cover their living expenses, those expenditures are not reimbursable in the event of dissolution. Indeed, it would seem quite bizarre to most folks if a husband retroactively billed his wife for the housing and travel expenses they incurred, as much as some would love to do that at the time of a divorce.

There are certain expressly demarcated exceptions to these rules; for example, in California some post-separation expenses are reimbursable as part of the final dissolution judgment, as are contributions from one spouse's premarital assets to the separate property asset of the other spouse. But a marital unit is considered to be a single economic entity, and so excess contributions are rarely reimbursed.

Life is not so neatly organized for unmarried partners. Generally speaking, there is no duty of support for one partner to voluntarily help pay the daily expenses of his partner. As one judge said in a case I consulted on some time ago, "being generous to a loved one in the reasonable expectation that the other party will reciprocate the generosity does not impose a legal duty on the recipient to do so." There may be a social expectation or even a moral obligation to repay the helpful partner, but rarely does this rise to the level of a legal obligation that can be enforced in court.

Judges tend to reach this conclusion from a variety of different paths. Some assert that these relationships are by definition family- or marriage-like in nature, where there is a presumption that any contribution is a gift, and thus there is no consideration for a contractual obligation. Others focus on the history of reciprocity within the relationship (e.g., where one year's assistance by one partner is followed by the other's help in a subsequent year or where there are some other nonquantifiable benefits that are seen as the exchange for the excess contribution). In some cases the evidence is so spotty and inconsistent that even the amount of money contributed by the generous partner cannot be readily determined.

The end result in just about every case is that any contribution that a partner makes to the other partner's ongoing living expenses will be considered a gift unless there is a legally binding contract—and usually this mandates a written document—setting forth the terms of the agreement. Writing these agreements is not complicated, and for your sake and your clients' sake, you should make a concerted effort to keep them simple. Assume that your clients will probably never return to you to update the agreement, so it's best to set forth some general rules that will apply well into the future rather than dealing solely with one set of preexisting transactions and expecting the clients to update their agreement in the future.

The following are things that you should generally include in such an agreement:

- *General Operating Rules.* It's helpful to have a set of presumed operating rules of the household, i.e., how housing, food, travel, and other expenses are going to be covered. The agreement should set forth distinct categories of "separate" obligations (student loans, extended family obligations, child support for a child who is not the legal child of the partner, and the like) and define which categories are shared expenses. It is also helpful to describe how incomes are going to be handled: Will everything be pooled in a single account or kept separate? Will bills be paid in part by each partner, or will there be a combined approach where some funds are pooled each month to cover joint expenses and others are kept separate to cover separate expenses or to be reserved for personal savings?
- *Presumed Default.* Generally, the default rule is that nothing is to be reimbursed unless there is a written affirmation of the obligation by the recipient or alternatively, (depending on how the

parties design their agreement) a written demand for reimbursement made within thirty days of the contribution. Your goal here is to avoid a situation where a partner acts generously but then retroactively sends a bill when feelings harden. Requiring a written demand for repayment or, for certain couples, an express affirmation by the recipient of the funds of a repayment duty also establishes a date of the promise to make the payment, which clarifies the statute of limitations for its enforcement.

- *Standards for the Reimbursement Agreement.* You will want to be clear about what constitutes an affirmation or a demand for reimbursement: Is it sufficient to write a note on a check, or does there need to be a separate written demand? Is email sufficient (generally yes, since that is how most partners communicate), and does it have to reference a specific transaction as opposed to a generalized category of assistance?

- *Repayment Obligations.* What does it mean to have a duty to repay someone? When is the payment due, and is any interest accruing on the debt? Is there a right to attorney fees if a lawsuit is filed? A reasonable default position is that no interest accrues and no attorney fees are awarded on these sorts of claims. A good rule of thumb is that claims for repayment must be made within two years of when the obligation arises rather than allowing the claims to rack up (absent renewal of the written obligation) and only be presented decades later when the relationship unravels.

- *Categories of Expenses.* For some couples, it makes sense to have certain categories of expenses shared while others are handled separately—with an agreement that if one partner pays more than 50 percent of the shared expenses and/or any of the separate expenses of the other partner, those excess contributions will be reimbursed. This is particularly useful in situations where one partner clearly needs help meeting his bills from time to time but the underlying assumption is that help in these categories of expenses is a loan, not a gift. This would be most appropriate when the payments are connected to something that is not usually considered a "family" expense, such as an expense for an unrelated family member or child, a business that is solely owned by the other partner, or an educational expense that will have a future benefit only to the nonpaying partner.

Lurking beneath many of these debates is the fundamental question of what is fair in unmarried partnerships, especially where one partner has significantly greater assets or income. Once again, marital law has this worked out for couples: The state's family law declares what is shared and what is not, and there is a set of rules for allocating debt and savings upon dissolution—either community property with its tight rules based upon the source of funds or marital property with equitable standards that are applied by family court judges. With unmarried partners, however, there is a wide spectrum of "fair" approaches, ranging from the "each keeps his own" autonomy to a marriage-equivalent sharing of assets. Unfortunately, most unmarried couples haven't thought through these issues, and their feelings are likely to evolve over time, especially if their financial needs change. As the couple's lawyer, you will have only a limited amount of input into this process. What you can and should do, however, is make it clear to your clients that absent a written agreement, they should assume that neither partner is obligated to share his separate assets, pay the other partner back for any support given during the cohabitation period, or provide post-separation assistance.[4]

DOCUMENTS FOR COUNSELING LOW-ASSET COHABITING RENTERS

(FORMS FOUND ON INCLUDED CD)

Form 04: Apartment-sharing agreement

Form 05: Sample shared co-ownership agreement

Form 06: Agreement for sharing of expenses with limited rights of reimbursement for excess contributions

NOTES

1. Marital status is a protected class under many local and/or state antidiscrimination ordinances, and this can be a problem in low-income or public housing situations. If there is a public benefits aspect to the rental (e.g., Section 8), then the issue of marital status and the income of the co-occupant can indeed become a legal problem.

2. Most cases in this arena come from New York City, and many of them arose when renters with AIDS died, leaving their unmarried partners as occupants of valuable rent-controlled apartments. While the decisions are somewhat inconsistent, most of them favored the rights of the long-term survivors. *See* Braschi v. Stahl Assocs., 74 N.Y.2d 201 (1989).

3. *See, e.g.*, Lee v. Yang, 111 Cal. App. 4th 481 (2003) (a soon-to-be ex-fiancée was determined to have the right to withdraw all of the funds from a joint tenancy banking account even though she had not made any of the deposits, and her fiancé had no reimbursement rights against her).
4. Couples who are both legal parents of minor children at the time of a breakup will be bound by the rules of child support, which cannot be waived in advance by agreement of the parents. A high percentage of unmarried partners, however, either have no children or are living with someone who is not a legal parent of their child.

CHAPTER FIVE

COVERING THEIR ASSETS: DEBTS, LIABILITY, AND INSURANCE

A. The Basic Principles of Nonliability

Each unmarried partner constitutes a separate economic unit; thus, unless one or both of the partners does something affirmatively to trigger joint liability, each partner will be solely responsible for his own obligations. The one major exception is if your clients have signed up under a state registration system (either as civil union or domestic partners) that is fully marriage-equivalent—then the marriage rules of joint liability generally will apply to their debts.

During these rapidly changing legal times, however, most creditors seem blithely unaware of the consequences of the marriage-equivalent registrations, especially those that operate on a national basis. Thus, if your state-registered clients honestly report that they are legally "single" (which is how they are categorized under federal law), most out-of-state creditors will not pursue the assets of a registered partner. But be careful—the debtor/creditor treatment of these marriage-equivalent registrations is quite fluid, and over the coming decade it is most likely that the reach of liability to registered partners will be expanded. But one core truth will remain certain: Absent some sort of marriage-equivalent

In general, a local or employer-based registration as a domestic partner will not by itself impose joint liability. Many local registrations—and even a limited number of employer-based registrations—include language stating that the partners are responsible for each other's basic living expenses during the period of their registration; these provisions were meant to restrict registration to those who have taken on some degree of shared financial obligations as opposed to casual roommates or those in a dating relationship, especially since marital obligations are not (and cannot be) triggered by these local registrations.

Lawyers have expressed concerns over the past thirty years as to whether those declarations could bestow upon creditors a third-party beneficiary claim for joint liability on the grounds that the registration constitutes a form of contract between the parties. Given the people who were signing up as domestic partners in the 1980s, the primary concern in the early days was that insurers or medical providers might seek to recover for unpaid bills from wealthier partners of judgment-proof ill or deceased debtors. Such concerns turned out to be without cause, and to date there are no reported instances of local registrations being used in this way—and the likelihood of a claim seems remote. It is highly unlikely that a creditor would even know of this sort of registration, let alone act on it, because the parties are legally single and can describe themselves as such. But as with the broader concerns over a potential claim against a common law marriage spouse, such a registration could in theory impose a legal liability on the part of the registered partner. Therefore, if there is a significant risk of a future collection action or a large amount of debt is involved, it would be most prudent to avoid any form of registration that includes a joint obligation provision. However, because these registrations do not impose any post-separation obligations, a termination should eliminate any risk of a trailing third-party claim.

registration, your clients will not be forced to cover each other's debts as a matter of marital law.[1]

Your primary focus with regard to loans or other forms of contractual liability should address two crucial tasks: (1) a determination of whether or not your clients have voluntarily created any form of joint liability; and (2) client education and preventive work to minimize the likelihood and resulting risk of them doing so in the future. To that end, you will want to review with your clients any loan documents that they have signed or are considering signing, as well as any purchase or lease contracts that specify which party is obligated under those agreements.

Partners may be confused as to whether they are a coborrower on a credit card account (i.e., someone who has a duty to repay the debt) rather than an authorized user (i.e., someone who can make charges but isn't liable to the bank) and whether their partner is a coborrower or merely an authorized user on their own accounts. They should be aware that the name listed on the monthly bill is not always an indication of this legal status since some creditors only list one name on the statement even when both partners are legally coborrowers.

Odd as this may sound, this is not always a simple matter to analyze. Sometimes an unmarried person co-owns a residence with a partner, but only one of them is considered a borrower. One of them may have a business loan or a government assistance loan for which the lender demanded that both partners sign a deed of trust or mortgage securing that loan with their jointly owned property. This can be especially problematic in states with mortgage loans that generally are recourse in nature. One partner may have taken on a student loan as an individual but then paid off that loan with a joint credit line on a co-owned residence. Overdraft protections, for example, are typically tied to the owners of the checking account being protected by that overdraft, but there may be a credit card account functioning as overdraft protection that only has one borrower of record. In each instance you will want to see—or at least have your clients review—the initial loan or account documentation or try to check with the lender to ascertain who is the legal borrower.

Your clients should make every effort to bring every account's legal status into alignment with their agreement and their own understanding and should attempt to modify the account status where there is an inconsistency. For credit card accounts, this often requires closing an account and creating a new account in the proper names because in most instances a borrower cannot simply be added to or deleted from the account. For other loans (such as a secured line of credit), it may be impossible to modify the borrower status to resolve any inconsistencies. In those instances, you would want to recommend a private indemnification agreement to minimize the impact of a default on the partner who is primarily responsible for the debt. A debt may have been incurred for a combination of multiple purposes—some joint and some separate—and in those instances a private agreement allocating responsibility between the partners may be advisable. Remember, however, that unless the creditor agrees to limit liability to just one party, the other partner will still be at risk unless the defaulting party has other assets to satisfy the indemnification claim.

B. MANAGEMENT OF JOINT LIABILITY SITUATIONS

Joint liability messes arise in surprising ways. Because your clients are legally single, they are likely to have kept their financial lives mostly separate; and so, with few exceptions, their individual credit ratings will rise or fall based upon their independent financial behavior. Those who co-own their home may encounter joint reporting on their home mortgage, though even there the credit reporting often is done only with reference to the "primary" borrower (i.e., the one whose Social Security number is used for the annual tax reporting). Because of the autonomy that flows from this nonmarital aspect of financial independence, your clients have more flexibility when it comes to taking on debts, and frequently they can elect between separate versus joint liability. But, ironically, it is this very independence that can lead them inadvertently into a joint debt situation, or, even worse, result in one party being solely liable for a debt that is truly the other partner's obligation. It is in these contexts that you may be called upon to guide them (either in advance or retroactively) with regard to their respective exposure to various types of debts.

As a threshold matter, you will need to distinguish between those debts that are rightfully joint, either because the obligation is considered a joint obligation or because the funds or assets obtained in connection with that debt were shared; and those where the joint liability is a result of misguided convenience, a mistake, or an underlying uncertainty in the partners' relationship. Your clients may regularly encounter payment and reimbursement conflicts regarding the genuinely joint debts, but the really ugly messes are those that unfold when the shared liability was unintended.

The Genuinely Joint Debts

The authentically joint liability situation arises when the partners expressly and knowingly took on the debt as a shared obligation, either because they wanted to use the funds for a joint purpose (home improvement, vacation travel, payoff of a joint credit card debt) or because the funds were used to cover their shared living expenses during a time when they had agreed to share obligations. In these situations, it is only fair that both parties be liable to the creditor and that both incur the consequences of a default. This is true as a contractual matter even if only one partner has signed on the bottom line.

The two tasks that need to be addressed in joint liability situations are (1) the allocation of ongoing payment obligations between the partners and (2) remedies for a default. As to allocation of the payments, the partners have to determine whether or not they want to enter into a formal arrangement as opposed to informally covering the payments as they decide from month to month; and then they have to determine how to divide up the obligations. For some partners, it makes the most sense to allocate obligations based solely upon the nature of the debt: That is, if it was all for joint purposes, they would each cover 50 percent; but if 60 percent was used for joint expenses and 40 percent solely for one partner's personal expenses, one partner would pay 70 percent and the other would pay 30 percent. For other couples, it may seem fair to split up the burdens based upon their respective incomes even if the debt was for a joint purchase such as a car. This is especially appropriate if their incomes are wildly disparate but they consider themselves a family, albeit an unmarried one. If the couple has elected to pool its incomes into a joint account, a variant will be whether or not the payments will come out of that joint account as opposed to being paid solely by one partner from a savings account. Your primary advice in all of these situations should be to remind them that in the absence of a written agreement, the actual payments will likely be deemed the agreed-upon allocations and each of them will likely be held responsible for 50 percent of any unpaid portion of the debt.

Default is harder to address. If the partners are jointly liable, the creditor can pursue either one for the entire amount, and a private agreement (even a written one) will not shield either party from a collection action for the entire amount owed. It is rare for one partner to pursue an indemnification and collection action against an ex-partner who defaults on his share of the debt, mostly because of the difficulty of collecting on a judgment, but having such an agreement nonetheless can be very useful. Consistent with the generalized concerns regarding shared obligations, it can be very difficult to enforce an equitable claim for reimbursement in the absence of a written agreement, even when one partner pays out more than his rightful share of the debt. Likewise, it is never simple to enforce an alleged oral contract, and thus a written agreement confirming the oral agreement of the parties can be useful. It's not just a matter of court enforcement: The agreement drafting process itself reinforces the obligation and thus increases the likelihood of voluntary compliance. At the same time, the more responsible partner should acknowledge that because repayment is highly unlikely to occur, taking on joint liability or covering the debts of a partner is fundamentally signing up for a partner's share of the debts in the event that the partner fails to pay them voluntarily.

The Inadvertent Joint Debts

The more problematic questions arise when both partners end up being liable for a debt that was never meant to be shared or, worse, when one partner ends up facing sole liability for the other's debts even though neither of them truly considered it a shared debt when they were taking on the debt.

This can arise in a wide variety of contexts, including the following:

- One partner has a poor credit score or has maxed out credit limits so the other partner either (1) agrees to take out a loan or signs up for a credit card for the first partner's sole benefit, (2) agrees to take out a joint account, or (3) agrees to shift the balances from the first partner's high-interest-bearing credit card to the lower-interest account of the partner with better credit.
- One partner's loan ends up being tied to or collateralized by a joint asset such as a checking account or home loan, usually just for the sake of convenience, and so it evolves into being a joint debt or the debt of the other partner even though only one partner withdrew or used the loan funds.
- The partners are taking on a project (such as a home renovation or the purchase of a company), and it is in their strategic advantage to allocate the personal loans of each of them in an unconventional manner, such as using one partner's business line of credit or a stock margin account either for a joint use or for the sole use of the nonborrowing partner; frequently there has been some attempt to game the loan system to maximize the borrowing potential, especially where lenders may be concerned about extending the debts of an already overburdened debtor.

- One partner has student loans that are not tax-deductible or has a business debt with a high interest rate, so it is less expensive to shift the debt to a joint account or a secured line of credit.
- One partner is trying to help out her partner on a limited basis in good faith, but then the limits of the assistance get extended incrementally such that over time one partner is either carrying a debt that is entirety the other partner's liability or has agreed to share joint liability for a debt that is considered partially joint and partially separate.
- The partners have vaguely discussed sharing their incomes and debts, and so they begin to act as if they had reached such an agreement but later on decide (either jointly or unilaterally) to manage their assets separately.
- The partners are undergoing a trial separation or have already broken up, but there are older debts remaining from an earlier phase of their cohabitation relationship or newly acquired debts that one person has taken on using a preexisting joint credit source.

In most of these instances, there probably wasn't a dispute when the debt was incurred as to who was responsible for the obligation, but partners nonetheless may be reluctant to put their agreements (whether oral or implied) in writing. Asking for a written confirmation may be seen by one of them as a lack of trust, which indeed it may be—and for good reason. Sometimes one partner may be coming to terms with a genuine and long-simmering disappointment that the richer partner refused to shoulder the entire debt, but the poorer partner may be reluctant to make these feelings explicit, perhaps because of a past history of raised expectations and subsequent letdowns. You will want to be attentive to the underlying dynamics because sometimes raising the issue of repayment may be seen as a surrogate for voicing a sense that a breakup may be imminent. For some couples, there may be a genuine dispute about what is considered a joint expense, and therefore working to formulate a written agreement may force into the open an issue that one of the partners prefers to keep buried under the proverbial household rug.

It won't hurt to operate under the conservative assumption that your clients always are worried about the consequences of a possible breakup, either as the initiator of the split or the "victim" of the other partner's election to move on. After all, if things were clear and simple in the partners' relationship, they probably wouldn't be calling on you for legal services. Similarly, it won't hurt to work under the assumption that the partners are to some degree uncertain as to how they want to handle their finances, and so this liability wrinkle is going to rattle those cages. Even when the debt is taken on for a good reason, the underlying issues of who owns what and "Aren't we a family?" may lie just beneath the liability uncertainties, which can transform the simple task of signing a one-page I.O.U. into a deep and dark journey into the underworld of the relationship. Often, you will be relieved to learn that the rumblings are not so severe, but it can't hurt to tread carefully in these situations.

In some instances, a joint liability situation morphs into an issue of a debt between partners. There are a variety of settings for this predicament: Sometimes one partner makes a loan to the other partner using funds from a refinancing or credit card loan, or there may be a debt that started out as a joint obligation but was paid off (in whole or in part) by the partner who wasn't entirely benefiting from the use of the funds. As with the other liability problems, what is important is that the obligations on paper don't match the couple's private arrangement; thus, if there is a default, the one on the hook legally (and also the one whose credit reporting suffers) isn't the true debtor. And as with the other bad-news scenarios, the creditors aren't going to care about the couple's

Sorting through the debt issues can be made even more complicated by the errors caused by financial institutions that don't understand the law that applies to unmarried partners. This is especially the case for those who are in marriage-equivalent registrations because title companies, lenders, and financial institutions regularly fail to treat them as state law. In California, for example, state-registered domestic partners are equivalent to married spouses, and they can take title to property as community property with rights of survivorship. Federally regulated lenders often don't know how to treat unmarried partners, let alone state-registered domestic partners, and loan applications and promissory notes often misstate the marital status of the borrowers. Similar problems arise when it comes to purchase contracts or leasing agreements for cars or mobile homes, especially where agents or sales representatives persuade their customers to rely on incorrect legal notions. Mortgage brokers or sales agents often persuade unmarried couples to put all the debt in the name of the one with the better credit rating, whereas married partners would almost always be listed jointly as debtors.

private agreement; instead, they will seek out and collect from the liable party, and it will be up to him to pursue the other partner, usually with little likelihood of recovering anything in the end.

C. The Bigger Picture of Debt Liability

Sorting through the legal dimensions of shared debt and contractual liability can be complicated, but most often the legal analysis is relatively straightforward once all of the documents are compiled and reviewed. Thus, advising clients as to who is legally liable and how to avoid joint liability rarely will invoke sophisticated contractual analysis. Nonetheless, counseling clients in this arena can be extremely challenging in ways that may well seem inexplicable to attorneys who are new to this field.

Most likely the source of this complexity lies in an undisclosed thicket of ambivalent feelings on the part of the partners with regard to who *should* be responsible for their financial obligations, a situation that differs dramatically from what happens in a typical marital relationship. Marriage imposes normative guidelines on the finances of family life, establishing which expenses are to be shared and which are legitimately separate expenses, and which assets are separate and which are shared. Many couples argue over how much to spend and what their spending priorities should be, but sociological research indicates that most married couples adopt a shared-finances model of marriage and do not question the marital law assumptions. And for those who have concerns, especially in a second marriage or if one partner has inherited assets, there is a well-established protocol for modifying those rules (i.e., by means of a premarital or post-marital agreement).

The essence of nonmarital cohabitation is that the marital rules don't apply, and therefore there are no preset rules for managing the household finances. For some partners, this will be liberating as it allows them to weave their own fabric of monetary policy. They can elect to share housing expenses but not educational and professional costs, or they can agree to share travel expenses but not the costs of helping out each partner's aging parents. Some may agree to share all of the household expenses equally, and others may prefer to allocate them in proportion to their respective incomes. There is no norm that must be followed or ignored; the couple is creating its own arrangements in its own organic individualized fashion.[2]

Many lawyers consider themselves comfortable engaging in such discussions, and so entering into such negotiations seems eminently manageable. But for a sizable minority of unmarried partners, the absence of a marital financial structure creates an ambiguity and uncertainty that can be tortuous. If one partner has significantly lower income than the other one and has (perhaps unconsciously) concealed a desire to be taken care of, making explicit the allocation of debt burdens can be extremely painful. So, too, if one partner is increasingly resentful of the other partner's lack of financial success but is drawn to the role of caretaker, watching the joint credit card balance mushroom can foster resentments that can spoil any attempt to forge an indemnification agreement. The social expectations of marriage impose a duty of caretaking that may not be embraced by traditionally married spouses, but the presumption exists as a social norm and sets a default rule for the couple to accept or reject. Sorting through each partner's emotions is far more difficult when there is no underlying norm.

The tensions can balloon exponentially if the financial dependency is itself tied to deeper relationship problems. If one of the partners has lost a job due to perceived malfeasance or if one partner has a drinking or drug problem that is causing the financial problems, the mounting debt may become the rack upon which the many-layered hats of relationship discord can be hung. Never forget that many unmarried couples are unmarried specifically to avoid any joint financial obligations; thus, when one partner's debt morphs into an expanding joint obligation, the more solvent partner may perceive the situation as an unwanted trap. As a result, what started out as an occasional act of loving generosity can become a major financial burden, to the great regret of the now-overburdened lover.

Similar problems arise when the overspending of one partner ends up imposing a financial burden on the other one. Once again, unlike married couples who make their financial decisions jointly and act as a single economic unit, many unmarried cohabitants think of themselves as financially separate, which often encourages them to disregard their partner's profligate spending habits, comforted by the repeated mantra of their nonmarital financial independence. If there is a slide into using shared credit cards or a payoff of one party's debt with the proceeds of a joint line of credit or (even worse) if the thrifty partner agrees to refinancing a solely held mortgage to pay off the debts of his spendthrift partner, the loss of that safety net of financial separateness can be devastating to the thrifty partner and thus to the relationship as well. Suddenly, the financially prudent partner feels trapped or even betrayed, and chances are that the financially troubled partner (who may have harbored fantasies of being rescued by her lover) will soon feel abandoned. Each one may end up feeling that the other one has "broken the rules" of their nonmarital relationship, with horribly painful consequences.

In light of these emotional dynamics, it may be hard for your client to face these problems openly, let alone ask you for advice or follow your recommendations. You will need to learn how to balance your justifiable legal concerns with an acceptance of your client's emotional hesitations, even when it results in their failure to follow your advice. And when that happens, you will need to be open to assisting them when they sheepishly return to your office a few years later, seeking help in protecting themselves from third parties.

D. Tort Liability—As Plaintiff and As Defendant

Unmarried Plaintiffs

One of the most important legal rights bestowed on married spouses is the right to bring a tort action as a married person. Most typically,

Providing meaningful counsel to unmarried partners in these sorts of situations requires a delicate balance of emotional, practical, and legal skills. It's rare for married couples to consult with lawyers in the midst of their financial matters simply because the marital rules are so clear and the assumptions about shared obligations are rarely questioned. Unmarried partners, by contrast, are less certain about how they want to arrange their finances, and working with you may be the first time that either partner has conferred with a professional about any aspect of these concerns. Rarely is it sufficient to merely summarize the legal rules of joint liability, but, at the same time, the couple isn't coming to you for "nonmarriage counseling." Let the clients know that you're aware of the deeper concerns, let them voice those concerns when they are pertinent to the matters at hand, and keep the focus of your discussions on the legal tasks that they've asked you to handle.

such a claim seeks compensation arising out of the wrongful death or injury of a spouse, based upon a loss of future financial support. In other instances there may be a claim for loss of consortium (defined as the emotional, affectional, and sexual comforts that a married spouse typically provides). Such claims would typically be raised in a civil action based upon the state's statutory wrongful death laws, which can include emotional distress as well as economic damages. In other instances a spouse can file a claim under workers' compensation laws or similar employee benefit systems, such as may exist in union plans or military compensation programs. Occasionally there may be special purpose compensation programs for surviving spouses, such as those set up for the widows and widowers of victims of the September 11 terrorist attacks.

With very few exceptions, unmarried partners do not qualify for any of these benefits. State-registered partners in a marriage-equivalent program are eligible for state-granted benefits as spouses (e.g., wrongful death claims), but no such benefits will be extended to couples who are neither married nor state-registered. Moreover, same-sex married or registered couples do not currently receive any federal benefits because DOMA will preclude any recognition of their legal marriage or registration. Only a limited number of courts have extended protections to unmarried partners,[3] and only a limited range of workers' compensation survivor benefits can be provided to unmarried partners who can demonstrate a history of financial dependency on the injured worker.[4] In general, therefore, assume that no statutory spousal or survivor benefits are available to unmarried partners unless they are in a marriage-equivalent registration that is recognized by their state.

The one broad area of exception to this "no claim" rule will be for couples who are in a contractual relationship that justifies an independent claim by either partner. So, for example, if the partners have a business venture that suffers at the hands of a tortfeasor, both of the business partners will have a financial claim. Similarly, with any jointly owned real estate, if someone damages the property, then they will both have a valid claim for damages. Difficulties in these situations can arise, therefore, where the business or asset is only titled in one partner's name, as that partner will be the only one with a valid legal claim. It is crucial that unmarried partners understand that there won't be any derivative claims simply because they are cohabiting, and so if there is any possible avenue of future claims, they would want to be sure that the names on the business documents reflect their intended partnership arrangements.

Unmarried Defendants

Similar rules apply to the question of which partner is a proper defendant in a civil action brought by a creditor, a tort plaintiff, or a business claimant. The liability will be based upon either the legal ownership status or the identity of the contracting partner. Except for couples who are state-registered in a marriage-equivalent registration, their cohabiting status will not extend liability from one partner to the other as it would for a married couple. Thus, if someone is injured in a store owned by one partner alone and there is a claim that is not covered by insurance, only that partner will be liable, not his wealthy girlfriend or boyfriend. Likewise, with a business dispute, if only one partner owns the restaurant and there is an unpaid bill owing to a supplier, her partner is not going to have to pay the bill if the owner defaults on her obligation.

Clients need to be educated as to how their designation of owners or operators of businesses and other ventures will determine who is a proper defendant should a claim or conflict arise. In light of the absence of spousal joint liability, a high-asset partner should *not* sign on as a co-owner of a risky business and should not guarantee a business loan taken out by a lower-asset partner. You will want to convey directly to your

Keep in mind that nonspouses lack the protections of the spousal evidentiary privilege, and so unmarried couples should be careful in their conversations if there is a serious risk of litigation. And even if your clients are registered in a marriage-equivalent state, it is unlikely that federal spousal exemptions will be applied to their relationship. It is important, therefore, to remember that if you are going to meet with both partners, they both must be signed up as your clients in order to keep your conversations with them protected by the attorney-client privilege. Your joint representation should be confirmed in writing, with a waiver of any conflicts of interest. Don't let your clients learn this lesson the hard way: The absence of a spousal privilege became a major source of contention in the lawsuit against Rosie O'Donnell over the failure of her magazine when the opposing party deposed her unmarried partner and learned a great deal about what Rosie was saying behind closed doors.

clients, repeatedly, that they risk losing the advantage of having no spousal liability if they intentionally add their names to a business or debt of their partner. Oftentimes, clients are tempted to help out their partners by assisting with access to credit or insurance, but doing so can create a serious risk of liability on the partner who is trying to be helpful.

E. The Rules of Bankruptcy for Unmarried Partners

With very few exceptions, your clients will be treated as unrelated people when it comes to a bankruptcy filing even if they have signed up as marriage-equivalent domestic partners with a local or state registration. Most of the bankruptcy code provisions refer to partners using the term *spouse* as defined by federal law, and so only those who are in heterosexual marriages will be viewed as spouses.[5] Thus, a same-sex married couple cannot file a joint bankruptcy petition, and the wealth of one partner will have no impact on the bankruptcy filing of her indebted partner.

There are a few instances, however, where cohabiting partners could be affected by their partner's bankruptcy filing and vice versa:

- Certain provisions of the bankruptcy code defer to state law, such as the determination of a homestead exemption. Thus, if both partners file bankruptcy and the couple is considered married under state law (such as domestic partners, both straight and gay, under a marriage-equivalent registration), they will be limited to one homestead exemption since that is how married spouses are treated under state law.
- If the partners have state registered in a marriage-equivalent registration, then their state's rules about marital property or community property probably will be applied, resulting in potential claims against the nondebtor partner's "share" of the community or marital property.[6]
- Even if the couple is unregistered and unmarried, if the partners have any joint assets such as a house or a car or a business, a trustee or a creditor may pursue a claim that challenges the extent of the debtor's interest in the joint asset. Thus, any vagueness or question about the true allocation of the partners' interests may create problems in a bankruptcy proceeding. This is yet another reason

why having a written co-ownership agreement can be useful to an unmarried couple.

- To the extent that the couple continues to live together or shares any financial obligations, its financial relationship may play a role in the bankruptcy proceeding. Questions can arise as to the validity of a prior transfer between partners or a payment to the nondebtor partner, and the nondebtor partner may end up being a claimant (or a creditor holding a debt that is discharged).

For all of these reasons, it is crucial that your unmarried clients work with a bankruptcy attorney who is familiar with these rules and can handle the filings appropriately. In some situations it makes sense for both partners to file bankruptcy at the same time, whereas in other situations that is not even feasible. If at all possible, it would be wise for your clients to meet with counsel well in advance of any planned bankruptcy filing so that they can organize their affairs appropriately in advance.

F. Insurance Coverage Challenges for Unmarried Partners

Navigating the many-layered maze of insurance coverage is not easy. Different companies have different practices, state antidiscrimination laws are inconsistent and rarely enforced, and real-life complications

Consider the following real-life scenario. "Alan" and "Beth" co-own their residence but are having serious relationship problems and are in financial distress as well. Alan allowed Beth to draw money out of their joint line of credit to pay off her personal credit card, but now she's racked up substantially more credit card debt, some of which is on cards that Alan took out in his name. Beth is unemployed and wants to file for bankruptcy, but Alan is a high earner and has very little personal debt. If Beth proceeds with bankruptcy, she may get relief from her personal liability on the line of credit and the joint credit cards, leaving Alan with piles of debt in his name—and a valid claim against Beth's share of the house equity. It would have been far wiser if all of Beth's debt had been solely in her own name so that her bankruptcy filing would not adversely affect Alan's situation.

can arise in all varieties of situations. Unmarried couples can face very serious problems when it comes to the purchase of insurance, access to coverage, extent of protections, and the costs of the premiums. And while many couples consider the treatment they receive to be discriminatory, chances are there won't be many viable arguments you can raise in their defense. Instead, you will want to focus your efforts on helping your clients sort out the available possibilities and solutions, working to minimize gaps in coverage, and reducing the premium costs wherever possible.

Homeowners Insurance

Most typically, only the partner who owns the house, and no one else, will be covered by the homeowners insurance unless the unmarried couple is state-registered in a marriage-equivalent registration. This can be very detrimental to a nonowner, most pressingly because her personal belongings will not be covered by the homeowners policy. The rules in most states establish that a married spouse's personal property is covered by the policy even if that spouse is not a homeowner (perhaps because the nonowning party may have some ownership interest as a spouse), but that rule does not apply to unmarried partners. Making matters worse, quite often it is far from clear who actually owns which items of furniture, art, or household furnishings. Fortunately, insurance companies do not always require legal proof of ownership in the event of a fire or theft. But couples should assume that if something was purchased by or given to the partner who is not the legal owner of the residence, that partner's things will not be covered by the homeowners insurance.

Homeowners insurance also covers thefts from automobiles and can provide a variety of other benefits, such as replacement housing in the event of a fire or other damage. Short of being added to the title, there is generally no way to bring the nonowner under the umbrella of the insurance coverage, and it rarely is wise to add someone to the title just to obtain an insurance benefit. But if someone is considering staying off or going off the title for financial reasons, it is essential that he understand the insurance coverage consequences of doing so. Some companies may be willing to sell a coverage rider extending protections to the belongings of an unmarried partner, as a de facto domestic partner, and your clients should inquire into that option whenever possible.

Renters Insurance

If either or both partners are renters, they should consider purchasing a renters insurance policy. In most markets, the cost of a policy is not great, and it will cover losses in a fire, theft, or other disaster. Renters policies typically cover a limited amount of damage, and usually only about $25,000 of coverage is needed. If one or both partners are operating a business, either at home or in an office location, they should consider having a comprehensive business policy that includes basic liability insurance as well as personal property losses. Keep in mind that the insurance decisions can have an impact on a subsequent dispute between the partners, e.g., if one of them contends that he is not a renter but rather an off-title equitable owner. To avoid this conflict, it would be wise for them to have a written agreement with the legal owner so that their purchase of a renters policy is not later used to support an argument that they acknowledged not having an ownership interest.

If both partners are renters, they may be required to purchase two separate renters policies as opposed to the single policy that is often offered to married spouses. This can result in a doubling of premiums, but it also may provide for double the amount of coverage. However, if the amount of coverage offered to the two renters combined is no greater than what is offered to a married couple, then your clients may be able to challenge the imposition of a double premium if they live in a state that offers protection from marital status discrimination.

Umbrella Policies

An umbrella policy can be extremely useful, especially for clients who have significant assets. It covers a car accident claim that exceeds the amount of the auto policy's coverage (though an insured is typically required to "buy up" to the maximum amount of basic coverage as a condition of obtaining the umbrella policy), as well as a house-related claim that is not covered by or is above the limits of a homeowners policy. Oftentimes, such policies include additional benefits such as libel and slander coverage, as well as protection from an assortment of rare but possibly devastating non-property related claims. The cost of such policies is fairly reasonable, even for $1 million or $2 million in coverage, since they can only be tapped after the regular insurance policies are tapped out. However, bringing the auto insurance up to the maximum amount of coverage usually turns out to be as expensive as the umbrella policy.

Unmarried couples face two problems here. First, if they don't co-own all of their major assets (i.e., the house and cars), it can be hard to obtain a single umbrella policy. Many umbrella policies are sold by insurance companies that only market to those who buy coverage for all of their major assets—and those who are jointly covered on all such policies. Thus, your clients will want to be sure that the umbrella policies cover claims arising out of all of their assets, such as cars and houses. Sometimes the insureds can convince a company to cover all the underlying assets even if some of them are owned by just one partner (such as an out-of-state house or a prerelationship car).

The second problem facing unmarried partners is that most companies won't sell a joint umbrella policy to an unmarried couple, and so your clients will have to pay double for their coverage. In this case, however, they will collectively get twice as much coverage, and so they don't each need as much coverage on their individual policies—thus, the financial consequences of the double purchase should be relatively minor.

Health Insurance

Notwithstanding the very real benefits of health-care reform, medical care costs and health insurance premiums continue to soar, and many unmarried partners are justifiably concerned about obtaining health insurance coverage. In many instances unmarried partners can obtain coverage at work solely based upon an employer, insurance company, or local ordinance-based registration as domestic partners. Some employees in a marriage-like relationship can obtain coverage for a nonemployee partner at a reduced cost or at no cost at all. This should always be explored whenever one of the partners is unable to obtain affordable insurance on his own. As has been previously mentioned, such de facto domestic partnership registrations do not carry with them any marital rights or obligations and can be terminated simply by written notice to the company or local government registry.

Other challenges of the health insurance decision-making process include the following:

- Some employers will only provide domestic partnership benefits to same-sex couples on the grounds that straight couples have the option of getting married to receive the benefits. There is a certain logic to this position, and yet some courts have said otherwise, ruling that this is just another form of sexual orientation discrimination. Many employers have preferred to avoid an outcry over these rules and so have included opposite-sex couples in the domestic partnership program. Generally speaking, this is a decision by the employer, not the insurance company.

- Sometimes it is preferable for couples to register under their local or employer-based programs rather than signing up for the state marriage-equivalent registration, unless they clearly want to be considered married under state law. The local registrations do not carry with them any of the marital obligations of joint liability and shared assets, and the broad statements in such registrations about providing assistance to the other's financial needs are rarely, if ever, enforced. Most important, a local or employer-based registration can easily be terminated by a simple document, filed by either of the parties, and does not require compliance with the judicial dissolution process.

Most local and employer-based registration systems were set up years before any marriage-equivalent state-registration programs existed. Many local employers did not want to bother with their own registration systems, so they extended domestic partnership benefits to couples who had registered locally. The primary beneficiaries of these programs were gay and lesbian employees who couldn't marry; to the extent that straight couples were included, this was either for political expediency or because of a reluctance to delve into the sexual orientation of employees. Now that marriage-equivalent registration or marriage is available for same-sex couples in approximately fifteen states, many employers are retreating from the use of local or employer-based systems. Instead, they are requiring that all couples, gay and straight, enter into a marriage or its equivalent in order to obtain benefits. This is only fair since that is what was historically required of all straight couples. And it is a trend that is growing. Partners who obtain coverage through a local or employer-based registration but live in a marriage-equality state should be on the watch for a change in policy rules and be prepared to either get married (or its equivalent) or lose their domestic partnership coverage.

- Nearly every domestic partnership program requires that the partners live together, and the partnership will end if the couple ceases living together (unlike coverage based upon marriage, which does not require cohabitation and can be extended post-separation). It is vital that the parties be honest about their living situation so that they don't find themselves losing their insurance coverage, due to noncompliance with this requirement, just when they need it most. A temporary separation between the parties should be documented as such so that an insurance company doesn't use the short-term break to terminate coverage.

- Unlike insurance benefits provided to married spouses tax-free, the Internal Revenue Service (IRS) taxes these payments as an additional benefit to the employee to the extent that the employer is paying the premiums. The tax is based upon the value of the insurance, not the out-of-pocket cost, so this can be a significant amount. Thus, as much as 35 percent of the value of the nonemployee's premium will be deducted from the employee's paycheck. State-registered partners won't be taxed under state tax laws, but they are still subject to the federal taxation of this benefit. For this reason, if a partner can obtain coverage for anything near the same price as the employer-based coverage after adjusting for the tax liability, it probably makes more sense to go with the separate nonpartner coverage.

- If the employed partner loses the job or if the relationship breaks up, the nonemployed partner might be able to keep the coverage under COBRA for several years; but this option is not always available, and the premiums can be exceedingly high during that coverage period.[7] Given the volatility of many jobs and relationships, it may be more prudent to try to get separate policies for each partner, even with the new health insurance reform rules.

Life Insurance

For partners who have children or who are financially dependent on one another, life insurance can be a useful long-term planning tool. Except for those who are older than sixty years of age or have serious health problems, even fairly large-sized policies are relatively low in cost (the reason is that most folks let their policies lapse before they ever get used either because the premiums get so expensive as they reach the end of their lives or because their partner predeceases them so there is less need for coverage). Of course, life insurance remains a luxury for those of limited financial circumstances, especially for those who are older or have medical problems. Unmarried partners generally will not face discrimination in obtaining life insurance, and thus the only significant issue here is whether they can obtain a policy on the other's life.

Here's the scoop: Sometimes it makes sense for one partner to buy a policy on the other partner's life rather than on his own life because the policy owner is in control of the payments and the designation of the beneficiary (i.e., oneself) and the policy proceeds are not considered part of the decedent's estate. Insurance companies require that there be an insurable interest before someone buys a life insurance policy, and married partners are considered to have the required mutuality of concerns to buy a policy on the other's life. If unmarried partners co-own a residence, they probably can do so as well, up to the amount of the mortgage or perhaps the value of the residence. There is little that a person can do to challenge a denial on this basis, but now that estate tax limits are so high, this is not likely to be a problem for most of your clients.

One of the most compelling situations in which buying life insurance is prudent is where the partners are sharing a house but one or both of them have children from another relationship. They may want to leave the residence to their surviving partner but also provide something for their children, so they bequeath the house in trust to a partner with the remainder interest going to their children or leave their share of the house directly to their children. Both of these approaches can create messy problems, however. The kids may be viewed as hovering over the surviving partner, waiting for a death to liberate their inheritance, and this arrangement can pit the needs of the surviving partner against those of the children. It is far wiser in most instances to leave the residence to the partner and provide for the children by means of a life insurance policy.

Automobile Insurance

Most companies will sell a joint auto insurance policy to unmarried couples who live together even if they are unmarried. However, in some instances they will require that the car be titled in both names, with separate policies if the ownership is separate and then separate policies again if there are multiple cars with different ownership. Even GEICO, which seems to want everyone's business, told me a few years ago that my partner and I could not be co-insureds, insisting that one of us had to be the secondary insured, which dramatically reduced the extent of coverage for the secondary driver. Thankfully, they quickly changed their tune when I told a supervisor that this practice was illegal in California as marital status discrimination, but I'm sure that others have not been so lucky. Your clients' main goal is to have both partners treated fully as co-insureds rather than having one partner be an authorized user or secondary driver, and to combine the policies whenever possible. The main reason for this is that unless both partners are coinsured, there are categories of coverage that will not be extended to the secondary partner.

Driving records are generally assigned by individual and not by joint ownership, and sometimes this can work to an unmarried couple's advantage. It may be possible in some instances to designate one of the drivers as the first-listed driver, even on a joint policy, if she has the better driving record and obtain a cheaper policy that way. Your clients also should explore whether or not there is any benefit to tying their automobile insurance to a homeowners policy as that can result in a reduced premium. Keep in mind that as long as your clients share ownership of their cars or have a joint policy, they must coordinate their insurance limits and policy choices, which can be onerous if they are in vastly different financial situations or have different attitudes regarding insurance. In these sorts of situations, it may make more sense for them to own and insure their cars separately, and you should be equipped to advise them on this issue if it arises.

This is an area where marital status discrimination can be very real, and you should be aware of your state's rules and be prepared to file a complaint with the state insurance commission if your clients face discriminatory treatment.

DOCUMENT FOR COVERING THE COUPLE'S ASSETS (FORMS FOUND ON INCLUDED CD)

Form 07: Agreement for allocation of shared debt and indemnification

NOTES

1. Even in common law states, it is rare that a creditor could assert a claim based upon an allegation of a common law marriage. However, if significant risks exist, it may be prudent to have the parties sign a "nonliability" agreement.

2. *See* PEPPER SCHWARTZ & PHILIP BLUMSTEIN, THE AMERICAN COUPLE (William Morrow 1983) (surveying the different ways that married and unmarried couples, both gay and straight, tend to manage their financial decisions).

3. *See, e.g., Smith v. Knoeller and Noel, San Francisco Superior Court; see summary of case at http://www.americanbar.org/publications/human_rights_ magazine_home/irr_hr_summer03_expanding.html.* In this closely followed dog-mauling case in San Francisco, the unmarried lesbian partner of Diane Whipple won a wrongful death claim at the trial court level. However, the trial court's decision was not appealed, and the issue was soon rendered moot by the extension of statutory wrongful death coverage to California-registered domestic partners. Some surviving same-sex partners have asserted that the preclusion of claims by unmarried partners is unconstitutional if they are not allowed to marry.

4. MD. CODE ANN., LAB. & EMPL. § 9–681(a) (2007), for example, provides workers' compensation survivor benefits to anyone who is "wholly dependent" on the worker, without regard to marital status. In NANCY POLIKOFF, BEYOND (STRAIGHT AND GAY) MARRIAGE (Beacon 2008), Polikoff argues that it is better social policy to award such benefits based on the actual economic interdependency of the two adults rather than on the legal status of marriage.

5. *In re* Kandu, 315 B.R. 123 (Bankr. W.D. Wash. 2004).

6. *See* Robert F. Kidd and Frederick C. Hertz, *Partnered in Debt: The Impacts of California's New Registered Domestic Partnership Law on Creditors' Remedies and Debtors' Rights, Under California Law and Under Federal Bankruptcy Law,* 28 CAL. BANKR. J. 148–93 (2006) (same-sex California couples).

7. Some states have their own COBRA rules for smaller companies, and these rules may provide greater benefits for state-registered couples (gay or straight) as well as same-sex married couples. The rules for dissolutions of nonmarital relationships are neither consistent nor clearly enunciated in many jurisdictions, and your clients may face wrongful denials of COBRA coverage that will need to be challenged.

CHAPTER SIX

TAX CONSEQUENCES, LIABILITIES, AND BENEFITS

A. A SURVEY OF THE LEGAL BACKGROUND

History of Tax for Married Couples

Before exploring the many-layered tax rules that apply to unmarried couples, it is important to first take a short historical excursion in order to understand the legal background of the tax privileges currently extended to married couples. Odd as it may seem nowadays, once upon a time the IRS didn't pay much attention to marital status. Congress simply did not address the issue of whether or not married partners should be taxed as a couple or as individuals when the modern tax code was adopted in 1913.[1] There was no such thing as a joint return, and transfers between spouses were not given special consideration. Individuals were taxed as such, and transfers were taxable or not as the nature of the transaction warranted, wholly apart from the parties' marital status.

But soon after the income tax system was established, the federal tax implications of the community property rules of several states caused a great deal of consternation, and a series of court filings challenged the federal tax treatment of community property income. There was uncertainty in the early decades as to whether or not earned income in community property states was considered equally owned by both spouses at the time it was earned or if, by contrast, the nonearner's rights to the spouse's earnings were vested only upon death or divorce. The issues in non-community property states were less complicated since each spouse's earnings undoubtedly remained separately owned, and so questions about transfers of assets typically only arose upon dissolution or the death of one of the spouses.

The debate was lively and a series of state and U.S. Attorney General opinions and court rulings emerged, with different results regarding the disparate community property states. Eventually, in 1928, the U.S. Supreme Court issued its landmark ruling and determined that the income tax obligations should be borne by the "owner" of the income.[2] Under the dominant rules in the community property states, the non-earners (generally speaking, the wives) had a vested property right in the community property income as soon as it was received (typically by the husband), and so they were deemed to be co-owners of the income—and thus each spouse should be taxed on one-half of the spouses' total income. Consistent with this approach, over the course of the middle decades of the twentieth century, married spouses came to be recognized (for the most part) as a single economic unit for income tax purposes,[3] and they were allowed to file joint returns combining all of their income.

Similar approaches were eventually adopted for asset transfers even in non-community property states, and eventually (but not until 1981) all asset transfers between spouses—not just those in community property states—were effectively rendered "nonevents" when the marital deduction was increased to 100 percent under the gift and estate tax rules. Over the course of the twentieth century, various state tax codes also were revised to extend the same marital privileges and to achieve consistency between state and federal law for married spouses. As a result, lawyers and accountants have grown accustomed to the luxury of not having to worry about any potential tax consequences of financial support and payments and transfers of assets between spouses.

Tax Rules and Unmarried Couples

Unlike the free pass bestowed on married couples, unmarried couples (defined for tax purposes as those who are neither legally married nor registered under any state's marriage-equivalent regime) are treated as unrelated single people under all state and federal tax regimes. As such, none of the spousal rules apply, and they pay their taxes as single people. They

Until the passage of DOMA in 1996, federal tax officials didn't pay much attention to the characteristics of the spouses in a marriage. If they were considered married under the law of the state in which they resided, that was good enough for the IRS. Granted, there were a few areas of uncertainty (common law marriages typically wouldn't be given much credence unless they were confirmed by a state court), but the variations in state rules about minimum ages or degrees of consanguinity (relation, i.e., cousin marriages) wouldn't disqualify a married couple from a federal tax benefit. But once same-sex marriage was legalized (starting in 2005), the mess anticipated in the passage of DOMA materialized: Suddenly there were couples who were state-married but federally single, and in some states they also still had community property income. Under the terms of DOMA, the federal government will only recognize a heterosexual marriage, and the law has been applied to deny same-sex married couples the federal status of being married.[4]

Thus, until DOMA is repealed by Congress or invalidated, judicially gay and lesbian spouses will be taxed as single individuals by the federal government but treated as married by their state tax authorities. Further complicating the situation, there are couples in marriage-equivalent domestic partnerships or civil unions who are treated as married under state law but also are federally single. The anomalies caused by these rules are enormously complicated and full of uncertainties, and they are discussed comprehensively in the last section of this chapter.

file their tax returns as single individuals, and any transfers between them are considered arm's-length and thus not subject to any spousal transfer exemptions. These rules apply to couples at all phases in their relationship: when they are forming their partnership, while they are cohabiting, if they subsequently break up, and if one of them dies during the course of their relationship. As discussed more fully below, some scholars have argued that if an unmarried partner has vested rights to income or assets under the nonmarital laws of his own state, then the sharing of that asset or income with his partner should not be taxable; however, there is no direct authority dealing with that issue, and attorneys counseling unmarried partners should assume that this approach generally will *not* be accepted, by either mainstream accountants or the IRS.[5]

Since almost every unmarried couple over the course of its relationship engages in a wide variety of transfers of income or assets, either during the relationship or upon its demise, it is continually at risk of incurring some kind of tax obligation. It is critical to bear in mind that this does not necessarily mean that each transfer is taxable; rather, it means that the transfer is not exempt under the broad spousal exemption from taxation and must be analyzed in the absence of such exemption.

The basic tax rules for unmarried partners are as follows:

1. If a transfer or payment was made in consideration of some kind of service provided by the recipient, it may be considered taxable income and thus subject to income tax owed by the payee. Depending on the nature of the (nonsexual) services rendered (e.g., a business expense), the payment may or may not be deductible by the payer.

2. If there was another kind of consideration for the payment or transfer (such as paying someone else's bills or offering relief from debt or a waiver of a claim or a transfer of an asset such as real property), there may be taxable gain resulting in capital gains taxes owed by the party who "gained" from such a transaction.

3. If there was no consideration for a payment or transfer (such as paying someone's debt or simply giving another person money to live on), it will likely be considered a gift, which should be reported if its value exceeds the annual reporting exclusion (currently $13,000 per donor/donee), and would be taxable only when the accumulated amount of gifts exceeds the donor's lifetime exemption (currently $5 million).[6] In theory, a payment in some circumstances can be both taxable income to the recipient and a gift from the donor's perspective.

4. Adding someone's name to a bank account typically isn't treated as a "present gift" for tax purposes, but putting someone on the title to real property usually is.

5. Depending on the nature of the transfer, there may be other secondary tax exemptions, such as an exclusion from taxation for up to $250,000 in gain on the sale of a personal residence.

6. If the payment or transfer is construed as the repayment of a loan or reimbursement of an advancement, there will not be any tax owed on the repayment or reimbursement, but there may be taxes owed on interest paid or an imputed gift regarding any waiver of interest.

7. Depending on the nature of the payments, the payor may be entitled to a step-up in tax basis if the payment is connected to the acquisition of all or a portion of an asset such as real property.

8. Each partner owns his own investments, retains his own basis in each investment, and "owns" his own income and thus is entitled to his own deductions. If an asset is jointly owned, each partner's tax obligations are analyzed separately, both annually and at the time of a sale of the asset as to income tax liability, deductions, and capital gains obligations.

9. The spousal estate tax exemptions do not apply to unmarried couples.

Frequent Concerns

While the tax questions facing unmarried couples can be tortuously complicated, several recurring situations trigger the most frequent concerns. Detailed discussions of these issues are contained within this chapter and in the real estate, dissolution, and estate planning chapters, but the following is the basic analytical framework for the most frequent scenarios.

- Partner A is supporting Partner B either (a) by paying living expenses associated with the shared lives of both partners, (b) by paying some of B's separate expenses, or (c) by giving money directly to B.[7]

  Tax concerns: (a) Payment of expenses for the parties' joint benefit is theoretically a gift from A to B or perhaps a form of income to B in consideration of B's domestic services; however, if A would have incurred the expenses in any event (i.e., for her own housing, travel, entertainment, or food), then the benefit conferred to B probably doesn't result in a taxable event. (b) Payment made directly to the creditors of B for B's sole benefit (e.g., student loans, personal credit card bills, or prerelationship debts) likely will be considered either a gift to B or taxable income to B, but often clients will ignore this simply because they are unlikely to be a subject of audit, especially if payments are below the amount of the annual exclusion. (c) Payment made directly to B definitely is either a gift from A to B or, if made in consideration of B's services, taxable income to B.

- Partner A transfers a partial interest in real estate or a bank account to Partner B, either by adding B to an asset already owned by A (typically as joint tenants) or by transferring the entirety of an asset from A to B.

  Tax concerns: Transfer of the equity in real estate most definitely will be either a gift or a sale; though even if nothing is paid by B to A prior to or at the time of the transfer, there may be future payments by B in excess of the value of the benefit enjoyed by B (if real estate is involved), which could render the transfer an installment sale. The biggest uncertainty involves the use of a joint tenancy deed or account, where the parties may think of the transfer as a form of estate planning and not as a present gift (which may be consistent with state and federal tax law); however, if the parties use the account jointly or the noncontributor withdraws any funds, the IRS may deem it as a present gift of 50 percent of the asset. Additional problems arise with regard to the tax basis for the partner who was not an original owner of real estate but may have contributed to the purchase or improvement of the property and was never put on the title.

- Transfers of assets or support payments are made in connection with a dissolution, either in settlement of a palimony claim or out of a sense of moral obligation to assist a dependent partner.

  Tax concerns: In the absence of a legal duty of support or a court-ordered palimony judgment or settlement, the payment may be considered voluntary and thus construed as a gift made without consideration. It is clear that statutory provisions for the shifting of taxation onto the party receiving support will not apply (Internal Revenue Code (I.R.C.) sections 71 and 215), nor will the marital exemption of I.R.C. section 1041 apply to an asset transfer. However, depending on the nature of the claim, the transfer also may be seen as payment for prior domestic (nonsexual) services, in which case it is taxable to the payee. In some situations, it may be possible to assert that the asset or income has already been taxed once and should not be taxed a second time on the grounds that it is exempt as an extension of the partner's duty of support to an unmarried partner or possibly a reimbursement of prior contributions or part of the buyout of a real estate interest. It also may be possible to argue that the transfer was a distribution of an asset that always was held in trust for the nonown-ing partner.

- Bequests, of either assets or a retirement account, are made upon the death of a partner.
  Tax concerns: *Because the partners are not spouses, there is no spousal exemption under state or federal tax law, and so any amounts in excess of state or federal estate tax limits will be subject to inheritance or estate tax unless some other exemption can be asserted. Additional problems may arise in the transfer of a retirement plan upon the death of an unmarried partner.*

B. PRACTICAL STRATEGIES FOR AVOIDING TAXABLE TRANSFERS

In light of the likely risks of any variety of taxable events happening on a regular basis, your first priority should be to educate your clients about the concept of taxable transfers and then offer practical suggestions to help them minimize their tax exposure in a manner that is legally valid (i.e., tax avoidance), without straying into the darker realms of tax evasion. "Not likely to get caught" does not meet the standards of appropriate legal advice.

Often, you will only be brought into these situations long after your clients have gotten themselves into trouble—or fear that they have. But when you are able to intervene earlier in the process, try to explain the basic rules to them and suggest the best strategies in the most helpful and practical terms, as follows:

1. Spending money on something for one's own benefit and sharing it with a loved one isn't a taxable transfer, so it's fine to share housing, meals, hotel rooms, and the like with a partner without fear of tax consequences. If the big spender would have incurred the expense anyway and enjoys the benefit of a partner's company and there are no "consumables" left over to benefit the lover (such as would happen if the couple takes a vacation), this probably is not going to be a taxable event.
2. Sharing the use of an asset that would cost the same even if it weren't being shared (e.g., a car, computer, or motorcycle) isn't a

Dealing with the tax ramifications of transfers and payments between unmarried partners opens up a hornet's nest of ethical and professional problems, in two respects. First, most attorneys are not qualified to opine on tax issues, and so, in most instances, clients should be referred to qualified tax experts; however, most clients cannot afford such counsel, and even if they could, many tax accountants and lawyers don't understand the rules that apply to unmarried couples. A lot of bad advice is offered, even in sophisticated circles. Given these concerns, it's totally appropriate for nontax lawyers to point out the issues and ask pertinent questions and even provide general guidance about the rules. But when it comes to complex questions involving large amounts of money, a referral to a tax expert is essential.

The second set of problems is ethical: When have you crossed the line from lawful tax avoidance to unlawful tax evasion, and what is your role in guiding the actions of your clients? I have often sat back and watched my clients engage in all sorts of questionable tax behavior, from treating their partner as an employee (when no real work was being done) to paying bills in cash for the other partner's benefit to changing title without reporting anything to the IRS. I repeatedly tell my clients that I am not an IRS agent and I won't turn them in, but, at the same time, I am not going to facilitate tax fraud. There's not an absolute bright line. For example, I have drafted settlement agreements that characterize transfers in ways that other lawyers might find inappropriate, yet I have turned clients away that other lawyers would readily help. You have to find your own baseline when it comes to dealing with these questions. The central points to remember are that you didn't write the rules or enter into the nonmarital relationship, and the essential requirement of your job is to accurately inform your clients of the applicable rules, even when they are unfavorable. There's no reason you should jeopardize your license to practice law in furtherance of a client's fraudulent tax reporting!

taxable transfer or gift, and you don't have to charge your lover "rent" for using the car.

3. Gifts below the annual exclusion amount (currently $13,000 per year per donee) need not be reported, and transfers of partial interest in real estate can be discounted for their minority interest percentage rather than valuing them based upon a proportion of the total market value.

4. Selling an asset to a partner at a "friends and family" discount usually isn't considered a taxable gift as long as the price is still reasonable and is reported as such.

5. Paying a partner's personal bills for expenses not related to shared debts (e.g., student loans, prerelationship obligations, or business expenses) or making a payment directly to a partner is generally considered a gift that should be reported if it's over the annual exclusion event, though the penalty for late reporting is not significant until the total value of the gifts exceeds the tax-exempt limit, which currently is $5 million per donor. But bear in mind that it is likely that the gift tax limit will go down over the next few years given the larger economic problems of this country.

6. If there's an oral understanding or a written document that provides that the payment is made in exchange for nonsexual services rendered by the payee, the payments probably are taxable as income to the payee; they may, if made for a legitimate business activity, be deductible by the payer.

7. Making gifts to a partner early on and in smaller amounts that appreciate over time is a great way to shift assets to a lower-income partner, avoiding a much greater gift tax problem upon dissolution or death. For example, giving your partner the down payment for a property that she retains over time is much smarter than waiting until a breakup and then giving her the property at its appreciated value. But remember, the essence of a gift is that it can't be retrieved no matter how awful the lover's behavior was. And while the gift tax exclusion may be $5 million this year, that doesn't mean it won't be reduced in future years—and a person never knows how wealthy he may be later in life!

8. How you characterize assets and transfers while you are together will likely be binding upon you at the time of dissolution or death; you can't suddenly argue that the house is "all yours" if you have been treating it as owned fifty-fifty while you were together—unless you want to voluntarily confess to having committed criminal tax fraud!

9. A couple who subsequently marries (and if the DOMA restrictions for same-sex married couples are lifted) will at that future date be able to benefit from the unlimited marital deduction for gifts made after that date, but you can't "revise" the date of earlier gifts retroactively. Couples should be realistic about their future plans and try to make reasonable predictions about political

change, knowing that they may regret the decisions they make if things turn out differently than expected.

10. Being unmarried has some definite tax advantages: You can engage in arm's-length transactions for sales of assets and take deductions and obtain step-ups in tax basis if you plan your transactions carefully.

Your greatest challenge is to convey to your clients the risks that they are taking when they act in a loving way to provide financial support to their unmarried partner. For the most part, they will ignore your counsel and continue doing what they've always been doing, blithely assuming they won't be subject to an audit—and they may be correct on this prediction. Your highest priorities are to be candid with your clients about the legal rules and to assist them in minimizing their tax risks and documenting their generosity in ways that are most helpful to them—within the bounds of legality.

C. THE HEAD-OF-HOUSEHOLD RULES

One of the benefits of being unmarried is that one of the partners can qualify as "head of household" under I.R.C. section 2(c). In many instances, this will enable that partner to pay taxes at a lower tax rate and also claim additional tax deductions at a federal level. Most states, moreover, have revised their income tax rules for heads of households to offer parallel benefits with regard to state income taxes.

In order to qualify for head-of-household status, the partner must meet all three of the following criteria:

- must be unmarried as of the last day of the calendar year,
- must pay more than half of the cost of maintaining the home for the calendar year (that's why both partners can't claim the benefit), and
- must be living with a "qualifying person" for more than half of the year.

The qualifying person must be a legal relative (and thus not an unmarried partner's child) or a dependent who lives in the household. The qualifying person can be an adopted or foster child as long as the child is living with the claimant pursuant to a legally recognized relationship. In some instances, the claimant's mother, father, or even a sibling can count as a qualifying relative. And an unmarried partner who earns less than the maximum income (around $3,500) and does not file his own tax return can be a dependent and thus a qualifying person as well.

A claimant who is still married but living apart from a former spouse may still qualify as head of the household. To qualify under this rule, the claimant's situation must be such that the spouse cannot have lived in the claimant's house during the last six months of the calendar year and the dependent must be living in the claimant's home for more than half of the year.

A partner of a same-sex couple who is state-registered or in a legal marriage probably still qualifies for head-of-household status because the partners are not federally viewed as spouses. However, if the partners pool their incomes or are living in a community property state, it's most likely that they will be contributing equally to the household expenses, so they would only be able to qualify if one of them spends some of his separate property assets on living expenses.

D. Effective Strategies for Minimizing Long-Term Tax Liabilities

Given the current high limits on exempt gifts under federal tax law, many clients simply ignore the tax consequences of their cohabitation

One of the trickier issues for unmarried partners is the allocation of tax deductions. If they are both owners of real estate, it may be possible for the higher income owner to hoard the deductible expenses by allocating his contributions to those expenses and allocating the other's contributions to the nondeductible expenses. In most instances it makes the most sense for the partners to use a joint account into which they both contribute and then allocate their contributions in a tax-minimizing way at the end of each year. It also may be possible in some instances for one partner to pay both partners' medical expenses or make charitable contributions on behalf of both partners. Your clients should be working with a tax adviser who understands the rules for unmarried partners so they can take advantage of these rules whenever possible.

and share their assets and income in a casual manner. Gift tax returns will rarely be filed, but as long as the lifetime limits are not exceeded, the consequences of this are not significant as long as the returns eventually get filed.[8]

Thus, the primary issues that are likely to require significant legal intervention are those that arise in the following settings:

1. Moderately high-asset or high-income couples living in states with gift and estate tax thresholds significantly lower than the current federal levels.
2. High net-worth or high-income partners who wish to make significant gifts and/or bequests to their unmarried partner or situations in which one partner is paying significant sums toward the ongoing living expenses of the couple.
3. Couples facing a dissolution or those who are open to planning for a possible dissolution, either as part of a cohabitation agreement, co-ownership agreement, or financial arrangement that specifically addresses their tax concerns.

Detailed descriptions of tax-minimizing strategies for each of these situations are presented in the substantive chapters dealing with property co-ownership agreements, cohabitation agreements, and estate planning, but it is useful as a preliminary matter to set out a broad-based conceptual understanding of the most useful approaches overall. This is especially important in view of the likely client responses to an effective tax-minimizing strategy: Clients will need to address their ongoing financial and emotional needs and priorities, the possible consequences of an unanticipated dissolution, and the tax implications of the death of one of them—all of which are highly complicated, and each of which may require the assistance of several legal and tax professionals.

Managing this process is not simple, but here are a few substantive and strategic tips to guide you in this effort:

•   In most instances, the earlier the high-asset partner makes gifts to his partner the better. Minority discounts can be used to reduce the value of real estate interests, and the filing of a gift tax return with a reasonable valuation of the asset transferred will trigger a three-year statute of limitations on the valuation. Gifting a down payment for a real estate purchase or the purchase of an investment asset will set the gift value at its lowest amount, and any appreciation (or paydown of the mortgage principal from rental income) will already be owned by the lower-asset partner. Early gifting also can have the psychological benefit of balancing the financial inequality of the relationship to some degree and can begin a process of "financial empowerment" for the lower-asset partner. On the other hand, some couples will resist engaging in what they perceive to be "divorce planning," and the high-asset partner may not be willing to give up the financially dominant role in this way. In order to avoid a premature gift of an excessive amount, the asset transfer should be phased in over time with an increasing percentage given in each year of the relationship.[9]

- It is almost always better to encourage the lower-asset partner to save his earnings and not contribute to any joint expenses, especially toward a residence that is owned by the high-asset partner. The couple should embrace the shared goal of increasing the net worth of the lower-asset partner even if it means having the high-asset partner pay all of the living expenses. Having a lower-asset partner contribute to joint expenses and then ask for post-separation support upon dissolution is not just ill-advised tax-wise—it also intensifies the dependency that only is harder to address if the relationship unravels.

- In most relationships there are effective strategies that can be adopted to reduce one partner's financial dependency, such as a savings plan (with the high-asset partner matching the lower earner's savings), a shifting of joint expenses toward the higher earner, or an educational or investment plan that builds toward the financial security of the lower earner. Pay particular attention to maintaining a level of earned income for both parties that results in a decent Social Security payment upon retirement and some kind of provision for housing for both parties in the event of dissolution. One popular option is for the high-asset partner to make a gift of a down payment for the purchase of a condominium unit that can provide income or alternative housing for the lower-income partner in the event of dissolution.

- While the gift and estate tax exclusion limit is currently very high, clients should understand that there is a reasonable prospect that it will be reduced in future decades. Thus, for high net-worth partners, some consideration should be given to creating a limited liability company (LLC) or a family limited partnership where assets can be transferred at a lower tax basis to the lower-asset partner. These approaches should be integrated into the estate planning tools, such as a grantor retained trust or an insurance trust, with an understanding of how these tools may need to be unwound in the event of a dissolution.

- In many jurisdictions there are local or state transfer or property taxes that can be significant for unmarried couples. Most counties have transfer taxes on real estate with marital exemptions, and these taxes can be triggered anytime there is a transfer between partners, either in a buy-in or buyout situation. Careful thought should be given to how real estate is titled so that the couple can

One of the benefits of marriage is that it sets out a road map for each spouse's financial roles and responsibilities. Most couples aren't aware of the rules, but as long as they stay together, that's probably just fine—for most of them. And because of the "toll-free" approach to transfers between spouses, they don't need to concern themselves with tax issues for the most part. By contrast, the tax concerns for unmarried couples are inextricably tied to the larger issues of each partner's financial obligations, especially whenever one partner has greater assets or income and is supporting the other partner to some degree. Thus, diving into the tax discussions almost always will trigger deeper personal concerns and will lead to difficult conversations about who has what obligations, both during the relationship and after it ends by death or dissolution.

It's not up to the lawyer to adjudicate what each partner's duties are as there is no legally correct stance and there are many fine nuances in each relationship that properly influence each partner's decisions. In many instances, the best stance for the lawyer to take in this realm is as a mediator or counselor, bringing the concerns to the surface, allowing each partner to retain his dignity and legitimacy, and working with the partners as a team to build a framework that honors the personal concerns while managing the financial and tax considerations as best as possible. If it emerges that there are undercurrents of resentment, anxiety, or disrespect that are making it impossible for the partners to engage in this sort of decision-making process, it usually is best to refer them to a therapist or relationship counselor so they can work out the interpersonal issues before returning to the tax and financial bargaining table.

avoid an excess or avoidable transfer. For example, it usually is more prudent to have both partners listed on the title from the outset rather than adding a partner afterward. In some states (especially California), there are property tax consequences of a transfer between unmarried partners, and the benefits of lower property taxes (based upon Proposition 13) can be lost in the event of a transfer or buyout of one partner's interest upon a dissolution or death unless he is covered as a state-registered domestic partner.[10]

- Unmarried partners with children should approach their tax strategies in an entirely different manner. They may wish to prioritize the needs of their children with regard to tax consequences and will want to address the absence of a marital exemption in a manner that is consistent with a child-centered gift and estate plan.

- In almost every instance, the tax analysis will end up with three different sorts of preferred plans: one that makes the most sense for the partners as they are living their lives together, another one that will be most prudent in the event of a dissolution, and a third plan that works best in the event of the death of the high-asset partner. Unfortunately, the future is always an unknown, and so only the clients can make an educated guess and choose between these three possible scenarios after they've been educated as to the tax consequences of each potential outcome.

E. Tax Considerations for Same-Sex Domestic Partners and Married Couples

Initial Tax Concerns

When marital rights were extended on a limited statewide basis to same-sex couples in 2004 and 2005, first as civil union partners in Vermont and then as domestic partners in California and as married spouses in Massachusetts in 2005, it didn't take long to see that there were going to be federal tax problems. It seemed likely that the policies of DOMA would lead the IRS to treat same-sex partners as legally single even though they would be classified as married under their respective state's tax laws. It was not outlandish to conjure up dramatic visual images of the IRS computers boiling over as they tried to process an income tax return on California community property income filed by a state-married domestic partner who was at the same time federally single.

While the tax problems in the northeastern states lay dormant for several years, not spilling out into high relief until high-asset couples broke up and transferred assets or paid alimony, there was immediate turbulence on the West Coast. Ironically, the tax questions that arose from that region resulted from the complex issues of how the federal government should tax each spouse's share of the community property income—the same issues that had fueled the marital deduction conflicts of the 1920s. Similar to how the tensions unfolded back then, the established rules of community property in California already had established that earned income is "owned" equally by both spouses from the moment it is received by the earner, and so the uncertainties about the IRS recognition of state marital rights surfaced immediately. Commentators started discussing the ramifications of the doctrinal issues from the month that the expanded domestic partnership law was passed in 2003, wondering whether the IRS would treat the de jure transfer of 50 percent of the community property income to the nonearner as a taxable event or would defer to the state law and disregard the income sharing—or maybe just ignore the issue as too messy to handle.

The 2006 Memorandum

The drama took many unexpected steps. Anticipating that the IRS would not allow same-sex domestic partners to split their community property incomes on their federal tax returns and not wanting to burden couples with filing state returns on a different basis than their federal ones, the California legislature initially ruled that registered partners should not report their earned income as community property income. Instead, each partner would file her state return as a single person, with each one taxed on her earnings without regard to its community property characteristic.[11] Consistent with that approach, the IRS issued an advisory opinion in 2006 stating that the same rules would apply for federal returns, and so each partner would report her earned income as if she were legally single.[12]

Most commentators and scholars believed that this was a legally incorrect approach, but nonetheless these rulings provided a bit of clarity on the income tax reporting front for a few years—while the broader tax issues remained unresolved. Eventually, as relationships lasted longer and couples eventually broke up, the gap between the legal doctrines and the tax agency's practices became unbearably wide—and in time the parallel tax liability problems in non-community property states emerged as well. The story took a surprising new turn later in 2006 when the California legislature shifted position and mandated that registered domestic partners would henceforth be required to report their community property income on their state tax return in the same manner as married couples. The legislation was packaged politically as an expansion of "marital" rights to same-sex couples, whereas in fact it saddled couples with the absurd burden of having to create dummy federal returns as married spouses so they could fill out their state returns using the federal return figures.

The 2010 Approach

A few years later, a new constellation of events led to a major shift in IRS policy, after the Obama administration came into office in 2009 and a series of private letter ruling requests prompted the issuance of a Chief Counsel Memorandum opinion in May 2010. The IRS agreed with its earlier critics and concluded that because federal tax law generally respects state property law definitions, the doctrine of *Poe v. Seaborn*[13] mandates that each domestic partner should henceforth report one-half of the couple's combined community income on his own federal tax return.[14] Partners would be required to report their income as such starting in 2010, and they were given the option of amending their returns for the past three years as well if it would result in lower tax obligations.

For domestic partners (both straight and gay) living in community property states (Washington, California, and Nevada), this ruling has great significance. Most dramatically, the federal government is effectively recognizing their state-granted marital property rights despite the specter of DOMA. And because the couples are still filing as "single" on their federal returns, they are not subject to the marriage penalty, and thus many of them may enjoy significantly lower tax rates. A great many technical issues remain unclear, such as whether the same rules will apply to same-sex married couples in community property states (probably yes), and there are many aspects of the tax reporting process that remain unclear, but this is an important development that will have many repercussions.[15]

Related Tax Uncertainties

Perhaps of even greater importance over the long run, the recognition of community property rights for income tax reporting purposes by the IRS is likely to greatly ease the tax complications of a dissolution or death of a partner. Once it has been acknowledged from a tax perspective that each partner "owns" 50 percent of the couple's community property income, it follows logically that a subsequent transfer of that 50 percent share of the assets to the nonearner will not be a taxable event. Thus, if half of a bank account funded by the high earner's earnings or a half-interest in the family residence that was titled in the high earner's name is transferred to the lower-earning partner—either during the relationship or upon a breakup or death—there won't be any concerns about potential gift or income tax obligations as the recipient is merely receiving that which was already his.

Though nothing is certain at this time, it is most likely that the IRS will act in a consistent manner going forward, and so couples in non-community property states also will receive similar rulings when it comes to the asset transfers that occur in connection with divorce or death. The doctrinal analysis in these instances is different in two respects: First, the dissolution of a same-sex married couple will more squarely confront DOMA because that couple's relationship is a marriage and not a marriage-equivalent partnership; and second, because the spouse/partner's rights in a non-community property state generally are not considered vested property rights (but rather equitable transfers based upon the many-factored state dissolution rules), a somewhat greater leap of logic will be required to avoid considering these transfers as taxable.[16]

The arena of even greater uncertainty, both in community property and marital property states, involves the tax treatment of alimony or spousal support payments. While it is quite certain that the tax-shifting provisions of the I.R.C. will not apply to these payments (until DOMA is repealed or invalidated), it is not at all clear whether the IRS will seek to tax the payee, even after the payor has already paid income tax on the receipt of the income used to fund such payments. To the extent that support obligations are imposed by state law, these payments certainly should not be viewed as a gift (and very few divorcing spouses feel much donative intent toward their ex-partners), and the recipient certainly isn't providing labor or services to the payer. Rather, the payment is imposed as an extension of the marital duties of support. From that perspective there should be no tax consequences of the payment, and yet the policy of DOMA would seem to lead to an opposite conclusion.[17] It will be some years before the IRS or the courts rule on this issue, but in light of the recent legalization of marriage between same-sex couples in New York State, there are likely to be quite a few such cases in the coming decade. Hopefully the repeal or invalidation of DOMA prior to then will obviate the need for such a ruling.

There is also great uncertainty with regard to the tax treatment of asset transfers for opposite-sex domestic partners in states that allow opposite-sex couples to register. In these situations there is no doubt that the partners are not spouses, but, at the same time, there is no DOMA issue for these couples. Transfers of one partner's share of the community property assets should not be taxable under the *Seaborn* doctrine, but the unmarried straight partners in non-community property jurisdictions may face problems because they don't have an equitable interest in the other's assets until there is a breakup. Most observers predict that the approach based upon a legal duty of support will prevail, and so the transfers that are made pursuant to the duties of registration will be nontaxable. It is also hoped that the same approach will prevail regarding the payment of spousal support. Straight couples do not suffer as a result of the DOMA policies, and so even though they still are not spouses, the payments will be seen as an outgrowth of the partner's legal duties of support and thus not be taxable.

The Best Advice

Advising state-registered domestic partners, civil union partners, or same-sex married spouses on any sort of tax issue is overwhelmingly difficult. There are very few pockets of legal certainty, and the clash between state family law doctrines and IRS policies toward nonspouses will continue to create confusion and uncertainty for years to come. At the same time, it is inappropriate for lawyers simply to refuse to handle these questions as it is just not true that there is "nothing" that can be done to help these clients.

Given this complex legal climate, it is essential that lawyers are cautious and nuanced in their counsel, keeping the following lessons in mind at all times:

- The notion of state-married partners who are federally single is without precedent in our legal system, and so it is generally not possible to offer legal certainty as to how the tax problems of these clients will be resolved in the long run.

- The politics of same-sex marriage are likely to lead to a great deal of turbulence in the coming decade at both the state and federal levels. IRS policies are likely to change over the next few years, and many states will shift courses with regard to recognition of same-sex relationships. To the extent that the recent legalization of same-sex marriage in New York will expose many high-asset and high-income partners to such tax uncertainties, we may see more private letter rulings—and hopefully public rulings—that shed light on these darker corners of tax law.
- In many instances there is no right answer, which hopefully will reduce the concern about the malpractice consequences of giving a wrong answer.
- Unpredictable changes in the lives of your clients make it extraordinarily difficult to do any planning that assumes one life course: How assets are characterized for tax purposes could have surprising effects over the long haul, depending on the financial trajectory and personal events in the lives of the couple.

With these concerns in mind, the prudent attorney should respond to inquiries regarding tax issues for state-registered and same-sex married couples as follows:

1. Provide basic information about the dichotomy between state-granted marital rights and the nonrecognition of the federal tax authorities so that clients have a clear understanding of the complex underlying legal predicament.
2. Describe the political and legal uncertainties covering the areas that are relevant to the immediate concerns of the clients so that they are realistic about the potential problems going forward; to some degree this information should be included in the initial retainer letter since, in many instances, there may not be any subsequent opinions rendered to the clients.[18]
3. Whenever significant sums are involved (perhaps when incomes are over $100,000 or the asset has a value of over $1 million), refer clients to competent tax advisers.
4. Provide advice in shaded tones and with express qualifications so that the clients have a realistic appreciation for the uncertainties—and so that you have a clear record of the concerns you have conveyed.

In many respects, the great uncertainties surrounding state-registered partners and same-sex married spouses have forced a change in the way I approach my role as an attorney. At one point, I quipped that I had never been paid so much to tell clients "I don't know" in such sophisticated ways! Many attorneys have found the uncertainties in this realm to be too great for them to endure, choosing simply to decline any counseling or representation requests by domestic partners. This is irresponsible, both in terms of your obligations to serve your community and also with respect to the marketing of your legal practice. Gay and lesbian clients understand the turbulent climate for same-sex relationships, and as long as you are clear about the uncertainties and are humble about the limits of your knowledge, they are likely to be appreciative of the counsel you can provide. Bear in mind that even where there is no certain right answer, there often are better or worse strategies that can be followed. Stay humble when you are making recommendations, don't conceal the gray areas, and engage your clients as partners in a voyage across uncharted water, and you are likely to be both helpful and able to sleep at night—but don't cancel your malpractice insurance if you are working in this arena.

NOTES

1. *See* Patricia Cain, *Taxing Families Fairly*, 48 Santa Clara L. Rev., 2008, No. 4 at 805 (cases cited).
2. Poe v. Seaborn, 282 U.S. 101 (1930).
3. I.R.C. §§ 151, 1041 (enacted 1984).
4. 1 U.S.C. § 7 (2000). Attempts to challenge the lack of recognition of same-sex relationships for tax purposes under DOMA previously had been unsuccessful, *see* Mueller v. Comm'r, No. 02-1189, 200 WL 1401297 (7th Cir. June 26, 2002), but more recent federal court challenges to other ramifications of DOMA have succeeded though are on appeal.
5. *See* Cain, *supra* note 1, at 825. *But see* Reynolds v. Comm'r, 77 T.C.M. (CCH) 1479 (1999).
6. This same issue is discussed in an appellate case on the related issue of whether an estate can properly deduct amounts paid in settlement of such claims or whether they are nondeductible as gifts. Estate of Bernard Shapiro v. United States, D.C. No. 2:06-cv-01149-RCJ-LRL (9th Cir. Feb. 22, 2011).
7. As discussed in Chapter 9 on benefits, health insurance and other benefits provided by an employer for the benefit of an unmarried partner are not exempt from taxation under I.R.C. §§ 132, 106 (unless the partner is a dependent), and thus the value of those benefits will be taxable to the employee partner.
8. However, if income spent on a partner's expenses is considered a gift, it is quite likely that many partners will exceed the $5 million limit over the

course of their lifetime even if their accrued savings are far less than this amount.

9. One gray area is whether a promise to make annual gifts transforms a gift into a contractual obligation, especially if it is done in consideration of a waiver of palimony claims. In most instances an agreement can provide that *if* a gift is made, then there is a waiver of claims, thus avoiding the contractual bind.

10. Cal. Const. art 13A.

11. Cal. Fam. Code § 297.5(g) (now revised); *see* Chief Couns. Mem. 200608038 (Feb. 24, 2006).

12. I.R.S. Chief Counsel Advice 200608038.

13. 282 U.S. 101 (1930).

14. I.R.S. Chief Couns. Mem. 201021050 (May 28, 2010) (citing U.S. v. Mitchell, 403 U.S. 190 (1971)).

15. Tax preparers are struggling with an array of reporting challenges, mostly because the partners cannot file a joint federal return as married spouses. Tax withholding cannot be transferred to the nonearning partner, not all deductions can be split between partners, separate property income is reported by the earning taxpayer, and many individual adjustments will need to be made on the tax returns. Many tax preparation software programs do not address these concerns, resulting in higher tax preparation charges for clients.

16. Even though the global exemption on divorce transfers (I.R.C. § 1041) will not apply to same-sex spouses until DOMA is repealed or invalidated, a transfer may nonetheless be nontaxable, either as consideration of a release of rights or an allocation of an equal share of property owned "in trust" for both partners. *See* Imel v. United States, 375 F. Supp. 1102 (D. Colo. 1974), I.R.S. Gen. Couns. Mem. 37716, Rev. Rul. 81–292 (1981), 2 C.B. 158. *But see* United States v. Davis, 370 U.S. 65 (1962).

17. *See* I.R.C. §§ 215, 61; Comm'r v. Duberstein, 363 U.S. 278, 285 (1960); Gould v. Gould, 245 U.S. 151, 153 (1917) (alimony found to be nontaxable as created by the relationship and not by contract); U.S. v. Davis, *supra* note 16, at 69 (alimony treated as a property settlement in exchange for inchoate partnership rights and thus not taxable).

18. It is unclear whether or not attorneys have an ongoing duty to contact past clients to notify them of changes in the tax laws that might affect them. Wherever possible, it is advisable to notify existing clients of these changes, and it is always prudent (and a good marketing practice) to issue a newsletter to past clients describing the latest developments in this field. In most jurisdictions, estate planning clients are considered ongoing clients, and so the duty to keep them informed of tax changes may be greater.

CHAPTER SEVEN
REAL ESTATE OWNERSHIP AND MANAGEMENT

A. The Ins and Outs of Title

Unmarried couples who acquire real estate together are not allowed to hold title as community property or by the entireties, as are married couples. In most every state they are limited to three options: joint tenancy, tenants-in-common as individuals, and tenants-in-common as trustees of their respective revocable trusts. While clients often will call asking which is the best manner of taking title, your response should always be that the answer to this question depends entirely on their underlying intentions and understandings. There is no uniformly best answer to this question.

Rather than explaining the legal rules in dry doctrinal terms, try to help your clients by taking them through a decision tree process.

- First, if they don't want their share of the property to pass to their co-owner upon their death, they should not use joint tenancy.
- Second, if they don't have a trust, then their only option is to take title as tenants-in-common in their individual names. Make sure they understand that as unmarried partners, their heirs-at-law will not be their partner but rather their parents, children, or other legally recognized relatives.

- Third, if they want their share to pass to their partner and they don't have a will or trust set up, then joint tenancy (with right of survivorship) is the only viable choice for them. A few states allow an owner to be the sole owner of property with a "transferable upon death" option, which also will achieve the inheritance goal.
- Fourth, if both of the partners want to leave their share to the other partner and they each have a will and/or a trust in place, then they have the option of any of these three alternatives. Ordinarily, it is best to leave it to their estate planner to help them make this decision.

Oftentimes, the partners haven't completed their estate planning when they are buying the house, or one or both of them may have an outdated will that leaves assets to former partners or family members. In this situation, joint tenancy is a reliable stopgap measure until they've had time to complete or modify their wills or trusts. Changing the title to tenants in common is simple enough, so this is not an irrevocable decision.[1] There are, though, two problems associated with owning property as joint tenants: The first one is an estate tax problem; the second, the much more serious of the two, is the presumption of equal ownership in the event of a breakup.

The tax problem (which is much less of a problem now that the estate tax limit is so high) is that the IRS presumes that the first owner to die owning a joint tenancy property owns 100 percent of the asset, unless the surviving co-owner can prove a financial contribution or clear evidence of ownership by a predeath gift of his share from the decedent owner. The legal reason behind this rule is that each owner is presumed to be the "owner of the whole" as opposed to owning an equal 50 percent; most likely this concept derives from the use of joint tenancy as a "poor man's will," where the surviving owner had only an expectancy interest. For decedents with valuable estates or those owning property of a high market value, this presumption can tip the estate of the first one to die into the taxable category (though much less likely now that the estate tax limit is $5 million). For this reason, it's generally better not to use joint tenancy titling for high net-worth partners unless both owners are clearly contributing to the acquisition and maintenance of the property and the surviving partner can prove that contribution.

The second problem occurs far more often; indeed, it was the source of more than half of the nonmarital litigation that I handled in the first twenty years of my practice. In most states, including California, joint tenancy creates a strong presumption of fifty-fifty ownership because the equal ownership is inherent in the deed. This makes sense, as the reciprocal rights of survivorship would not really be fair if one partner owned a greater share of the property (then one partner would inherit more than the other one depending on which partner died first). Accordingly, in most states there is only a weak presumption of equal ownership for tenants-in-common owners, and a tenancy-in-common owner is entitled to reimbursement of any excess contribution (or a greater ownership share) without having to prove the existence of any contractual agreement. By sharp contrast, joint tenancy owners are only able to recoup their excess contributions if they can prove an agreement. Softening the consequences of this rule, in many states (including California), such a claim can be based upon an express and even an implied agreement, and a written contract is not required. However, if nothing was ever said or thought about the consequences of the excess contribution, there will be no reimbursement or excess ownership share allocated in the event of a dispute.[2] And, since the burden of proof in most jurisdictions for overcoming a deed presumption is clear and convincing evidence, even a well-stated recitation of the oral or implied agreement by one partner is not likely to win the day in a contested trial.

Many couples are told about the survivorship aspect of joint tenancy, and they naïvely assume that they need only worry about a catastrophic death; they don't worry as much as they should about the more likely catastrophe, which is a dissolution. Since most unmarried couples don't ever sign a co-ownership or cohabitation agreement, one partner's excess down payment or years of excess monthly payments can become the major item in dispute in the event of a breakup. Thus, it is crucial that you do your best to point out to your clients that in the absence of a written agreement or a percentage allocation set forth on the deed, they should assume that a joint tenancy property will be divided up fifty-fifty without regard to who contributed more to the down payment or ongoing payments. If they aren't okay with this arrangement, then they should not be taking title as joint tenants.[3]

This is one topic where having a written summary of the various titling options available to unmarried partners in your state will

There are endless misconceptions about the fifty-fifty presumption rule, and many accountants and real estate lawyers misunderstand the doctrine. Moreover, few lawyers acknowledge the true difficulty of overcoming the presumption of a deed, especially in a contested trial between hostile co-owners. The informality of couples' financial arrangements makes it very hard to do any sort of forensic accounting, and the reciprocal arrangements of generosity and shared obligations make it difficult to isolate one set of transactions (the house ownership) and disregard all the other ways that money was spent. Most judges have very little tolerance for these sorts of claims, especially for couples who voluntarily chose to remain unmarried and didn't bother to put together even an informal agreement covering the basic terms of their co-ownership. It took a series of disappointing losses in court (both mine and those of other lawyers to whom I've spoken) before I really came to understand how forceful the fifty-fifty presumption is in a joint tenancy co-ownership.

be helpful. The title companies often misstate the information; and in states where lawyers handle closings, it should not be assumed that the standard real estate closing attorney knows the rules for unmarried partners. The down payment is often the single largest asset of an unmarried partner, and mishandling the deed titling can result in a terrible loss of the bulk of the down payment contribution—so this is not a task to be taken lightly.

Some lawyers recommend that if one partner is contributing more than 50 percent of the down payment (or has an oral agreement to contribute more each month), that unequal percentage ownership should be declared right on the deed. While this approach certainly avoids the downside of a presumed fifty-fifty allocation that leaves the excess contributor out of luck, in most instances you should discourage putting a percentage on the deed. The financial lives of most unmarried couples are not so fixed and certain, and so it is likely that the ownership interests will end up shifting over time. A fixed percentage becomes hard to change, both because of tax consequences and also the need to record a new deed, usually at a substantial fee. It would be preferable to make sure that your clients have a written contract that covers any future shifting of contributions and ownership so that the actual ownership shares or reimbursement entitlements can be determined with the subtlety of detail that only a written agreement can provide.

B. THE PROBLEMS OF THE OFF-TITLE CONTRIBUTOR

Even worse than the problems facing the excess contributor are those of the off-title contributor. Why, you may ask, would someone invest their life savings in a house they don't own? The reasons are manifold, ranging from reasonable to unreasonable to downright stupid or even illegal. Your goal, whenever possible, is to ensure that the legal ownership matches up with the "real" ownership and to explain clearly to your clients the risks of doing otherwise.

The most frequently stated reason for one of the partners being off the title is that he has bad credit, and the couple believes that keeping the low-credit-score partner off the title is crucial in order to obtain a mortgage loan. First, in many instances this turns out to be untrue; more likely, the real problem is that getting the loan will take more work on the part of the loan broker, or it may result in a higher interest rate but not an outright denial. Increasingly, lenders are even willing to allow both partners to be on the title from the outset with just one of them as the borrower on the mortgage loan. But even if one partner must stay off the title at the time the loan is granted, in nearly every situation the co-owner can be added to the title the very next day.[4]

In other situations, one partner may be reluctant to share true legal ownership with the other, either because the other has bad credit or because the buying partner is concerned about the messiness of a co-ownership situation. If that is the case, then the other partner is not really an owner and should not pretend to be one. In many instances the concerns about co-ownership are well founded, but that is why there should simply be one owner! If a partner has a spotty enough history to warrant keeping him off the title, then chances are he should not be considered an owner under any perspective, even as an equitable co-owner. Occasionally a couple has a legitimate reason for one partner to stay off the title, such as privacy (for a same-sex couple) or a temporary uncertainty about titling or paying a large transfer tax, but the non-titled partner still wants to be considered a co-owner for other reasons, such as honoring the value of his financial contribution. For those partners, having an agreement for equitable co-ownership should be considered.

But bear in mind that this also will be an agreement that a creditor can rely upon, and therefore most of the supposed benefits of staying off the title will be lost as well.

Then there are those who are trying to hide assets, perhaps from a government regulator or maybe a former spouse or some other aggressive creditor. In these situations, the lawyer should simply stay away from the matter and not get involved at all. You don't want to ever be accused of facilitating a fraud against creditors, and there certainly is no right answer about titling in this sort of scenario.

There are two sets of risks of your client staying off the title when he is truly a major financial contributor to real estate: (1) those posed by the tax authorities and (2) the more serious ones presented by the client's own partner.

As to the tax risks, not being on the title creates a presumption that a person is not an owner, and therefore it is most likely that such person will not be allowed the tax deductions that owners regularly enjoy. For many of your clients, this will be a minor risk as the value of their 50 percent share of the interest deductions may not be that great. But the same restriction can be very expensive when it comes to selling the house; if the IRS were to determine that the nontitled contributor was not an owner, that partner could lose out on nearly $250,000 in the capital gains exclusion under the residential sale provision of the Code.[5] If you only learn about the situation after it is too late to add a partner to title, you can always try to assert that the nontitled partner had an equitable interest in the property, but at a minimum there should be a written agreement that details the terms of the equitable ownership.

Most clients are able to comprehend the tax risk and analyze the situation appropriately, and if they fail to deal with the issue, the consequences are not usually that dire. In many instances the actual tax deductions are not of such great value since in most instances the legal owner can amend his return and take the entire deduction, though he then would have to report the off-title contributor's contribution as taxable rental income. But the much greater problem is one that arises in the event of a breakup, where the off-title contributor may be denied any share of the appreciation in the property.

These situations can be cruel: I once represented a man who had shared his paycheck with his partner for decades, and his income constituted nearly one-third of the monthly housing payments. But when they broke up twenty-five years later, the titled owner claimed 100 percent of the San Francisco property, then worth nearly $1 million. The dispute went all the way to trial, and in the end the judge ruled that my client had only been paying rent since there was no "clear and convincing" evidence of an oral or implied agreement for ownership that overcame the presumption of sole ownership in the titled partner's name.

Sorting through the stories that clients tell about the ownership history after the fact is messy and painful. Usually the titled owner will have an explanation for his position: Perhaps the other's credit scores were too low, maybe there was a risk of a judgment being attached to the property, or perhaps the couple hadn't reached the requisite level of commitment to justify legal co-ownership. Most often, the titled owner will claim that the contributions by the partner were for occupancy (as a form of rent, even if undeclared as such in the owner's tax returns). Sometimes there is a claim that an oral agreement was made, but more typically the off-title contributor genuinely relied on the unspoken assurances of his partner or was too insecure about his own relationship status to press to be added to the title. In any case, though, the outcome is likely to be horrible for the one off the title unless there is an abundance of good faith and generosity on the part of the titled owner.

A brief note about gift letters: Lenders sometimes require that nonowners sign a gift letter stating that their down payment is a gift and not a second loan on the property. Most often these requests are made when a parent or other family member is contributing to the purchase. Lying about this situation is criminal bank fraud, and if the bank loan doesn't get paid and the lender is looking to blame someone, he could pursue a borrower for this wrongdoing. If the contribution truly is a gift, it is important that the generous parents make it clear whether they are giving it to one or both of the co-owners. These letters are evidence of the ownership arrangement and obligations and will be binding upon co-owners if there is a subsequent dispute. The same goes for any gift letter between partners: if one partner is asked to sign a letter stating that his down payment is a gift and not a loan (or co-ownership investment), then it won't be possible to press a legal claim if the legal owner decides not to pay it back at the end of the ownership history.

This is one area where you should be absolutely frank with your clients: Tell them in no uncertain terms that if they are not on the title and if they don't have a written agreement for some kind of equity sharing, they should assume that they have no ownership interest and act accordingly. Tell your clients not to renovate the kitchen in a house they don't own and not to contribute more on a monthly basis than the value of the rental occupancy they are enjoying; it just is too risky to do otherwise.

C. PRELIMINARY ISSUES REGARDING CO-OWNERSHIP AGREEMENTS

Clients often ask whether or not they need a written co-ownership agreement, and the correct response is a two-part answer. Every co-owning couple would benefit from having such an agreement, but such agreements become essential whenever one partner is contributing more than half of the down payment or the monthly expenses or if one partner is not going on the title but is contributing to the purchase or monthly expenses.

The primary value of an agreement for a couple equally contributing is that it allows the partners to design their own exit plan, which surely will be more rational than the co-ownership legal process that will be binding on them in the absence of an agreement. In California and most other states, either co-owner has a statutory right to seek partition of the property if they cannot agree in the event of a breakup. When this happens, the court takes over the property and appoints a referee who sells the property for the best price under a tight timeline (which usually is shorter because of the forced-sale aspect of the court process), and then the parties return to court to fight over the meager proceeds of sale. Clearly, this is not a rational way to part ways, and that's the main reason why having a written agreement is useful to a couple.

The second reason that an agreement is useful for an equal-contribution couple is that the agreement-formation process usually provides useful educational and emotional benefits to the partners. It forces them to address their underlying issues of financial capacities and concerns and gives them an opportunity to see how well (or poorly) they communicate about financial matters. Interestingly, I've discovered that the couples who come into my office for a first meeting but never complete the agreement tend to have a high dissolution rate; my hunch is that the inability to address the co-ownership questions indicates a broader relationship dysfunctionality.

The main benefits of an agreement when there is an excess contribution or an off-title contributor should be self-evident: Absent a written agreement, chances are that the contributor will never see any return on his contributions. Even in states where oral and implied agreements can be enforced, it's just about impossible to prove such agreements, which is why the excess or off-title contributor absolutely needs the protection of a written agreement.

Lawyers need to be flexible regarding the scope of these agreements. In my first decade of drafting co-ownership agreements, it was rare for me to cover anything but the ownership of the residence. That was the primary asset of the couple, and that was the partners' chief concern. Over the course of the next decade, a growing number of couples broke up and fought over financial issues unrelated to the property. While it was rare to see litigation arising out of these disputes, it sometimes did get to that point, and I regretted not having pushed my clients harder to deal with the nonproperty issues up front. As a result, my approach has shifted somewhat, and I now always try to persuade my clients to address to some degree the separate financial issues as part of their co-ownership agreement.

For some of your clients, this will mean entering into a comprehensive cohabitation agreement that addresses all of their financial concerns, both during their relationship and in the event of a separation.[6] For others, they simply want to have a waiver of all claims, confirming that absent a subsequent written agreement to the contrary, they each own whatever is in their own names and neither one owes any post-separation support to the other one. If the partners are unable to reach any agreement about these issues at all, consider including a provision that expressly states that they are not entering into any agreement on any other issues—period. This clause serves as a reminder to them that they don't have any such agreement (and thus are likely to be subject to the default "no valid claims" rule of the jurisdiction for unmarried couples in the event of a breakup). It also will remind them, if they should ever have a dispute about finances in the future, that the issue was raised and they consciously chose not to deal with it in advance.

D. The Basic Ingredients of Every Co-Ownership Agreement

Early on in my career, I undertook a review of the dozen or so versions of co-ownership agreements that I had drafted or reviewed, and I compiled a list of all the key issues that should be covered in any comprehensive agreement. I also analyzed the degree of complexity of the various agreements, seeking to achieve a balance between the overly simplistic agreements (some of which seemed defective in my opinion) and the excessively complex agreements (including some that were so detailed that they probably wouldn't even be understood, let alone followed, by a typical unmarried couple). Out of this analysis, I developed a standard template for my own model co-ownership agreement, and this is the document that serves as the basis for the discussion in this chapter and is included in the Forms section of this book.

Keep in mind that this is a recommended approach for a typical unmarried couple. If the couple is state-registered as domestic partners, then their rights and obligations are set by marital law, and so the agreement needs to be framed as a premarital (or preregistration) agreement. In other instances, a parent or sibling will be added as a co-owner as well, and that calls for a different sort of agreement. And, in the San Francisco Bay Area, oftentimes couples end up buying a duplex or triplex with another couple or an unrelated individual, and so those agreements require additional terms and conditions.

But there are a few essential components that make up the standard unmarried partners' real estate co-ownership agreement, which are discussed below.

The Ownership Structure

Always start with a recitation of the initial investment arrangements: How much is each partner putting in as a down payment, what is the amount of the loan (or loans), and what amounts are being invested in improvements undertaken immediately upon the purchase. This section usually is not controversial, but it serves as an excellent summary of the deal if the parties subsequently lose track of their closing documents. State the manner in which title was vested and describe the marital status of the parties. You should include a provision for straight couples describing how the agreement may be superseded by marital law if they end up getting married later on (but stating that it is their intention that these terms survive if allowed by law), as well as including a similar provision in your agreements for same-sex couples. Try to summarize in a paragraph or so the essence of the co-ownership plan (i.e., equal, proportional, or with a reimbursement of the down payment) so that if disputes arise later on that aren't directly covered by the specific terms of the agreement, there is a statement of general principles that can be applied to resolve the dispute.

Co-owners usually present two different sorts of uncertainties in this regard. Some couples are in sync about the basic terms (e.g., equal or unequal ownership) but are confused about how to monetize their contributions and come up with a fair agreement that reflects their shared values. For these folks, you will need to make sure you understand the core of their basic agreement, and then you can focus on explaining the different ways of calculating value and the likely consequences of their

Is it best to treat an excess contribution as a loan to be repaid, an entitlement to a greater ownership share, or simply a gift by the higher-asset partner? There is no right or wrong approach here, and the real-world outcome hinges on what happens to the value of the property. If the value soars, then an excess percentage of ownership will be a windfall to the excess contributor; if the value drops or stays level, the reimbursement approach will be best for the excess contributor. And if it totally tanks, there's nothing there to recover for either party. Suggest to your clients that they do some simple calculations using a few likely outcomes over a five- or ten-year horizon as then they can see for themselves how the different outcomes would play out.

For those who want to be especially fair, one suggestion is a blended approach, where there is an initial reimbursement for the excess contribution but with a minimum amount and a ceiling as well, above and below which some share of the profit or loss is shared equally. The marriage model typically provides for the reimbursement of premarital contributions without interest, whereas the business model typically goes for proportional ownership; let them choose what is most appropriate for their lives. It's crucial that they understand that if the property gets sold before there is any appreciation, there will actually be a loss of some portion of their down payment since the costs of sale (especially real estate commissions) will have to be paid out of their equity.

differing approaches to unequal ownership. Typically, they will need some time to decide on the best formula to use, but their discussions will be mostly technical in nature.

Other couples are still at odds about the basic framework they want to follow, and typically this touches on the underlying debate about whether or not they are sharing their assets. This is most difficult if one partner has greater savings or enjoys a higher income and, as previously discussed, goes to the heart of their relationship as an unmarried couple. It's essential that you be attuned to this sort of conflict as clients will sometimes want to conceal it (in part because they don't want to face it themselves). For these clients, you will need to shift gears and engage in a more therapeutic kind of counseling, and, depending on how the conversation unfolds, they may need to take a break from the legal process and work with a relationship counselor or therapist to address these deeper conflicts. Unfortunately, many clients come to you just before they are closing escrow on their purchase, which often results in them proceeding with the purchase without an agreement and never reaching consensus later on. You should always remind your clients that there is only one deadline for having such an agreement: anytime before they are split by either death or a breakup.[7]

Payment of Necessary Expenses

The agreement should recite the default provisions for making payments for the ongoing and predictable expenses: mortgage, property taxes, insurance, and utilities. Some couples agree from the outset that these expenses will be paid for equally, regardless of income, and others prefer to allocate them proportionally based upon net incomes. The relative fairness of these various approaches has to be evaluated in terms of the ownership agreement, either equal or unequal. One of the most common arrangements is where one person contributes more to the down payment and the other pays more each month; in this situation, you can either treat the excess down payment as a loan to the other one that is repaid through the excess monthly contributions, as a precursor to a greater ownership share, or as an excess contribution to be reimbursed. In any event, you should typically add a provision that says that the actual payments are deemed to be the agreed-upon payments unless the excess contributor makes a demand for reimbursement within a set period of time, no later than the end of each calendar year. Keep in mind that you can never assume that the down payment loan will ever be fully paid back as most folks refinance their loan, break up, or sell their house long before the original mortgage is paid back.

One frequent phenomenon that you will learn about in these partnerships is the powerful role of "regretted generosity," an emotion that can occur when one partner contributes more than his legal obligation. One partner feels loving and generous at the time that the payment is made—but then regrets that generosity when the relationship goes sour (especially if the recipient of the generosity has an affair or initiates the breakup). Some folks are honest about their regrets and can accept the painful consequence (i.e., you can't take back a gift), but many others engage in a bit of historical revisionism and try to construe the "gift" retroactively as a loan. As you can imagine, such a claim is usually not well received, especially by a partner who probably would not have signed on for receiving the "gift" if he thought he'd ever have to pay it back. Quite often the payment was made when one partner was having financial troubles, either because of a job loss or medical condition, or where one partner was the higher earner and was willing to contribute more or pay for other expenses, wanting to enjoy some of the bounty she had earned in the form of a vacation or some other luxury. Knowing how likely it is that this sort of dynamic can arise is one of the reasons that you should require some form of notice or consent as a prerequisite for demanding reimbursement for an excess contribution, especially if it's for a nonnecessary expense such as a renovation.

Improvements and Capital Contributions

Design your agreements to be ignored by the partners until there's a conflict, and always include default provisions that match the intent of the parties. Unless it's really necessary, you don't want to require that your clients "take action" on any regular basis to carry out the terms of their agreement; they simply won't do that, and so their intentions will be frustrated. Silence should usually equal consent or should leave the partners where they want to end up in ways that make sense for their values and intentions. It would be prudent to fill your agreements with clauses that start out "In the absence of a written agreement to the contrary, . . ."

The one exception to allowing silence to imply an agreement is when it comes to making major improvements to a residence. This is one of the touchiest areas in co-ownership, as oftentimes the parties have very different values and tastes and are in different economic classes, especially when they aren't sharing their income or other financial assets. A major improvement does not always increase the value of the property, and so one person's expensive renovation can eat up much of the equity if the paying partner is entitled to be reimbursed. Make sure that your clients understand that the value of an improvement is not the same as its cost. If the partners have already decided what they are going to do, recite those terms; otherwise, set out a procedure for them to follow, letting them decide for each particular improvement how the costs are going to be shared and, if one partner is paying the entire freight, how that will be reimbursed. Encourage your clients to keep a simple ledger of approved improvements that will be reimbursed, and typically recommend that they use a set dollar figure (either the true cost or some percentage of that amount) rather than trying to estimate the value of the work.

Use the same approach for post-purchase capital contributions. Most real estate lawyers would assume that capital contributions should always be reimbursed, but given how unmarried couples organize their lives, this isn't necessarily the case. In some instances one partner is making an excess contribution because she is the richer partner or is expecting an inheritance, or it may be because the lower-earning partner is contributing "sweat equity" more regularly. Numerous people live in the cash (i.e., underground) economy, and sometimes they will do things such as pay for vacations and other purchases in exchange for their partner paying down the mortgage. Because of these anomalies, it doesn't make sense to assume that the excess contributor should be reimbursed; that should either be listed on an amendment to the agreement or a ledger, or at a minimum there should be a written demand for reimbursement within thirty days of the excess contribution. The one thing you don't want to have is someone thinking that her partner has made a generous gift or a reciprocal payment, only to have the gesture surface as a demand for reimbursement years later.

Planning for the Dissolution

There are two aspects of the exit strategy discussions that need to be addressed: the dissolution process and the financial allocations. As to the process, encourage partners to consider including a "first dibs" as a right of first offer and not a right of first refusal. A right of first refusal refers to the refusal of a third-party offer by matching the outside buyer's price, whereas a right of first offer involves a buyout using an appraisal before the property is marketed to the public. In most markets having a right of first refusal will hamper a market sale, as it forces a partner to list the property but then discourages buyers from putting much effort (or money) into the offer. For that reason, it's always better to allow for a buyout based upon an appraisal. Then, if that doesn't work, your clients can put the property on the market for sale. Some partners are reluctant to give one of them first dibs, especially based upon an appraisal that might not be reliable. In that event, the partners can rely on a coin toss, a mediation process, or an "internal auction" where the one who pays the most keeps the property. If the parties are unwilling to consider such an approach (often they think it comes too close to planning their divorce), then include a provision that confirms that no one has such a right and that if the issue is not resolved in mediation, the house will have to be sold.

It is also helpful to cover the basic elements of the buyout or sale process. One party gives notice of wanting to end the co-ownership relationship (or the relationship overall), and then the couple determines if either partner wants to and is able to undertake a buyout (which usually means getting a new loan on his own as neither party is bound to remain a co-borrower after he is no longer a co-owner). If so, then an appraisal process is used to set a fair market value. You should recommend a moderately complicated process, using appraisers rather than real estate agents but only bringing in a second or third appraiser if really necessary. You should also recommend that the market value for a buyout calculation be reduced by some percentage to reflect the future real estate commissions that will be incurred when the buying partner becomes a selling owner. Because there's never any certainty as to what will happen, recommend a 3 percent reduction rather than the full amount of the likely commission. In some instances it may be appropriate to provide for a moving expense reimbursement for the one who has to leave.

Strongly discourage any kind of fault-based allocation of sale or buyout expenses, as tempting as it is to clients who want to include such a charge. I recently met with a client whose girlfriend walked out on her barely three months after they purchased a home; they are now incurring nearly $50,000 in real estate commissions, plus losing the $8,000 tax credit because they aren't staying in their house for at least three years. To me, it seemed that the girlfriend owes something for these costs; but, in fact, every breakup results from actions by both partners in some way or another, and trying to allocate fault is simply impossible. You might want to consider including provisions stating that if either partner unilaterally elects to leave within a year or two, he has to continue to pay his share of the property's expenses for a minimum holding period until the property is sold—but even that is tricky. It would be preferable to have your clients understand the risks that they are taking on when buying property with a partner and accept them as facts of life that can't be avoided.

The main priority in designing the exit strategy is to avoid the forced sale of a court-ordered partition action; you want to do your best to set up a rational process for your clients, one that is realistic given who they are and how they live their lives.[8] Some folks move slower than others, so you might want to extend the notice and compliance periods in those cases. Some partners have kids or a disability or vulnerable jobs, and so they may need special protections in the form of a willingness to stay on a loan or a longer period of time to complete a buyout process. Others may have been excessively generous at the front end (e.g., paying a larger down payment or doing construction work on the home), and they should be given some special consideration at the back end. If there are disputes about valuation or a credit for an excess contribution, you want to provide a system that isolates those problems and deals with them in a focused arbitration process rather than having the entire buyout or sale process come to a grinding halt. You also want to think about and draft the provisions covering these issues in general terms: you can never be certain how their lives are going to unfold, and you can't engage in the kind of hyperdetailed lawyering that might be appropriate for a multimillion dollar shopping center development.

Be sure to include the basic requirements of a joint sale: hiring an agent (don't ever use more than one, even for warring partners), paying the marketing costs, and an obligation to participate in the sales process in a reasonable manner. The last point is often an area of high conflict in a nasty breakup, but it really isn't possible to prevent contentious outbreaks in a co-ownership agreement, and it is unrealistic to think that you are going to include sufficient details to cover every instance of misbehavior that might arise.

The financial element of the dissolution should, of course, be based upon the ownership structure. You will want to come up with a formula that applies to the actual proceeds of sale as well as estimated proceeds if a buyout is happening. Typically, the formula should be the same for both outcomes other than the additional details that only arise in the event of a buyout (allocating expenses of refinancing, title transfer, and reimbursements and credits). Try to keep the formula simple: Pay the costs of sale, pay off the mortgage loans, reimburse any agreed-upon advancements, and then distribute the proceeds according to the ownership formula.

One subtle nuance that often needs to be explained to the partners involves the concept of "half from the half, whole from the whole." In other words, if one partner has paid $100,000 for the down payment, he should either receive $100,000 "from the whole" (i.e., out of the proceeds before they are divided in half) or $50,000 from the other partner (out of his half of the proceeds). This concept can be very difficult for nonprofessionals to master, and you might need to use drawings or even torn pieces of paper to explain how receiving 50 percent of the advancement from the other party makes the excess contributor whole.

Death-Related Provisions

Even though a co-ownership agreement will not meet the standards of a will or trust, it can still include provisions that are applicable in the event of the death of one of the partners. The most crucial such term is a contractual agreement not to terminate a joint tenancy or do anything that would disinherit the other partner with regard to the property. You should always explain to your clients that a joint tenancy usually can be terminated, and in most states this can be done unilaterally by either of the owners. Thus, taking title in joint tenancy does not preclude one of the partners from converting the property to tenants in common and then bequeathing her share to someone other than her partner. Sometimes that is just fine with the other partner, especially if one or both of them have children from another relationship that they want to protect. But even then, encourage them to provide for their children in other ways, either with other assets or with insurance. Most kids do not want to end up co-owning property with their parents' surviving lover, and most partners don't want to co-own with their stepchildren. The best solution is to have each partner take out a life insurance on her partner's life (or her own life), with the children as beneficiaries, in exchange for a promise of not terminating the joint tenancy except to put the property in trust for each other's benefit. Such an agreement will be binding on the heirs as a contractual claim in probate if the partner breaches the agreement before death.

Conflict-Resolution Procedures

Always encourage a mediation provision, usually setting forth a minimum number of sessions over a set duration of time, typically three or four sessions within a month's time. Generally I recommend arbitration, but you need to be careful here. In some states an arbitrator has limited powers over ownership of real estate and can't issue injunctive orders (such as a requirement to sign a property listing or a deed). But binding arbitration can be especially useful, in particular because an appeal isn't possible, which is appropriate for this scale of conflict. But if an arbitrator can't issue an appropriate ruling, then it might be better to rely on court adjudication or, at a minimum, have an attorney fees clause in place in case an owner refuses to abide by an arbitrator's order and an enforcement action in court needs to be filed. Binding arbitration typically isn't allowed for marital disputes, and so if your clients end up getting married, they will find themselves in the family court of their county, not in front of a private arbitrator.

You should include a paragraph that expressly recites that it is likely that conflicts will arise that are not expressly covered in the agreement, and that in such event they should be resolved in a manner consistent with the overall structure of the co-ownership arrangement and the basic terms of the agreement. While this is simply reiterating that which is already the legal rule, it is important to include such a provision for two reasons. First, it reminds the clients that it wasn't a mistake on your part to have left out certain possible outcomes but, rather, part of a deliberate strategy to have a simpler agreement and keep the attorney fees as low as possible. Second, it encourages the parties to honor their underlying purpose in the agreement when dealing with unforeseen circumstances or an unanticipated conflict, especially while in mediation. This is a personal relationship and not a corporate merger, and the parties should be encouraged to view their inevitable conflicts in this context.

There are two ways of looking at the idea of attorney fees clauses for these co-ownership agreements. In most instances, the conflicts are not terribly complicated, and you should encourage folks to resolve their conflicts through mediation or arbitration without getting expensive lawyers involved. At the same time, some exes can be extremely difficult in a high-conflict dissolution, and one partner often feels that he desperately needs legal counsel. For these reasons, a worthwhile recommendation is a "bad faith" standard for attorney fees awards, where a judge or arbitrator can still issue such an award but only when there is a finding of bad faith.

Optional Additional Provisions

There are some additional provisions that should be considered in appropriate circumstances, including the following:

- *Space Allocation.* If one of the parties is using part of the house for an office or studio or if one partner has a relative living in a portion of the residence, it may be helpful to have a paragraph covering these intentions, sometimes with a particular allocation of some of the extra expenses that are associated with this usage.
- *Extra Expenses.* If one of the parties has children, it may be helpful to clarify how they will share in the occupancy, sometimes including an allocation of some of the additional costs associated with their presence.
- *Labor and Materials.* For some couples, it is useful to clarify from the outset that one of them will be taking on the bulk of the labor for maintenance and repair in exchange for the other one paying the bills for the materials.
- *Bank Accounts.* You might want to leave it open as to whether or not they are going to share a bank account, but some couples like to have these details worked out in advance.
- *Insurance.* Again, this is something that you might want to let the owners work out for themselves over time, but some partners find it useful to specify a minimum insurance commitment, both as to homeowners insurance and life insurance to protect each other's ability to keep paying the mortgage if one owner dies while they

are co-owners. This is just the sort of provision that most co-owners end up ignoring, however, so it seems unwise to include it.

- *Sales Restrictions.* Typically, neither party can unilaterally sell his share to a stranger (and who would ever buy into such a co-ownership arrangement?), but it can be useful to specify this in advance.
- *Interest on Advancements.* You might think it's inappropriate to charge interest to a loved one, but others disagree and want to include the right to charge interest. The one area where this is most appropriate is when there is a major default that is not cured for a significant amount of time, often leaving the other party to have to use a credit card (at a very high interest rate) to make up the shortfall.
- *Recordation.* Having your clients record these agreements is something that should happen rarely; they are private documents, and recording one version means you have to record all amendments. Given the informal way in which most couples operate, it is best if they keep their private lives private. If there is a particular reason why something needs to be recorded, then, to protect an equitable co-owner, it is best to simply record a memorandum of agreement stating that an agreement exists but not disclosing all of the details to the entire world.
- *Tax Allocations.* Don't put tax allocations into the agreement as those situations change and the parties always are bound by the applicable tax rules anyway. It is better to have these arrangements worked out from year to year, as the law allows and as the couple's financial situation mandates—and that is what the agreement should state.
- *Expenses Pending Separation.* Most states have default rules as to how expenses are to be paid during a co-ownership pending a sale or a buyout, after the parties have separated. In some instances, it is prudent to prenegotiate a specific set of guidelines for this possibility in order to minimize the conflicts. Usually the occupying owner is responsible for the "fair rental value" of the property, and the excess expenses, if any, are borne by the parties in proportion to their ownership shares.
- *Lack of a Business Partnership.* You will probably want to include a provision that expressly states that this is not a business partner-

ship so that no one is tempted to invoke the state rules about business ventures.

- *Roommates and Guests.* Some couples want to include from the outset a provision that allows for a child or other family member (typically an adult child from a prior relationship) to move in but otherwise precludes inviting roommates without the other's consent.

- *Debt Allocation.* If one of the partners has contributed more of the down payment, it may be prudent to put into the agreement the details about the shifting of the monthly mortgage payments so that the lower-contributing partner can "catch up" by paying the larger share of the mortgage.

- *Rental Unit.* If the property includes a rental unit, it is useful to confirm that the rental income will be shared and that any excess above property expenses will also be shared in proportion to ownership interests.

- *Maintenance and Management.* A standard agreement should have a provision that says that neither party is going to be paid for excess maintenance work unless the parties agree in writing. If your clients have an arrangement where one is more than simply a "stay-at-home" partner and is doing significant maintenance and improvement labor, some sort of compensatory scheme may be appropriate.

- *Ordinary Domestic Chores.* It probably isn't wise to include provisions about taking out the garbage or washing the dishes. If the partners aren't able to work this sort of stuff out without paying a lawyer to write up rules for them, they probably shouldn't be buying a house together.

- *Liens and Judgments.* A standard agreement should include a provision that each partner will be liable for any liens or judgments that she has incurred. If one of the partners has particular exposure, perhaps because of a high-risk business, some further provisions about how this is to be handled should be included. The main point to include is that the liens or judgments can only be satisfied out of the debtor's share of the property and that if the other partner ever finds herself on the hook, there will be full indemnification by the liable party.

- *Post-dissolution Co-Ownership.* Some couples end up remaining co-owners even after their relationship ends, perhaps renting out the house during a downtime in the market or keeping it as a joint investment for the long term. This can sometimes work out fine, but the new business relationship should be structured as such at the time. It's simply too difficult to conceptualize such an agreement in advance.

E. REAL ESTATE TAX CONCERNS

Even though you probably are not a tax accountant, you need to have a basic understanding of the recurring tax issues that are likely to arise for nonmarital co-ownerships. It is appropriate to refer your clients to tax specialists to answer complicated questions or to prepare their tax return, but you will want to be able to offer general guidance on the central tax issues—and, at a minimum, you don't want to miss the essential issues.

Off-Title Contributors

As mentioned earlier, one of the worst risks of being an off-title contributor is not being able to take the tax deductions as an owner. If there is a clearly written equitable co-ownership agreement and the owners follow its terms, there is a plausible argument that an off-title contributor should be able to take the tax advantages, but it is not certain that they can do so. The IRS doesn't require titling in order to prove ownership, but it is considered the only reliable proof. There are inconsistent reports from accountants who have prepared returns and handled audits; some will be willing to take a chance and claim ownership deductions on behalf of an off-title contributor, but some won't.

Keep in mind when evaluating the risks the reason behind the decision to stay off the title: if there's something improper at the heart of that decision, the tax problems could be serious. You certainly don't want to have your clients take a tax deduction when the reason they are off the title is that they haven't paid taxes on the money they used to help purchase the property. And keep in mind that if the off-title partner contributes to expenses directly, the other partner can't take those payments as a deduction; so if the non-titled contributor can't take the deduction, it is lost entirely. Alternatively, if the non-titled contributor makes the payment to the titled owner, the payments should be treated as rental income, which is itself taxable.

The much greater problem, of course, arises when the property is sold, because then the off-title contributor may not be entitled to the residential tax exclusion that is given only to those who have been an owner for at least two years. As with the annual deductions, being off the title is not fatal to the claim of ownership, but it can create a serious risk in the event of an audit.

Allocation of Deductions

Deductions can be taken based upon actual contributions for the most part, and it is usually possible for one owner to hoard some of the high-deductible expenses as long as there is no double deduction of any contribution. Recommend to your clients that they open up a joint account for all property expenses because then they can allocate the expenses in the most tax-advantageous way at the end of the year. No one can deduct more than the total contributions to the joint account, but oftentimes all or a greater share of the nondeductible expenses (insurance, utilities, etc.) can be allocated to the lower earner, and the deductible ones (mortgage interest) can be clumped on the higher earner's return. Of course, it is only fair that if this results in a disproportional tax benefit, the higher-earning partner should share the benefit of that extra deduction with the other partner. Some expenses, such as property taxes, are only deductible in proportion to ownership interests, so your clients need to be mindful of the limits of this sort of tax-benefit shifting.

Capital Contributions and Tax Basis

One of the stickiest problems for unmarried co-owners is the allocation of capital contributions for the tax basis calculation. Because the partners are not married, they won't be filing a joint return, and each of them has to separately track his capital contributions to the down payment, mortgage paydown, and improvements. If a joint account is used for these expenditures, it is typical that the basis contributions be allocated fifty-fifty, which usually is fine for the partners. The real problem arises when major improvements are made. From a doctrinal perspective, each partner's actual contributions make up the contributor's individual basis, but as with the allocation of annual expenses, some shifting can be done where the partners combine their assets.

In other words, as long as nothing is being double counted and no one claims more than his total contribution to the joint account, the IRS probably isn't going to care how the contributions are allocated. But, in some instances, this can become a major source of conflict at the time of a sale or buyout. If the total appreciation is under $250,000 per owner and both partners lived in the house within three years of its sale, this isn't going to be a big problem as neither partner will owe any capital gains taxes. However, if there is significant appreciation above this amount or if one or both of the owners have moved out of the property more than three years before it is sold, then the owners may find themselves arguing over who should be able to take the lion's share of the tax basis and benefit from a reduction in capital gains tax liability. In effect, each partner will want to hoard a greater share of the basis so that he can claim a lower gain and thus avoid any capital gains tax liability.

While you probably can't monitor your clients' conduct on an annual basis, the best advice to give them is to keep good track of which partner is contributing what amounts to any improvements. And, if they are pooling their funds in a joint account and one partner is contributing significantly more than the other one, they should keep track of those contributions on an annual basis. And, if their home is likely to appreciate greatly in value, they may want to document a portion of the higher-contributor's payments as a gift to the lesser-contributor, so that the overall contributions to capital expenses are closer to equal in amounts.

Local Tax Concerns

In many jurisdictions there are transfer taxes imposed on the transfer of any interest in real estate, and in some locations (especially in California) the assessment for property tax purposes can be increased to the market value whenever there is a sale or transfer. Most of these tax rules have spousal exemptions, but only those couples who are legally married under state law (or are state-registered in a marriage-equivalent registration) are entitled to any of these exemptions. A few jurisdictions have a local registry that can entitle your registered clients to an exemption from local tax burdens if they have signed up as domestic partners, and this should always be considered (though generally it won't work for a couple who is already breaking up).

The lack of knowledge of these rules in the real estate community can create severe financial burdens. One of the most challenging situations, and it comes up way too often, is where a mortgage broker has encouraged a couple to take title in just one partner's name to improve the loan approval outcome, assuring the partners that they can simply add the other partner to the title after the fact. However, in the San Francisco Bay Area this strategy can result in a transfer tax when the unmarried partner is added to the title. The tax can be more than $5,000 (the typical tax is about $15 per $1,000, so even a 50 percent transfer of an $800,000 property results in a $6,000 tax), which is usually far more costly than what the added interest costs would have been had both partners been on the title from the outset. In addition, an increasing number of lenders will allow a partner to be added to the title from the outset even if that partner is not considered a borrower under the terms of the mortgage loan.

Anticipation of Taxes upon Dissolution

While it is always difficult to get your clients to focus on the potential future dissolution issues, it is important to make an effort in that direction simply because the tax consequences can be so significant. The allocation of deductions while the couple is together rarely has great monetary impact, whereas the tax ramifications of a sale or buyout upon dissolution can be consequential. If the property has gone up significantly in value (above the $250,000 in residential exclusion) or the partners don't stay together for at least two years, the one who is selling (or both of them if they are selling jointly) will have a hefty tax bill to pay. If one of them moves out for more than three years before selling his share (or the entire property), he will have lost his residential exclusion since he won't be able to extend the sale deadline based upon a marital dissolution as married couples can do. Whenever possible, you should be thinking through the most likely dissolution outcomes, either a buyout by one of the parties or a sale on the market, and try to envision what the tax consequences will be. It may not be possible to avoid all of the negative outcomes, but they should be minimized whenever possible.

One of the few tax benefits that is not dependent upon marriage is the residential capital gains exclusion, which is $250,000 per person regardless of marital status. However, there is one aspect of this rule that hits unmarried couples particularly hard: the two-year ownership rule. For a married couple, one spouse can be the sole owner for decades and if the other spouse is added as a co-owner just before sale, they each can take the $250,000 exclusion (and save as much as $37,000 in federal taxes and as much as $25,000 in state capital gains taxes), as long as both of them lived there the requisite two years.

F. Creative Alternative Ownership Arrangements

Various lawyers have proposed alternative ownership arrangements for unmarried partners, such as an LLC or a family limited partnership or some kind of creative trust arrangement. This sort of approach is not optimal for most clients for several reasons. First, the tax savings are not likely to be all that great by the time the complicated legal and tax structures are set up. Second, many of the LLC and similar schemes are not legally valid as there isn't a profit motive that is necessary for most business ventures. Third, they are simply too complicated for most folks to figure out. And finally, the couple probably will lose the benefits that are extended to owner-occupied residences, from the availability of lower-interest purchase loans and lines of credit to the property tax benefits in some states and the deductibility rules while the couple owns the property and to, most generously, the $250,000 per party residential exclusion from capital gains taxes. All these add up to a far greater benefit in keeping ownership in the name of the partners. Keep it simple and avoid these fancy schemes.

Document for Real Estate Ownership and Management (Forms Found on Included CD)

Form 08: Residence co-ownership agreement

NOTES

1. A few states offer other forms of taking title; this section's analysis is for the vast majority of states that offer the tenants in common and joint tenancy options.

2. Kershman v. Kershman, 192 Cal. App. 2d 23 (1961); Milian v. DeLeon, 188 Cal. App. 3d 1185 (1986).
3. In theory, a joint tenancy co-owner cannot "own" more than 50 percent, even with a written agreement. However, most attorneys believe (as do I) that such an agreement can provide for a reimbursement of an excess down payment or even an unequal distribution of appreciated equity without jeopardizing the equal ownership required for a joint tenancy co-ownership.
4. Adding a co-owner to the title is not always simple or easy; many owners are afraid of a due-on-sale clause, though this is rarely a problem where the borrower is staying on the title. The more significant concern is that there may be a local transfer tax (with an exemption only for married spouses) that might be triggered by adding the partner to the deed.
5. I.R.C. § 121 (2010).
6. *See* Chapter 8.
7. Several times a year, I am hired to draft an agreement that never gets signed; I jokingly said once that I was tempted to charge a monthly "file storage fee" to encourage clients to finish up their agreements, but instead I simply send regular reminders at no charge.
8. In many agreements, you will want to retain a partition clause but only as a "final step" that can be invoked if one party refuses to participate in the buyout or mediation process. You should include this option mostly to cover the situations where one party is disabled, demented, or extremely angry, such that having court supervision will be a useful tool in resolving the conflicts.

CHAPTER EIGHT
COHABITATION AND FINANCIAL AGREEMENTS

A. The Background Context

The Doctrinal Framework

Unlike a premarital or post-marital agreement for a married couple. which is necessarily structured as an opt-out of the statutorily prescribed marital rights and duties, a nonmarital cohabitation agreement at its core is primarily an opt-in contract (i.e., one that bestows rights and imposes obligations on the parties that would not exist but for the contract). In other words, most often a marital agreement is fundamentally deductive in nature in that it typically reduces the obligations of one or both parties. True enough, occasionally it also might be drafted to impose additional obligations where marital law is perceived as inadequate for meeting the needs of one or both of the parties. By contrast, an agreement between unmarried partners is almost always additive, in that it typically grants rights to one or both of the partners that either would not exist at all or, in states that honor implied agreements, might only exist in the abstract sense of one party having the technical right to pursue a palimony claim.

Because of this difference in doctrinal context, the practical approach to crafting a nonmarital agreement cannot be directly analogized to that involved in creating a premarital agreement, even when the financial terms end up being quite similar. The starting point for a nonmarital agreement is that neither party has any rights or obligations to anything owned or owed by the other partner, whereas in a marital agreement there are likely to be extensive rights established by law that the parties may wish to abrogate. Maintaining a clear distinction between these two conceptual paradigms is crucial as you guide your clients through the agreement-formation process.

The Waiver of All Claims

For those who practice in one of the numerous states that allow non-marital claims to be based upon alleged oral or implied promises, there is one other type of agreement that also can be useful for an unmarried couple: a simple waiver of any and all oral or implied contractual claims. It is not unusual for some clients to ask a partner to sign such a waiver at the outset or in the midst of a long-term relationship, usually because they were previously in a dispute with a partner or have heard of a friend or relative who was in such a fight. It's important to recognize that in technical legal terms, a document that simply waives all potential claims does not really memorialize an agreement per se. Rather, it is an acknowledgment that there have been no such agreements made in the past and a stated willingness to forgo any such claims in the future. From the perspective of legal doctrine, such a document is analogous to executing a quitclaim deed, where no certain rights to a property ever existed. The written document does not reflect a change of position for either partner (as would typically be the case for an agreement), nor is it a waiver of any actual claims that would likely have any real value, given how hostile most courts are to granting any awards in such cases, even in states where such claims are allowed. Rather, it is simply an affirmation of the status of the parties' existing positions and a confirmation of their willingness to be bound by that truth forevermore.

But precisely because the rules for unmarried partners are so vague in most states and because there are rarely any statutorily imposed rights or duties, there may be underlying tensions between the partners as to whether there *should* be any obligations. For this reason, what is legally a very simple process may itself be perceived as an aggressive act or a demand to give away perceived rights or, alternatively, may be taken to reflect a degree of mistrust by one partner of the other. Oftentimes, the lower-income partner will be happy to declare orally that she has no interest in the other partner's assets and would never present a legal claim upon a breakup, but asking that same partner to "put it in writing" nonetheless may feel very foreign—and downright hostile.

You should never minimize the emotional risk of commencing the waiver process. And, for these reasons, it always is best to frame such an agreement as providing reciprocal benefits for both parties, whenever possible. At a minimum, if your client is initiating the process, some thought should be given as to how to present the request for an agreement in a positive light so as to minimize the potential negative impact on the relationship simply by the making of the request.

There are two situations that frequently recur that can facilitate such a request, and they are directly connected to the process-related questions about the format of the agreement. As mentioned in the prior chapter, asking clients about their broader financial expectations is entirely appropriate whenever a house co-ownership agreement is being drafted. The larger financial questions of sharing or keeping separate each partner's assets and debts often will be linked in some way to how they handle the down payment and monthly expenses for their residence, and so adding provisions to the co-ownership agreement regarding the non-real estate financial issues will make sense to most couples. Additionally, if one of the parties is making a significant sacrifice, such as supporting a partner for a few years or making a financial gift to a partner or even relocating to another city to keep the relationship together, discussing the partners' long-term financial obligations should be accepted as an appropriate task.

Incorporating non-real estate financial terms and addressing potential cohabitation claims in a co-ownership agreement is noticeably more viable when the agreement is fundamentally a waiver of oral or implied contract claims, rather than one that includes an extensive set of financial terms. As mentioned above, a waiver of all claims does not inject any new obligations, but rather the parties are simply affirming that the provisions regarding their real estate co-ownership are their only financial obligations to each other. But even in situations where the parties also have agreed to some other financial arrangements not connected to co-owned property, it usually is prudent to integrate the terms of their real estate agreement into their broader financial contract. Only when there are other parties to the real estate agreement (such as when the couple co-owns the property with other family members or friends) or when there is no jointly owned property will you need to document the couple's financial arrangements in a separate document.

Four Optional Templates

Given this background and these concerns, there are four basic formats that can be considered in documenting the parties' agreements regarding the overall financial rights and obligations of their nonmarital relationship:

- A simple waiver of all claims as part of a property co-ownership agreement;
- A simple waiver of all claims as a stand-alone agreement for partners who do not co-own any real estate or who have previously signed a real estate agreement or who co-own property with third parties;
- A comprehensive agreement establishing the parties' defined rights and financial obligations, included as part of a real estate co-ownership agreement; or
- A stand-alone comprehensive agreement for a couple who does not own any real estate, who has previously entered into an agreement about its co-owned property, or who co-owns property with third parties.

A brief word about terminology: Avoid using the terms *community property* or *separate property* in agreements that you draft for unmarried partners, and those of you in non-community property states should similarly avoid using your state's marital property language. You do not want to suggest that you are confused about your clients' marital status, and you never want them to forget that they are unmarried. So, too, try to avoid terms such as *dissolution* or *divorce* in your agreements; instead, refer to the termination of their personal or nonmarital relationship. If you work in a state where there is any risk of invalidating the agreement on the grounds that the consideration was improper sexual relations, you will want to focus on the business or property aspect of your clients' lives. And if common law marriages are recognized in your state, it is crucial that you include a statement nullifying any such contention.

Using the right terms can be tricky when you are drafting agreements for civil union registrants or domestic partners because they are technically unmarried, but in several states their lives may be subject to the marital law rules. As cumbersome as it can be, whenever possible, use words that are legally correct but with a sensitivity to your clients' perception of their own relationship status. For example, you can describe them as civil union partners, and also state that they are waiving their rights under the marital law of their state of residence. And be sure to include in the recitals a description of your clients' legal relationship to each other in very clear terms so that they have no doubts about where they stand legally.

B. The Essential Ingredients of a Cohabitation Agreement

Waiver of All Claims

If your agreement is simply a waiver of all potential claims (rather than a detailed recitation of specific financial terms), the agreement can be quite short. It should include a summary of the basic facts and a description of the legal status of the relationship and some degree of disclosure of assets and debts, however general in nature, or at a minimum an express waiver of any disclosures. Beyond that, all that is needed is an acknowledgment that each party may otherwise have the legal right to make claims as an unmarried partner based upon alleged oral or implied agreements (or, in some states, on any type of equitable grounds), followed by a statement that neither party has any such claims at the time the agreement was made and a comprehensive waiver of all such potential claims based upon future conduct.

Make sure that the waiver is both retrospective and prospective. It needs to cover all the assets (and debts) that exist at the time the agreement is being made as well as any that could conceivably be accrued afterward, in addition to any claims for post-separation support. A mutual waiver of claims will be sufficient consideration for this agreement, especially because in most instances it is not a waiver of any actual claim or relinquishment of any particular asset, but rather, is an acknowledgement that no such claims exist at the present time as well as a mutual commitment to not raise any claims based upon an alleged oral or implied agreement. In nearly all states, your clients cannot waive future child support claims or defenses if they are both legal parents to a minor child at the time of a breakup.

A limited version of such a waiver also will be included in a more comprehensive agreement in that the parties will be waiving all rights or claims *other* than what is being provided for in the cohabitation agreement. In this context, the language of the waiver would be similar and simply prefaced by the phrase "Except as so provided in this agreement."

Additional Provisions

There are additional provisions that should be included in a comprehensive cohabitation agreement that expressly provides rights and benefits that would not exist in the absence of such an agreement.

Summary of the Basic Facts. Begin with recitals that describe the basic facts of the relationship, including the duration of the relationship, the lack of marriage and/or registered partnership or common law marriage status, a description of any children of either party or of the two of them together (including adult children), and a description of their living arrangements. If your clients are planning to register privately for any particular benefits that require cohabitation, you want to be especially careful in describing their living situation in case they ever have to produce the agreement to support a claim for benefits. While it is not necessary to do so, it can be useful to include a brief statement of each partner's employment status and current salary, as well as a statement as to any disabilities or significant medical conditions. Though separate counsel for each partner generally is not legally required, it is good to include either a waiver of a right to have the agreement reviewed by independent counsel when none is being sought or a statement confirming the independent counsel's review if it has been obtained.

Confirmation of Prerelationship Assets. While it is not legally necessary to provide detailed disclosures of each partner's prerelationship assets (as it would be for most premarital and post-marital agreements in most states), you should encourage your clients to make some degree of disclosure. There are two reasons for this: It is healthy for the relationship for the parties to be up-front about their finances, and the disclosure removes any potential claim down the road that consent to the agreement was obtained by misrepresentation. The disclosures can be general in nature. For example, it usually is sufficient to include a paragraph that states that one partner owns two other properties subject to mortgages, and a retail business or a retirement account. You might prefer to separately describe any assets acquired post-relationship (but preagreement) because those are the assets that could arguably be subject to an oral or implied contractual claim. You do not need to require a formal accounting of the precise increases in the post-relationship values of prerelationship assets, as you might in a prenuptial agreement; rather, you may simply state that the account or asset has increased during the relationship period.

Confirmation of Debt Liabilities. A brief summary of each partner's debts also is useful, again in general terms. If either partner is carrying debt in his own name but the partners consider it a joint debt, or vice versa, that should be spelled out carefully. The agreement should also describe any debts that either partner owes to the other partner, including the details of any interest accruing and the repayment obligations.

Detailed Disclosures of Assets and Debts. As mentioned above, the underlying purpose of disclosure is to protect your client from any claim of misrepresentation or fraudulent inducement should her partner later claim that she would never have signed the agreement if she knew the extent of her partner's financial condition. So, even though it is not legally required, you should press your clients to provide a detailed disclosure, especially if you're concerned that the other party may want to undo the agreement later on. Given the lack of statutory requirements, there should be no great concern about the agreement ultimately being overturned for a lack of full disclosure, but why take the risk?

There is yet a deeper reason to encourage disclosures, however. If your client tells you that he is afraid to disclose the extent of his assets to his partner, then you should be worried that the waivers of claims won't really be entirely genuine or that there are underlying emotional tensions that are not being addressed. In some instances, you could compromise on this point and only insist on a range of asset values being disclosed so at least you will be sure that the other party wasn't being deceived about your client's assets generally. But when in doubt, lean toward more disclosure rather than less. One other option is to include a statement that confirms that the parties have generally disclosed their assets to each other outside of the written agreement, though that is a risky approach given the lack of documentation of any disclosure.

Try to motivate your clients to be transparent overall about financial issues in their relationships, and try to frame the disclosure process as a step in that direction. If someone is sufficiently intimate with a partner to decide to live together, then sharing each one's respective financial stories should be an acceptable risk. Moreover, in most instances, the other partner will learn the financial details soon enough; and if there has been a concealment of sizable assets (or debts), there could be resentment and even anger about a prior lack of disclosure.

If your client tells you that he doesn't think his partner would sign the agreement if the extent of his assets were known, my recommendation

The disclosure process carries a great many risks, in ways that lawyers all too often minimize. Consider the following situations: A client of mine recently learned that his longtime partner had failed to file income tax returns for more than fifteen years and was facing penalties and fines in excess of $1 million. In another instance my client lived with a much younger man who was a recent immigrant with limited assets, and he was concerned that disclosing the extent of his assets would be overwhelming to his impoverished partner who had never been involved with anyone of substantial means. A few years back, one of my clients was under enormous pressure from his parents not to reveal anything about their finances, fearing that the disclosure would fuel the attachments of a partner whom they perceived as a gold digger. And just last year, a client of mine inherited a great deal of money and was afraid to tell her partner for fear that it would distance them emotionally and create resentments on the part of her financially struggling partner.

In each of these instances, my clients had to wade through some very difficult waters, and I worked with them from the vantage point of encouraging as much disclosure as possible. Happily, I can report that each of them overcame the challenges, made the disclosures, and emerged with more solid relationships and legally binding agreements. And while I consider such counseling to be part of my role as a lawyer, in most instances it took some time for them to come around to making the disclosures—and in several instances some serious counseling work with a skillful therapist also was required. Most important, they could only take on the legal agreement process after this underlying relationship bridge-building work had been completed.

is that you should then decline to work on the agreement. It may not be a matter of fraud or a breach of legally imposed duties, and unmarried couples don't generally have a fiduciary duty to one another. But concealment of these facts is not healthy for the relationship, and it can surely cause big headaches later on, including legal challenges. Fundamentally, I don't feel comfortable getting involved in a process that is grounded upon concealment, and you probably shouldn't be either.

Confirmation of Preagreement Relationship Assets. For couples who have already been together for a longer period of time (more than five years), you should be a bit stricter about the disclosure of any assets that were accumulated during the course of the relationship. Apart from the real prospect of a legal claim over such assets, there is a greater chance that one of the partners will feel entitled to some of those assets than is the case for prerelationship assets or in shorter-term relationships. Also, quite often there has been some commingling of assets or shared liabilities for the debts. Titling the asset or debt in one partner's name may not mean that the other partner has no claims on that asset, and the partners should not be afraid of disclosing what they have each accumulated while they have been living together. If one of the partners has a plausible claim on some of these assets, then this should be acknowledged from the outset, and it should be addressed in the document either by an express provision in the agreement or as something that is waived in consideration of some other provision.

Again, because there is no statutory duty of disclosure, it would be fine for the parties to make general statements about these assets in narrative paragraphs. It is usually sufficient to state that each partner has a retirement account of an estimated value or that one partner owns a consulting business of unknown market value or that each partner has separate credit card debt. If your client feels very strongly about not disclosing the assets accumulated during the parties' relationship, you should certainly inquire about their actions and their concerns. If you do go forward with the agreement, then at a minimum you should insist that your client sign an acknowledgement (as part of your retainer letter or in a subsequent letter) that the failure to disclose assets could jeopardize the validity of the agreement if there is a claim of fraudulent misrepresentation.

Usually you can approach this situation differently if the other party has legal representation. If she does and if her lawyer is willing to sign off on the agreement in an absence of any financial disclosures, you can feel more confident that the agreement will survive a subsequent legal challenge. When you are representing the lower-asset partner, always try to learn the basic facts of the partner's financial condition as a prerequisite for waiving financial claims or support. Occasionally your clients will say initially that they don't really care to learn the details of their partner's financial condition, though when asked if they would feel differently about the agreement if they learned that their partner was worth $20 million, they usually understand the need for some degree of disclosure. However, as with the parallel nondisclosure situation when representing the higher-asset partner, if your client is willing to sign an acknowledgement that she waived the receipt of any detailed disclosure of her partner's assets, you can often proceed with the agreement. It's a potential malpractice risk, but sometimes it is an acceptable one.

Ongoing Living Expenses. There are two philosophies on this topic: Some couples like to work out a solid understanding in advance regarding how they are going to pay the bills, while others are willing to let things flow in a more fluid manner. Occasionally the couple takes a midway approach, preferring to nail down the arrangements for the big-ticket items but leaving things open-ended for the smaller expenses. In either event, you will want to include a waiver of any reimbursement claim for excess contributions in the absence of a written agreement or, at a minimum, in the absence of a written claim for reimbursement within a set time (usually thirty days) after the excess contribution was made. This allows the couple to make its financial decisions in an evolving manner without being worried that what was presented as generosity will later morph into a repayment demand.

The more daunting challenge in deciding how to handle future expenses arises when one partner has significantly greater income or assets than the other one. This is always a touchy subject, but it cannot be avoided, and you have to approach the topic delicately. Whether representing just one partner or serving as a mediator, you should lead off with an exploration of all the different factors involved, both financial and emotional. It is not just a matter of utilizing current income; it also is connected to what savings each partner already has, whether each is likely to receive an inheritance, and what other obligations each may have (for example, minor children or elderly parents).

You also need to be attuned to the stage of the partners' relationship, since many couples may be coming to you before they have truly decided to share their lives together for the long haul. This is especially true for straight couples, where being unmarried can represent a vote for a "separate property" relationship that is accompanied by a vague expectation of merging assets once they enter into a legal marriage. Each partner will approach this discussion from the perspective of his own core values and expectations as well as his own fears and anxieties about being (or becoming) financially vulnerable. Keep in mind that in many instances you may be the first person who has openly raised these topics, and thus you should be prepared for some awkward discussions.

It is also of great importance to try to uncover *why* each of them is in his particular financial situation. You must distinguish between impoverishment as part of a family plan (e.g., when one parent quits a high-paying job to be a stay-at-home parent or when a partner has quit a lucrative job to move across the country to be with a partner) and impoverishment stemming from discrepancies that predated the relationship (e.g., when one person has lesser education or health limitations or has pursued a lower-paying career). There is an arguable ethical responsibility for the partners to share the wealth in the first instance, whereas the obligations are far less certain in the second.

The partners' intentions regarding payment of the future bills also must be integrated into their long-term financial plans. If each partner is going to retain individual savings, then the allocation of living expenses can have dramatic consequences where one partner is a higher earner. However, if savings are going to be shared equally or in some proportional manner, then the partners' spending habits during their relationship will be less consequential.

As with the real estate arrangements, try, whenever possible, to design an agreement that does not require ongoing documentation or any ledgers to be kept. When there is a preset allocation of expenses, you should provide for some form of annual review, with a stated presumption that each party has met his obligations in the absence of a complaint within a few months of the end of the year and with a waiver that is conclusively presumed by the absence of such a complaint. Very few couples keep decent records over the long haul, and so an annual review process assures that if there is a dispute in the future, they will be limited to fighting over the accounts for just the most recent year and won't be able to go back decades in an attempt to calculate a lifetime of obligations.

Agreements About Future Accumulated Assets. This topic has the biggest financial consequences for the parties, and therefore it requires the closest attention. The major challenges aren't in drafting the terms; the terms are relatively simple. Rather, the biggest hurdles involve helping your clients figure out what they believe to be fair and discerning what is their real intent in light of the many future uncertainties. For some couples, it is quite simple: They may have already decided to keep their assets separate and be ready to sign a full and complete waiver of any of the other's separately titled assets. In this case, you want to be clear that the definition of *separate* is based upon what is stated on the title of the asset, and typically you would also provide that any asset that is jointly titled is presumed to be owned fifty-fifty. If there is a waiver of all oral or implied agreement claims, that waiver also would apply to a claim of an excess share of a joint asset, as well as a claim to any asset titled in the other partner's name. You will want to make it clear that once such an agreement is in place, a partner can only establish an ownership interest contrary to the titling of the asset through a subsequent written agreement.

At the other extreme of the spectrum are couples who want to adopt a marriage or community property model, where all of the assets accrued during the relationship will be shared equally. If that is their intention, try to design an equalization model that takes into account the tax issues; for some couples, that means a minimization of the transfers of significant assets during the course of their relationship. For such arrangements, rather than dividing up their assets on an ongoing basis, it is better that the value of the saved assets be calculated only in the event of a breakup. If that happens, each partner would keep anything in his own name, and then they would divide up the joint assets equitably. Only if one partner has ended up in a richer position (all assets included) would that partner owe an equalization payment to the other one. The best strategy is to set forth the basic philosophy of the plan in the agreement as well as a detailed process, acknowledging that the mechanisms of distribution (and tax consequences) will need to be worked out at the time of a breakup. Most often the agreement empowers an arbitrator or a judge to carry out the distribution in an equitable fashion.

A third option is to provide a defined safety net for the lower-asset partner, acknowledging that it may be less than an equal sharing of all assets but may be better than simply leaving each partner with everything in his own name. This also can be conceptualized as a proportional distribution, for example, where the parties agree that the lower-asset

It's essential that you be prepared to check your biases at the door when working on these tasks. You may have a set notion of what partners in long-term relations (married or unmarried) owe to one another, but this may not be how your clients view their relationship. Many in the legal field presume that parties always know how to look after their best interests and are able to stand up for themselves in this sort of negotiation, but this may not be true either. This process is very difficult for some folks, especially those who have had personal and financial problems in the past. Interestingly, though, highly educated women do well in these negotiations, as often they have been taught since childhood about the sexism of the workplace and the risks of becoming the displaced homemaker after years of domestic service. At the other end of the spectrum are men who may be deeply attached to an identity of self-sufficiency even when their work or medical history puts that in doubt over the long term.

It can be hard to authentically engage clients in these discussions. Try to describe hypothetical futures that are conceivable for the lives of the particular clients to get them to understand why you are worried for them. I counseled a guy recently who had given up his low-level marketing job to become an artist when he partnered with a wealthy older partner. My client initially was overly willing to sign a release of all claims, so I walked him through a doomsday scenario (a major injury resulting from his art making, no savings at age sixty, and not even any Social Security because he had stopped working at age thirty), and eventually he was able to see the reason for my concerns. Unfortunately, once he felt empowered to ask for some degree of protection from his partner, the relationship fell apart, though in the end he felt that this was inevitable given the lack of understanding on the part of his boyfriend.

Ironically, the conversations can be even more difficult when the relationship has passed the honeymoon phase. Most likely the couple has already experienced tension stemming from money issues, and each may have strong opinions about the other's financial situation. Unlike married couples who conceptualize their budgets as a unified plan, unmarried partners tend to stand in judgment of the other's business practices; and so if one of them has lost a job or racked up credit card bills, the discussion of any future sharing of assets will be delicate.

partner will end up with no less than one-third of the couple's total assets. With this approach, most typically the proportion is based either upon their respective financial positions at the commencement of the relationship or upon some notion of fairness, and the parties can agree that the shared percentage is increased depending upon the duration of the relationship. For other couples, it makes sense to provide a specific dollar amount as a safety net, perhaps unrelated to the duration of the relationship but rather based upon the financial needs of the vulnerable partner.

In one such agreement I drafted, for example, the wealthier partner agreed to pay her partner an amount annually that was roughly equal to what they estimated the poorer partner would have saved each year if she hadn't quit her job to spend her time with the richer one. In another instance, my client simply agreed on the estimated cost of her boy-friend's rental housing for three years, deciding that this was a sufficient safety net for her financially dependent boyfriend to get back on his feet if they broke up, regardless of how long they stayed together.

There is no set formula for all couples. What counts is that you spend the time understanding each partner's financial condition and concerns—whatever your role in the negotiations—and then work with them to develop a plan that is realistic and is accepted by both partners. Your job is to assume that life is going to be full of bad turns and trag-edies (illness, unemployment, loss of investments) and not let your cli-ents' optimistic notions blind them to the risks of things going wrong. There's a well-documented tendency of parties to be unreasonably opti-mistic in these discussions, and part of your obligation is helping them prepare for the bad times as well as the good ones.

Occasionally a couple will want to simply sign up for the marital rules, especially a same-sex couple who isn't allowed to marry in their state of residence. It isn't sufficient to just reference your state's marital rules in the abstract because a contract needs to include all of the basic terms and the parties need to understand them for it to be enforceable (as opposed to entering into a marriage, where the parties are never even shown the rules of marital law in advance, let alone required to understand them or expressly agree to them). If the parties want to abide by their state's marital rules, then you should include a fairly detailed summary of the basic provisions of the marital law rules and state that any disputes about the interpretation of the rules will be adjudicated in

One tactic for financially unequal partners is to have them set up a plan to "pay it forward" rather than looking solely to post-separation payments or distributions of assets to address financial dependency. In other words, have the higher earner or higher-asset partner give something to the other partner each year or, at a minimum, cover a greater share of the living expenses to enable the financially weaker party to build up some savings. Then, in exchange for this assistance during the relationship, the dependent one should waive any (or most) claims for post-separation support or a share of the other's assets. There are many advantages to this plan: The richer one doesn't have to pay support just when they may be the most angry at the ex-lover, there is a partial balancing of the financial inequities during the relationship, and any issue of duration of support or percent of assets to be shared is resolved by the accumulated payments made during the course of the relationship.

There are several problems with this approach, however. In addition to the tax concerns, many clients resist it as feeling too much like they are planning their breakup. It also doesn't address the risk of the receiving party squandering the gifted assets. I recently worked with a client who had given his boyfriend $200,000 just so he would have his own nest egg, and then the boyfriend lost all of it in an unwise investment. For some partners, there is a serious concern of overspending, and in those situations you can include a clause that says that each year's payment is dependent on the partner saving the prior year's payment.

accordance with the marital law rules and applicable court cases. This still leaves some area of uncertainty, but it is sufficiently comprehensive to avoid an invalidation of the agreement.

Allocation of Debt Liabilities. This is usually a simple provision that states that each party is responsible for his own debts, with a right of indemnification if one ever has to pay out for the other's debts. The main point to remember here is that a right of indemnification does not produce the funds out of a bankrupt ex-lover. And similar to the default asset provision, any jointly held debt should be presumed to be borne fifty-fifty in the absence of a written agreement to the contrary.

Consequences of a Subsequent Marriage. In most states marital law trumps any nonmarital agreement, at least as to assets or debts that are acquired post marriage. Most nonmarital cohabitation agreements will not meet the standards of a premarital agreement, and a prospective spouse can't waive marital rights years in advance as it is only when the agreement is signed shortly before the couple is about to get married that a premarital waiver will be enforceable. It is essential that your clients know that if they elect to get married in the future, they will need to redo their nonmarital agreement. Nonetheless, clients often request a provision stating that the parties intend this agreement to be binding even if they later marry unless they enter into a new agreement to the contrary. If you include such a provision, always explain the risks and include a statement confirming that to the extent marital law overrides this nonmarital agreement, the parties will be bound by marital law unless they enter into a new agreement in writing at the time of their marriage.

Managing the Breakup Process. Given the absence of the marital dissolution process, you should cover some of the most common sources of conflict in the cohabitation agreement in the event of a breakup. No one can know for certain what his life will be like decades into the future or even where he will living, but if one partner is living in a house owned solely by the other, it is prudent to include a provision about the notice (sixty to ninety days, perhaps) to be given to the non-owner to vacate the residence. If it is already known that one partner is underemployed or without much in terms of assets, it might be prudent to include a moving assistance payment to help cover the first month's rent and a security deposit for a relocation apartment. Sometimes you will need to integrate the issues about housing (e.g., who gets to stay in a rental apartment) with the allocation of who will cover certain expenses (e.g., mortgage) if they live apart for a while before their finances are settled.

Some lawyers draft agreements that include mandatory mediation and cooling-off periods, where the parties commit to spending some time in counseling and postponing any final decision about breaking up. It is preferable to keep those sorts of relationship provisions out of an agreement that is basically about money and property, but if it is important to your clients, you shouldn't object to including them. However, warn your clients that an obligation to participate in mediation may be unenforceable unless the obligations are strictly focused on the money and property issues. Judges just don't like being asked to adjudicate anything having to do with the interpersonal aspects of a relationship.

Agreement Regarding Post-Separation Support. Most couples will want to opt out of paying or receiving any post-separation support, consistent with their decision to remain unmarried. But there are exceptions, especially for couples who are unmarried because of legal impediments (i.e., same-sex couples), and it is important to tread carefully in this area. It is an emotionally difficult terrain to navigate, which is precisely why marital law imposes these duties without asking couples to negotiate them. Don't be surprised to hear your client ask to base any support obligation on a perception of fault (e.g., no support paid to the unfaithful partner), but it is highly inadvisable to draft such provisions. No fault is the rule for married couples in all states now, and it should be the same rule for unmarried partners. Using fault-based rules when it comes to financial obligations invites partners to make up stories, stage their departures to conceal their "bad" activities, or pathologize one of the partners inappropriately, and courts are not going to be interested in any sort of fault-based provisions.

Figuring out what is fair when it comes to post-separation support involves the integration of the following factors:

- *Amount of Support.* There are various approaches to this touchy issue. Some lawyers prefer to base the amount on a minimum standard of living for the dependent partner; others prefer to look to a percentage of each partner's income. You also have the option of electing by contract to have your state's marital rule formulas applied to any dispute. Some clients use their pre-relationship incomes to establish a proportional formula (e.g., if one earned double what the other made, then the support should ensure that neither partner ended up with less than half of the other's net income); other couples look to the average of their living expenses for the years prior to a breakup and base the support on a minimum percentage of that amount. In most instances, there is an offset for the dependent partner's actual or potential income, sometimes based upon a few years of income averaged over the pre-breakup period. Some kind of cost of living adjustment is appropriate in most instances.
- *Goal of Support Payments.* Usually the purpose is to help the dependent partner achieve some degree of self-sufficiency over time,

which envisions some kind of career restoration or other adjustment in living arrangements. In other situations, it is tied to housing needs or perhaps the costs of finishing up a college or graduate education; it also may be about replacing income lost because of a decision to become a stay-at-home parent or give up a lucrative job. The key here is that the purpose of the support should guide the determination of its conditions.

- *Appropriate Consideration of Other Assets and Income.* In most instances, it makes sense to reduce the support by the amount of income the dependent partner is receiving or by some percentage of the amount of other assets (e.g., real estate equity or other savings) she has accrued. Setting the limit for these thresholds is not simple at all, but you should try to keep it as simple as possible. For example, I recently worked on an agreement that said that the goal was to provide $60,000 net income to the dependent partner, with her actual income deducted before figuring out what the amount of support would be.

- *Duration of Support.* In some instances, it makes sense to extend the duration of the support based upon the duration of the relationship, as happens with most, but not all, marital divorces. If the purpose is to help with a readjustment period or to find alternative housing or employment, then the duration of the relationship may not matter.

- *Reciprocity of the Obligations.* Unless one partner expects to receive a very large inheritance or has some other form of financial security, it is preferable to make the obligations reciprocal, depending on who is in dire straits at the time of a dissolution.

- *Tax Consequences.* Given the absence of a marital exemption for payment of support, it is crucial that the agreement lay out who is responsible for any tax consequences of a payment.

Obligations Regarding Estate Planning. As unmarried partners your clients don't have any statutory duty to provide for each other upon death, but many couples want to include a binding agreement to do so, especially regarding a co-owned residence. If they have an agreement for shared assets or payment of post-separation support, you should include a provision that these terms are binding upon the heirs of the supporting partner and that the decedent provide no less in support upon death than upon a breakup. You cannot assume that unmarried partners will bequeath their assets to each other, so this should be discussed as part of this agreement. If your clients want to include such a provision, make sure that such contracts to make wills are valid in your jurisdiction. You can also include an obligation to maintain a specified level of life insurance coverage for the other. Another worthwhile inclusion is a provision that states that each partner will provide the other with a copy of the current testamentary documents, mostly as a reminder that they need to sign such documents in order to implement the contractual provisions of the agreement.

C. The Tax Aspects of a Cohabitation Agreement

Because of the lack of any spousal exemption for gift or estate transfers between unmarried partners, it is crucial that the lessons of this book's chapter on tax burdens be integrated into the design of any cohabitation agreement. You shouldn't build your clients' entire arrangement around the tax concerns; rather, you want to understand what their goals are and figure out an agreement that meets their goals as much as possible—and then refine it to minimize the tax complications and burdens. This is especially true for those with significant assets. You should work with them (with or without another lawyer, depending on your role) to put together the basic terms of the agreement and assemble a term sheet that is two or three pages long, with enough detail that an accountant can grasp the structure of the plan (without having to plow through a twenty-page detailed agreement). Then you should send your clients off to their accountant to review and comment on the agreement and make prudent suggestions from a tax perspective. Only then should you start drafting the substantive provisions of the agreement.

The key tax concerns to keep in mind are as follows:

- Covering some of a partner's ongoing expenses that don't result in ownership of an item probably won't have gift tax consequences.
- Paying a larger share of joint obligations probably will be below the radar and not considered a reportable gift by most accountants, or by the IRS.
- Giving someone a portion of an asset (e.g., a minority interest in real estate) is a reportable gift, but it can result in a lower declared

valuation amount for gift tax purposes compared to making a financial gift.

- Helping a partner buy a property early on can limit the value of the reported gift to the down payment amount, especially if the rental income covers the property expenses, and then the growing equity will already be an asset of the partner.
- Paying the separate bills of a partner is most certainly a gift that should be reported if the amount exceeds the annual exclusion limit.
- Paying the expenses of a child rarely has tax consequences, especially if the expenses are for medical or educational purposes.
- Transferring a large portion of a valuable asset (real estate or an investment account) probably will be viewed as a gift in light of the absence of any statutory duty of shared assets or support, though the value of the gift may be reduced using the minority interest or partnership discount.
- Retirement assets cannot be transferred to an unmarried partner, and so sharing a retirement account typically will require its liquidation, with taxes owed and likely penalties.
- There is no clear guidance as to the tax consequences of paying post-separation support to an unmarried partner, but the safest assumption is that it will be a reportable gift or income to the recipient. And watch out: In the future the gift exclusion limit may be reduced from the current $5 million as the economic and political climate changes over time.

D. ISSUES OF JOINT AND INDEPENDENT REPRESENTATION

There is no requirement that unmarried partners each have independent legal counsel to sign a cohabitation agreement, nor is there any presumption that the agreement is invalid for lack of independent review. This is primarily because unlike married spouses, partners in an unmarried relationship generally are not giving up any rights that they would enjoy by statute.[1] However, in a long-term relationship, one or both of the partners may have acquired some equitable or contractual rights, and as their legal counsel you will need to analyze this situation; thus, the standard requirements of effective representation and managing potential conflicts of interest definitely will apply. In other words, the issues of representation will need to be addressed in the same manner as in any sort of agreement that involves two parties in a preexisting and forward-looking financial relationship.

There are several options as to how to structure the representation arrangements:

- A lawyer can act as a mediator for the two partners and draft an agreement in that role and then have each partner consult with independent counsel before it is signed—or not, as they prefer.
- Each partner can work with separate counsel, with one lawyer drafting the agreement and the other one acting as reviewing counsel.
- The same lawyer can represent both partners without independent counsel reviewing the agreement.
- One partner can hire a lawyer who prepares the agreement, and the other partner can review it without legal counsel.

As with all of the other tasks for unmarried partners, you should try to strike a balance between (a) your duties to take care of the long-term needs and protect the interests of your client or clients (which usually will lead you to prefer to have only one client) and (b) your clients' limited budgets and an oft-expressed desire to work with just one lawyer. On balance, my recommendation is that you can often safely agree to serve as the joint attorney for both parties, though only when the agreement is simple and where neither partner is giving up any significant rights or assets that he has already acquired.

For example, if the parties co-owned the house equally and contributed equally to its costs and they simply wanted to include a basic waiver of all other financial claims (and each of them was earning good money and had sufficient assets for his own support), you should be willing to serve as their joint counsel. You can properly advise both of them as to the legal consequences of their actions and be confident that neither party is being disadvantaged by the agreement—after all, the purpose of the agreement is to confirm an agreement that was already in place.

Interestingly, the scope of agreements that I am willing to handle as joint legal counsel has increasingly narrowed over the past ten years as partners have increasingly complicated lives and their marital and

registration options continue to expand. Even for gay and lesbian partners, the choice to remain unregistered (in California) or married (in
recognition states) can have dramatic financial consequences, and it is
hard to work with clients (either straight or gay) on a nonmarital agreement without facing questions about whether or not they should register
or marry. It is possible to represent both partners in a simple agreement
that does not waive significant rights or impose new obligations as long
as there is a valid waiver of the conflict of interest (that is a must-have
document). It's just that the number of situations in my office that safely
fall into this narrow slot seems to shrink each year.

For parties that truly want to work with a single attorney but don't
fit your standards for joint legal representation, you can be designated
as a mediator so that you can still help them out. But this role creates
its own set of challenges whenever the partners elect to not consult with
independent counsel. As a mediator, you can give the parties legal information, but you will have to determine where to draw the line when it
comes to not giving out legal advice. These are fine lines, though, and
some lawyers are reluctant to take this risk, legitimately fearing that clients will inevitably perceive the "information" as advice. You will need
to make some difficult judgment calls if you are representing folks who
are unwilling to retain independent reviewing counsel.

Where should you draw the line when it comes to providing legal
information? Here are some examples: You should feel comfortable telling the parties jointly that in California an oral or implied agreement
can be the basis of a claim, but it must be proven by clear and convincing
evidence. What you can't do is say whether either of them would win in
court if they made a claim based upon the history of their relationship or
advise them as to whether or not they should give up a claim for the house
in exchange for a portion of a stock account. In most instances, as long
as you give them the full scope of information (which you should always
do in a joint session), they generally have the capacity to make their own
decisions. If you find that one or both of them are feeling stuck or are
in need of a deeper sort of legal counseling, then you should refer the
concerned client(s) to independent counsel. You can also urge a client to
obtain independent counsel if you feel that the client is unable to grasp the
language and terms of a complicated agreement without legal assistance.

Whenever possible, it is preferable for each party to have separate counsel, whether you're in the role of drafting lawyer or mediator.

There are many advantages to this approach: Two sets of professional eyes will be reviewing the agreement, and two skilled attorneys will be working to set up the structure of the agreement. You won't have to worry about being the only professional looking after the needs of both parties, and you can be assured that the other party will have a chance to think about and talk through the provisions with the aid of counsel. At the same time, you will want to be sure that the attorney process is constructive, collaborative, and relationship-supporting and not unnecessarily adversarial or contentious. It is always appropriate that opposing counsel protects the needs of her client because that is what is supposed to happen. However, it is unacceptable when the other attorney injects personal agendas or ramps up the conflicts, disregarding the needs and priorities of the two partners.

One way to achieve the desired goals is to use the joint session approach of collaborative law, where both counsel and both partners meet together before anything is written down. Neither attorney should draft the agreement until such a meeting has occurred or before there has been a substantive discussion between counsel. A written agreement should never be presented as a "take it or leave it" proposal. Rather, the written agreement should be based upon an oral discussion that addresses the major terms, and this should be a discussion that is led by the parties, not the lawyers.

Lawyers have different approaches to how deep their counseling should be. I recently worked on a premarital agreement with one of the top lawyers in this field, and he emphatically said that he didn't do any touchy-feely counseling and would only serve as a scrivener of the parties' agreement. His attitude was that if the parties had issues to resolve they should do so with a therapist, not their attorney. This isn't necessarily a workable approach because there always needs to be an integration of the emotional and the legal aspects of the agreement, and it is rare that a therapist can handle all of these issues. My belief is that as long as the chasms are not too enormous, a sensitive interaction between counsel and clients can resolve issues fairly quickly without sending the clients out for a multiweek therapy program.

The hardest task in drafting these agreements is translating the clients' emotional and practical concerns into valid legal terms. The only way to build this bridge is to be able to work on both aspects of the process.

Here is the protocol to use when each side has independent counsel, which is pretty much the same as handling a marital agreement process.

1. Each party retains counsel; if your client's partner doesn't know whom to call, you should provide a short list of qualified attorneys that are sensitive and competent.

2. Each party meets with her or his independent counsel, preferably in person, engaging in a substantive discussion of the key concerns and issues; if the clients have written up a term sheet or have a good idea of what they want their agreement to say, have them send a joint email or letter to the two attorneys summarizing the terms so that they are both working off the same page.

3. The parties talk with each other to see what issues they are in agreement on and explore what's left to be resolved, either substantive (e.g., what do to about financial support) or procedural (e.g., the need to consult with a tax attorney).

4. Each party talks again with her or his lawyer to report back on their post-consultation discussions.

5. The two lawyers talk and determine whether the process is far enough along to move to the drafting stage; if not, and especially if there are delicate emotional issues or complex financial arrangements to discuss, a joint meeting is scheduled. Only in rare situations is the lawyer-to-lawyer negotiation process appropriate to handle difficult issues, since that can escalate the conflict and wrongly takes the decision making out of the hands of the parties.

6. One lawyer drafts the agreement and reviews it with her or his client; after the client approves it, it is sent to the opposing counsel and the partner, usually at the same time.

7. Final negotiations over the precise terms of the agreement typically are handled between the lawyers, since usually the remaining issues are more technical in nature, and only rarely is a second meeting necessary.

8. Once everyone is in sync, the agreement is finalized and signed. Notarization is not necessary in most jurisdictions, but it can be useful to impress on the clients the importance of the document. In most instances, however, you can simply send the clients the final document (either as a hard copy or as a PDF) and let them

handle the signing themselves. Some attorneys insist on having a signing ceremony in their office, in part to ensure that the signing gets done and also to avoid any subsequent claims of duress or forged signatures. If you let your clients handle the signing, follow up to make sure that it gets done.

You won't always have the luxury of this sort of step-by-step process, and oftentimes the process has already gone off-kilter when you are

Mishandling the agreement-formation process can create tremendous problems for your clients. On the positive side, a few years back, I represented a very wealthy guy whose partner was in a very vulnerable situation, having become overextended financially and then walking away from a lucrative job. Their relationship itself was a bit shaky as one of them had recently had an affair, but they wanted to try to stay together. They knew they needed to sort out their financial arrangements, so my client convinced his partner to hire a collaborative lawyer, and we met for three sessions. There were some very rough passages, but an agreement was forged, drafted, and promptly signed—and last I heard, the couple is still living happily together.

By contrast, I once met with a woman whose partner's lawyer had gone ahead and drafted an agreement that she initially thought was just fine, though she really didn't understand its consequences. Once we met, she realized that the agreement had problems. She told her boyfriend about my concerns, and he was furious (especially because he had paid my bill and expected that I would simply sign off on the agreement, as she supposedly had already done). We tried to present a moderate package of revisions that I thought was fair, but the boyfriend's irritation at the way the process had unfolded and the suspicion that I had "turned her" against the agreement tarnished the process. The couple is still together, but the partners still haven't reached an agreement on any of the major terms of their financial relationship.

One thing I'll never do again is walk into a joint meeting without having met with my client in advance. I made this mistake once, and I was hopelessly lost in trying to figure out my client's real goals and concerns, all in the midst of negotiating the terms with the other side. An opposing counsel in another matter made this same sort of mistake, and when she failed to "stand up" to the very well-enunciated positions of my client (whose thoughts were well organized since she had met with me in advance), her client fired her the next day. The resentments over the meeting have badly damaged the couple's relationship.

hired. But it is always useful to have a well-developed model of how things should proceed in an ideal world and then use that road map as a touchstone in effectively managing the agreement-formation process.

Documents for Cohabitation and Financial Agreements

(Forms Found on Included CD)

Form 09: Simple waiver of claims agreement

Form 10: Comprehensive financial agreement with shared assets/payments (setting up account with salary-equivalent provision)

NOTES

1. To the extent that the partners are registered in a marriage-equivalent registration and they wish to disclaim any such rights, their agreement will need to meet all of the requirements of a marital agreement in their state, including the rules regarding independent representation.

CHAPTER NINE

PUBLIC AND PRIVATE BENEFITS

First, a few preliminary words about benefits. If your clients are not registered or legally partnered as a couple in any governmental sense, then they are legally single individuals and thus not entitled to receive most public or private benefits as a couple. Thus, your primary task will be explaining to your clients the benefits that they do *not* receive as an unmarried and/or unregistered couple, a conversation that might motivate some of them to marry or register if the consequences of being legally single are unacceptable. But there remains a narrow range of benefits that may be available to some unmarried couples, and this is where your expertise is most particularly needed.

When it comes to accessing benefits, it helps to think about your unmarried clients as sitting somewhere on a wide spectrum ranging from de facto cohabitants to employer or insurance company registrants to local city or county registrants, all the way to state-registered couples in a marriage-equivalent registration, either gay or straight. For each type of benefit being analyzed, you should ascertain where along this spectrum your clients are sitting so that you can advise them as to what benefits they are entitled to, what actions they will need to take if they wish to partake in any particular benefit, and which will remain unavailable to them unless they are legally married or state-registered.

A. ACCESS TO GOVERNMENT BENEFITS

This section discusses the most frequently sought-after federal benefits. Local or state governments administer many of these programs, and in some jurisdictions there may be particular state-issued rules. Some states may also provide additional benefits that are not included in this list, and the rules for those programs also should be reviewed. The most important rule to remember is that city and county registrations or employer or insurance registrations will not entitle an unmarried partner to any benefit that is limited to legal spouses, and that state-registered partners in marriage-equivalent registrations will only receive benefits that are state-funded and regulated entirely by state law.

Social Security

With very few exceptions, Social Security does not pay any attention to unmarried partners; the existence of an unmarried partner is simply a nonevent. Some Social Security programs are true entitlement programs (such as Medicare and Social Security) that have no income or asset limitations, whereas others are needs-based, evaluating assets and income available to an applicant in determining eligibility or the extent of assistance (such as Supplemental Security Income (SSI) or Medicaid). The central two-pronged starting point for any analysis in this arena is that being federally single will disqualify an unmarried partner from receiving any spousal benefit based upon a partner's earnings, but, on the other hand, the income of an unmarried partner will not disqualify an applicant from receiving a needs-based federal government benefit.

Thus, federally unmarried partners (which includes unmarried cohabitants, state-registered partners of any sexual orientation, and same-sex married spouses) will not be eligible for any of the spousal benefits that are extended to opposite-sex married couples. They will not receive the benefits that widows and widowers, surviving ex-spouses, parents, and dependent children of deceased eligible workers receive based upon a percentage of the deceased worker's entitlement.[1] For someone whose income over the years has been significantly lower than her partner's income, this preclusion can make a dramatic difference in monthly Social Security income, either after a divorce (and the subsequent death of the former spouse) or upon the higher earner's death during the parties' marriage. Take note: For those in federally recognized marriages, the widow(er) benefits require that the marriage must have lasted at least a year before the higher earner's death, and for divorced widows and widowers the marriage must have lasted at least ten years.

It is important that your unmarried clients are aware of these rules so that they can take appropriate action if they want to enjoy any of these benefits.[2] State registration may be treated as a marriage for state law purposes but it won't be for federal purposes, so these benefits are not available to state-registered partners regardless of sexual orientation. On the positive side, however, state registration will not be considered a marriage for federal purposes and therefore will not disqualify a widow(er) from receiving benefits based upon a deceased former spouse's income and will not subject the couple to any Social Security income limits as a married couple.[3]

Until DOMA is repealed or invalidated by a higher court, same-sex married couples also will not be entitled to any Social Security survivor or spousal benefits, and their marriages will not be treated as marriages for any disqualification purposes. The same is probably true for state-registered opposite-sex couples in marriage-equivalent registrations even though they are equivalent to spouses under their state's law, and the same treatment probably will apply to same-sex domestic partner registrants if and when DOMA is lifted.

There are many aspects of the interconnection between same-sex couples and Social Security that remain legally unresolved at this time. In the past, most federal agencies deferred to state law in defining marital status, and so DOMA's disregard of same-sex married couples appears unconstitutional to many observers (including, most recently, President Obama's Justice Department). One definition of *spouse* under Social Security law is someone who inherits under the state's intestacy laws, which would include all state-registered domestic partners in marriage-equivalent states, both gay and straight. However, at this point, it would be most prudent to assume that domestic partners will *not* be treated as spouses under Social Security law.[4] If the couple is co-parenting minor children but only one of the partners is the legal parent of the child, most likely the child will not receive any Social Security benefits from the nonlegal parent. The safest strategy is to assume that any benefit available to spouses under Social Security law will extend only to legally married opposite-sex couples.

Social Security Disability Insurance

Access to Social Security Disability Insurance (SSDI) is not income-based as it is an entitlement program; however, the amount of benefits actually received will be reduced by other sources of income available to the applicant. This is an area where being single from a federal perspective can be beneficial as the earnings of an applicant's unmarried partner generally cannot be used to disqualify a partner from SSDI.[5] For purposes of SSDI, the value of these benefits probably will not be construed as imputed income even if a partner is providing free housing or other practical benefits, and so the monthly payments won't be reduced.

Supplemental Security Income

By contrast, SSI is a needs-based program that provides income to seniors (over age sixty-five) as well as to blind or disabled people of any age who have limited income and assets. Thus, even when the applicant is approved for the program, the amount paid to an eligible applicant is reduced by the amount of income received by the applicant. For this program, *income* is defined as anything a recipient receives in cash or in-kind for support or maintenance. Accordingly, even if the applicant is unmarried (and thus not legally entitled to any share of a partner's income), the value of any food or shelter provided by an unmarried partner would count as income and thus dramatically reduce the monthly payment. The income levels for SSI are very low (no more than $790 per month as of 2004). The greatest risk here is not that the benefit income will be very low; rather, the loss of that tiny benefit amount altogether could result in a loss of Medicaid eligibility for health-care purposes.

Medicaid/Medi-Cal

These programs offer means-based benefits that may be lost if a partner is married to a higher-income person under federal law or if the beneficiary receives any other payments or benefits from an unmarried partner that count as income. State registration will not automatically result in a marriage disqualification, but any benefits received from the unmarried partner or spouse could have that consequence.[6] Thus, it is important that unmarried partners who are applying for or receiving any such benefits keep their finances entirely separate from their partner's finances and not commingle any checking or savings accounts; they also should thoroughly document any payment of rent to their unmarried partner.

One important exception to Medicaid that is not available to unmarried partners involves the "spend down" rules, especially regarding a home. Current regulations exclude the value of a jointly owned marital home when determining eligibility for this means-tested benefit. Thus, an unmarried couple who jointly owns its home will have to sell it to allow either partner to qualify for Medicaid.[7]

Food Stamps

The rules for food stamps speak in terms of "household" income, without regard to marital status or shared assets. Therefore, the total household income of the unmarried couple will be used to determine eligibility and not just the separate income of the applicant, even where the incomes are never commingled. Unless the total household income is below the maximum income limits, neither partner will be able to qualify individually for this form of government assistance.

Section 8 Housing Assistance Program

As with the food stamp program, receiving Section 8 housing benefits is based on household income: The family gross income must be

There remains great uncertainty with regard to the implications of DOMA for same-sex married couples and domestic partners. Fortunately, the federal Health and Human Services (HHS) Secretary, Kathleen Sebelius, announced on April 1, 2011, that same-sex spouses will be treated like opposite-sex spouses in some respects in the federal Medicaid program and can save the home from an ill partner's nursing home costs:

> HHS will continue to evaluate ways its programs can ensure equal treatment of LGBT families. For example, HHS will advise states and tribes that federal law allows them to treat LGBT couples similarly to non-LGBT couples with respect to human services benefit programs such as Temporary Assistance for Needy Families and child care. The Centers for Medicare & Medicaid Services will also notify states of their ability to provide same-sex domestic partners of long-term care Medicaid beneficiaries the same treatment as opposite-sex spouses in the contexts of estate recovery, imposition of liens, and transfer of assets. This includes not seizing or imposing a lien on the home of a deceased beneficiary if the same-sex domestic partner still resides in the home. It also includes allowing Medicaid beneficiaries needing long-term care to transfer the title of a home to a same-sex domestic partner, allowing the partner to remain in the home.[8]

less than 80 percent of the local median income, with a preference for those whose total family income is less than 30 percent of the median.[9] The combined income of both partners will be taken into consideration without regard to their marital status, and thus the higher income of one partner may pull their family income over the maximum income threshold. The only way for a lower-income applicant to avoid this disqualification problem would be for the couple to cease living together so that the applicant would only have to report separate income.

First-Time Home Buyer Credits

Many counties and cities and some states offer financial incentives for first-time home buyers, and in 2009 the federal government offered a significant first-time home buyer tax credit. Most of these programs define *first-time buyer* as someone who has never owned a home as a principal residence; the 2009 federal program defined *first-time home-buyer* as a buyer who has not owned a principal residence during the three-year period prior to the purchase. Each such program has a rule about married taxpayers, and typically either spouse will be disqualified if either the buyer or the spouse owned a home previously.

If the program is federally run, then only federally married people will be disqualified based upon the home ownership history of their spouses; unmarried partners, state-registered domestic partners, and even same-sex married couples will be treated as single applicants. But if the program is run by or subject to the regulations of the state government, then anyone who is treated as married under the state laws will be disqualified, which would include state-registered domestic partners and same-sex married couples. If the program is entirely local in funding and regulation, review the specific ordinance and program rules to verify whether locally registered partners would count as spouse equivalents to disqualify an applicant. Generally speaking, it is safest to assume that if a local registration bestows any benefits under the jurisdiction's programs and rules, it will also disqualify an applicant whenever a spouse's income or home ownership history is relevant.

Low-Income Housing and Rent Control Protections

Many cities and counties offer to low-income people protection from rent increases, and others offer reductions in purchase prices or rental rates. Many of these programs treat the combined income of married couples as family income, and so an otherwise qualified applicant will be disqualified if the partner's income (or the combined income of the partners) is more than the threshold amounts. Some jurisdictions (such as New York City) exclude higher-income families from the full benefits of rent control programs, and others have specific rules for the transfer of below-market rental units between spouses. It is impossible to generalize as to the reach of any of these programs in terms of de facto cohabiting partners, locally registered partners, or state-registered partners. Where the rules are unclear after you make your review, you or your client should consult with supervisory staff in the specific program. As with the other nonfederal programs, it is most likely that registered domestic partners in a marriage-equivalent registration will be treated the same as married spouses, both in terms of eligibility and disqualification purposes.

Unemployment Compensation Benefits

One of my favorite provisions of unemployment law in most states is the right to collect benefits even when quitting a job voluntarily if the reason is to follow a spouse who has been relocated. This is one of the few areas of law where the government actually fosters family unification (as opposed to uttering vague statements to that effect that are rarely backed up by specific policies or laws). Several decades ago, I wrote an amicus curiae brief in a California appellate case that challenged the denial of unemployment benefits for an unmarried heterosexual partner who left her job to follow her boyfriend out of town, on the grounds of marital status discrimination. Sadly, we lost that appeal.[10] Similarly, in most other states as well, this benefit will be denied to unmarried partners.

State law generally regulates unemployment insurance benefits, even when the funding comes in part from federal sources, and so you will need to investigate your own state's laws to see what coverage they provide. As with other areas of state law, a registered partner in a state-sanctioned marriage-equivalent registration probably will be entitled to this benefit, but a city- or county-registered partner will not. A mere cohabitant definitely will not qualify for this benefit.

Workers' Compensation Benefits

Every state has its own workers' compensation rules; most such programs provide a death benefit. Fortunately, in most instances the benefits are paid to "dependent" family members regardless of a marital relationship.[11] Under California law, for example, *dependent* is broadly defined as a "good faith member of a family or household of the employee."[12] Ironically, however, in most states a cohabitation agreement stating that the partners will be separately responsible for each other's expenses probably would disqualify the survivor for a dependency claim under the workers' compensation rule.

Family Leave Benefits

The federal Family and Medical Leave Act allows employees to take up to twelve to twenty-six weeks of unpaid job-protected leave in a twelve-month period for specified family and medical reasons. The law applies to employers with fifty or more employees within a seventy-five-mile radius. The allowable reasons for time off include the birth of a newborn child (of the employee or legal spouse), placement of an adopted or foster child with the employee or legal spouse, a serious health problem of the employee, or caring for the employee's legal spouse, child, or parent who has a serious medical condition. An unmarried partner will not qualify as a spouse for this benefit even if the partners are locally registered or state-registered, nor will a same-sex married spouse.[13]

Some states, including California, have parallel state laws providing similar benefits. State-registered partners in a marriage-equivalent registration (such as a California domestic partnership) will be covered under the state law because they are recognized as spouses. Similarly, taking care of the child of an unmarried partner will not qualify under the federal law even if the couple is state-registered, but it will count under the state law version if the couple is state-registered in a marriage-equivalent registration even if the partner is not the legal parent of the child.

Veterans' Benefits

Veterans' programs are regulated by federal law and therefore will only provide benefits to federally recognized spouses. Unmarried partners of any variety (as well as same-sex married partners and state-registered domestic partners) are ineligible for federal spousal veterans' benefits (such as survivor payments upon the death of the veteran). In addition, it is only logical to assume that the children of an unmarried partner will be ineligible for children's benefits unless they are the biological or adopted children of the veteran, because all of the statutes and regulations regarding benefits refer to a child "of the veteran." Some states provide additional benefits to the spouses or children of veterans, such as tuition waivers or hiring preferences or limited property tax benefits. Same-sex married spouses and couples who are state-registered in a marriage-equivalent registration such as California's domestic partnership registration will be eligible for these state-issued benefits as spousal equivalents.

B. Governmentally Regulated Employee Benefits

The Role of ERISA

The federal Employee Retirement Income Security Act of 1974,[14] commonly known as ERISA, governs all employee benefit and welfare plans that are established or maintained by an employer, to the extent that the benefits are connected to retirement programs or to any medical or health-care benefits. It does not cover peripheral benefits such as bereavement leave, maternity leave, voluntary insurance coverage, or membership or travel discounts. Most significantly, plans offered by government entities (both state and federal) or religious institutions are not bound by ERISA even though they may voluntarily offer plans that are regulated by ERISA.

ERISA's strong preemption language prohibits any local or state laws that are in conflict with its provisions. In some instances employers can voluntarily provide additional benefits (benefiting lesbian and gay employees, for example), but they cannot redefine the basic terms (such as who is a spouse) of the programs that they generally offer to all employees. As a result, the federal definition of *spouse* will apply to any ERISA-regulated program, and neither unmarried couples nor same-sex married couples are federally recognized spouses. In addition, state-registered domestic partners, even straight ones, are not considered federally recognized spouses even if they are treated as equivalent to married spouses under state law.

Some states have passed their own laws that require insurance companies to provide domestic partnership coverage equivalent to spousal coverage. Because this is a requirement imposed on insurance companies, not employers, most analysts do not consider it to be pre-empted by ERISA. These rules only apply to state-registered domestic partners, not to cohabitants or locally registered partners.

Qualified Retirement Plans

Unmarried partners (including state-registered partners as well as same-sex married spouses) are not spouses under ERISA-regulated pension and retirement plans. Two main problems result from this rule, both of which arise upon the death or the divorce of an employee.

With regard to a death, most plans offer preferential survivor benefit plans for spouses upon the death of an employee, while the designation of a nonspouse beneficiary usually results in higher fees or lower payments, if allowed at all. Fortunately, the 2006 Pension Protection Act[15] allows a decedent to pass the entirety of a retirement investment account to a nonspouse beneficiary without triggering a major tax consequence upon his death, but this generally does not apply to the income stream of a defined benefit plan.

Equally serious problems arise for state-registered domestic partners and same-sex married couples with regard to the transfer of all or a portion of a retirement plan upon a breakup. State marital law typically considers the nonemployee spouse or partner to have a legal or equitable interest in the employee's plan (either a defined benefit plan or a retirement savings account), especially in community property states. However, as discussed further in the dissolution chapter, such accounts cannot be transferred at the time of a nonmarital breakup by means of a Qualified Domestic Relations Order (QDRO) or a retirement account transfer.[16] The same restriction applies to unmarried partners who contractually agree to share their retirement assets, either in a cohabitation or separation agreement, or those who are fortunate enough to win a palimony or cohabitation civil lawsuit.

Given these limitations, dissolution agreements between unmarried partners should look to a distribution of equivalently valued nonregulated or nonretirement assets, adjusted for the tax consequences of the eventual distribution of the retirement assets, or some kind of financial compensation (which can always be measured against the value of a retirement asset). This enables the partners to distribute their joint assets in ways that avoid the messy tax and penalty complications of a shared retirement asset.

Health Insurance Coverage

Even though unmarried couples and same-sex married couples are not considered spouses under federal law, employers can voluntarily provide health insurance coverage for the unmarried partners of employees without running afoul of ERISA. Moreover, in states where the insurance companies are required to offer domestic partnership coverage equivalent to spousal coverage, state-registered domestic partners of employees generally will be able to obtain such coverage.

In states that do not have marriage-equivalent registration, employers have the option of extending coverage to anyone who is identified by an employee to be a de facto domestic partner.[17] Some employers require some kind of public registration, and it is important that employees are careful in electing where to register. In the past, many employees chose to register under the state of California's domestic partner system regardless of their state of residence because California allows nonresidents to apply by mail. However, now that California's registration is a marriage-equivalent system, registered partners could face serious liabilities and must terminate their dissolution through the court system, even if they live in a nonrecognition state. For this reason, registering with a city or county registration system would be more prudent.

Here are some of the issues that arise in connection with unmarried partner health insurance coverage:

Eligibility. Most plans require partners to live together even though this is not required of married spouses. Some plans are limited to same-sex partners on the grounds that opposite-sex partners have the option of a legal marriage.[18] Every employer requires that the parties not be registered or married to someone else or be in a relationship that would be disallowed from marriage (e.g., where one or both parties are of minority age or where the parties' familial relationship would prohibit their legal marriage).

Statements of Dependency. Most plans require employees and their partners to sign a statement of financial interdependency. While these statements do not legally bind partners to pay post-separation support, the partner or a third-party creditor could argue that these statements should form the basis for collecting support or forcing the nondebtor partner to pay the debtor partner's debts.

Upgrade Requirements. In states that now offer marriage-equivalent registration or same-sex marriage, an increasing number of employers no longer will extend coverage to locally or employer-only registered partners. Instead, they are requiring that their employees state register or marry as a condition of receiving health insurance benefits in order to be equivalent to married couples in all respects. This is a reasonable requirement as long as the same requirement is imposed on opposite-sex unmarried couples, but it can be burdensome on a couple who has enjoyed domestic partnership coverage in the past without having to sign up for all of the marital rights and responsibilities as state-registered partners.

Proof Requirements. One of the more maddening details of unmarried life is a demand to prove registration, especially when that is rarely required of married couples. California's Insurance Equality Act (which mandates that insurance companies provide domestic partnership coverage) includes a provision stating that the provider can only require proof of registered partnership if it imposes the same requirement on married couples.[19]

COBRA Coverage. Continuation of benefits coverage is important in two settings: the loss of the job by the employee and the less-recognized loss of coverage of the non-employee arising from a breakup of the partnership relationship. Because unmarried partners (as well as same-sex married partners and any state-registered domestic partners) are not federally recognized spouses, they are not entitled to any coverage under the federal COBRA rules. However, some states have their own rules for smaller non-federally regulated employers, and those plans usually cover state-registered domestic partners and same-sex married spouses, and sometimes they will cover locally registered partners as well. Typically, they will not cover unregistered cohabitants of any sexual orientation.

IRS Issues for Benefits

Because of a little-known IRS rule, certain state- and federally mandated long-term care plans (which have specified tax advantages for government employees) can only extend benefits to legally married spouses and not to registered domestic partners. Thus, domestic partners are not covered by these plans, nor are same-sex married spouses, and this problem will only be resolved when DOMA is invalidated or repealed. Unregistered cohabitants, once again, will not be eligible for this benefit.

One well-documented IRS problem regarding medical and life insurance benefits is the taxation of health insurance benefits. Because the domestic partner of the employee (whether city- or state-registered, or even a de facto cohabitant who is recognized as a partner by the employer) will not qualify as a federally recognized dependent—and definitely is not a federally recognized spouse—the value of the premiums paid by the employer are taxable to the employee. Your client should shop around for nonpartner-based insurance since, in some situations, the overall cost of the partner-dependent premium may be higher than obtaining independent coverage elsewhere.

It is not always easy to establish what the tax on the partner benefit should be. Some suggest that the taxable value is roughly equivalent to the COBRA cost for that employee, apart from any group rate subsidy that the employee and his partner is enjoying while the couple is together. That is why the copayment by the employee plus the tax burden may turn out to be so expensive. A few employers have begun covering these tax penalties as additional compensation for their unmarried employees, though usually just for same-sex couples who do not have the option of a federally recognized legal marriage.

C. Local Registration Benefits

Employee Benefits

Many local city and county jurisdictions offer registrations for couples as domestic partners, some only for same-sex couples, and others for opposite-sex couples as well. The primary beneficiaries of these registrations are local government employees as oftentimes the domestic partner benefit packages are tied to local registration. Because these local government plans are not subject to ERISA regulation, the benefits provided by these registries for their own employees can be significant, including medical and life insurance, bereavement leave, and other valuable services. Because these are not marriage-equivalent registrations, they do not carry with them any of the rights or responsibilities of marriage, which may be a welcome relief to your clients. They still impose the eligibility requirements discussed above, and so it is important to be aware of the requirements (such as cohabitation) in discussing these options with your clients. In most instances, either partner can terminate the registration unilaterally with the mere filing of a notice of termination.

Private companies are often free to extend benefits to such couples. As discussed above, the benefits provided to locally registered employees (by private and public employers) can be vulnerable to a demand that the employees either marry or state register, if that is available to them. This is especially true for same-sex couples in situations in which employers may have been willing to use local registries in the absence of marriage equality or marriage-equivalent registration. Clients who elect to take advantage of local registration eligibility should be advised of the potential long-term consequences of the closing of this local registration loophole—most dramatically, the inability to retain insurance coverage without getting formally married.

Local Tax Benefits

Some localities, especially in the larger cities in California and New York, impose local taxes with spousal exemptions. Many of those taxes grant exemptions to city-registered and county-registered domestic partners, and many are open to straight as well as gay couples. For example, the cities of Berkeley and Oakland have a very high local tax on property transfers ($15 per $1,000 of transferred value), and so a buyout of one partner's half-interest in a residence by the other partner (in a dissolution, for example) could trigger as much as a $6,000 transfer tax on the value of the 50 percent interest transferred. A city registration, which is not a marriage-equivalent registration, exempts the couple from that tax. Local registration also can be useful for obtaining spousal-equivalent benefits under local rent control laws, such as the transfer of a rent-controlled apartment upon the death of a partner or the breakup of the relationship.

D. DISCRETIONARY EMPLOYMENT BENEFITS

Insurance

Many enlightened employers provide free or discounted medical insurance for the partners of their unmarried employees, either voluntarily (typically to attract younger skillful employees) or as part of a collective bargaining agreement. Some employers only provide benefits to same-sex unmarried couples on the grounds that the opposite-sex couples have the option of marriage, and others provide them to all unmarried partners. Some employers require some kind of governmental registration, which can be difficult if your clients live in a city or county that does not offer such registration, but others do not. If a registration is required, your clients probably can sign up for one of the out-of-state local registrations, but you would not want them to state register in a marriage-equivalent registry just for this limited benefit. Many other employers allow their employees to self-disclose or sign an affidavit as cohabitants without requiring any formal registration.

It's important that clients think long-term with regard to these benefits because the employer can withdraw them or the covered employee could leave his employment, thus leaving the partner uninsured. Depending on the contribution required for the partner's premium and the income tax owed on the value of the premium, the cost can sometimes be greater than an otherwise available policy (and one that would not be jeopardized by the partner's job loss or a breakup of the relationship).

In a wonderful development by a small number of companies, some employers recently began covering the tax burdens imposed on unmarried employees for the value of their partner's health and life insurance coverage. For the most part, such a top-up is only being offered for gay or lesbian state-registered partners or same-sex married employees on the grounds that straight employees have access to tax-exempt coverage for their spouses.

Some employers also offer free or discounted life insurance plans that provide additional coverage for cohabitants, and unmarried employees should carefully investigate the available options and conditions for such coverage. In general, most employers will not extend benefits based upon a claim of a common law marriage, and clients should be warned of the risks of intentionally misstating their legal marital status.

Other Benefits

Larger companies frequently offer a wide range of noninsurance benefits, some of which may be of interest to the unmarried partners of employees. These may include day care for children who are not the legal children of the employed partner, membership in various health or social clubs, tuition (primarily for employees of schools or universities), prepaid legal services, or purchasing discounts. Everyone's favorite partner benefit is the right to free or reduced-cost airline travel as the "loved one" of an airline employee. Each airline company has its own rules: Some limit the benefit to legal spouses, some honor state registration or even city registration, and others let the employee decide who is their allowable "significant other" or dependent. Two details need to be looked into, however: Some airlines only offer reciprocal benefits to the spouse of an employee and not the unmarried partner; and, most important, the value of the benefits conferred to a nonspouse will be taxed (just like the health insurance premium value), whereas a spouse's benefits are typically tax-free.

E. MISCELLANEOUS NONEMPLOYMENT BENEFITS

Many private businesses offer domestic partnership benefits to cohabiting couples without requiring any formal registration. These include family discounts for health and fitness clubs, reduced insurance premiums if both partners purchase long-term care policies at the same time, and rental car insurance benefits—my favorite. I learned about the importance of these last benefits the hard way when I was driving a rental car that had been rented by my (unmarried) partner. We had a minor car accident, and 364 days later I was served with a lawsuit filed by the other driver. To my great relief, National Car Rental simply asked for proof that we lived at the same residence and then provided me with free legal defense as a domestic partner of the renter. The case settled for less than $5,000, but it was great to know that I was covered.

For most of these benefits, no specific registration is required, and most often they will be extended to any cohabiting couple without regard to gender or sexual orientation.

A final word about benefits: I am highly skeptical about anyone marrying just to receive benefits, just as I am about those who choose to marry to gain a tax benefit. The long-term consequences of being married (or state-registered in a marriage-equivalent registration) or staying single are too significant to be invoked solely to save a relatively small amount of money on a limited benefit. I always encourage my clients to know what they are missing and what they may be able to obtain as married people, but given the magnitude of the consequences, they always should base their decision upon the overall legal and financial consequences of marriage.

NOTES

1. 42 U.S.C. § 402(e)–(h).
2. Generally speaking, a common law marriage will entitle a widow(er) to these benefits, even in the absence of a court order confirming the marital status and even if he has relocated to a state that does not recognize common law marriages. *See* 42 U.S.C. § 416(a)–(b), (h).
3. It is for this reason that some states, including California, allow opposite-sex couples over the age of sixty-two to register as domestic partners, thus enabling them to obtain state benefits as a married couple without jeopardizing any federal Social Security benefits.
4. Given this problem, same-sex couples in marriage-equivalent registrations would need to "upgrade" to marriage if and when the preclusions of DOMA were lifted if they wished to obtain any of the spousal benefits under Social Security.
5. For many government programs, the answer to the questions of disqualification lies in how the applicant's income tax return is filled out. This is especially true for applicants in community property states, where each spouse would report 50 percent of the total community property income. If the community property rules apply (as they do for state-registered partners), then the applicant probably will be disqualified.
6. It is possible that the rules may change in the next year or so to extend all protections (and restrictions) to same-sex married couples, despite the seeming prohibitions imposed by DOMA.
7. 42 U.S.C. § 1396p(b)(2)–(2)(A) (2000).
8. Kathleen Sebelius, U.S. Dep't of Health & Human Servs., U.S. Dep't of Health and Human Services Recommended Actions to Improve the Health and Well-Being of Lesbian, Gay, Bisexual, and Transgender Communities (Apr. 1, 2011), http://www.hhs.gov/secretary/about/lgbthealth.html.
9. 42 U.S.C. § 1437f(a); 24 C.F.R. § 982.201(b).
10. Norman v. CIUAB 20 Cal. 3rd 55 (1983).
11. California's rules are covered in Cal. Lab. Code §§ 4700–01.
12. *Id.* § 3503.
13. 5 U.S.C. § 6381.
14. 29 U.S.C. §§ 1001–61 (1974).
15. I.R.C. § 402(c)(11) (2006).
16. A recent 9th Circuit case has held, however, than an unmarried straight partner could enforce a Washington state judgement by means of a QDRO. *Owens v. Automotive Machinists*, 551 F.3D 1138 (9th Cir. 2009).

17. Because these benefits are voluntary, they are subject to withdrawal, as recently occurred when there was a change in governor in the state of Arizona, with regard to coverage for partners of gay and lesbian state employees.

18. There has been litigation in the past asserting that such restrictions are a form of sexual orientation discrimination, but in most instances the restrictions have been upheld as a reasonable attempt to correct an otherwise discriminatory restriction on marriage.

19. Cal. Health & Safety Code § 1374.58(a); Cal. Ins. Code §§ 381.5(a), 10121.7(a).

CHAPTER TEN

THE RULES AND PRACTICES OF PARENTAGE

A. A Brief History of Illegitimacy

Up until just a few decades ago, the legitimacy of a child made a substantial difference in the life of that child and her parents. Illegitimate children were defined generally as children whose natural (i.e., biological) parents were not married to one another at the time the child was born, either because they never married or because they had already gotten divorced by the time of the child's birth. Interestingly, the parents' marital status at time of *conception* did not seem to matter, and so a last-minute marriage could salvage an otherwise unacceptable family arrangement. Illegitimate children (and their mothers) suffered many emotional and financial injuries, ranging from rejection by their extended family to neglect by the broader social community. But, of greatest importance, these children also were forced to endure many legal burdens.

Nolo Press's *Sex, Living Together, and the Law* legal guide (first published in 1974) illustrates how serious the problem was at the time, devoting no fewer than ten pages to the legal problems facing illegitimate children and their parents. The law in most states at that time deprived the father of any presumption of custody unless the relationship was legitimated by the father "accepting the child as his own" with the consent of the mother. If the couple never lived together or if the partners broke up before the father had established a continuing relationship with the child, the father could be denied custody entirely, and perhaps regular visitation as well, even if it were clearly established that he was a biological parent. Only if the father had helped to support the child financially and had maintained regular contact with the child would a court be sympathetic to a demand for postseparation custody or visitation by the father.

Interestingly, the father's consent would not be required if the mother decided to give up the child for adoption or if the mother's subsequent partner (or legal spouse) wished to apply for a stepparent adoption of the child. Adoption agencies did not notify the dad or ask for his consent, and neither did the courts. If a father intervened and could prove that he was the biological father of the child, a court might pay attention to his concerns; but in light of the fact that there was no requirement that he be given notice of an adoption proceeding, this intervention had very little practical consequence. Fathers of illegitimate children existed, for the most part, only as potential sources of child support.

So, too, with regard to abortion. Because the father was not a legal relative of the mother or of the unborn child, there was no requirement that the biological father be notified or asked to give his consent to the mother's decision to obtain an abortion. Absent a marriage between the parents, the father was fundamentally disconnected to his biological child as a legal matter.

Financial issues abounded for the illegitimate child. Before a father could be ordered to pay child support, the court would have to determine that he was a biological father, and this was not a simple proceeding. By contrast, if the parties were married, the husband would owe a duty of support to the child even if he were not the biological father. In most instances, illegitimate children would not benefit from any pension plan or other retirement benefits based upon the father's employment when the father died, and until the 1970s the Social Security programs disfavored illegitimate children. In effect, the illegitimate child could only look to her mother for long-term financial support, which generally resulted in a dramatically thinner financial cushion.

These problems were all very real, but perhaps the worst consequences of illegitimacy—and those that caught the greatest attention of the courts—involved intestacy disputes. Most states' laws up until the late 1970s provided that if a father died without a will or trust, his biological children would not inherit anything from him (or from any of his relatives) unless he and the mother had subsequently married and he had acknowledged the child as his own or formally adopted the child. Speaking with great prescience on the issue, the Nolo book's authors stated in 1974 that "many legal scholars think these discriminatory laws are unconstitutional and there is some case authority to indicate that this is true."[1]

And so it was to be. In the late 1960s and early 1970s, a series of cases had touched on the subject of illegitimacy but without reaching any final resolution. Then, in 1977, the U.S. Supreme Court ruled in *Trimble v. Gordon*[2] that the doctrine of equal protection invalidated any state law that limited intestate succession by an illegitimate offspring from the father when there was no equivalent preclusion upon the mother's death. The father in the *Trimble* case had been acknowledged as a parent and had been ordered to pay child support, and the court concluded that it was therefore unfair to penalize the children for the illicit sexual activities of their parents. Instead, the state was required to provide some method of determining paternity in order for children to qualify for intestate succession. In response to this ruling, some states imposed rather stiff burdensome requirements on proving paternity, such as setting early deadlines for establishing legal parentage, and courts have subsequently thrown out requirements that appear unduly strict or "not reasonably related" to the legitimate purposes of the regulation.[3]

As a result of these decisions and the social shift against these biases, the generally applicable doctrine now is that any provision of benefits based solely on the marital status of the parents is invalid. The Uniform Parentage Act (UPA), first adopted in 1973 and currently in effect in nearly half of the states of this country, unambiguously abolished any need to determine legitimacy of a child, stating that all rights and obligations should be imposed regardless of the marital status of the parents.[4]

The borderline of legal significance with regard to the welfare of children has shifted, therefore, from that of legitimacy to one of parentage.[5] While marital status still is relevant to the extent that it establishes one of the rebuttable presumptions about parentage, marital status is no longer the end of the legal inquiry—it is just one component of the analysis.

B. THE LEGAL PRESUMPTIONS OF HETEROSEXUAL PARENTAGE

Once a person ventures beyond the traditional notion of parentage (based upon a marriage between the heterosexual biological parents of the child), an entirely new set of questions arises: How did the child come into existence? Who are the biological parents of the child? Who should be the child's legal parents? What will the ongoing parent-child and partnership relationship between the parents and the child be? And most crucially with respect to your work as an attorney: What are the applicable legal rules, and how should any disputes that arise with regard to any of these issues be resolved?

Uniform Parentage Act Framework

While many states have their own rules and practices with regard to issues of parentage, the UPA is the dominant framework, and it has been codified to some degree in about half of the states in this country.[6] Of necessity, the discussion of the parentage issues in this chapter will be general in nature, and attorneys must research the specific statutes and relevant case law in their state before advising the client. Given the local particularity and complexity of parentage law, this is an area that particularly calls out for referral to an experienced lawyer in this field. And since the UPA (and all similar state laws) is framed entirely in heterosexual terms, unique issues will arise for determining parentage where the parents are lesbian, gay, or transsexual.

Briefly stated, the UPA establishes clear definitions for both the mother-child and the father-child relationship, framed in terms of the assumptions of a heterosexual partnership.[7] According to the UPA, the mother-child relationship can be formed in any one of four ways: (1) the woman gives birth to the child and does not relinquish parentage through adoption or as a surrogate, (2) a court adjudicates the woman as the mother, (3) the woman legally adopts the child, or (4) the woman is confirmed as the legal parent of a child born to a gestational mother (a surrogate) as allowed by applicable state law.

There are six ways that a man can become a legal father: (1) the proper application of a presumption of parentage (either because of a legal marriage or a cohabitation relationship with a mother) that is not legally rebutted, (2) an effective acknowledgement of parentage (which requires the mother's consent), (3) a valid court adjudication of parentage (usually as a result of a paternity or reverse-paternity suit and genetic testing results showing a 99 percent probability of parentage), (4) a legal adoption, (5) consent by the man to an assisted reproduction procedure that led to the child being born, or (6) confirmation of the man as a legal parent of a child born to a gestational mother (a surrogate) as allowed by applicable state law. Other than the inclusion of a rebuttable presumption arising from a marriage between the parents, the marital status of the parents has been expressly declared as irrelevant to the parent-child relationship.[8]

There are three basic ways that a father becomes a presumed parent under the UPA: (1) he is married to the mother when the child is born (or the child is born within 300 days after the death of the husband or the parties' divorce), (2) he marries the mother after the birth of the child and agrees to be named on the birth certificate as the father and to support the child, or (3) he lives in the same household with the child for the first two years of her life and "openly holds out" the child as his own.[9] Keep in mind, however, that a presumption of parentage can be rebutted if there is evidence that supports the conclusion that another man should be designated as a legal parent.

Most states require clear and convincing evidence in order to rebut any of these three presumptions. The proponent of the presumption has the initial burden of proof to establish the foundational facts supporting the presumption, and then the burden of rebutting the presumption shifts to the other party.[10] Interestingly, not being a biological father does not necessarily deem the man a nonparent. As a result, there may be two competing rebuttable presumptions of parentage, and in most states there are equitable social policy doctrines that will be applied to resolve these conflicts. The overall goal as stated in most such codes should be the protection of the child's well-being. Given the nuances of these policies and rules, it is crucial that any attorney handling a disputed parentage action be aware of the local court's practices and prior rulings and be prepared to bring forth evidence and testimony that addresses the particular issues that are likely to be of greatest concern to the court.

The second primary method of establishing parentage, acknowledgement as a father, is a statutorily created documentation process fostered to a great degree by a push from federal officials (seeking to designate fathers who might be liable for child support) that confirms all the rights and duties of parentage on the father. The acknowledgement document must clearly state that there is no other presumed or acknowledged father, such as the married spouse of the mother, and both parents must sign it and acknowledge that they understand its legal consequences. Interestingly, under the UPA, there is no requirement of any genetic testing of the father as part of the acknowledgement process. Conversely, in certain circumstances, the parties may elect to sign a denial of parentage document, which is appropriate if the mother is married to a man who would thus be a presumed father. A declaration of either position can only be challenged on the basis of fraud, duress, or material mistake of fact, and the challenge must be brought within two years of the signing of the acknowledgement or denial of parentage.[11]

In addition to establishing these categories of parentage and setting the substantive rules for determining parentage, the UPA also contains detailed provisions for the process of adjudicating parentage, including burdens of proof; standards for the use of genetic testing; and recommended approaches to appropriate and necessary parties, court jurisdiction and venue, statues of limitation, and civil procedure.

The goal of the act, as its title implies, is to provide clear rules for establishing legal parentage on a national basis, especially of the father-child relationship, in a way that deals with the wide variety of social and biological arrangements between sexual and emotional partners.

Likely Legal Conflicts

Because unmarried heterosexual cohabitants by definition will not be subject to the presumptions based upon their marital status, the legal parentage issues for your clients will most likely arise in one of the following four settings: (1) a dispute over the presumption arising out of the parties' cohabitation and whether the father has "held himself out" as the parent of the child, (2) a court adjudication of parentage based upon genetic testing of the alleged father, (3) the decision as to whether or not to sign a formal acknowledgement of parentage as authorized by applicable state law or the validity of a previously signed acknowledgement, or (4) a second-parent (or, for registered domestic partners in marriage-equivalent registrations, a stepparent) adoption by the non-biological parent. In each of these situations, your first responsibility will be educating your client (or clients) about the specific rules and procedures in your state for each of these options and then, if appropriate, representing your client in an application for an order in one of these settings, or a response thereto.

Approaching these situations requires a delicate balance of detailed legal knowledge, a practical understanding of how the court system in your jurisdiction adjudicates these matters, and good client counseling skills, in particular an ability to help clients make clear decisions and act consistently to implement them. These are not simple tasks. Thus, whether you are advising the mother or the father or both (with an appropriate conflict of interest waiver), it makes most sense to address your client's needs by following the path of initial inquiry, open discussion, research, and decision making:

1. Start with an inquiry as to who is the genetic/biological parent of the child, and if this is unknown, decide whether it is appropriate that the alleged father undergoes genetic testing to obtain further clarity on the genetic parentage issues. If one or both of the parents do not wish to allow genetic testing, you will want to educate them as to what is the risk, if any, of another man emerging as the genetic parent.

2. If both partners are clear that they wish to be considered legal parents in terms of custody, decision making, and the long-term duties of support, determine what legal procedures are most effective to formalize their parent-child relationships; often, this only will need to be addressed with regard to the father. This analysis can be problematic if either of the parents is not a biological parent (especially if a second-parent adoption is not feasible, and even more so if the parents are a same-sex couple). You will need to evaluate to what extent the personal relationship of the parents will affect, and perhaps determine, how they wish to approach the parentage issues.

3. If a legal parent resists having a partner deemed a legal parent, either because of genetic uncertainty or because of the couple's uncertain or nonexistent partnership relationship, you will want to evaluate what is the appropriate legal strategy to effectuate that goal. This analysis will be different if there is a likely legal parent who is not one of the relationship partners.

4. Separate from the question of establishing the child's legal parentage, you will need to work with your clients to determine how they wish to organize their co-parenting lives, especially if they are not currently living together or if it seems reasonably likely that they will not be living together in the near future. As part of that discussion, you will want to consider whether there is good reason to formalize their relationship in a written agreement, even if such an agreement may not be legally binding.

Parentage Actions

Once it is determined that there is legal uncertainty about parentage, you will need to decide how best to resolve that uncertainty. Some couples may be fine with taking no legal action at all, and this may be acceptable, especially if there is no question about the father's genetic connection to the child and they are living together as a family when the child is born. In situations where there may be ambiguities about the parentage and their living situation, or if things are in flux, the partners may want some legal certainty. In those instances, a formal parentage action may be appropriate. The questions for the attorney in a parentage action are as follows:

1. Who is your client? Usually you will represent just one client, either the mother or the alleged father, though in some situations there may be legal relatives involved (e.g., a former or estranged spouse or perhaps a grandparent of the child). They may not be parties to the legal action, but they still may be your clients.
2. What are the biological and emotional facts that are most relevant to the dispute, and how do those truths factor into the legal strategy? What is the nature of the personal relationship of the parents, what are your client's main concerns and priorities, and what is in the best interest of the child?
3. What are the substantive rules for establishing parentage in your jurisdiction? How is the court case initiated, and what are the substantive and procedural requirements for proving (or disproving) parentage?
4. Who are the appropriate and necessary defendants in a parentage action? Is there anyone whose parentage rights will need to be terminated or determined to be nonexistent in this proceeding?

5. Should any other professionals be involved in the process? Is there a need for a counselor or a mediator or someone with experience as a custody evaluator? Does your client need personal assistance from a therapist or social worker? What sort of testimony or documentation, if any, will be needed for the court hearing, and who is most capable of gathering that evidence?

6. What will your role be as an attorney? Will you be formulating the overall approach or merely appearing at the court hearing? What sort of fee arrangement should you be making with your client, and is there a way to farm out some of the work to minimize the financial burden on your client? What tasks are more appropriately delegated to a paralegal or a savvy assistant in your office?

For the specific practice tips on initiating or responding to a parentage action, you should consult with the appropriate treatise and practice guide for your state.

C. The Legal Challenges of Same-Sex and Transgender Parenting

The legal landscape for lesbians and gay men raising children as a same-sex couple (apart from those—primarily women—with children from a prior heterosexual relationship) was quite bleak back in 1980 when Nolo published its first edition of *A Legal Guide for Lesbian and Gay Couples*. Lesbians who left their straight marriage faced daunting obstacles when they tried to retain custody, and the chapter on becoming parents as a couple started out with the stark statement that under the then-existing law, only one of the partners would be able to be a legal parent or obtain legal custody of the child. By definition, only one member of a lesbian couple could be the biological mother; and by law, only a single person could adopt a child—thus, in "all these situations the other member of the couple will have no legal rights to custody of the child."[12] The only practical suggestions that the book could offer were a private agreement for co-parenting (which probably would not be legally enforceable) or some kind of short-duration or limited-purpose coguardianship arrangements.

One particularly prescient section of the Nolo book, however, discussed the new idea of artificial insemination for men, well before the term *surrogacy* was popularly recognized. The authors described how a few men had advertised for a woman to bear a child "fathered" by the sperm of the gay man, where the woman would contractually agree to give up the child for adoption to the donor dad. There was little settled law on these practices back then, but the section ended with a hopeful statement that this procedure "will become more common and legally acceptable in the future."[13] How true that has turned out to be.

Things were somewhat improved a decade or so later when April Martin wrote her comprehensive guidebook for lesbian and gay parents in 1993, *The Lesbian and Gay Parenting Handbook*. She quipped that "heterosexuals who are planning to become parents do not usually consult with lawyers first. They don't have to. The laws which protect the families they create are already in place."[14] While the discussion in this chapter of straight unmarried parentage issues demonstrates that these laws are still somewhat uncertain for unmarried partners, the parentage conflicts of straight unmarried parents are relatively rare (as opposed to custody and support disputes upon dissolution of the nonmarital relationship), and there are readily available legal methods of resolving these conflicts. Genetic testing, formal acknowledgements of parentage, or court adjudication of parentage disputes can resolve many parentage conflicts, though new issues arise regularly. When in doubt, marriage or second-parent adoptions can address most other issues.

Same-sex parents face a much more complicated and legally uncertain terrain. As summarized in Martin's book, the legal issues then (as well as now) are as follows:

1. Who is a legal parent, especially when the laws of many states do not honor any functional definitions of parentage for de facto parents?
2. What are the legal rights of a nonbiological or nonlegal parent, especially in the event of a breakup of the couple's relationship?
3. What happens if one of the parents dies while the child is still a minor?
4. Under what conditions (and in what states) is it possible for the nonbiological or nonlegal parent to obtain a second-parent or stepparent adoption of the child?

5. What steps are available and appropriate to define the rights of a sperm or egg donor or surrogate mother who was not intended to be considered a parent?
6. How are the potential disputes between opposite-sex biological co-parents resolved where a gay man and lesbian or straight woman have decided to co-parent but were never in a romantic or marriage-like relationship?

Some of these issues will affect all same-sex couples, some are particular to one or the other gender, and others only transgender parents will encounter.

Perhaps more than any other area of law discussed in this book, the rules on same-sex parentage are changing quickly, and dramatically. Advising clients in this arena is especially difficult given the uncertainties about future trends and legal decisions. Consider, just as an example, the situation in North Carolina. Over the past two decades, hundreds of lesbian couples obtained second-parent adoption decrees from local judges, confident that the parentage rights of the nonbiological mother were certain. However, the procedure had never been statutorily authorized in North Carolina, and in a devastating decision by the North Carolina Supreme Court, all such adoptions were retroactively invalidated.[15] Depending where your client lives and the available legal procedures under consideration, counseling your clients will require a careful balancing of encouragement, caution, and legal flexibility.

Notwithstanding all of the uncertainties in this field, there are several strategies that can be used to confirm the parentage rights and obligations of same-sex couples, as follows.

Second-Parent Adoptions

While a conventional adoption involves the termination of the biological parent or parents' rights in favor of the adoptive parent or parents' designation as the legal parent(s), in a second-parent adoption the nonbiological or nonlegal parent adopts her partner's child as a "limited consent adoption," without modifying or terminating the legal rights of the biological or legal parent. In most instances, the original parent is a birth parent (for lesbians) or a genetic dad (a gay man who contracted with a surrogate to bear his child), or a lesbian or gay man who became the legal parent of a child through adoption as a single parent.[16] In most instances, there is no formal legal relationship between the two partners; but even when they are married or registered in a marriage-equivalent registration, it is often advisable to obtain a second-parent or stepparent adoption in case a government agency or court challenges the partnership or marital relationship as a basis for parentage.[17] Which method is more appropriate depends on whether the partnership relationship is recognized; in most states, however, if the second parent is a spouse or domestic partner of the legal parent and the couple is living in a recognition state, then a stepparent adoption procedure rather than a second-parent adoption is more appropriate.

As of 2010, second-parent adoptions were available to same-sex couples in about half of the states in this country and in the District of Columbia.[18] In about fifteen states they are expressly permitted in all courts of the state, and in about thirteen states there are some local courts that will grant such adoptions but without statewide authorization.[19] Six states expressly prohibit such adoptions (Arkansas, Florida, Nebraska, Ohio, Utah, and Wisconsin), and the remaining states have no clear law on this issue at this time.

Given these legal ambiguities and the newness of the procedure, it is crucial that clients work with an attorney who is experienced in the local courts. In some jurisdictions, there are particular judges who are known to be more open to such applications, and certain social service agencies or evaluators may be sympathetic to the couple. Since a social worker's evaluation of the applicant will likely be necessary, the couple will need to be educated on how to handle the application in a sensitive and locally appropriate manner. In addition, given concerns about the validity of these methods in certain states, procedural requirements should be scrupulously adhered to and clients should be advised as to the risks of future validity questions, especially if they relocate to a non-recognition state. In most instances, the child's birth certificate can be amended after the second-parent adoption is approved, but even that can be difficult depending on where the child was born.[20]

Interestingly, most states do not require independent counsel for the biological or legal parent consenting to a second-parent adoption by her partner. In most instances, the lawyer will only represent the adopting partner, and while the first parent will usually be required to participate in a counseling session, typically there is no requirement of separate legal counsel.

Uniform Parentage Act Recognition

It is possible for nonbiological or nonlegal parents to be adjudicated as legal parents based upon the provisions of the UPA in a small number of the states where it has been adopted or where there are equivalent state provisions. For the most part, these cases arise in one of two contexts: a claim of intentional or de facto parentage, most often when there is a dispute after a breakup of the parents' relationship;[21] or where one of the parents (typically a gay man in a surrogacy situation) has a proven genetic connection to the child, usually at the time of the child's birth or shortly beforehand. A parentage decree under the UPA also can be used where one of the lesbian partners is the genetic mother but the other is functioning as a surrogate and thus will be the birth parent. In some instances it is only the genetic parent that is seeking the legal determination of parentage, but in other situations both parents will be seeking an order of parentage.

There are only a few state courts that authorize UPA decrees for intact couples, primarily for genetic dads using surrogates, and there is lingering debate as to whether or not the decrees will be recognized across state lines or by the federal government.[22] It is crucial that your clients work with a local attorney who has experience in this area and that they recognize the risks of nonrecognition in the future. For the most part, the preferred approach is for the decree to be sought only after the child is born and a DNA test can be conducted so that the presumed parental rights of the surrogate mother can be terminated at the same time. A limited number of trial courts in a variety of states have entered prebirth decrees naming one or both of the same-sex partners as legal parents, typically based on the child's genetic connection to one parent and the parental intentions of the other parent, but this is only available in states like California, where the surrogacy contract is clearly valid— and even in those situations a decree has been subject to court challenges in other states, such as what happened in the *Berwick* case, cited above.

Presumed Parentage as Registered Partners or Spouses

Once same-sex couples began to be allowed to register in a marriage-equivalent registration (in 2000) or get married (in 2004), a new legal issue arose: how to apply the statutory presumptions of parentage that are created based upon heterosexual procreation and marriage. The enabling state legislation (or, in some states, appellate court rulings) establishing marriage or its equivalent for same-sex couples typically said simply that all rights and duties of married spouses should be applied to same-sex partners or spouses. However, it is not at all obvious how that can be done in this context given the gendered differences of opposite-sex partners and the heteronormative language of the marital presumption statutes. California's presumed parentage laws, for example, refer to the spouse of the birth mother as a presumed parent "unless the father is impotent or sterile,"[23] and it should be readily apparent that it makes no sense to apply these rules to the partners of lesbian moms (who are never impotent and whose "sterility" really is not relevant to the child's conception) or gay male couples (neither of whom are birth mothers).

Given the awkwardness of this situation and the legal uncertainties of applying these rules to lesbian or gay parents, and especially in light of the potential problems of basing parentage solely on the partnership relationship between the parents, most expert attorneys advise couples to not rely on such a presumption but rather to obtain a stepparent adoption wherever possible, even when they contend that they are presumed parents as domestic partners or spouses.[24] The child will have an established legal relationship with both of its parents in the form of a judgment that should be recognized across state lines under the doctrine of full faith and credit even if the partnership or spousal relationship of the parents is subsequently challenged. Attorneys should recognize that many parents will resist such advice, finding it offensive (and unnecessarily expensive) to adopt a child that they consider already theirs legally, but it would be unwise to assume that the rebuttable presumptions of parentage will be sufficient to prove parentage in a future contested proceeding.

De Facto Parentage / Intentional Parentage

Even in states where the UPA is not in effect and second-parent adoptions are not authorized, there may be legal doctrines that allow non-biological or nonlegal parents to be designated as legal parents based upon their actual conduct as a parent. Some states use the concept of psychological parent, some intentional parentage, and others de facto parent. In most instances, however, this sort of claim only arises if and when a couple breaks up and the biological or legal parent is contesting the parentage or custody of the former partner. It is rare, but not unheard of, for a state to authorize a designation of parentage for an intact couple. Some couples understand the need for legal certainty and may wish to apply for such a determination even while cohabiting; others may be drifting apart or may even have broken up but may have a mutual wish to establish a legal co-parent relationship in the best interest of the child. Again, a local attorney with experience in this area is vital in this situation so that the clients can be effectively counseled as to their legal options.

Private Contractual Agreements

Couples who live in states that do not allow any form of legal recognition for the nonbiological or nonlegal gay or lesbian parent are left with a very limited set of options. The best available option is to engage an attorney or mediator to help them draft a private co-parenting agreement, knowing that it probably will not be legally enforced if challenged (either by an angry ex-lover or a third party, such as a grandparent or government agency) but hoping that it will constrain the behavior of the parties to some degree. In some situations, they also can take some minor legal steps, such as designating the partner as a legal guardian in the event of the death of the legal parent and signing a consent to medical treatment for the child. Many attorneys encourage a co-parenting agreement, despite the questions about its legal validity, in the hope that the agreement-formation process will solidify the intentions of the parties and hold them to their commitments, even in difficult times. However, in the absence of full court-approved legal parentage, there is tremendous risk of a legal problem if the partners' relationship unravels in a nasty way.

There has been a lively debate for decades within the lesbian and gay legal community over the true benefits of a private co-parenting agreement. A strong faction, which historically has been the dominant one within the alternative legal segment of the gay community, has argued that writing up such agreements is a good thing. It rightly points out that the agreement-formation process usually flushes out many of the underlying concerns and doubts, with some couples deciding not to co-parent and others addressing their deeper issues in a positive way and then putting in writing their intentions and plans. This by itself is tremendously useful, even if a conflict arises later on. Furthermore, a written agreement may be admissible as a declaration of the parties' intent and thus could be influential on a court decision even while not legally binding on a court because parentage cannot be established by contract. It may influence a judge's decision, especially in states where there is a doctrine of intentional parentage or where there is contested evidence about the parties' actions during the early years of co-parenting.

Other attorneys have taken a more conservative approach and are reluctant to draft an agreement that as a matter of law is not legally enforceable. They are concerned that it is impossible for a parent to predict how she is going to feel years in the future regarding something so deep and important as her relationship to her child. Some of these lawyers believe that such an agreement not only is unhelpful but also worse, in that it could mislead the nonlegal parent by encouraging false impressions of her rights when none exists. It is better, these lawyers would say, that the nonparent be aware from the outset of her extreme vulnerability should the relationship unravel.

Your approach should be customized based upon the needs and intentions of your client and the state of the law in your jurisdiction, bearing in mind that the law itself can change. In California, for example, the courts had tightly closed the door on implied or de facto parentage for decades; then, in 2005, the California Supreme Court issued a series of rulings on nonbiological same-sex parentage cases. One involved a woman who had donated her eggs to her partner (but had signed a release of parentage as a condition of the implantation by the hospital), one involved an incomplete UPA parentage decree, and the other involved a claim by the county for reimbursement for child welfare payments that it had made to a disabled child (where the nonbiological parent was disclaiming legal liability as a nonparent).[25] These cases totally changed the rules of the parentage game in California, and now the practices of the parents and the written documents will be compelling evidence in disputes over the application of the standards for intentional parentage established by the court in these cases. Thus, even if you are practicing in a state that doesn't provide this avenue of legal parentage now, it may do so in the future.

Donor Insemination Issues

Most state laws (and the UPA) provide that a sperm donor who supplies sperm through a medical service or a sperm bank agency is not a legal parent of the child that results from the donation. While these clear rules will address most donor concerns, difficult problems still can arise in a limited variety of situations: (1) where the mom uses sperm that is directly donated by the man, most typically by a close friend or even a sibling of a partner, such that the statutory rules of nonparentage do not apply; or (2) where the initial donation was done through a medical facility, but, subsequently, the donor becomes involved openly in the child's life in a father-like role. Many state courts have ruled that the legal moms may be estopped from denying future involvement by the donor once they have opened the door to his participation in the child's life, thus justifying some degree of custody or visitation even where the donation process would preclude his being considered a legal parent.[26]

As is true in so many other parentage situations, when working on these matters, you will need to bring to the process an integrated capacity to explain the legal rules to your client, gauge the real needs of the client, and give due consideration to the best interests of the child. Then, with all of these factors in mind, you must try to figure out a legal strategy that is viable, constructive, cognizant of the long-term issues, and not harmful to the children involved. You should also be mindful that while you may have a duty to "zealously advocate" for your client once you have taken on a case, you always have the option of not representing a client or of setting limits as to what strategies you will or will not attempt as part of your representation.[27]

Special Issues for Transgender Parents

Gender transition can challenge the interpersonal parent-child relationship and can also give rise to legal issues. Sometimes the problems arise from conflicts within the partners' relationship, but more often they arise in connection with the difficulty of meeting the rules imposed by regulatory agencies or legal decision makers. Typical problems include the following:

- ambiguities regarding a partner's perceived gender, especially in presentations to adoption agencies or social services agencies reviewing adoption applications;
- disclosures to birth parents in private adoption situations;
- questions about the legality of a partner's legal gender designation, especially for those living in states where gender changes are not

authorized or where the state requirements (usually full genital reassignment surgery) are not consistent with the intentions or past decisions of the transgender person;

- concerns regarding the validity of a marriage (if the partners described themselves as an opposite-sex couple) or domestic partnership registration (if they registered as a same-sex couple) where their legal gender has changed or where a partner's self-identified gender is at odds with his legal gender;
- issues involving medical insurance coverage, resulting from disqualification based upon spousal or partnership rules; and
- conflicts between partners or between the transitioning partner and the child, especially where the court system or social worker "blames" the conflict on the transitioning partner.

You will need to approach these situations with humility and compassion, recognizing that you may not understand the motivations or concerns of the transgender client (or opposing party) and that the legal rules may not fit snugly with the realities of the parties' situation. Whenever possible, it is wise to consult with a transgender law expert or, at a minimum, with someone who has worked with the transgender community either as a social worker or a therapist. Remember, sexual orientation (i.e., the gender of the person who is the object of another's sexual or emotional attraction) is not the same as being transgender, and there are unique and important concerns that are particular to transgender individuals that should be taken into consideration at all times.

D. Adoption Practices and Concerns

Helping a client through a conventional adoption process (as opposed to a second-parent or stepparent adoption) is hardly conventional when your clients are an unmarried couple, either gay or straight. While the legal procedures may be the same as those facing straight, married adopting parents, managing the application and selection process will be quite different. Some couples will feel pressured to marry if that is an available legal option, and others may be inclined to conceal their relationship status and have one partner present himself as a single person. Whether they are working with a private agency or are attempting to do an independent adoption, in most instances it is essential that your clients work with an attorney who has familiarity with the adoption practices in your jurisdiction and who has a history of working successfully with unmarried couples, straight or gay.

It's also important to recognize that the scope of work undertaken by an attorney in an adoption process varies dramatically. Some lawyers will focus solely on the legal technicalities, helping the parties file the necessary court paperwork, but most others provide a much wider range of services, including help in preparing letters sent to prospective birth parents, selecting an appropriate agency and home study consultant, and working to negotiate the terms of the independent adoption process. Many lawyers who specialize in adoption law of this kind also have social workers and other nonlawyers on their staff to help their clients in essential ways that are not typically provided by attorneys.

The Adoption Process

Before diving into a discussion of the specific challenges that unmarried partners face in the adoption process, it is important to have a broad understanding of how the process works overall. Here is the essential framework:

1. Some states have categorical bans on certain types of individuals or couples as adoptive parents, and these generally will apply both in the state of the expectant or birth parent and that of the adoptive parent.[28] Other states have stated preferences that discriminate but do not wholly prohibit certain types of parents from adopting.[29]

2. Adoptions are often facilitated through private agencies, though most of these are open adoptions where the expectant parent has a direct say in the selection of the adoptive parents. The agency plays two roles: It can exercise discretion in the matching of prospective parents and expectant or birth parents, and then it can influence the outcome in how it manages (or directly performs) the home study of the prospective adoptive parent(s). In a closed adoption, the expectant or birth parent will relinquish the child to the agency without restrictions, and then the agency will have exclusive decision-making authority regarding the selection of the adoptive parent.

3. Even when there is an independent adoption (where the adoptive parent directly contacts an expectant or a birth parent or where

a private attorney makes the connection), an agency (either a private adoption agency or a state agency) still must approve the prospective adoption, and there may be discrimination or preferences in this process. In many instances this process is commenced before the child is born; by law, however, the adoption cannot be finalized until after the child is born.

4. There are additional rules that apply for international adoptions. For example, nearly all of the countries that have babies available for adoption prohibit known lesbian or gay male parents from adopting, and the Hague Convention imposes strict rules on agencies that participate in international adoptions.[30] Many countries do not approve of single or unmarried applicants, either— the preference for opposite-sex married couples is very strong in foreign adoptions.

5. The rules for adoption through the foster parenting system work differently and are handled locally by the governmental foster parent agency.

6. In almost every instance, married heterosexual couples will be preferred, and so anyone who does not fit into this preferred category will need special assistance and will need to work with agencies and individuals who are open to and supportive of their adoption efforts.

Adoption by a Single Straight Parent

Rarely will a single straight adult face legal problems attempting to adopt a child based solely on her single status, either from an agency or as an independent adoption, unless she resides in one of the few states that have statutorily imposed preferences for married couples. However, she may face challenges as to her financial or psychological capacities, and she is definitely at a disadvantage when competing with married opposite-sex couples. It is essential that she work with an attorney and/ or an adoption agency that has a history of placing children with single parents and knows how to present such applications in the most positive light.

It is crucial that the prospective parent not misrepresent her relationship status. Being in a romantic relationship does not preclude a single parent from adopting a child. However, if the prospective adoptive

Part of the challenge is that the adoption process can take many months or years, and people's lives change over the duration of the process. Consider the problems that "Ann" is facing: She began the adoption process as a single woman living in Atlanta, using an agency that specialized in helping single women obtain children through an overseas adoption process. Then, after five years of waiting "in line" for a child, she got involved with a man living in Boston. He's a great guy, employed and emotionally secure, but he's in the midst of a nasty divorce and a custody dispute with his estranged wife. Ann wants to move up to Boston to live with her boyfriend, but if she is open about this, it could disqualify her from the "single mom" adoption process. There is no obvious way to resolve this dilemma, and it's not clear what the lawyer's ethical and professional duties are here.

What is most important is that the client be aware of what the rules are and how the interview and site visit process will work. Ultimately, the client will need to make up her own mind as to what to do and how to manage the information flow during the approval process. But the lawyer can help sort out the issues, making sure that the client is aware of her vulnerabilities and the risk of concealing crucial relationship information.

parent is living with a romantic partner, questions will be raised as to who will really be parenting, and the partner should expect to be investigated as part of the home study, as would any roommate sharing the home. If the partner has a personal history that would preclude her from adopting independently, this could be a problem even if the partner is not seeking to be a legal parent.

Adoption by Cohabiting Opposite-Sex Couples

Some states expressly prohibit cohabiting unmarried straight couples from jointly adopting children, including Florida, Michigan, Mississippi, New Hampshire, and Utah.[31] These rules will probably apply both to couples in those states seeking to adopt as well as out-of-state parents seeking to adopt a child born in one of those states.[32] Even outside of those most restrictive states, unmarried couples are likely to face serious obstacles in adopting a child. In a few states (Arizona and Utah), there are statutory preferences that will create obstacles.

But even where there is nothing in law that imposes burdens, social workers or judges may presume a lack of commitment, in ways that may make it even more difficult than applying as a single parent. The partners will be questioned about their decision to remain unmarried, and the answer (whether it's financial, political, or emotional) probably will raise further questions, especially in a competitive situation where there are a limited number of available babies. Some observers perceive this to be a greater problem for expectant or birth parents than for agencies, which may have a more nuanced understanding of the cohabitation situation. In any case, both partners will need to be investigated, and the investigators (either from a state social service agency or, in some states, a state-licensed private agency) will want to know why the couple has remained unmarried, and most expectant or birth parents (to the extent that they are making the decision) will prefer married couples. The partners should be prepared to be told that if they are not willing to get married, their most viable option is to have just one of them seek legal parentage rather than taking on the struggle to become legal co-parents notwithstanding their legally single status.

As with the other nonconventional adoptions, the most valuable service that an attorney can provide to a client is to help her find an experienced adoption attorney who has worked in the local area and is familiar with the special challenges facing unmarried partners.[33] That professional should be able to advise the client as to the available options, especially on the issue of whether they should seek a joint adoption as co-parents as opposed to just having one of the partners become the legal parent and on how to present the situation for someone adopting as a single person who is in a romantic cohabitation relationship.

Adoption by a Lesbian or Gay Single Parent

Lesbians and gay men can adopt in about forty-four states, but in many places they can only do so if they adopt as single parents.[34] International adoption, however, is effectively closed to lesbians and gay men as a result of the stricter enforcement of each country's regulations under the Hague Convention. While in the past lesbians and gay men were able to adopt internationally with a "don't ask, don't tell" approach by the agency, those days have passed for the most part. Your clients may ask you about the possibility of misrepresenting their sexual orientation on an international adoption application; you cannot encourage them to do so, nor should you sugarcoat the very serious risks of lying.

One of the trickier issues is how to legally treat same-sex couples who have entered into a marriage or domestic partnership but are living in a nonrecognition state. They will probably be considered legally single, and thus one of them may be encouraged, or at least allowed, to adopt as a single person. In fact, depending on the attitudes of the agencies or prospective birth parents (and the applicable local law), this approach may be preferable. The most delicate aspect of this arrangement is where the couple intends, either expressly or vaguely, to subsequently seek a second-parent adoption by the partner. Clients should be careful with regard to how they describe the existence and involvement of their partner or the legal status of their relationship (even if not recognized in their state of residence) so that they do not encounter any allegations of misrepresentation at the time of a subsequent second-parent or stepparent adoption.

Joint Adoption by Same-Sex Couples

Same-sex couples are expressly allowed to adopt children in eleven states, and another twenty-two states do not explicitly prohibit or permit same-sex couples to jointly adopt. Up until recently, there was a total ban in Arkansas, Florida, Mississippi, and Utah, and the Florida ban only fell (by an unchallenged appellate court ruling) in 2010. Other states permit adoption by same-sex couples in practice, despite the lack of any statute or judicial ruling. Fortunately, the clear trend is toward increased openness to lesbian and gay men as adoptive parents, given the strong research showing that their children do just as well as those of heterosexual parents.

Sometimes the problem is an outright ban on same-sex couples adopting, but more frequently the problem is an indirect consequence of a ban on any unmarried couple adopting a child since it is only the same-sex couples who are unable to get married to get around the ban. However, even when there is no outright ban, there can be serious problems. As with the other varieties of unconventional families, same-sex couples often face disfavor in competition with straight couples when it comes to expectant and birth parent selection, and they also may face significant discrimination on the part of public and private agencies, both at the time of initial evaluation and when it comes to the home study. Many same-sex couples report being steered toward special needs children or foster adoption programs on the assumption that they will otherwise be rejected by the birth parents or agency staff. Others believe that there is persistent discrimination against same-sex couples in the adoption world, where agency staff favor straight couples when it comes to adopting healthy babies.

One of the most delicate ethical issues in the adoption process, especially for same-sex couples or lesbian or gay male single applicants, is the lawyer's duty to disclose the applicant's sexual orientation or relationship status. There are many social workers who find the outright ban on adoption by lesbians and gay men to be morally offensive, and they are willing to cover up an applicant's sexuality to some degree. In general, this is quite risky with regard to international adoptions (where the agency could face problems with respect to its compliance with the Hague Convention standards), or in communications directly with the expectant or birth parent (where misrepresentation could lead to a revocation of the consent to adoption). There is less risk where the expectant or birth parent is aware of the applicant's situation and it is the agency or home study coordinator that is willing to mask the sexual orientation facts—and may be willing to do so even where the adoptive parent intends to participate in a second-parent adoption with his partner subsequently.

Ironically, as there is greater acceptance of same-sex marriage and more states are recognizing same-sex legal partnerships, you may soon find that couples who live in recognition states but are not married or registered may be disfavored, similar to the treatment of unmarried straight couples.

E. Miscellaneous Parentage Issues

Custody of Children from Prior Relationships

Cohabiting with a new partner can generate conflicts with a co-parent from a prior relationship. Sometimes the problems are financial, where a new partner provides an abundant source of income that the former partner wants to tap (or use as a basis for reducing spousal or child support payments). Most states have laws that allow a modification of support on a discretionary basis where the supported partner is cohabiting with a romantic partner (though many such laws focus only on heterosexual relationships), and you should be prepared to advise your client as to what constitutes cohabitation and how to deal openly with these issues. The problems also can involve scheduling of the child's activities, especially vacations or after-school lessons. In more extreme cases, the new relationship may raise an issue of a long-distance move, which can create terrible pressures on a shared-custody arrangement.

Problems can arise when the new partner or a child of a former or new partner is considered dangerous or harmful to the co-parented child. This may occur when the new relationship is of a different sexual orientation (either a straight spouse in a new gay or lesbian relationship or a formerly lesbian partner in a new relationship with a man), but it can also arise when the new partner is (or is perceived to be) violent, abusive, or an abuser of drugs or alcohol. It can even arise when an adult child from a former relationship (perhaps of the new partner) joins the household and is perceived as a danger to the co-parented child.

In some instances it is best to avoid the legal adjudication process. Child-centered mediation can be effective, and there are excellent resources in every county for this sort of intervention. In other situations a court motion to change the custody arrangements will be necessary to achieve the desired protection.

The Child's Surname

The legal parents will have the right to select the child's surname, and so the determination of who is a legal parent will establish the legal authority over this designation. The choice of surname could, in some instances, be seen as evidence of acceptance of a partner as a parent, especially if the legal indicia of parentage are ambiguous. What is most important is consistency so that the child has the same surname throughout life and will be recognized for all governmental purposes as the same person.

Federal and State Agency Recognition

Formal recognition by state and federal agencies can be of enormous importance for the children of unmarried partners. State law issues involve health insurance coverage, access to scholarships or other educational benefits, social service benefits, or housing or disability benefits. If the child is not the legal child of the applicant adult, the child may be denied the benefits even if the applicant is functioning as a parent. The federal issues mostly involve the children of same-sex parents. If the nonlegal parent has not adopted the child, then the spousal relationship (or its equivalent as a registration) will not suffice to extend the parent-child relationship to the nonbiological parent. This is especially relevant with regard to qualifying for Social Security benefits upon the death or disability of one of the parents. It can also arise with regard to obtaining a passport for the child and especially for meeting immigration requirements. Legal parentage also can have a significant impact on taxation issues, especially with regard to dependency determinations.

Insurance and Other Benefits

In the context of insurance and other benefits, the issue is who is eligible for medical insurance on the policy of the adult. In some situations only a legal child can be included on a parent's policy, whereas in some instances a stepchild will qualify if there is a legal spousal or parental relationship between the parents (even same-sex parents in recognition states). In the absence of any legal relationship between the parents, the child won't qualify for benefits under the nonbiological, nonlegal parent's policy. For those working in companies or for public institutions that provide benefits to the child of an employee (such as reduced tuition for the children of employees), the lack of a legal relationship with the child or between the parents generally will result in a denial of such benefits.

Authorizations for the Nonlegal Cohabiting Partner

In most states a legal parent can designate a nonmarital partner as a medical decision maker for the children even if the partner is not a legal co-parent. Parents should inquire at the child's school to make sure that the proper forms and authorizations have been signed and, in the case of medical authorizations, put on file with the pediatrician. A legal parent can nominate a significant other as a guardian of a child in the event of a disability or death of the legal parent. While not strictly binding on the court, there is a strong policy in favor of deferring to the nomination. However, if there is a surviving legal parent (perhaps from a prior relationship or a casual sexual encounter), there may be a statutory presumption in favor of that legal parent. In these situations, it is strongly advisable for the client to talk directly with the legal parent, whenever possible, to inform that parent of her guardianship preference. A personal request can have an enormous emotional impact on a surviving legal parent and can greatly reduce the risk of a court battle over a guardianship nomination.

Most states also provide for a written authorization for medical decisions or for similar authorizations for school decisions—even the right to pick up a younger child from a school location. Your clients should consult with the authorities of their school and medical facilities to be sure that the forms are familiar to the institution and will be honored by them.

F. SPECIAL CONCERNS FOR ASSISTED REPRODUCTIVE TECHNOLOGY SITUATIONS

Assisted reproductive technology (ART) is defined as any means of causing pregnancy through methods other than sexual intercourse.[35] The growing acceptance of ART has evolved in many ways as part of the changing attitudes towards the family overall. While infertile heterosexual married couples have always relied on ART to create their families, many of those using the new technologies are same-sex couples or single parents. In their book, Charles P. Kindregan and Maureen McBrien list six varieties of same-sex couples who benefit from ART, including lesbians using a sperm donor, surrogate mother, in vitro fertilization (IVF), or even an egg donor or gay men using a surrogate; three varieties of heterosexual partners (whose marital status is irrelevant to the use of ART); and three varieties of single parents.[36] As Kindregan and McBrien point out (and as supported in the many appellate decisions and law review articles and books cited by them), the link between the acceptance of nontraditional families and the use of ART is a direct one: "[O]nce procreation became separated from sex with the advent of alternative methods of human reproduction, nonmarital unions were also seen as an appropriate means of childbearing and ultimately child rearing."[37]

The rise of ART has also led to a rethinking of the legal framework for parent-child relationships. The new technologies allow for parentage that is not connected to biology or even legal adoption, and therefore the issues of de facto parentage need to be resolved. As a result, concepts such as intentionality and involvement in the ART process become increasingly important, and such involvement now can even lead to an imposition of child support obligations.[38] The UPA and similar model codes focus on the particulars of the parents' involvement in the creation of the child rather than the formal legal relationship between the parties involved. Thus, for the most part, the marital status of the participants is no longer determinative of the parent-child relationship, but it is not irrelevant to the process either.

Marital status is particularly relevant when it comes to the presumed parentage of husbands. The existence of this presumption leads to the obvious requirement of the consent of the husband to the wife's use of donor sperm, as otherwise he could end up being liable for supporting a child whose creation was done utterly without his knowledge or consent (and, by definition, without his participation). In those states where same-sex marriage or marriage-equivalent registration is recognized, the same rule should apply to same-sex couples. There remains a significant lack of clarity in this area of the law, compounded by the multistate issue of sperm being obtained in states that don't recognize same-sex partnerships but being used in states that do. An ABA Model Act permits a legal spouse to challenge the parentage of a child conceived by ART and born to the person's legal spouse without the consent of the claimant.[39]

In light of the lack of any presumption of parentage in the absence of a marital or registered domestic partnership relationship, it is reasonable to not require the consent of an unmarried cohabitant to the use of ART in either an opposite-sex or a same-sex relationship. If the cohabiting partner would not have any legal rights over the child and could not be forced to pay any child support, the absence of consent should not be legally relevant, though most certainly it will have social and emotional ramifications on the lives of the couple.

The issue for unmarried partners, therefore, is the reverse, where the nonmarital partner and the mother intend to treat the partner (whether male or female) as a legal parent. The UPA advocates allowing an unmarried man to obtain parentage by his consent to ART with donor sperm, and the UPA also provides that a nonbiological partner (referring in existing versions only to the male partner) can be determined to be a parent if he lives with the mother during the first two years of the child's life and both partners openly hold out the child as their own. A variety of court cases, involving both lesbian and straight couples, have upheld that doctrine.[40]

Marital status also plays an important role if the couple breaks up and there was never a second-parent or stepparent adoption that clearly established the nonbiological parent's rights. A wide range of problems can surface in the context of a dissolution, as follows:

- If the parent-child relationship was never formally established with the gestational mother, there may be a serious dispute as to whether the other parent can meet the standards of the legal rules of their particular state.
- In the absence of a demonstrable biological connection with the other parent (either as an egg donor in a lesbian relationship or through intercourse in a straight relationship), conflicts may arise

as to whether any of the available state law doctrines of presumed, de facto, psychological, or in loco parentis parentage rules apply.

- Even where there is a biological connection to the gestational mother, a delay in confirming legal parentage and/or a failure to act consistently with the parentage claim will bar the claim on grounds of estoppel.
- Disputes can arise as to how to handle conflicts regarding the future use of frozen embryos produced for IVF.

Surrogacy raises many of the same legal questions as other forms of ART, but in uniquely complicated ways. The most troubling set of issues arises when one (or both) of the partners is not biologically or genetically connected to the child, either because a sperm donor was involved or because the surrogate was acting as only a "gestational" surrogate and thus the female parent's egg was not used in producing the child. In these situations, one or more of the participants will not be able

There is no lack of astounding hypotheticals that have arisen in the past few decades in the area of ART and parentage disputes between couples in dissolution. One of my gay male clients got into a nasty dispute with his ex-partner over the use of the frozen embryos. My client had contributed sperm, and the same woman whom the couple had used as a surrogate for its first child donated the egg, and the legal mess was truly mind-boggling. First, because they were not married (or state-registered as domestic partners), their dispute was not within the jurisdiction of the family court. Second, they had signed an agreement to submit any dispute about their home "and any personal property" to binding arbitration, and it wasn't at all clear if frozen embryos could be considered "personal property." Third, the private company continued to send an annual bill each year for the storage of the embryos while the conflict was continuing, and they considered the embryos to be co-owned because both names were listed on the storage contract. And finally, it remained utterly unclear as to which of the partners would be considered a legal father if a child was born from the embryos if this was done over the objections of the other partner.

In the end, the matter was submitted to binding arbitration. The arbitrator ruled that neither partner could use the embryos without the other's consent and that if either partner failed to pay his share of the annual storage fee, he could not object to their destruction if that is what the other partner demanded.

to assert parentage based upon biology or genetics; and if the parents have not obtained a second-parent (or stepparent) adoption decree, the nonbiological parent can face significant legal hurdles. In many states there is no regulation of the surrogacy process, and so the terms of a private contract (extending parentage rights to the nonbiological parent) may not be considered legally valid. The right to claim parentage based upon involvement in the surrogacy process (including helping to pay the expenses) is a valuable first step in presenting such a claim, but the complicated facts of many such situations and the significant cost of pursuing such a claim could make establishing the claim very difficult.

Another issue is that, in some states, unmarried people and partners in a same-sex relationship may simply be barred from access to ART. Refusing to provide ART services to a same-sex couple was ruled unconstitutional in California, but no other states have weighed in on this issue.[41]

Finally, professional responsibility and ethics questions can arise in advising and representing clients involved in ART. At a minimum, an attorney should not advise more than one person involved in the process (i.e., both the sperm donor and the donee or a services provider and a recipient of those services). While in theory the conflicts could be waived by the parties, it is strongly recommended that no such waiver be sought given the serious potential consequences of a future conflict. Lawyers also need to be particularly careful to preserve the confidentiality of client information, and support staff should be thoroughly trained and monitored with regard to this concern. The attorney should make a focused effort to advise his client on the potential consequences and risks of using ART, should be sure to not accept a fee from a nonclient, and should be attentive to the issue of whether any particular agreement is or may in the future be deemed unenforceable.[42]

G. ESTATE PLANNING CONCERNS

Estate Planning for the Parents

There is nothing in the law that prevents anyone from making a bequest to an unrelated person, nor are there any requirements that legal children be provided for in a testamentary plan. Still, protecting inheritance rights in the absence of a legal parent-child relationship requires well-drafted paperwork. This is most typically a problem where the child is a functional stepchild of one of the parents but is denied this legal relationship because the co-parents remain unmarried.

Issues to consider include the following:

- In the absence of a valid will or trust, a child with no legal relationship to the decedent may have no intestacy rights either because there is no factual basis for such a claim or because a statutory deadline for making such a claim of parentage has lapsed.
- Even in the absence of a valid will or trust, there may be rights of intestate succession, but the legal or factual complexity or simply the cost of establishing such rights may be prohibitive.
- Language in a will or trust may be generic with respect to "legal heirs" or children and thus may exclude a functional stepchild who has no legal relationship to the decedent.
- Unresolved family tensions over a relationship deemed illicit (such as an affair by a married man resulting in a child born to his non-marital girlfriend) that surface only upon the death of the father may lead to an inheritance dispute.
- Legal restrictions on survivor benefits, such as might exist for certain pensions or employer-provided insurance programs, can cause problems.

More on estate planning can be found in Chapter 12.

Issues Involving Grandparents' Estates

You should always inquire as to whether the terms of a grandparent's testamentary documents unintentionally exclude a grandchild who may have been treated as a family member but in fact is not a legal descendant of the grandparent whose estate is being administered. If the bequest uses traditional categories (e.g., "the legal descendants of my heirs"), then the grandchild who is living with and being raised by a son or daughter but is not the legal child of that parent will be excluded from any inheritance. The two ways to resolve that issue are either to have the estate documents modified to name specific individuals or to include all minor children living with the heir.

H. NONDISSOLUTION CONFLICTS BETWEEN CO-PARENTS

Couples don't always wait until a dissolution to face conflicts, especially when it comes to dealing with complex parentage issues. Whether you are working with a straight or gay couple, unmarried partners can face serious issues when they are making decisions about children, in ways that play out differently than for married couples. Again, you always want to stay focused on the legal issues since that is your job, but you will want to be attentive to the broader social and emotional issues when managing your legal tasks.

There is quite a bit of disagreement as to the appropriate boundaries of the lawyers' role in helping resolve parentage disputes. Some situations are obviously outside of the legal parameters, such as where there is a fundamental argument about whether to raise children together or where the relationship of the partners is on the rocks. In these situations, clients should be told, gently but firmly, that they are not ready to address the legal tasks but need to work with a professional counselor before taking on the legal process. In other situations, it will be quite evident that the nonlegal problems are secondary and manageable, such as how to present a particular partner's past actions in ways that will not jeopardize the adoption process. But between these two extremes lies a wide swath of blended problems for which an emotionally intelligent attorney or a legally savvy therapist could be helpful. You will want to approach these tasks with an open mind, aware of the other professional resources available to your clients and willing to talk openly with them about who is the most appropriate adviser in their particular situation.

DOCUMENTS FOR THE RULES AND PRACTICES OF PARENTAGE
(FORMS FOUND ON INCLUDED CD)

Form 11: Joint representation retainer provision re: parentage
Form 12: Parentage agreement
Form 13: Nomination of guardian form

NOTES

1. CARMEN MASSEY & RALPH WARNER, SEX, LIVING TOGETHER, AND THE LAW 104 (Nolo Press 1974).
2. 430 U.S. 762 (1977).
3. *See, e.g.*, Parham v. Hughes, 414 U.S. 347 (1979); Gomez v. Perez, 409 U.S. 535 (1978); Picket v. Brown, 362 U.S. 1 (1983).
4. *See, e.g.*, CAL. FAM. CODE § 7602.
5. Interestingly, new issues regarding illegitimacy have arisen in the context of same-sex parenting, where the absence of a legal partnership or spousal

relationship has been raised to defeat claims by a nonbirth mother for de facto or intentional parentage or for joint custody of a child born to the claimant's nonmarital partner.

6. It has been adopted in its entirety in Alabama, California, Colorado, Delaware, Hawaii, Illinois, Kansas, Minnesota, Missouri, Montana, Nevada, New Jersey, New Mexico, North Dakota, Ohio, Rhode Island, Texas, Washington, and Wyoming, and to some degree in numerous other states.

7. UNIF. PARENTAGE ACT § 201.

8. *Id.* § 202.

9. *Id.* § 204.

10. *See, e.g.,* CAL. FAM. CODE § 7612; 32 Cal. Jur. 3d § 272. *In re* Nicholas H., 28 Cal. 4th 56 (2002).

11. UNIF. PARENTAGE ACT § 308.

12. HAYDEN CURRY & DENNIS CLIFFORD, A LEGAL GUIDE FOR LESBIAN AND GAY COUPLES 142 (Nolo Press 1980).

13. *Id.* at 178.

14. APRIL MARTIN, THE LESBIAN AND GAY PARENTING HANDBOOK 156 (Perennial 1993).

15. Boseman v. Jarrell, No. 416PA08–2 (N.C. Dec. 20, 2010).

16. Most (if not all) foreign adoption agencies, as well as many domestic agencies, prohibit adoption by a homosexual parent, and thus it is not always possible for a same-sex couple to openly adopt a child as a couple.

17. While some have argued that a person cannot adopt his own child, the lack of certainty with regard to the presumptions of parentage through registration or same-sex marriage have led to a general understanding of the need for a "confirming" adoption in those situations.

18. *See* A. FREDERICK HERTZ, EMILY DOSKOW & DENIS CLIFFORD, A LEGAL GUIDE FOR LESBIAN & GAY COUPLES 85 (chart) (Nolo Press 15th ed. 2010).

19. *See* Sharon S. v. Superior Court, 31 Cal. 4th 417 (2003).

20. *See, e.g.,* Adar v. Smith, Case No. 09–30036 (5th Cir. 2011) (ruling that a Louisiana birth registrar was not required to amend the birth certificate of the child even after his gay parents had jointly adopted him in New York State).

21. *See In re* Marriage of Buzzanca, 61 Cal. App. 4th 1410 (1998); *In re* Nicolas H., 28 Cal. 4th 56 (2002).

22. A highly contested Texas case resulted in the validation of the prebirth UPA decree from California, even to the extent of adopting its implied findings of shared custody. Berwick v. Wagner, No. 01–09–00834-CV (Tex. App. 2011).

23. CAL. FAM. CODE § 7820 et seq.

24. Unlike a partnership registration or marriage (which is a legal action but not a judgment), an adoption is typically awarded "full faith and credit," even in states that would not otherwise approve of a second-parent adoption for same-sex couples. *See* Miller v. Jenkins, 276 Va. 19, 661 S.E.2d 822 (2008).

25. Elisa B. v. Superior Court, 117 P.3d 660 (Cal. 2005); Kristine H. v. Lisa Ann R., 117 P.3d 690 (Cal. 2005).

26. *In re* Thomas S. v. Robin Y., 618 N.Y.S.2d 356 (N.Y. App. Div. 1994).

27. A group of attorneys practicing in this area has promulgated a set of ethical guidelines for lawyers, arguing that it is not ethical (from a community perspective, rather than a professional responsibility angle) for a lawyer to help a biological parent take advantage of a biased legal system that has prevented his co-parent from obtaining legal recognition. *See* Gay & Lesbian Advocates & Defenders of Boston, Mass., Protecting Families: Standards for Child Custody in Same-Sex Relationships, *available at* http://www.glad.org/rights/publications/c/parents-kids.

28. *Expectant parent* is the proper term for a pregnant woman (and possibly the biological father of the child); once the child is born, the appropriate term is *birth mother* and/or *birth parent(s)*.

29. In 2011 Arizona enacted a law that mandates a preference for married heterosexual parents in adoptions by public and private agencies. A similar law is in place in Utah.

30. Hague Adoption Convention on the Children and the Cooperation in Respect of Inter-Country Adoption (May 19, 1993), www.hcch.net.

31. Arkansas' ban on adoption by unmarried couples (both gay and straight) was struck down by the Arkansas Supreme Court in April 2011. Ark. Dep't of Human Servs. v. Sheila Cole, 2011 Ark. 145 (2011).

32. *See* Interstate Child Placement Compact, which has been enacted in all fifty states and the District of Columbia.

33. The best approach is to select a member of the American Academy of Adoption Attorneys or to work with an agency such as the Independent Adoption Center, which has a strong commitment to serving nontraditional parents.

34. *See* Ill. Inst. for Continuing Legal Educ., Unmarried Partners: Estate Planning and Property and Parental Rights chart, § 4 (2010); *see also* Human Rights Campaign, http://www.hrc.org/issues/parenting/adoption .asp.

35. *See* CHARLES P. KINDREGAN & MAUREEN MCBRIEN, ASSISTED REPRODUCTION TECHNOLOGY: A LAWYER'S GUIDE TO EMERGING LAW & SCIENCE (ABA 2011).

36. *Id.* at 10–11.

37. *Id.* at 15.

38. *See* Elisa B. v. Superior Court, 117 P.3d 660 (2005); E.N.O. v. L.M.M., 711 N.E.2d 886 (Mass. 1999). *But see* T.F. v. B. L., 813 N.E.2d 1244 (Mass. 2004). *See also* Courtney Joslin, *Protecting Children: Marriage, Gender and Assisted Reproduction Technology*, 83 S. CAL. L. REV. 1177 (2010).

39. ABA Model Act Governing Assisted Reproduction Technology §§ 102(21) (definitions) and 605(a) (2008).

40. *In re* Parentage of M.J., 787 N.E.2d 144 (Ill. 2003) (dispute involving heterosexual couple); Paraskevas v. Tunick, 1997 WL 219831 (dispute involving heterosexual couple); *see* Kristine H. v. Lisa Ann R., 117 P.3d 690 (Cal. 2005) (dispute involving a lesbian couple); Elisa B. v. Superior Court, 117 P.3d 660 (Cal. 2005) (dispute involving a lesbian couple).

41. Benitez v. N. Coast Women's Care Med. Group, 44 Cal. 4th 1145 (2008).

42. *See* KINDREGAN & MCBRIEN, *supra* note 35, at 328, ch. 10 (on contractual documents and services).

CHAPTER ELEVEN

ILLNESS AND DISABILITY PLANNING

The major tasks involving illness and disability planning revolve around the simple truth that unmarried partners are legal strangers to each other unless they are state-registered in a marriage-equivalent registration. Because of that legal status, if they want to be involved in any sort of legal decision-making in the event of either partner's illness or disability, they need to do that by means of a valid legal document.

A. MEDICAL DIRECTIVES

As of 1992, every state had established a procedure for setting up a decision-making process for future illness, disability, or incapacity. In some states it is called a living will, which simply provides instructions for doctors and medical institutions regarding the parameters of care. In other places it is labeled a medical power of attorney, advance health-care directive, or medical directive, which designates a person to act on behalf of the one who signs the document and may also provide a summary of the patient's wishes about care.[1] Regardless of its name, the document has two functions: the authorization or designation of a person or medical institution to make medical decisions when the affected person lacks the capacity or competence to do so, and a set of instructions or statement of philosophy about medical care to guide the agent's decision making. In many states there is a statutory form that is widely available; but even where available, that form is not required for the directive to be effective.

The technical requirements for a medical directive are simple. It must be dated and signed by the patient (or in the patient's name by another adult in the patient's presence and direction, if the patient is unable to sign). In most states it must either be witnessed by two disinterested individuals or notarized; you should confirm the particular requirements for your state's rules (and those in any state where your client is likely to reside or be hospitalized) to make sure it will be effective. In most instances, the medical care staff cannot be witnesses, nor can the designated agent or anyone who is entitled to receive anything under the patient's will or trust documents (or by intestate succession). Because there may be some suspicion—or at least heightened concern—whenever a nonmarital relationship is involved, it is a good idea to describe in the document the significance of the relationship of the designated agent in order to explain the basis for the designation. Lastly, there should always be an alternate agent designated. In some states the principal can specify who is *not* to be consulted when medical decisions are to be made, and this option may be especially relevant in certain nonmarital situations.

Because the unmarried partner is generally not the legal next of kin, having a valid and readily available medical directive document is crucial. Unlike the unquestioned deference to a married spouse, the unmarried partner may be shut out of the decision-making process in favor of a legal relative if there is no valid directive. This is true for both opposite-sex and same-sex couples, and it can happen whenever the legal relative (most typically a parent, sibling, or adult child, but possibly a niece or nephew) feels entitled to make the medical decisions. In some parts of this country, the medical facility may be reluctant to follow instructions issued by a nonrelative in the absence of a valid directive, even where the legal relative may be willing to include the unmarried partner in the decision making. You should always assume that the nonmarital partner will be ignored and draft the documents accordingly.

Choosing an attorney-in-fact for medical decisions requires serious thought. If a relationship is new or still informal, naming the partner on a legally binding document could feel awkward or premature or even a betrayal of the family's assumed authority. This is especially the case for older couples if one or both of the partners have adult children who assume that they should play this role. It is essential that your client be practical here: He should think about who is going to be notified if an injury or illness occurs and which relatives are going to assume that they should have legal authority. If your client wants to name someone else, you should help him think through the consequences.

This decision should always be aired with the designated partner as well as any close relatives. In most instances, it is prudent for your client to speak with legal relatives in advance so that they know who has been selected for the role and can hear it directly from the client. Also, you want to be sure that the selected agent has the emotional and intellectual capacity to function in this role, especially during a stressful time. Don't just assume that the partner makes the best agent here; it may be prudent to designate a son or daughter or even a close friend, especially if the partner may not be emotionally equipped to handle these obligations.

Be sure that a substitute agent is properly named in case the designated agent is also ill or incapacitated or has died before the document ever has to be used. This task should be taken seriously as there is always a possibility that the substitute will be called upon. As with the other designations, the substitute agent should be told about her assignment in advance, and the close family members should be told as well.

Clients must seriously consider their advance medical decisions. Many states provide detailed forms describing various medical conditions and posing a variety of treatment options, allowing the signer to state what he would like done under a variety of medical conditions and quality-of-life situations. In most instances the law provides that if the principal declines to set forth any particular philosophical statements, the agent is obligated to make decisions based upon what the principal would have wanted and what is in his best interest. It is always a good idea for the principal to discuss core values and priorities with the designated agent even if nothing is specified in the document. Elderly clients should be aware that most nursing homes require some kind of formal authorization or designation as part of the admittance process, and these forms will generally supersede any documents signed earlier.[2]

Any medical directive also should include an authorization for a hospital visit and a release of medical information (also known as a HIPAA release).[3] Without these provisions in place, it will be very difficult for the medical agent to actually carry out the duties delegated under the medical directive.

If your clients are state-registered in a marriage-equivalent registration, they will have all of the same state-law rights as married couples, which typically include medical decision-making authority and hospital visitation access even in the absence of any express declaration in a medical directive. But even where the spousal-equivalent statutory provisions apply, it is prudent to have your clients sign the appropriate medical directive forms for two reasons. Some institutions still are not always willing to recognize the statutory authority of domestic partners, especially for same-sex couples; and, more importantly, these spousal-equivalent statutory rules probably will not apply if the hospitalization takes place in another state. A newly issued set of federal guidelines now mandates that any hospital receiving Medicare or Medicaid funding accept any valid medical directives or powers of attorney, but your clients will need to have such forms in place; even if they are state-registered, they want to be fully protected under these rules.[4]

Signing the required forms isn't the end of the process; clients also should be realistic about where they store them and what institutions are given copies so that they have ready access to them, especially when traveling. There are companies that will store them electronically so that your clients will have access to them at any time (even if they lose access to their own computer-stored or emailed documents), and some attorneys recommend that couples make extra copies to have with them when they are traveling, just in case. At a minimum, your clients should know where they are, and they should delegate someone such as a friend or relative to have an extra copy that can be faxed to a hospital in an emergency. It's also helpful to post a copy on the refrigerator door as well so that a paramedic coming to the home in an emergency will be alerted.

B. Hospital Visitation

Patients in hospitals generally have the right to determine who is allowed to visit them, and most hospitals will include any person living in the household of a patient on the list of allowed visitors. Implementing these rules has not generally been a problem for married spouses of patients, but it can be a serious problem for unmarried partners, both gay and straight. It can also be a serious problem for state-registered domestic partners or civil union partners, especially if they are living in or visiting nonrecognition states. Most typically the conflict arises when there are legal relatives (i.e., parents, siblings, children, ex-spouses) who dislike or disrespect the unmarried partner, but it can also be a problem if conservative hospital administrators or staff try to impose their moral judgment and exclude unmarried partners.

The best way to avoid these problems is to provide for hospital visitation in the medical directive document and to be sure that the partner has ready access to the document in case of a hospitalization. Under the terms of the new federal rules that apply to all hospitals that accept Medicare funding, any written directive that includes visitation designations must be honored by the medical facility.

C. ACCESS TO MEDICAL RECORDS

A designation of a partner as a medical agent is not particularly useful unless the designated agent has access to the partner's medical records.

Some of the most tragic stories of unmarried couples involve emergency medical decision-making and hospital access. One of the more recent stories comes out of Florida, where a lesbian couple was visiting before boarding a Caribbean cruise. One of the partners suffered a serious stroke, and her partner was not allowed into the emergency room even though the couple had signed valid medical directives. In fact, this was the very case that led to the new federal rules imposing a duty on hospitals to recognize valid medical directives. As more and more straight couples are living together outside of marriage (especially older couples), this same sort of situation is likely to arise more often. End-of-life decision-making raises similar types of decision-making and access issues, especially where a sibling or parent or adult child does not respect the relationship with an unmarried partner.

The newly enacted federal rules provide the following protections:

- Hospitals are required to explain to all patients their right to choose who may visit them during their inpatient stay, regardless of whether the visitor is a family member, a spouse, a domestic partner (including a same-sex domestic partner), or other type of visitor, as well as their right to withdraw such consent to visitation at any time.
- Hospitals must have written policies and procedures detailing patients' visitation rights, as well as the circumstances under which the hospitals may restrict patient access to visitors based on reasonable clinical needs.
- Hospitals must make sure that all visitors chosen by the patient must be able to enjoy "full and equal" visitation privileges consistent with the wishes of the patient.[5]

In the past medical directives always included authorization of access to records, and they still should, but it is not enough anymore. The Health Insurance Portability and Accountability Act of 1996 (HIPAA)[6] provides that health-care providers can face criminal and monetary penalties if they violate medical record rules, which were designed in part to protect the privacy of the patient. Concern over the strictness of these rules has resulted in greater caution on the part of the health-care provider.

The HIPAA rules provide that a designated health-care agent (under a valid medical directive) should be recognized as a "personal representative" for purposes of medical record access, as would a family member or a person identified as such by the patient. However, just to be certain that no problems arise, you should always include specific provisions covering these rights in the authorization document. The best practice is to draft a specific HIPAA-compliant release as a separate document so that the medical care provider can review a simple single-purpose document that meets immediate legal needs. As a further protection, you should also include a medical record release in any medical directive or power of attorney.

D. Financial and Asset Powers of Attorney

Another document that most unmarried partners should consider signing is a financial power of attorney. For many unmarried partners, the standard "durable power of attorney regarding all financial affairs" is most appropriate. With this document, the designated attorney-in-fact is given authority over all of the principal's financial affairs, commencing from the day it is signed and continuing even after a disability of the principal. But this is not always the most appropriate approach. In many instances these sorts of powers are only needed when one partner is unable to exercise management over his affairs, and in that situation a springing power of attorney (which only takes effect upon the principal's incapacity) makes more sense. But except for time-limited situations (such as the sale of property when the principal is out of town), it is generally appropriate for all powers of attorney to be durable so that they remain in effect even after the principal partner is disabled or incapacitated. You will want to evaluate the specific requirements of your client's needs in light of the particular options available under the laws of your state.

If the power of attorney is only supposed to spring into effect under certain conditions, then the document will need to specify how those conditions are to be determined. Some drafters provide that a certification by a physician (or two physicians) is required, though that can be cumbersome if there is an urgent need for the attorney-in-fact to use the document. Such conditions also mean that the agent will need to have access to the principal's medical records in order to obtain the required certification. For these reasons, it usually makes more sense for the power to be immediately effective, which does not in any way preclude the principal from making his own decisions while still competent.

It is important that you interview your clients closely about their financial affairs and their personal relationship to be sure that the standard power of attorney forms make sense for them. If any decisions about real estate will need to be made, the document typically has to specifically designate the property in question; and because it will have to be recorded along with the sale or purchase (or refinance) documents, it will need to be notarized, whereas powers of attorney generally do not require such formalization. Some financial institutions or title companies will insist on using their own particular forms, so it is important that you or your clients speak with a representative of his financial institution when filling out the requisite forms.

Helping clients sign these documents is not something to be taken lightly. Every lawyer practicing in this area has heard stories of horrible abuse, and your clients should understand that they are effectively giving their partner a blank check—and that this is a power that can be abused. Be sure that you are meeting only with the principal and not with the agent in the room, and be attentive to any indications of undue influence or lack of capacity. There is a fine line between being sensitive to abuse and not respecting the relationship, especially if your client is lesbian or gay or is in an unconventional relationship, so be very cautious when first expressing any doubts or concerns about the appropriateness of the requested delegation.

Your clients also need to understand that it's not very easy to cancel a power of attorney, short of notifying all of the financial institutions that might be asked to honor it. Pay attention to any feelings of doubt that your client expresses. Most of your clients rarely need these documents in advance as they are only really necessary in a medical emergency. For most other clients (especially those in new relationships), it may be better to suggest that they refrain from signing any broad authorizations in advance. They can always come back to you when a particular situation arises (such as a home purchase when one partner is out of town). You should point out that in the absence of a power of attorney, they could be faced with a complicated conservatorship application if one of them suddenly becomes disabled. However, such a task may be preferable to allowing a "loved one" to abscond with one's life savings.

E. CONSERVATORSHIPS

A power of attorney is very useful for an immediate business situation, such as when a partner is temporarily incapacitated or out of the country when an important financial decision needs to be made. It also can work very well in connection with a specific transaction, such as the sale of a property, when documents need to be signed in person and the time deadlines are tight. In the opinion of most practitioners, however, powers of attorney are not the best solution when it comes to dealing with long-term disability or incompetence. In those situations, it is best to use a conservatorship appointment or, even better, a trust appointment.

Conservatorships generally come in two forms: "of the person" or "of the estate." Some people need help in both realms, others just in one. A personal conservatorship covers the decision-making tasks of the daily life of the conservatee in connection with housing and access to personal care, food, and clothing. A financial (estate) conservatorship is limited to the handling of financial and business affairs and is more appropriate for someone who is able to handle the simple tasks of daily life but has troubles managing the more complicated demands of financial affairs. There is no prohibition on the same person serving in both capacities. However, some division of conservator labor may be appropriate, and, if so, that will affect the selection of the conservator. In many situations a financial professional is best for the financial conservatorship, whereas a family member can easily handle the personal issues.

Each state has its own rules for appointment of a conservator, but every state provides that a judge must make the appointment; it is not something that can be done solely by a private agreement or attorney-drafted documentation. In most states there are statutory preferences for appointment of a conservator, and an unmarried partner generally is not going to be high on that list, if mentioned at all. A state-registered partner in a marriage-equivalent registration will have the same priority for appointment as a married spouse, but only if the partners are living in a jurisdiction that recognizes that registration as equivalent to marriage. Thus, for every other variety of partnership, a nomination of conservator is what is needed to avoid having the court appoint a more distant (but legal) relative. In most states there will be a strong preference for the person who was nominated by the principal as long as it is clear that the nominator was competent at the time of the nomination and there was no undue influence. In most states the nomination can either be included in the medical directive (for the personal conservatorship) and in the financial power of attorney (for the financial conservatorship), or they both can be set forth in a separate combined conservatorship nomination document.

Filing a conservatorship petition is not a simple court procedure, especially if there are legal next of kin who may object to the appointment of an unmarried partner as the conservator. While judges and family members are ordinarily quite accepting of a married spouse functioning in this way, concerns about undue influence or outright self-interest may arise when the nonmarital relationship is not honored as being equivalent to a marriage. Most often this occurs when parents or siblings don't accept the partner of their lesbian or gay family member, or when an older parent has a younger unmarried partner or a former caregiver has become a romantic partner and children from a prior relationship are suspicious of the new partnership. If there is any likelihood of such a challenge, an experienced attorney who is respected in the local probate court should be retained to prepare and present the conservatorship application. This is especially true where, as is the case in most states, a private evaluation of the nominated conservator by a court investigator is required prior to any conservatorship hearing.

Once appointed, a conservator will have all the legal rights of the principal, including financial decision making and property decisions and any medical care decisions. A conservator must be prepared to post a significant bond and will be required to submit formal reports on a regular basis to the local probate court.

F. TRUST DESIGNATIONS

Though significant, a conservatorship nomination is not always honored, and the appointment process requires public notice, so the court requirements may invite or, at a minimum, facilitate a family challenge to an unmarried partner's nomination. For this reason, and because of its overall simplicity, many estate planning practitioners strongly recommend the use of a trust appointment rather than a conservatorship nomination. With this approach, the same revocable trust document that is used to make testamentary bequests that will be effective upon death can be used to appoint a substitute trustee to take over the principal's financial affairs while the principal is still alive in the event that he becomes incapacitated or incompetent.

As with the conservatorship appointments, you need to be careful in setting up these arrangements, especially if any challenges from legal family members are likely to arise. Most trust documents require certification by two physicians before the partner takes over as substitute trustee, but rarely is any court action required unless there is a challenge to the trustee's authority.

If challenges to the appointment are anticipated, it may be prudent to name the partner as a co-trustee from the outset to demonstrate to everyone concerned that the partner is a trusted family member. This will also allow the co-trustee to demonstrate reliability while the trustor is still active and involved. Financial institutions and family members can thus learn to trust the decisions of the partner, which should reduce the level of suspicion and distrust if and when the trustor becomes incapacitated and will thus enable the co-trustee to do a better job.

In most states there is no formal process of certification of a substitute trustee when the trustor becomes incapacitated. Rather, the financial institution will review the trust documents and the physician certification if required. Unlike the process with powers of attorney, however, financial institutions generally don't have their own forms of trust documents, so typically they aren't likely to raise a fuss over the form of the documents. If real estate is involved, it always makes sense to have the trust document notarized so that it can be recorded as part of a real estate transaction.

One final point about trusts: Whenever there is any risk of nonrecognition of the relationship or allegations of undue influence either by a financial institution or a relative, it is crucial that the trust be drafted by an attorney and the signing be done under the attorney's supervision. This will help ensure that the technical requirements are met, and perhaps more significantly, it will give more credibility to the designation process if anyone challenges the competency of the principal who signed the documents.

While it's not really a legal issue, you should also be talking with your clients about the option of purchasing long-term care insurance. Some companies may be willing to offer a domestic partnership discount to cohabitants who each buy a policy at the same time, regardless of their legal relationship status. If the discount is sufficiently large, it may make sense for the younger partner to buy a policy earlier than she otherwise would since the discount might cover a few years' worth of premiums. Chances are the discount will remain in effect even if the relationship ends since each partner owns her individual policy. If the premiums are significantly different (because of age or health conditions), the couple will have to decide whether or not to share the cost of the premiums as part of its overall family budget planning.

G. Undue Influence and the Role of Extended Family Members

As the number of unmarried partners continues to increase, especially in older populations, the risk of financial abuse or, of equal impact, concerns about such abuse will likewise continue to rise. In some instances there may be blatant financial or elder abuse, such as when a caregiver obtains access to a bank account without the authorization of the account owner. In other situations there may not be any abuse at all, such as where there is a loving relationship between the partners and a mentally competent principal knowingly delegates authority to a loved one. The reality may also lie somewhere in between these extremes, which is why it can be so difficult to sort through the allegations of financial abuse.

Unconventional relationships can lead to unconventional problems and unexpected conflicts, and the lawyer working with unmarried couples needs to be attuned to the complex dynamics that may be at play. Be mindful of when you might need to try to persuade your client to take the difficult step of saying no to an intimate partner in order to avoid being a victim of financial abuse. And you should be savvy when it comes to meeting with or talking to the relatives and friends of your client, who may have negative opinions about what is going on and what to do about it, oftentimes without any legal justification for their fears.

Consider, for example, the following situations, all of which have come up in my practice:

- "Bill" is an older gay man who has been living with a much
  younger man named "Bobby" for the past few years. They have a
  genuinely close relationship, but Bobby has serious money problems and tends to drink too much, and Bill is a bit worried about
  Bobby leaving him. Over the years Bill has given Bobby quite
  a bit of money and has given him a credit card that Bill pays off
  monthly. Bobby has come to you to ask that you prepare a power
  of attorney for Bill designating Bobby as the attorney-in-fact for
  Bill, telling you that Bill will sign it at home with a notary whom
  Bobby will bring to the house. Quite rightly you have some serious
  concerns about whether or not this is an appropriate arrangement,
  from a legal perspective.
- Imagine that it's the same sort of situation as with Bobby and Bill,
  except that this time it is Bill's niece who has come to you, with
  Bill in tow, asking that you take legal action to cancel the power of
  attorney in favor of Bobby that Bill signed a year ago. The niece
  is convinced that Bobby is stealing from Bill, and she also wants
  you to report this suspicion to Bill's bank and to Adult Protective
  Services. Bill seems to share his niece's concerns, but, at the same
  time, he is worried about hurting Bobby and seems especially anxious about being abandoned by him.
- "Sandra" and "Anthony" have been living together for nearly a
  decade, and Anthony has been the primary source of financial support for both of them. They have come to you to write up their
  wills and powers of attorney, and each of them wants to designate
  the other one as attorney-in-fact for all purposes. Anthony tells
  you that his daughter is very suspicious of Sandra and doesn't
  want her to have any decision-making authority, especially since
  Anthony's former wife only recently passed away and his daughter
  is upset about Anthony's relationship even though it's been going
  on for nine years. Anthony wants to be sure that his daughter can't
  do anything to displace Sandra as the decision maker for him.
- "Steve" and "Arnie" are brothers in their mid-forties, and their
  mom is a lesbian with a longtime unmarried/unregistered partner.
  In principle, the brothers respect their mother's relationship, but
  they don't agree with many of the decisions that her partner has
  been making since their mom's health started declining, and they
  are especially concerned that she is depleting their mother's finan-

cial resources on unnecessary at-home care. They are their mother's only heirs, and they are concerned that her partner doesn't really care if all of her mother's funds are spent before she dies. They are interested in seeking to be nominated as their mom's conservator, over the objections of her unmarried partner.

There are no simple answers for any of these situations, but here are a few guidelines that will help you minimize the likelihood of making matters worse:

- Make sure that you are clear on who your client is, and always speak directly to that client when decisions are made. If there is any question about undue influence, be careful that no one else is in the room when key decisions are being made, and confirm in writing the details of your professional relationship with your client.
- If you sense that your client is uncomfortable making hard decisions, especially where an emotional partner is involved, consider referring your client to a counselor or therapist to help him sort through the personal dynamics. Stay in touch with your client as the counseling process evolves so that you can figure out the best time for you to commence the legal tasks.
- If a friend or partner is raising legitimate concerns about possible challenges or if you are concerned that a family member will create problems even when none is warranted, you may want to set up a meeting between your client and that the potentially troublesome family member(s) to discuss the situation. In some instances you may want to refer them all to a family mediator, either a lawyer or therapist mediator, to help address some of the underlying tensions.
- Don't ignore any signs of undue influence or elder abuse. The last thing you want to do is facilitate something that is improper or fail to protect a client from an abusive situation. If you begin to have concerns, try to voice them openly with your client before you call in any outsiders or public agencies in order to avoid triggering adverse consequences prematurely.
- Give some thought to proposing a mediation of an underlying dispute, either with a lawyer or a therapist mediator, before any

legal challenges are commenced. Remind your client that showing up at a mediation does not mean that anyone is giving up his legal rights. Explain how mediation can be very useful in airing out the conflicts and reaching nonlegalistic solutions that are in everyone's best interest.

- Document, document, document! Keep good notes of your conversations, and be sure to follow up with written advice to your client when you are concerned about his condition. There are two reasons for doing this: first, it will reduce the risk of you being wrongly blamed for a subsequent problem; and second, and even more importantly, it will raise your client's awareness of a possible problem. This is one area where email is *not* sufficient—a real letter in a paper envelope is needed to be sure that your client is taking the problem seriously.

Documents for Illness and Disability Planning (Forms Found on Included CD)

Form 14: Medical directive with hospital visitation and HIPAA release provisions
Form 15: Financial power of attorney form

NOTES

1. *See, e.g.,* Health Care Decisions Law, Cal. Prob. Code §§ 4600–06.
2. Some states also have implemented rules for a more focused set of instructions, called Physician Orders for Life-Sustaining Treatment (POLST). These documents are signed by the patient but also by his doctor, making them "doctor's orders" that are then binding upon healthcare workers and emergency responders, thus increasing the likelihood that they will be followed in an emergency situation.
3. 42 U.S.C. § 1320d.
4. 42 C.F.R. §§ 482.13(h), 485(f).
5. Changes to the Hospital and Critical Access Hospital Conditions of Participation to Ensure Visitation Rights for All Patients (CMS-3228-F).
6. 42 U.S.C. § 1320d.

CHAPTER TWELVE

ESTATE PLANNING CONCERNS AND PRACTICES

Estate planners working with unmarried partners should always be mindful of three core doctrines. First, unmarried partners, unless they are state-registered in a marriage-equivalent registration and live in a recognition state, are legal strangers, and therefore none of the rules of intestate succession will apply. Second, because they aren't married spouses, the rules requiring a "forced share" of estates will not apply to them. And third, state and federal spousal estate tax exemptions don't apply, and until DOMA is repealed or invalidated, the federal exemption won't apply to same-sex married couples.

These three principles are what distinguish nonmarital estate planning from conventional estate planning—which is why your clients should always be working with an attorney who has the requisite knowledge and experience in this specialized field.

A. WILL-DRAFTING ISSUES

The single most important piece of estate planning advice for unmarried partners is this: Have a will in place. You should repeatedly tell your clients to get a simple will in place as soon as possible, even if they use a store-bought form or an online source. The beneficiary designations don't have to be perfect, and they don't have to resolve every one of their deep uncertainties about who should inherit any particular piece of artwork. The purpose is to have a stopgap document in place in case of an unforeseen calamity. Your unmarried clients need to accept the fact that unless they get *something* in place, they will have failed to protect each other from potentially losing everything.

Motivating your clients to sign a simple will has additional indirect benefits as well. If you are able to motivate your clients to draft and sign a simple will, even without a lawyer's assistance, it actually inspires them to tackle the more comprehensive estate planning tasks. It is as if they've overcome their initial resistance to thinking about their inevitable demise and can see where their first version needs refinement. Most likely, they will have also confronted some of their big-picture questions about their relationships and may even have begun to think about tax issues, all of which may motivate them to seek legal counsel. And along the way, they also will become better prepared to talk about the detailed estate planning issues.

You should take a look at the statutory will forms available in your particular state, as well as commercially available forms that are most frequently used by your clients, so that you are able to assist them if asked. The main problem with most such documents is that they presume that the testator is married, so you will need to be prepared to explain to your clients how to modify the standard documents accordingly. You also will need to explain the relevant rules to state-registered domestic partners or civil union partners, whether gay or straight, since the marital rules might apply to them under certain features of state law. You will also want to be ready to point out to your unmarried clients that they must be particularly careful to meet the procedural requirements for signing their will if they anticipate any protests or claims by disinherited legal relatives.

While every will-drafting assignment presents its own challenges, these are the key points to be attentive to when drafting a will for an unmarried partner:

- No one can create an estate plan until he knows what he does and does not own, and oftentimes this is a more complicated issue for unmarried couples than for married folks. Bear in mind that many couples have at least a vague sense of what is their separate property and what assets they consider to be shared. For some unmarried partners, this will be an easy task, especially if what's "in their name" matches what they consider to be theirs. Unless your client is state-registered and lives in a state-registered partnership that imposes marital law property rules on him, there won't be any marital property or community property presumptions that apply to his assets.

Ironically, it's because title will generally rule the day that the will-drafting process can be so delicate. The rules of most states that allow claims to be based upon oral or implied agreements will force your clients to face up to any discrepancies between what they think is theirs and what is really theirs, legally speaking. If either partner contends that he has an ownership interest in an asset titled in the other partner's name, he will have to address those discrepancies as part of the estate-planning process. Be prepared to learn that you may be the first person who has raised these issues with the partners.

- An estate plan does not allocate assets should the relationship end, and so a bequest to a partner doesn't mean that the partner gets that asset in the event of a dissolution. Odd as it sounds, this may come as surprising and disturbing news to your clients. Complicating things even further, *how* an asset is characterized can be evidence in a dissolution dispute. Having one partner state in a will that he owns no real estate can end up being cited as an admission that could be used against him if he should later try to claim that he had an equitable ownership interest in his partner's house.

- Because there is no marital estate tax deduction, every estate plan must provide a formula for how the inheritance taxes are going to be paid. High net-worth clients should always consider probate-avoidance tactics on transfers to their partners, if at all possible.

- You should never assume that unmarried partners want to leave everything to each other. One or both of them may have children from a prior relationship or even a prior partner or spouse whom they want to help out, and they may have charitable or other purposes that prevail over their partner's needs. For many couples, being unmarried means being open to think freely about making such bequests; and as a lawyer helping unmarried partners, you also should be open to thinking flexibly as well.

- For many unmarried partners, dealing with estate planning will raise lots of deeper issues about the nature of their relationship,

especially if their unmarried status is an unspoken reflection of
some underlying commitment issues for one or both partners.
Don't be surprised if the drafting and signing process gets delayed
or seems unreasonably complicated even when the legal and financial issues are fairly simple.

• It is entirely normal for unmarried partners to have different contingent beneficiaries. They may not have children that they raised
together, and they may have had many years of close bonds with
other friends or partners before they got together as a couple.
They may be less connected to each other's extended family, and
so they each may want to provide something for their own relatives
in case their partner predeceases them.

• Decisions about a jointly occupied house can be particularly
complicated regardless of how it's titled, especially if one of the
partners owned it before the partners entered into their current
relationship. Using joint tenancy as a simplified estate planning
method usually is not a wise idea, especially because joint tenancy
means a present co-ownership, which is binding upon dissolution.
Moreover, in most states either owner can unilaterally sever the
joint tenancy and thus defeat the stated testamentary intentions.
A few states allow property to be titled as joint tenancy for testat-
mentary purposes only, which avoids any claim that a present gift
of 50 percent was made when one owner adds a partner as a joint
tenant.

• In most states a will can be used to create a life estate with a
remainder beneficiary, and this can sometimes work fine for a
shared home, even when owned solely by the testator. The problem
of using a will for this arrangement is that you can't specify any of
the financial conditions or management arrangements for the life
estate as you can do in a living trust.

• Whenever either partner's family doesn't respect a same-sex
marriage-like partnership, be extra attentive to the possibility of a will challenge. Take special care to ensure that all of the
technical requirements for signing the will are being honored. In
extreme situations, the partners should each use different estate
planners, with neither partner involved in any way in the hiring of
the other's planner or the conveying of information to the other's

lawyer. While it is entirely proper for a lawyer to draft both partners' plans with an appropriate conflict of interest waiver, doing so
could be used against a partner in a subsequent will challenge. Presumptions about undue influence should be considered, especially
for older partners or those in newly formed relationships.

- If you have clients whose estate plans may be challenged, educate
  them about the public nature of the probate process and urge them
  to set up a living trust to avoid this. While it is true that trusts can
  be challenged, it is much more difficult for an angry relative to
  launch a challenge in the absence of a probate process.

- Take special care in addressing issues involving children who are
  not the legal children of one of the partners. In general, this means
  guardianship nominations and bequests. Nominations of guardianship should take into account the concerns of the other legal
  parent, if there is one.

- Because the partners are not married spouses, none of the statutory protections for spouses will apply, such as a homestead right
  of occupancy. These will have to be created by the language of the
  will.

- Choosing an executor is never a simple matter, and it's especially
  tricky in the case of an unmarried partnership. If there is likely
  to be dissension between heirs and especially if there are children
  from a prior relationship, it may be prudent to name someone
  other than the partner as an executor. That way there should be a
  greater sense of trust and neutrality, and the chances of a will contest may be less likely.

- Clients should be reminded that under the law in most states,
  bequests to married spouses are automatically revoked upon dissolution, but this does not apply for unmarried partners unless they
  are state-registered in a marriage-equivalent registration. This rule
  can come into play with regard to a will that provides for a former
  partner and also can be relevant with regard to a subsequent dissolution from a current partner.

- Beneficiary designations on retirement and pension plans generally
  supersede will and trust bequests, so it is essential that your client
  review and possibly revise their designations, to be sure they are
  consistent with their current intentions.

Joint representation is not improper for both partners in a nonmarital relationship as long as there are proper conflict waivers. Typically, estate planners require a full disclosure between partners as a condition for working for both partners because they don't want to—and ethically shouldn't—keep secrets from one or both clients. Thus, if one client doesn't want the other to know the identity of a contingent beneficiary or doesn't want to disclose any asset, this will make it impractical for the same attorney to advise both parties.

The stickiest consequence of joint representation arises if the couple breaks up or has major conflicts. One of the partners may want to keep changes in an estate plan confidential, especially if he hasn't fully disclosed a new romantic interest to his partner, but he can't ask a joint attorney to help him out behind the back of the attorney's other client.

Notwithstanding these risks, most attorneys are fine working for both partners, and most couples prefer it that way. Just be certain to handle the conflicts of interest issues thoroughly, and clearly document in full your clients' consent to the joint representation. Also, point out that the manner in which the assets are characterized in a will can be used as evidence in a dissolution challenge, with particular mention of anything of special significance, such as the titling of a house.

B. Particular Issues for Trusts

A revocable living trust can be enormously useful for anyone with a complicated life—and by definition that includes most unmarried partners. It enables the testator to make a bequest that is time-limited in nature (equivalent to a life estate), with the residual benefit passing to someone else, outside of the control of the life estate owner. This can work well for those who have children from a prior relationship whom they want to help in the long term without neglecting the shorter-term needs of a surviving partner. A living trust avoids the public probate process and thus is less likely to be challenged by resentful relatives. It allows for detailed provisions for conservatorship-like protections while the trustor is still alive, and it can be administered by a successor trustee who knows how best to manage the assets.

Ironically, the sheer complexity of a trust (if it is prepared by an attorney) makes it less vulnerable to challenge since it's more likely to have been crafted by a lawyer who spent significant time with the testator and thus can testify as to her competence. For similar reasons, a trust that is already funded and is operating during the lifetime of the trustor has a sturdiness that can discourage most outsider challenges. And perhaps most important to clients, it allows for the use of complex tax-avoidance strategies that may be needed in light of the lack of a marital exemption from estate taxes.

Estate planners often draft a joint trust for a married couple, and there is nothing legally wrong with doing so for an unmarried couple. However, most lawyers who specialize in this area discourage the use of joint trusts for several reasons. First, the partners may be less likely to have legally shared assets because they are not subject to marital law and thus are less likely to have any community property, co-owned property, or marital income or assets. Second, a fairly high percentage of unmarried partners formed their relationship later in life, so they are each more likely to have acquired separately owned assets that they prefer to keep separated. Third, they may have very distinct estate planning goals, especially if either or both of them have children from a prior relationship. Fourth, breakups happen frequently, and a breakup will require a complete redoing of their estate plans as they each will have to create new trusts rather than simply modifying the bequest designations of their separate trusts.

On top of all of these practical reasons, neither same-sex nor opposite sex unmarried couples are protected by the marital estate and gift tax exemptions. Forming a joint trust could create an implication of a present gifting of significant assets, which would not be a good thing. Still, some couples feel very strongly about wanting a joint trust as it reinforces their own sense of being a united team. If that is what your clients want, and as long as they understand the downsides of a joint trust, in some instances it is fine. It just should not be embraced as the default plan for every unmarried couple, and your clients should be warned of the problems inherent in such an approach.

Most trust-drafting issues are similar to those that arise in the drafting of a will; it's just that they are handled in a different context and with greater flexibility than in a will-drafting situation. Here is a list of the crucial components to consider:

- The designation of the successor trustee is of vital importance and should take into account the present needs of the trustor (which may include having a partner be a co-trustee from the outset); the scope of the tasks being assigned to the trustee; the likely age and possible limitations (both physical and mental) of the surviving partner upon the death of the trustor; and the possible suspicion and resentment of the surviving partner's assertions of authority, especially if there are children from a prior relationship who may feel shut out by the choice of the partner as the successor trustee.

- As important as estate tax considerations are (see the following section), they should not be the sole determinant of how the estate plan is structured, especially in light of the very high gift and estate tax exemptions at the present time. You should think practically about the needs of the surviving partner and other potential heirs and also think about the charitable intentions of each partner. You also need to remember that tax laws change, and the discriminatory tax treatment of same-sex partners and spouses is especially subject to change. As much as you would hope that clients will return to modify their estate plan as the tax laws are revised, you cannot count on this happening.

- The absence of most marital survivor benefits (Social Security, traditional pensions, automatic IRA rollover provisions) mandates a creative rethinking about how retirement assets should be handled. The lack of spousal survivor benefits not only affects the financial abundance (or lack thereof) for the surviving spouse but also will affect the tax treatment of any bequest of such assets.

- Using separate trusts can be tricky when partners co-own real property, but it is not impossible. In this case you must be especially careful to sync their estate plans so they don't end up with incompatible arrangements. For example, if they have agreed that one partner is entitled to reimbursement of a down payment or similar capital contribution, both trusts must say so. Just as with your married clients, think through the ramifications of a death of either partner and be mindful of what is likely to happen if the couple breaks up so you don't end up with a co-ownership arrangement that works for death but not dissolution.

- Counsel your clients to be realistic about the financial needs of each partner in the event of an early demise of one of them, especially because the surviving partner may remarry or find a new partner. While this is also a problem that can arise for married partners, your unmarried client's feelings can be quite different if the assets were accumulated prior to the relationship or, at a minimum, were not considered joint or marital assets even during the relationship. One aspect of being unmarried is that many such partners may have a reduced sense of obligation for the long-term care of a partner, and there may be a greater sense of individual ownership of certain financial assets.

- Whenever a trust allows for discretion in the amount to be distributed to a survivor, whether it's a surviving partner or an adult child, there can be disagreements or resentments among the beneficiaries and the successor trustee. You will want to be sure that the trustee can handle these demanding pressures and that the procedures and standards for payouts are realistic and fair. The duties and protocols can be extra sticky if a partner is also going to be the successor trustee of assets designated for the deceased partner's children from a prior relationship.

- As with any trust planning, be sure to have your clients execute a pour-over will to capture any assets that are not transferred into the trust, and, of course, monitor your clients' diligence in transferring into the trust.

C. EFFECTIVE TAX STRATEGIES FOR UNMARRIED PARTNERS

The limit on federal estate tax exemptions, both for inter vivos gifts and for bequests, has vaulted up to $5 million, so most of your clients won't be particularly worried about federal inheritance taxes. But some states have much lower inheritance tax limits, and, given the state of our economy, the federal limits may well come down in the future. And for those of you with extremely high net-worth clients, even the present limits may seem too low. For all of these reasons, it remains vital that every estate planner working with unmarried partners be mindful of the absence of an unlimited marital exemption and aware of the repertoire of possible estate tax reduction strategies.

Every couple presents its own particular challenges, and part of the distinction that marks a truly skillful estate planner for unmarried partners is an ability to discern which strategies are truly appropriate for the couple who is sitting in your office. Some plans get wildly and unnecessarily overcomplicated without really helping the clients, whereas others make terrific tax sense but are not a good fit emotionally.

Below are descriptions of the most frequently used tax-avoidance strategies for unmarried couples in the arena of estate planning: early gifting of low-value assets, savings plans to equalize estates, transferring portions of a jointly owned asset, gift tax exemption, bypass trusts, charitable trusts, life insurance policies, life insurance trusts, grantor retained trusts, and community property asset accumulation.

Early Gifting of Low-Value Assets

Having a higher-asset partner give the other partner funds for a down payment on a condominium or commercial property that is titled in the partner's name can avoid significant estate taxes. The property should pay for itself each month from rental income, and the appreciated value (and the paydown of the mortgage principal) will be an asset of the recipient, not the donor. A gift tax return will have to be filed for the amount of the down payment, or the down payment can be partially structured as a loan that is forgiven each year in amounts that are below the reporting threshold. This same approach can be taken for the transfer of low-valued stock or personal property. The motto here is "give early and give low-value assets." There is one real downside to this strategy, of course: The gift cannot be taken back if the couple breaks up. Many couples are uncomfortable with this approach, either because it feels like they are planning for support in the event of their death or a breakup or because of a perception that the receiving partner is not qualified to manage a complex asset such as real estate.

Savings Plans to Equalize Estates

Another way of avoiding significant estate tax burdens is to encourage the higher net-worth partner to pay a greater share of the couple's ongoing expenses, thus enabling the lower-asset partner to save more income for her own future financial needs. It also may be possible to top off such savings by having the richer partner make gifts below the tax-reporting threshold to supplement the lower-asset partner's savings. Either of these approaches also can be useful in providing a safety net for a dependent partner in the event of a breakup of the relationship.

You need to be careful that the payment of shared expenses is not itself construed as a reportable or taxable gift, and so it is better to allocate such payments to joint expenses or shared expenses such as travel or housing. It also is crucial that the benefiting partner follow through with the intention to save the unspent earnings and not just take advantage of the generosity of a partner to spend more on discretionary purchases. Some couples are uncomfortable with this plan to the extent that it reinforces the notion that the richer partner is paying more of the bills, but in fact it is one of the best ways to protect both partners from a later tax burden.

Transfers of Portions of a Jointly Owned Asset

Like the early gifting approach, transferring portions of a jointly owned asset can be very beneficial from a tax standpoint. The higher-asset partner can buy property alone and then transfer a percentage each year to the lower-asset partner. If the asset is real estate or a limited partnership that is encumbered by a co-ownership or partnership agreement, the value of the transferred portion for gift tax purposes can be lower than its market value as a percentage of the whole. Thus, property can be bought entirely in the name of the partner with greater assets, and then a percentage can be transferred each year to the lower-asset partner. The goal here is to create estates of roughly equal value so that neither partner is excessively dependent on the other one in the event of the death of one of them, thus freeing up each partner's assets to be used for charitable bequests or other gifts or at least reducing the amount needing to be bequeathed to the lower-asset partner. You can use a similar approach with LLC business ventures or family limited partnerships.

Gift Tax Exemption

The current high threshold for gift taxes ($5 million) enables a wealthy client to provide more than ample resources to an unmarried partner during the lifetime of the partners without any concern for estate or gift taxes. Of course, such gifts cannot be taken back if the relationship breaks up, and so typically you would want to integrate the gifting plan with a waiver of postseparation support or any other palimony kind of claim and in most instances phase it in over time. This approach also can result in a depletion of the gift tax exemption early in the donor's life, depriving her of using the gift tax exemption for a bequest or gift to a subsequent partner or a child. One of the most unfair challenges in this area involves same-sex married couples; at the moment, they are not protected by the marital transfer exemption, but that situation may change in the near future once DOMA is repealed or judicially invalidated.

As a result of this uncertainty and in light of the prospect that the gift tax limit probably will decrease in future years, there's a real tension between making significant gifts now (which can't be retrieved even if the relationship unravels) while the gift tax limit is high and waiting, either because of a concern that the relationship may not last or, for same-sex couples, a hope that the spousal exemption will be extended to them in the future. There is no single right answer here: It's a balancing of needs, political predictions, relationship analysis, and figuring out what feels most right to your clients. Your job is to be clear in explaining the law and the risks going forward; your client has the more difficult job of making the final decisions.

Bypass Trusts

A bypass trust provides that the surviving partner can use some portion of bequeathed assets during his lifetime, with the bulk of the assets being held in reserve for a child or another beneficiary, to be transferred upon the death of the surviving partner. Under this sort of plan, the larger value of the underlying asset is not considered as part of the decedent's estate at the time of his death but rather is only taxed when the surviving partner dies or uses some of the assets. This strategy is particularly attractive where the assets are probably more than the surviving partner needs during the remainder of his lifetime but where income from those underlying assets may be needed to support the surviving partner for some time to come. This arrangement also enables the testator to select the successor beneficiaries and thus not have to worry about a surviving partner turning over the assets to someone the testator would not want to benefit (such as a subsequent new partner).

Charitable Trusts

Whenever partners have sufficient assets to meet their financial needs and are charitably inclined, give serious thought as to how best to integrate the charitable intent with tax-avoidance strategies. It is a different sort of analysis than what is appropriate for married partners, who don't have to worry about the absence of a spousal exemption. The best strategy is to use nontaxed assets, such as retirement accounts, for the charitable purpose. Another useful tool is a charitable remainder trust, where income is used to support the surviving spouse but the underlying asset is reserved for the charity. Alternatively, a charitable lead trust can be set up, giving the income stream to the charity with the underlying asset left to the surviving partner at a designated time. These approaches also can protect the testator's charitable intentions from a change in plans by the surviving partner.

Life Insurance Policies

Reasonably priced life insurance can be a useful tax-avoidance strategy because benefits are paid outside of the decedent's estate. In most states an unmarried partner has an insurable interest in a partner's life, especially if the couple owns a home together, so that should not be an obstacle to its purchase. Partners should avoid an obligation of reciprocal bequests of such policies as that could render the transfers as being "for consideration" and thus taxable. If the wealthier partner is paying the insurance premium, it could be considered a reportable (but probably not taxable) gift.

Life Insurance Trusts

One of the more advanced techniques is an irrevocable life insurance trust. Under this approach, a special-purpose trust holds a life insurance policy on the life of the grantor. The beneficiary pays premiums from gifts made by the grantor, which should be lower than the annual gift tax exclusion, or at least not that much greater than that amount. Moreover, in some instances the grantor can name a group of beneficiaries at the outset and grant each beneficiary a withdrawal right that can later be waived, which allows the grantor to name more than one potential beneficiary, at least on paper. This can enable the grantor to convert the secondary beneficiary's interest to a present interest, which in turn reduces the tax consequences of the gift of the annual premium and allows the grantor to spread the premium over multiple low-value annual gifts.

If properly structured, the proceeds of the policy are excluded not only from the grantor's estate but maybe even from the surviving partner's estate, to the extent that the partner does not use up the entire policy amount during his lifetime. You need to be very careful here and make full disclosures to your client as these are generally irrevocable trusts and cannot be terminated even if the personal relationship ends. It may be possible to draft the trust to allow the beneficiary to be changed should a new partner come into your client's life. More likely, it can be written so that if the relationship ends, the successor beneficiaries will become the primary ones, which may not be a terrible result.

Grantor Retained Trusts

Unmarried couples can take advantage of a variety of options not available to married couples, including a grantor retained trust. Under these arrangements, a grantor sets up an irrevocable trust and retains ownership for a designated period of time, after which the asset is transferred to the remainder beneficiary. According to the tax code (see IRC Chapter 14, Sections 2701–2704 on "freeze transactions"), the grantor has made a reportable gift of the remainder interest when it is set up, but this is generally much lower in value than the market value of the asset. As long as the grantor survives the term of the trust, the remaining trust value will not be included in the decedent's estate for inheritance tax purposes.[1] A similar technique, called a qualified personal residence trust, involves the grantor's personal residence.[2] Another alternative is an annuity trust (called a GRAT), where the grantor receives an annuity for a limited period of time, after which the remainder interest passes to the partner (or remains in trust for the partner's use in the future).

Community Property Asset Accumulation

A recent IRS ruling established that same-sex married spouses and registered domestic partners in community property states (as of 2011, California, Nevada, and Washington) must average their income. This suggests that the IRS is recognizing community property rights for same-sex couples generally. If this turns out to be the case, then retaining savings and other assets as community property will eliminate any issue of taxable transfers upon the death of either partner, to the extent that the surviving partner is merely receiving "his" half of the community property (though the deceased partner's half could be considered a taxable transfer). Don't let your clients forget that characterizing assets as community property is binding on them in the event of a dissolution, thus preventing the higher earner from taking back what might otherwise be considered his own, separate savings.

One additional method of avoiding the tax burdens is for one partner to adopt his unmarried partner. As discussed previously, this is not necessarily an optimal approach, in part because it is almost impossible to undo an adoption and in part because it just doesn't seem right. But in some highly unusual situations, this might be an effective strategy, especially when you need to find a way to bring a partner into the ambit of a class of beneficiaries under an existing will or trust. For more detailed information and some excellent strategic suggestions on this and other advanced estate planning techniques for unmarried couples, see Wendy Goffe's comprehensive article "Estate Planning for the Unmarried Adult."[3] As she explains there, in some instances an adult adoption can help a surviving partner avoid some adverse generation-skipping trust tax consequences.

D. RETIREMENT BENEFITS / PENSIONS / IRAs

Historically, nonspouses (a group that now includes those in a same-sex marriage that is not federally recognized due to the provisions of DOMA) did not do well when it came to inheriting a retirement benefit. This is still the case for most nonretirement plan IRAs (such as SEP IRAs or privately funded IRAs). For these accounts, the beneficiary has to set up an "inherited IRA" account in the name of the decedent, and there are strict rules that limit what the beneficiary can withdraw after the death of the retiree and when, without incurring significant tax penalties.

The rules for retirement plan accounts (such as 401(k) or 403(b) plans), however, have loosened up to some degree in the past few years. In the past, an unmarried partner (or a spouse in a same-sex marriage that is not federally recognized) would have been forced to take distributions of the entirety of an inherited qualified retirement plan within a fairly tight schedule or, in some plans, immediately following the participant's death. Then, in 2006, the Pension Protection Act was enacted. As part of its provisions, a nonspouse beneficiary of a qualified retirement plan is allowed to roll over, via a trustee-to-trustee transfer, the deceased partner's benefits into an "inherited" IRA, which allows for an extended payout plan. The act also permits the postmortem transfer of qualified retirement plans to inherited IRAs held by trusts for the benefit of nonspousal beneficiaries. Once the benefits are in the inherited IRA, the beneficiary may stretch the benefits over his life expectancy.[4] This is still not as good as what a federally recognized spouse is entitled to, which is the ability to roll it over to his own plan with much more liberal payout schedules, but it is a dramatic improvement over what existed prior to 2006.

Each private retirement plan or pension plan has its own survivorship rules. Some institutions (such as some public pension plans and certain federal thrift savings plans) allow the employee to designate a "survivor benefit" to a nonspouse, but that has to be done at the time of retirement and generally cannot be changed, even in the event of a breakup. The amount paid each month to the employee will be somewhat less than what would ordinarily be paid, in exchange for a more generous payout to the surviving partner. Other plans, such as many union or government pension plans, pay nothing to unmarried surviving partners.

This is also an area where specialized knowledge is needed for same-sex couples who are state-registered in marriage-equivalent registrations. They will be entitled to all state-based spousal benefits as spousal equivalents, but not any of the federal benefits. In some instances, there are additional gray areas where the federal ERISA preclusion could limit the survivor benefits, even where they shade into state law. You should review your clients' retirement plans carefully so that the clients are aware of what they are being denied as an unmarried couple and where they could take early action to minimize the discriminatory consequences.

E. THE JOINTLY OWNED/OCCUPIED RESIDENCE AND THE JOINT ACCOUNT

Sometimes referred to as the "poor's man's will," holding title to a property or a bank account as joint tenants with rights of survivorship can effectively result in a transfer of the asset to the surviving co-owner without the need for any probate proceeding or even a will. In most states bank accounts can be held in one name with a transfer on death designation. This preserves the assets solely in the owner's name while he is alive, which means that the owner can retain the account and terminate the designation in the event of a breakup. Upon the death of the

Pension Protection Act of 2006: Maybe Unintended . . . But Positive Changes for Unmarried Persons

By Deb L. Kinney[5]

Used with permission. www.dlklawgroup.com

It's not unusual for people's eyes to glaze over when the topic of retirement plans comes up. But this is one time when you might want to pay attention because the Pension Protection Act of 2006 includes provisions that really are great news for same-sex partners and other unmarried persons. The first important modification is that a nonspouse may now be the designated beneficiary for an eligible retirement plan. The second change is that an employee who designates a nonspouse beneficiary may now tap into the employee's retirement funds in certain "hardship" situations to help the beneficiary. Each of these provisions is discussed in more detail below. However, in recognition of those glazed looks, some basic information about pension plans will probably be helpful.

There are generally two kinds of pension plans: defined contribution and defined benefit plans. Defined contribution plans are the most common type of plan. They are accounts into which an employee will make periodic contributions of a specified amount of pretax dollars or a defined percentage of her salary, and, usually, an employer will match those contributions up to a predetermined amount. The total assets ultimately available for distribution to the employee or the designated beneficiary will vary depending on income, expenses, and gains or losses experienced by the plan's investments. Examples of defined contribution plans include 401(k), 403(b), or 404(c) plans; stock options; and profit-sharing plans. Typically, the employee "owns" the plan and may choose the plan beneficiary who will receive the plan assets if the employee dies before the assets are exhausted. Defined benefit plans, on the other hand, are more like a contract between an employer and employee in which the employer agrees to provide a specific benefit amount at some future date, usually after a certain age or after the employee retires. Traditional public employee retirement plans that provide a retirement benefit based only on the age of the employee, the employee's final salary, and her years of service are the most common example of a defined benefit plan. In this case, the plan itself controls the funds and may restrict how and to whom the funds may be distributed. When the IRS approves a plan, it is called a "qualified" plan and, as such, is subject to ERISA regulations.

Historically, when a surviving spouse (as defined by the Internal Revenue Code) inherited retirement assets from a defined benefit or defined contribution plan as the designated beneficiary, the beneficiary could roll

(continued)

the assets into her own IRA without any tax liabilities and would only be taxed later when the assets were withdrawn from the IRA. Moreover, if a surviving spouse did not have an immediate need for the assets, she could wait to take the distributions until she reached the age of fifty-nine and a half. The distributions could also be "stretched" or withdrawn in small portions over the expected lifetime of the beneficiary (as determined by the IRS), thereby reducing the tax liabilities and increasing the amount of money actually available to the beneficiary.

In contrast, a nonspouse beneficiary was compelled to withdraw the entire amount of the retirement assets from almost all pension plans in a lump sum or, in the best case, take the distributions over a five-year period. Because the majority of contributions to retirement plans are made with pretax dollars, the government collects deferred income tax when distributions are made. The rate applied is the marginal income tax rate of the person who actually receives the distributions. The infusion of income in a short period of time that occurs when a retirement asset is distributed in these circumstances will often force the beneficiary into a much higher tax bracket than she would otherwise be in during that time. The result is that she will receive significantly less than she would have if she had been able to absorb the additional income over a longer period or if she had taken the distribution during retirement.

The first important change created by the act is that designated nonspouse beneficiaries of a defined benefit plan, such as an unmarried partner, parent, sibling, or adult child, are now provided with the same options as a surviving spouse with regard to asset distribution. A nonspouse beneficiary may now take a distribution in a lump sum or roll the assets into an inherited IRA in the name of the deceased partner and stretch the distribution over five years or even over the life expectancy of the beneficiary. This is likely to result in significant tax savings for nonspouse beneficiaries. It is important to note that while the act provides a nonspouse beneficiary with additional distribution options, the beneficiary is not permitted to merge the assets with her own retirement assets.

Of course, there are a few caveats. First, this new provision does not require a pension plan to allow distributions to nonspouse beneficiaries. The provision is applicable only if the plan currently permits nonspousal beneficiaries. Some plans, such as the Federal Employees Retirement System, allow distribution to spousal beneficiaries only. This amendment will not change that allowance.

Second, even if a plan is covered by the act, each plan participant must name her beneficiary(ies) on the form provided by the plan administrator in order to ensure that a nonspouse beneficiary will be eligible to receive the distribution. Since the federal government does not recognize a legal relationship other than marriage, registered domestic partners or other nonspouse parties will have no claim to the benefits unless they are specifically designated, in writing, as the beneficiary. These assets cannot be directed by estate documents—only by a beneficiary designation.

Finally, because the act does not specifically address Roth IRAs, for now it is safest to assume that they are not covered. Future Treasury Department regulations may clarify this situation.

The second significant provision of the act is that a plan participant may now make withdrawals from her 401(k) in case of certain medical or financial emergencies experienced by the designated beneficiary, irrespective of the parties' marital status. In the past, a plan participant was only allowed to make such withdrawals for her legally recognized spouse or dependent(s). This modification ensures that a plan participant has a source of emergency funds for her same-sex partner or any other previously designated plan beneficiary.

This new provision directs the Secretary of the Treasury to issue rules for purposes of determining whether a hardship or unforeseen financial emergency has occurred, so the criteria are not absolutely clear at this point. However, Internal Revenue Code section 409A(a)(2)(B)(ii) provides that an "unforeseen financial emergency" is

> a severe financial hardship to the participant resulting from an illness or accident of the participant, the participant's spouse, or a dependent (as defined in section 152(a)) of the participant, loss of the participant's property due to casualty, or other similar extraordinary and unforeseeable circumstances arising as a result of events beyond the control of the participant.

Furthermore, it is not clear whether a plan participant will be permitted to take a hardship distribution for the dependent of a nonspouse, such as the child of a same-sex partner, even if that nonspouse is a designated beneficiary. If the dependent meets the criteria for designation as a qualifying child (I.R.C. section 152(c)) or a qualifying relative (I.R.C. section 152(d)), it is possible that a hardship distribution would be permitted. This is likely to be determined on a case-by-case basis, although future Treasury Department regulations may clarify who else will be eligible.

The act does not specifically address or include any government or union pensions unless the plan itself addresses nonspousal distributions. It does not affect military or Social Security benefits. The Act also does not change the requirement that a beneficiary have a valid Social Security number or tax identification number to be eligible to receive benefits, nor does the act require or compel employers to provide pension benefits to domestic partners.

The Pension Protection Act of 2006 was signed into law by President Bush in August 2006 and is applicable to pension distributions made after December 31, 2006. Additional information can be found at http://www.irs.gov/retirement/article/0,,id=165131,00.html.

owner, there will be an immediate transfer of the account without any need for probate or a will. Indeed, in some states real property also can be held entirely in one person's name but with a right of survivorship granted to a surviving partner on the deed as a kind of transferable on death real property asset.

While a joint tenancy or payable-on-death (POD) account or title designation will work in many instances, it is not considered a preferred approach to estate planning for the following reasons:

- Under applicable IRS rules,[6] the full value of the asset is included in the estate of the first to die unless the survivor can prove financial contribution to the purchase or maintenance of the property.[7] The philosophy behind this rule is that most joint tenancies historically were set up as bequest mechanisms, where one partner was considered as the remaining sole owner from a tax perspective and a family member (other than a spouse) was added as a joint tenant to achieve the bequest intention without having to go through a court probate. Proving financial contribution of the second owner can be difficult, either because there was no such contribution or because records were lost. For especially valuable properties or high-asset decedents, this can create a serious problem upon the death of the original owner.

- Joint tenancy deeds can be severed unilaterally in most states, and if one partner does that, then the other partner's intentions are also frustrated. The property shifts to being owned as tenants in common, and so there is no right of survivorship in either direction, and the legal heirs (who usually are not the co-owners) end up inheriting the decedent's share of the property.

- Oftentimes, parties don't really understand what joint tenancy means, and so their true intentions may be frustrated. The vagueness of the rules and the very informality of the titling process also can make this technique more vulnerable to challenges by a relative who doesn't respect the relationship. This is especially possible when there is a will or trust provision that contradicts the title, raising the possibility that the decedent didn't really understand the significance of putting the property into joint tenancy or adding a payable on death beneficiary. Typically, the owners do not retain the instructions to the title company about the vesting of the title, and often these decisions are made informally or are handled by a real estate agent, so there is no evidence to show that the owners had a knowing intention to make their co-owner their beneficiary. There also can be a problem if one partner has contributed far more to the purchase of the property than the other one as that may not be described in a valid written agreement. If that is the case, a reciprocal right of survivorship will provide a greater benefit to the survivor in the event that the larger contributor dies first.

- Joint tenancy or POD designations don't allow for any flexibility or a residual beneficiary or life estate approach. The surviving partner has total discretion as to what to do with the property without any obligation to make any provisions for any children or charity or other secondary beneficiary.

Apart from the deeding issue of joint tenancy, you also will want to address the broader issue of what should happen with the jointly owned or jointly occupied house. Many older partners wish to eventually bequeath their house to their children from a prior relationship, and this makes sense when the house was in the family prior to the current relationship and where the testator is the sole owner of the house. In that situation, a life estate for the surviving partner can be an effective estate planning solution as long as the details of the financial and maintenance obligations during the life estate period are worked out in the trust document and the parties are comfortable with the arrangements. But even in this situation, there often are intense conflicts that only arise after the owner dies, where the children resent the power and presence of their deceased parent's partner. You should encourage your client to always consider other options, to avoid leaving a ticking time bomb that could blast apart an otherwise cordial relationship between the surviving children and the surviving partner.

Where the house is jointly owned and was not the family home of either partner prior to the new relationship, you should strongly discourage couples from choosing a plan that involves a life estate to the partner with a remainder interest to the children of just one partner. The children typically would prefer to receive a financial payment upon the death of their parent rather than waiting around for the partner to die to receive their inheritance. And there's no question that the surviving partner would prefer not to end up being a co-owner with the children of a deceased partner. These problems are hard enough to resolve when the older couple has married or has been together for many decades because then they truly are stepparents and likely will have formed a new blended family together. For many unmarried older couples, this is not the case.

There are two ways to avoid these unwanted outcomes. One approach is to have each of the partners purchase a life insurance policy, either on her own life or on the life of her partner, with the beneficiaries being the other partner's children so they can receive the policy proceeds in lieu of inheriting any portion of the house. Then, in exchange, each of the partners can comfortably bequeath her interest in the house to the other partner. Alternatively, the home ownership agreement (and the estate plan) can provide a buyout right to the surviving partner based upon the value of the house at the time of a partner's death, with a time limit (typically six months) for the surviving partner to exercise this right if she wants to do so. Of course, this approach only works if the surviving partner can afford to buy out the heirs, either through savings, other inherited funds, a life insurance payment, or a new mortgage. The first life insurance option is preferable simply because it avoids the need for a contested appraisal process, but it won't necessarily keep up with the appreciation of the house after the insurance policy is purchased.

F. INSURANCE STRATEGIES

Life insurance isn't just about tax minimizing: It should be considered a substantive part of any estate plan. The legal issues surrounding life insurance for unmarried couples are not really all that different than those facing married couples except that there are no issues of community property or marital property ownership of the policy, and there may be estate tax problems for particularly large policies or high net-worth decedents.

Thus, the insurance-related issues for unmarried couples involve the following questions:

1. Who needs a policy and, if so, for how much?
2. Who is paying for the policy, and should it be paid for out of joint funds?

3. What type of policy is best from a cost and benefits perspective?
4. As an unmarried couple, are there any employment-provided policies that can be tapped?

For each of these questions, you should engage your clients in a practical and financially thoughtful conversation, guiding them through the available insurance options in a manner that is mindful of potentially unresolved emotional issues. It probably makes sense for you to get to know some insurance agents who are working with unmarried couples, both opposite-sex and same-sex, so that you can confidently refer your clients to an agent who will be knowledgeable about any particular differences in premium pricing, benefits provisions, and tax issues for unmarried partners.

G. GUARDIANSHIP OF CHILDREN

While only a court can determine the legal parentage of a minor child, a parent can nominate a guardian to be appointed upon the parent's death. Unless there is a second legal parent who is competent and wants to step up and be an active parent, in most instances the court will honor this request. A nomination of guardianship can be included in any estate planning document or set forth in its own separate document. For those whose children have a second legal parent, it always is prudent to have an open discussion with that parent before nominating a partner who is not a legal parent in order to minimize subsequent ill will or potential legal challenges.

H. INTEGRATION OF THE ESTATE PLAN WITH THE OTHER AGREEMENTS

It is essential that estate planning documents are consistent with other agreements that your client has signed. If your client has a co-ownership agreement, you will need to review it to see whether it provides for reimbursement of a down payment or a right of first purchase by a co-owner. If so, the estate plan should acknowledge and honor that provision. Your standard co-ownership agreements should always provide for a buyout right if a partner is not the heir to the property, and the estate plan should refer to that provision. And if there is a cohabitation or relationship agreement that provides for a payment upon the dissolution of the relationship, most partners will want to include an equal (or greater) payment in their estate plan.

Your documents also need to be consistent with any will, contract, or mutual promises that your client has made with a partner because those agreements won't meet the formalization standards of a will and thus won't be self-executing. Most crucially, because a person can only bequeath that which he actually owns, you will want to review any ownership agreements and the title to any real property and bank or investment accounts to confirm that the provisions in your testamentary documents are consistent with those deeds and the other agreements.

I. UNDUE INFLUENCE CONCERNS

Any professional involved in estate planning needs to be attentive to the specter of undue influence and lack of capacity, but there is a special need to watch out for these issues when working with unmarried partners, for two interrelated reasons.

First, marriage in many ways acts as a gatekeeper on many relationships with its public nature and elaborate rituals, its deeply felt social meaning, and the many legal formalities it imposes. Thus, there is a lower likelihood of casual, unconventional, or disrespected relationships in the universe of married couples. This is not to say that there is anything inappropriate about unmarried relationships or that there aren't any impulsive or inappropriate marriages—of course this is not the case. Rather, it's just that more of the unconventional and controversial relationships are likely to be found within the pool of unmarried relationships simply because of the absence of the marriage threshold.

Second, and this is probably the most important factor, there is a much greater likelihood that legal relatives will challenge an estate plan that favors an unmarried partner, even when the relationship seems to you to be fairly conventional and appropriate. If you reflect back on the population that makes up your roster of unmarried couple clients, the reasons for this concern should be readily apparent. Many of your clients are gay or lesbian couples, older folks in a relationship with someone they met outside of their familiar social circle, disabled or elderly people in a relationship with someone who started out as a caregiver, couples who have only been together a short while, and a colorful variety of younger and older partners with adult children from a prior relationship. In each of these situations, there is likely to be a legal relative (son, daughter, sibling, former married spouse, or even a parent) who may feel suspicious about the nonmarital relationship to a degree that simply does not exist in the universe of married couples (even those who have children from a prior marriage).

Oftentimes, your client will be acutely aware of these suspicions and will tell you about them from the outset, giving you a head start on addressing the potential challenges. However, in many other situations, your clients may be quite unaware of the negative feelings of their family members, and so the hostilities may only surface after the death of your client. Try to keep an open mind, never forgetting that in many romantic relationships the line between genuine affection and undue influence is a fine one. Making matters more complicated, one outgrowth of your client's pride (which often includes a strong sense of self-sufficiency) in the path that he has taken may be a hostile reaction to anyone else's allegation of undue influence. This is especially true where there has been a history of disrespect for the relationship, such as what lesbian or gay couples have so often experienced. It can be difficult for an attorney to sort out a healthy concern over the possibility of undue influence from the suspicion that the relatives are simply continuing a course of pervasive criticism of the relationship.

Given these tensions, it is best to focus on the likelihood that others will be suspicious and to act accordingly (i.e., in a protective manner). Expressing concern about a potential challenge from outside relatives is the most tactful way of raising your own possible concerns without alienating your client unnecessarily. Your client should be able to understand that it really doesn't matter, in the end, what you as the lawyer think is going on. What counts most is what the relatives who might challenge the estate plan in the future will say and what a judge hearing their challenges will do.

Spotting undue influence is not at all simple as it involves a delicate interaction between a vulnerable person (who may still be competent in the legal sense of the term) and the actions of another person who is deemed to be "taking advantage" of the vulnerable person. The California Civil Code, which is typical of most state laws, defines undue influence as follows:

1. The use, by one in whom a confidence is reposed by another, or who holds real or apparent authority over him, of such confidence or authority for the purpose of obtaining an unfair advantage over him;
2. In taking an unfair advantage of another's weakness of mind; and
3. In taking a grossly oppressive and unfair advantage of another's necessities or distress.[8]

This definition reveals the fundamental flaw in the legal notion of undue influence: The statutory definition is really just a label, a set of words that are applied post hoc to behavior that is deemed to be "unfair." The definitions don't really describe in any detail what constitutes undue influence, and in most states the case law is decidedly inconsistent and unhelpful in many ways. The nuances of past cases also are not always particularly helpful in guiding you in your analysis of the issues when you are faced with real-life situations.

For that reason, a variety of mental health, legal, and social work professionals working in this field have tried to develop more precise definitions as well as a framework of analysis that actually can help sort out actions that are truly the result of undue influence from those that are not. The authors of a comprehensive study conducted for the San Francisco Superior Court in 2010 identified four primary factors that make up undue influence: the characteristics of the victim, the characteristics of the influencer, the specific actions or tactics of the influencer, and the transactions or outcomes that appear to be improper.[9] The particular components that constitute each factor are described in this report as follows:

> *Victim Characteristics.* Incapacity resulting from medical or psychological conditions, deficits in judgment, altered states of mind (due to medication or alcohol), emotional distress, personality disorders, or an especially acquiescent or passive personality.
> *Influencer Characteristics.* Being in a position of trust, either formal or informal; having a professional authority, superior physical strength, charismatic personality traits, privilege based upon gender or age or class, or special access as a caregiver; or being in a "reliant relationship" with the victim.

Actions or Tactics. Isolating the victim, playing on loyalties and excluding others, exercising control over the victim, limiting information to the victim, controlling the victim's thoughts, reinforcing a sense of hopelessness, making threats (especially of withdrawal of affection or sexual favors), manipulating information, or aggressively initiating the transactions (especially when the victim is vulnerable).

Improper Transactions or Outcomes. Giving away assets or signing a will or trust to unfairly benefit the influencer, or making gifts not commensurate with the length and quality of relationship or that diverge from the victim's expressed wishes or that suggest behavior by a professional outside of his professional roles and responsibilities.[10]

Analyzing a romantic relationship through these four lenses can easily result in a wide range of judgments depending on how much information you have, what your own biases are, and whether or not you have underlying suspicions based upon prior involvement with the parties. As an estate planning lawyer, you are (hopefully) free of biases, but not always—and the absence of personal history with the parties can make it hard to sort through the ambiguities.

The even more difficult question, of course, is what the appropriate course of conduct should be when a client's situation and the estate planning requests suggest the presence of undue influence.

Each situation calls for its own particular response, but the best plan of action is as follows:

• Structure your interaction with your client to ensure clear and reliable communication. Whenever possible, discuss the important issues in person rather than over the phone, and pay attention to any behavior that suggests improper influence (e.g., a partner listening in on the phone call or insisting on being present, or markedly different behaviors when the partner is or is not present). Make sure that the instructions you receive come from your client as opposed to hearing them from others and simply having your client assent to what the others say. Never use email to communicate with a client when the possibility of undue influence exists.

- Monitor the overall competency and capacities of your client. Pay attention to whether appointments are missed, try to engage in fairly detailed conversations about the technical legal issues (as opposed to just reciting the legal rules to a passive client), and observe your client's ability to discuss and manage his financial affairs. Make sure you ask your client to tell *you* what he understands about the legal principles, even in simple terms, rather than just explaining them and assuming that your client understands them.
- Talk openly with your client about possible challenges by legal relatives and observe how your client reacts to these claims. Whenever possible, encourage your client to talk directly with the potential claimant so that she can hear directly from her relative about the reasons for the decisions that he has made.
- Find a way to involve the partner even when you are concerned about undue influence, if only to reduce the likelihood that the partner will turn on you and force your client to withdraw from using your services. Even if you are meeting more often with just your client in the room, there is nothing wrong with having an additional meeting with the partner present.
- Suggest alternative estate plans that address the undue influence concerns, such as a spendthrift trust (rather than an outright bequest) or the nomination of a neutral trustee or executor. Where appropriate, propose deferred gifts (or gifts that start with lower amounts and increase over the years as the relationship flourishes) rather than immediate gifts of large amounts. Ask about past gifts so that you can discuss the overall scale of your client's generosity.
- If you have serious concerns about the undue influence of a partner, bear in mind that you can decline to represent the client or draft the documents. You probably will need to refund any fees already paid by the client, and you should explain your decision in a thoughtful and considerate letter. Chances are your client will find someone else to draft the documents, but you can feel good about the integrity of your own decision. Before doing so, however, express your concerns to your client openly, and explore what other options there may be to address your concerns.
- If you reasonably conclude that there is, in fact, no undue influence taking place, take appropriate steps to protect your client from a

possible challenge. Encourage your client to talk directly with the potential challenger, and make sure that the beneficiary has no participation in the estate planning process. You should not meet with or talk with the beneficiary except in an informal greeting type of context, nor should you have any email communication with the

I received a high-intensity crash course on the issues of competency and undue influence when I volunteered to write wills for people with AIDS in the early 1980s. Many of our clients were in very bad shape, both medically and emotionally, and they often had lovers who were disdained by the relatives of the ill client—or, in some instances, were completely unknown to the extended family. Emotions ran high, quick decisions had to be made, and we had a strong commitment to helping our clients. I'll never forget the bitter disappointment I encountered when I refused to help a client with a will on the grounds that he did not appear competent to understand that what his partner was saying was not the client's intentions. We soon learned a few vital lessons on how to reduce the incidents of inappropriate estate planning and how to bolster the validity of the documents that were signed.

The key is to think about how the story will play out in a trial on a claim of undue influence or lack of capacity on the part of the testator. It was in that context that we came up with a few additional suggestions:

- Call the medical provider or nursing home in advance, and have the dose level of any sedative medication (e.g., morphine) reduced a few hours before any documents are signed or discussed.
- Learn in advance who is being named as beneficiaries, and make sure that those people are not in the room or involved in the transportation to the lawyer's office.
- Find out who is most likely to challenge a will, and whenever possible include those people in a family meeting or discussion while the testator is still competent.
- Make an audio or video record of the will signing, showing the testator competent and clearheaded. If possible, supplement that recording with a narrative explanation by the testator of the reasons for estate planning decisions.
- Interview the client about the relationship history so that your own notes show the justification for the bequest, both in terms of the emotional connection and the help and support that the beneficiary has provided. If the beneficiary has made financial contributions that helped pay for a house or other assets in the name of the testator, make note of those facts as part of the background for the bequest.

partner that delves into confidential material. The partner should not be making the appointments on behalf of your client or even bringing the client to your office unless there is a particular reason and the meeting is appropriately documented. Be especially attentive to the witnessing process, and make sure you use witnesses who will likely be available to testify in future years. If your client is in the hospital, it will be useful to have a doctor or nurse enter a description in the medical record of the condition of the patient on the day of the will signing, and you may even want to bring along an independent person (such as a paralegal in your office) who will be able to testify as to the testator's competence.

J. PALIMONY AND PROPERTY CLAIMS

Though rare, it is not unheard of for a surviving partner to file a palimony or property claim against the estate of a deceased partner. Many states restrict such claims to those based upon written agreements or where there is a demonstrable obligation, such as an unpaid bill or a claim for services rendered. Other state courts have rendered appellate decisions expressly allowing such claims.[11] A surviving partner could also raise claims alleging breach of constructive trust, resulting trust, or breach of fiduciary duty, especially where the decedent owned property into which the claimant invested personal funds.

Typically, there is a two-year statute of limitations for oral claims, but in many states *any* claim against an estate must be filed within a much shorter probate claims deadline.[12] Just as with any palimony claim, the burdens of proof are going to make it hard for such a claim to be successful, especially in the face of a vigorous defense brought by the legal heirs or beneficiaries. In most such situations, the absence of a bequest to the partner will suggest a lack of intent to help the partner, at least where the relationship was in effect when the will or trust was drafted. The claim will be even more difficult to win where the relationship was on the rocks when the partner died.

In some states all such claims must be brought in the probate court, which usually means that there is no right to a jury trial. In other states the claim can be raised either in civil court or in probate court, so you should be careful to ascertain the proper venue and jury trial options. Ironically, the most difficult aspect of such claims is the challenge facing the defense, where there is no "witness" who can rebut the claims of the partner. Unless the decedent spoke openly of his feelings about the partner and the plans they had made—and assuming that those comments can overcome a hearsay objection—the defense has very little evidence to marshal in rebutting the claim.

In order to protect the client in a proactive manner, the estate planner should be aware of applicable rules on these claims so that the client can take appropriate preventive action. The best protection, of course, is a written agreement with the partner that defines the rights and obligations of each party and is binding upon the heirs of both parties. The agreement should also be integrated into the estate planning of both partners. Such an agreement would surely be persuasive evidence in response to any claim for assets in excess of what the agreement provided. In the absence of such an agreement, however, the testator should make a reasonable bequest to the partner with an explanation as to why the bequest is not any larger, and perhaps include a "no contest" clause. This would be the next-best evidence in response to a postdeath claim by a disappointed lover.

DOCUMENTS FOR ESTATE PLANNING CONCERNS AND PRACTICES

(FORMS FOUND ON INCLUDED CD)

Form 16: Estate planning retainer letter with conflicts of interest waiver

Form 17: Will

NOTES

1. Treas. Reg. § 25.2512–5(d)(2).
2. I.R.C. § 2702(a)(3)(A)(ii).
3. Wendy Goffe, *Estate Planning for the Unmarried Adult*, MARRIAGE, DOMESTIC PARTNERSHIPS, CIVIL UNION: THE DEVELOPING LANDSCAPE (Advanced Estate Planning Techniques, ALI ABA, San Francisco, Cal., Mar. 24, 2011).
4. Pension Protection Act of 2006, Pub. L. No. 109–280, 120 Stat. 780.
5. Deb Kinney is an attorney in San Francisco specializing in the estate planning needs of unmarried couples, both gay and straight. For more information on her practice, see www.dlkgroup.com.
6. I.R.C. § 2040.

7. Goldsborough v. Comm'r, 70 T.C. 1077 (1978), *aff'd per curiam*, 673 F.2d 1310 (4th Cir. 1982).
8. Cal. Civ. Code § 1575. Cal. Prob. Code § 6104 bolsters this provision by stating that a will is ineffective to the extent that it was procured by undue influence.
9. Mary Joe Quinn, Undue Influence: Defintions and Applications (S.F. Superior Court 2010), http://www.courts.ca.gov/xbcr/cc/UndueInfluence.pdf; *see also* Howard Klein, How Much Influence Is Undue? An Analysis of Family Law and Probate Perspectives (2008).
10. Quinn, supra note 9, at 13.
11. Byrne v. Laura, 52 Cal. App. 4th 1054 (1997).
12. In *McMackin v. Ehrheart*, 194 Cal. App. 4th 128 (Cal. Ct. App. 2d App. Dist. 2011), the court ruled that the one-year statute of limitations under Cal. Civ. Proc. Code § 366.3 applies to a claim by a surviving unmarried partner to a life estate in the decedent's residence. However, the court remanded the case to the trial court to decide whether doctrines of equitable estoppel would extend that deadline since the intestate heirs had waited three years before opening probate of the decedent's estate.

CHAPTER THIRTEEN

MOVING ON: THE SUBSTANTIVE LEGAL DOCTRINES

Working with couples as they squabble over the detritus of a broken relationship is never easy, but it can be exceptionally tortuous when you don't have the clear legal doctrines and established court procedures of a conventional marital dissolution. The lack of procedural protocols and the vagaries of the substantive law can lead to an amorphous and often unpredictable legal drama. But it is also a process that can be managed with a proper combination of legal knowledge, personal skills, and emotional discernment.

A. SUMMARY OF THE KEY LEGAL DOCTRINES

There are five segments amongst the class of unmarried couples for whom marital law may still determine some or all of the rules for their dissolution: (1) those whose relationship meet the standards of a common law marriage in a state that recognizes such marriages (or who formerly lived in such a state and now live in a state that will recognize a common law marriage formed in another state); (2) cohabiting couples in the state of Washington, for whom marital law is the presumed equitable rule upon dissolution; (3) state-registered civil union or domestic partners who have registered in a marriage-equivalent system and are living in a recognition state; (4) married couples who cohabited prior to marriage and have disputes arising from their premarital period, but

291

also must complete a judicial dissolution of their marriage; and (5) couples who had some kind of formal ceremony that might meet their state law standards of a putative marriage.[1]

For all other couples, however, property and financial disputes will be adjudicated according to the contract-based doctrines that apply in their state of residence.[2] While each state has slightly different rules—some imposed by statute but most by appellate cases—they generally fall into one of three categories (except for the equitable application of marital law in Washington state).[3] In three states (Minnesota, New Jersey, and Texas), courts will only honor written contracts between unmarried partners; oral and implied agreements will be disregarded. In a few states, only business or property contracts will be considered, such as those for a co-owned property or business asset, while personal agreements (even in writing) or cohabitation agreements are not considered valid. In the other forty or so states, however, written and oral agreements and, to varying degrees, implied agreements and equitable claims will be honored.

Thus, as with any area of legal practice, advising and representing clients in a nonmarital dissolution always starts with a detailed understanding of the applicable legal framework for your particular state. However, unlike other areas of law, the interpersonal dynamics and the relative unpredictability of any court outcomes impose a higher level of attention. You also will need to develop a capacity to integrate the legal rules with a practical understanding of the broader personal and financial issues facing your client, in the following manner:

- Because a nonmarital dissolution doesn't have to be processed through the court system (except for state-registered couples in a marriage-equivalent registration or those that subsequently married), informal approaches and alternative dispute resolution methods (i.e., client-initiated negotiation, lawyer-to-lawyer negotiation, mediation, collaborative negotiation, or binding arbitration) all can be effective to resolve your client's conflicts. While a visit to the courthouse usually remains an option, it is definitely not a necessity.
- When there's no court process, the resolution process typically flows unpredictably, driven by the practical problems facing the couple (e.g., moving out of the house, closing a bank account,

sorting through personal belongings) rather than based upon any court-imposed dissolution procedure. The absence of any preordained resolution schedule can itself create tensions; sometimes one of the partners will be eager to move on and will find the other's lack of response very frustrating. Over time, the eager partner (typically the one that initiated the dissolution) may trigger a conflict over a relatively minor issue, simply in order to get the other side's attention.

- Except for those couples who have been together a long time, saved a lot of money, or invested dramatically unequal amounts into a co-owned property, the dollar amounts at stake probably won't be that high. The driving force in high-conflict dissolutions will likely be the emotional dynamics rather than a substantive financial dispute.

- Given the vagueness of the legal rules in most states and the idiosyncratic histories of a great many nonmarital relationships, trying to resolve the disputes according to a strict interpretation of the law probably won't be very effective. Instead, it will be more useful to focus on the equitable claims and the practical concerns, with an emphasis on the history of how the partners actually organized their financial life. This is not to say that the law is irrelevant; it's rather that you and your client will both need to accept the legal uncertainties that are inherent in the situation unless there was a signed cohabitation or co-ownership agreement.

- If court adjudication is necessary to resolve a crucial issue, such as ownership of a house or control of a business, your client must understand what it means to litigate in the civil court of their local jurisdiction. The judges may not be particularly sensitive or attuned to the personal nature of the dispute, and the procedural rules certainly are not constructed around the needs of a couple in a marriage-like relationship. Generally, there will not be any award of attorney fees regardless of outcome, and so the cost of pursuing a legal remedy should always be taken into consideration.

- If you are representing the lower-asset (or lower-earning) partner or an off-title contributor to a property titled only in the other partner's name, you can expect that your client will express surges of anger from time to time, as well as resentment at the lack of marital law protections. This may seem surprising coming from opposite-sex clients who could have married, but it is something seen repeatedly. It definitely will be at play for lesbian or gay clients who were not allowed to marry. Pointing out to your clients that they could have signed a co-ownership or cohabitation agreement probably won't be very comforting, and they will be quite distressed at the gap between their expectations and the likely legal outcomes. It's essential that you express compassion for their feelings and a nonjudgmental response to their complaints, and you must not paper over these problems or pretend that the law can help them when it is not likely to do so. Most straight clients focus their anger at themselves or their partner for not honoring the implied or oral promises that they assumed would be upheld; for same-sex partners, the more common reaction is resentment at the political prejudices that prevented them from being able to get married earlier on—or ever, if they are living in a state that doesn't currently recognize same-sex partnerships or marriages.

B. THE DOCTRINAL GROUNDS OF NONMARITAL LEGAL CLAIMS

In most states, nonmarital claims are decided under the generic statutory rules that apply to any contract claim or to the titling of real property or a bank account, as well as a series of appellate decisions. It's not always easy to learn your state's precise rules since some may be buried in statutes and cases on partnership law, real property co-ownership, bank account ownership, and presumptions of titles and other evidentiary rules. Moreover, the financial vagaries of most couples' lives don't fit easily into any simple framework, and so it can be difficult to assemble your arguments. One of the most important tasks when working in this field, therefore, is figuring out how best to frame your client's demands in the context of the applicable legal rules.

Written Contract

Remember that a written contract need not have been drafted by a lawyer, nor does it have to be complete in every detail to be legally valid. If the basic terms of the deal have been written down and signed by the parties, that may be sufficient to constitute a written contract—with the equitable rules of contract interpretation applied to fill in the blanks or resolve ambiguous or inconsistent terms.[4] It's quite frequent that partners will have retained email exchanges (which may have effectively been signed by being sent from the writer), notes from a casual conversation, or even personal letters, some of which may suffice to establish a legally valid written contract. I once handled a case where one partner had sent his girlfriend a lengthy handwritten letter stating that they would always treat their finances as if they were husband and wife; while a lot of details were left out of that broadly worded promise, I was convinced that it would at least keep the legal door open to the girlfriend's claim for a portion of an asset titled solely in her boyfriend's name—though the case soon settled so I never had to test my theory.

Written contracts also need some form of consideration or some other legal grounds (such as a claim of equitable estoppel) to be enforceable. Vague social promises (such as "I will always treat you fairly" or "I will always consider our residence to be our home") probably won't suffice as legally enforceable contracts, nor will promises of inheritances where a partner has exited the relationship voluntarily rather than dying. Promises of future gifts generally are not enforceable as contracts, nor are those that are based solely on past consideration or on sexual favors. Keep in mind that some state courts have ruled that cohabitation alone cannot serve as adequate consideration but that the written contracts are otherwise valid as contractual agreements.[5]

Your search for an enforceable written contract isn't only for the purpose of trying to have it literally enforced in a court trial. Rather, bringing forth the documentation will lend credibility in a negotiation. In the context of a lawsuit, a claim that a written contract exists can overcome a variety of procedural hurdles (such as extending a statute of limitations or surviving a demurrer). And it can be looked to as a "window" into the deeper realms of the parties' understandings, expectations, and motivations, strengthening an argument as to why the claims are justified in light of how the parties talked about and even wrote about their relationship.

Oral Agreement

Most claims raised by unmarried partners will be based at least in part on an oral contract claim. As with any written contract claims, it is crucial that the terms of the oral contract be sufficiently specific to justify a legal claim and that there be valid consideration or some grounds for claiming equitable estoppel to legally support the claim. Given the uncertainties of memory—especially when it comes to emotionally tinged recitations such as those that are brought up in the course of a breakup—it is crucial that you be skeptical in your analysis of your client's claim of an oral agreement. Always ask your clients to send you a written narrative summarizing any such conversations, including the details of when and where the words were spoken. Give them a brief explanation of the general legal rules before they send you the narrative so that they will understand the details that you're looking for. Also, you will want them to set down their story as soon as they are able to do so, before too much time passes and before the battles become overly pitched and their feelings cloud their powers of recollection.

You might need to remind your clients that agreements always involve two parties; they cannot ever be based solely upon the inner hopes and dreams of just one partner. You should also explain that if there was an open disagreement about the terms of the agreement, then there probably wasn't a legally valid agreement: when there is a disagreement, there is never a "meeting of the minds." You should also point out to your clients that if they never envisioned their dissolution, they cannot have entered into an express contract that covered the terms of their breakup. Yes, they might still have an oral agreement about the ownership of their home or the payment of a debt that may be applicable in the event of a breakup, but there can't be claim of an oral contract for postseparation support if they never discussed separating.

Those old-fashioned rules of reasonable reliance also must be taken into account. One of my clients wanted to base her claim for a share of her partner's inheritance entirely on a remark uttered when she and her girlfriend were shopping for a car. She described how when she was considering an expensive model, her girlfriend said, "Go ahead and buy it; with my inheritance coming in, there will be enough money for both of us to enjoy life." Of course, I encouraged her to tell that story at trial, but fortunately she had other grounds for her claims because I'm not sure how persuasive this particular story really was. Vague statements like "We'll work something out" or "You'll get sweat equity credit for all the work you did on the renovation" may suggest some sort of obligation to compensate the other party, and that's a good thing; but you probably won't win a lawsuit based on such an allegation alone.

You also need to take into account how the parties' subsequent behavior plays out in the narrative of the trial. One of my clients lost his claim for reimbursement of his down payment when the arbitrator observed that just a year after the supposed agreement for reimbursement, they took out $50,000 on a line of credit and spent it on new cars instead of reimbursing my client. From the arbitrator's point of view, this was evidence disproving the existence of any such oral contract, especially when my client didn't even ask that the credit line funds be used to reimburse him.

Implied-in-Fact Contract

Most states allow claims of an implied contract, which is viewed as an enforceable "meeting of the minds" even though express contractual words were never written down or even uttered.[6] Unlike an equitable obligation imposed by a court as a matter of law, an implied-in-fact contract is based upon a judge's interpretation of the conduct of the parties: in retrospect, it seems only logical to suppose that they had an agreement in mind when they acted in the manner in which they did. For example, if every property expense was shared one-third/two-thirds for years on end without any express contractual discussion about percentages of ownership, the expense allocations clearly were not accidental nor did they vary over time. This strongly suggests that the parties had an implied agreement for a one-third/two-thirds ownership. In contrast, an erratic or varying allocation of payments based upon the available cash each owner had from time to time without any accounting or demand for reimbursement suggests the absence of any such set proportional ownership agreement. Conversely, if one partner had sole access to a separate bank account and never used it to pay any joint expenses and never even discussed its contents with the partner, that conduct suggests an implied-in-fact agreement that the titled owner was the sole equitable owner of the account.

As you can readily imagine, finding an implied-in-fact contract is a wildly subjective exercise. Virtually everyone (including most judges) holds assumptions about how life is to be led, many of which are unconscious, and everyone brings those assumptions to the table when analyzing someone else's conduct. For example, the assumption that the absence of a demand for reimbursement presumes the lack of any agreement for repayment is based upon expectations of social conduct; that is, we expect the entitled partner to "make a demand" in a timely manner. In a society where making such demands would be considered rude and inappropriate, that legal assumption simply is incorrect.

To a great degree, most judges undoubtedly operate in similar ways. They probably start from a conclusory vantage point of what they believe intuitively is the right outcome and then justify that decision based upon post hoc reasoning using the framework of an implied-in-fact contract. Thus, you can't evaluate the likely outcome of your client's implied contract claims without taking this likely dynamic into consideration.

Implied-in-Law Contract / Unjust Enrichment

Every state also has its own doctrine of implied-in-law contracts, usually framed in terms of unjust enrichment. The principle here is that if one party has benefited through another's actions that resulted in the detriment of the other party in a situation that does not usually imply nonreciprocal generosity, it is unjust for the benefited party to hoard all of the benefits for himself. It can be hard to explain these concepts to clients, but it's important that you try to do so. You might tell to your clients as an example a story of one partner giving up a job to follow his partner to another city and then taking on the bulk of the domestic chores, thus enabling the employed partner to get a higher-paying job. In this scenario, it only seems fair that the well-paid partner should share some of the bounty with the relocated partner who made it all possible. Similarly, if one partner takes $50,000 out of her savings account and spends it on a renovation for the house owned solely by the other partner and then they break up before the contributing party has any real enjoyment of the renovation, it only seems fair that the homeowner should reimburse some proportion of the $50,000 to the nonowning partner. In each of these situations, there is a direct connection between one partner's sacrifice (of time or money) and the other's financial gain, and so there is an equitable basis for imposing a duty on the benefiting partner to share some of the benefit with the contributing partner.

Rulings along these lines are even more subjective than those involving implied contracts, for several reasons. It is rare that the quid pro quo of the parties is direct or readily demonstrable in a court of law; more often, there are intermittent waves of sacrifice by each party over time and many gains by one partner that probably have many causes, not just the other partner's sacrifices. In most families, there are benefits going in both directions, even if not precisely equal, and so it is not so simple to compile a detriment and benefit analysis. Moreover, in most states there is an exemption to this doctrine for relationships where no legal obligation is assumed or where generosity is presumed, such as in parent-child or most friendship relationships.

You should always keep in mind that most judges, being fairly conservative lawyers for the most part, are reluctant to find a contract in the context of an informal cohabitation relationship. For opposite-sex couples, there seems to be a dark strain of dismissive disregard of the claim as sour grapes since the claimant could have insisted on marriage if he really felt that he was entitled to something. Same-sex claimants often suffer a different sort of barrier: the judges often feel that the partners should have signed a cohabitation agreement, knowing that they were not protected by the marital laws. And, as succinctly stated in the ruling by the judge in a case I worked on several years ago, being generous to a lover in the reasonable expectation of some kind of reciprocity does not impose a legal *duty* of reciprocity on the recipient partner. The lack of reciprocity may be socially or morally offensive, but that does not make it unlawful.

Good Faith Improver

This doctrine is derived from fundamental principles of real property law and is one of the more reliable bases of a claim by a nonowner. If one partner has made significant improvements to a residence owned by the other one and if those improvements actually raise the value of the house (as opposed to being cosmetic changes such as an interior repainting) and if the improver hasn't been able to stay in the relationship long enough to enjoy the benefit of the improvements (and thus hasn't received enough free housing to amortize the improvement's cost), then the owner of the house owes some amount of compensation to the contributing party. This is especially true where the improvement is out of scale with what a nonowner would typically pay for, as opposed to a small-scale project or something that is directly tied to the nonowner's shared occupancy of the property, such as a home office.

Keep in mind that the actual value of the improvement may not be very great, especially if it has already been in place for some time (and thus has diminished in value) or if the property overall has dropped in

In one of my last nonmarital breakup trials, the nonowner of the house claimed that she was entitled to half of the equity on the grounds that she had spent nearly two years renovating the place using her skills as a carpenter and tile setter. She claimed that the value of her renovation work was nearly $250,000, which was about the same amount that the titled owner had invested in the property. Her claim was based upon an alleged oral contract and an implied-in-fact agreement, as well as quantum meruit and a wide variety of equitable arguments.

I represented the owner, and our defense was multifaceted. We argued that the claimant had stated in a prior bankruptcy proceeding that she owned no real estate and that no one owed her anything on a contract. My client testified that while her ex-partner had always demanded an interest in the house, she had always refused to put her on title, and thus there was never any agreement between the two of them. We also brought in an expert who testified that in his opinion the real value of the work was closer to $100,000, and my client testified that she had spent more than double that amount on joint living expenses plus paying some of the separate bills of her partner. By the time the value of the free housing was included, the benefit conferred on the claimant was more than double what we asserted the renovation work was really worth.

Fortunately for my client, the judge denied the claim in its entirety, concluding that there was no clear and convincing evidence of an oral contract claim, that any equitable claim was defeated by the bankruptcy statements, and that the documented financial contributions and free housing provided to the claimant more than exceeded the value of the improvements.

value. Furthermore, as with any equitable claim, the value of the claim would be offset by any benefits conferred on the claimant such as free rent, other financial assistance, or shared repayment of student loans or other pre-relationship debts.

Quantum Meruit

Quantum meruit claims are most useful where one party has done work without compensation for the benefit of the other party. Most typically this arises in connection with a renovation of a home, but it also can be raised in connection with a business activity. There are two important questions underlying a quantum meruit claim: whether the work was something that would typically be compensated as opposed to provided freely, and what benefits in lieu of compensation the claimant has already received.

When explaining this doctrine to your clients, you should use examples of an extended family because this is the best way for clients to understand these concepts. If someone's brother came from out of town for a weekend to help rebuild a deck and was treated to dinner and maybe a hotel room, the homeowner sibling would probably be shocked to receive a bill from her brother a few weeks later. On the other hand, if another brother came to town, rented an apartment for a year at his own expense and did a complete renovation of his sister's house, it would be surprising if she didn't offer him something in return. So, too, with lovers: a partner who goes into the office of his boyfriend once a month or so and helps with the accounting and never sends a bill after several years of such generosity is not going to be well received if he submits a monetary claim after a breakup. But a girlfriend who devotes a decade or more of work to a company owned by her boyfriend whose value soars vastly in excess of what she was paid on an annual basis may indeed have a valid quantum meruit claim.[7]

Other Equitable Claims

There are a wide variety of other sorts of equitable claims, mostly under the rubric of breach of fiduciary duty or constructive or resulting trusts. As with the other equitable arguments, the claims should focus on how the claimant suffered to his detriment with a resulting direct benefit to the other party, either by a contribution of time or money.[8] It will be very hard to pursue an equitable claim without some kind of detriment on the part of the claimant and a benefit to the other partner. This contrasts with a contractual claim that does not require benefit and detriment but rather requires some kind of consideration. For example, remaining unemployed to take care of the kids would be sufficient consideration for a contract but might not be much of a detriment if the claimant had no prior work history at all. Similarly, helping a partner with the management of a business when the claimant would not otherwise be out making money may suffice as consideration for a contract but probably would not meet the threshold of detriment for an equitable claim.

Constructive trust cases focus on an assertion that one party invested funds on behalf of the couple or that one partner's funds were used by the other partner for a jointly owned asset. Resulting trusts, by contrast, generally involve situations where one party is using the other party's funds for making an investment that is titled solely in one party's name.[9] The most typical such claim is where one partner supplied the down payment for real property, but the title is held by the other partner, usually for credit-related reasons. Keep in mind the old adage, however, that to claim equity, one must do equity. If the underlying reason for one person being off the title was a suspect one, such as avoiding creditors or hiding from an ex-spouse or, even worse, trying to launder ill-gotten gains, most courts are not going to be very welcoming of an equitable claim of a constructive or resulting trust.

It is very difficult to persuade a judge (or jury, if that is an option in your jurisdiction) to make an equitable award in these sorts of situations. When it comes to cases brought by opposite-sex partners, most judges and jurors tend to believe that if the parties expected to enjoy any of the protections of marriage, they could have married; and so they interpret the absence of a marriage as a kind of informed consent to opt out of the marriage benefits. When it comes to cases brought by same-sex partners, most judges (and jurors) tend to see the parties as competent independent-minded folks who voluntarily opted out of "the system," and they aren't able to see a traditional husband-wife dependency relationship that would justify any sort of claim. In other words, the gay men are still men and the lesbians are tough women, and none of them is likely to win the sort of sympathy that a financially dependent wife might enjoy.

Real Property or Financial Asset Title Presumptions

Every state has its own set of substantive and evidentiary rules for property titling, and these rules generally apply to real property as well as financial assets. Putting both names on the title presumes equal ownership, and in some states holding title as joint tenants creates a stronger presumption, rebuttable only by proof of an agreement.[10] Where title is held as a tenancy in common, however, the presumption of equal ownership generally can be overcome simply by proof of excess contribution to a necessary expense.[11] Conversely, if only one party is on the title to the property or account, there will be a strong presumption that such person is the sole owner, rebuttable only by proof of a contract or equitable claim to the contrary.[12] Each state has its own set of procedures for adjudicating real estate co-ownership claims as part of the equitable partition process, with all of the attendant equitable bases for claims and defenses.

Claims by Noncohabiting Partners

Not every unmarried couple lives together, yet most states require cohabitation as a threshold prerequisite for any sort of palimony or property claim. A few courts have dealt with the question of whether noncohabiting partners are entitled to anything and for the most part have denied claims on the grounds that the parties did not have a "marriage-like" relationship.[13] The only exceptions would be for partners who co-owned property or had a business relationship, in which case a financial or property claim can be based upon this business venture rather than on any history of cohabitation.

C. Defenses to Nonmarital and Palimony Claims

Just as claims between partners need to be framed in terms of each state's legal doctrines, so must the defenses to such claims. When the parties or their lawyers are engaged in informal negotiations, the discussion may well focus more on specific issues unique to that particular couple's situation. At the same time, you should always be thinking about legal defenses and be ready to raise them in response to any legal claim. While predictions of court outcomes are notoriously unreliable in this volatile and uncertain area of law, it's an exercise that always should be attempted, even in the early stages of negotiation.

Statute of Limitations

The statute of limitations will always depend on the nature of the claim being presented: an oral contract claim in many states has a two-year limit, whereas written contracts typically have longer limits, such as four years in California.[14] Fiduciary duty claims, like constructive trust or other equitable claims, often have a specific limit based upon the nature of the claim, ranging from two to four years in most jurisdictions.

Figuring out the appropriate statute of limitations is the easy part; what is more difficult is determining *when* the time begins to run and what actions might toll the deadline. In most states time limits on a claim for reimbursement of a real estate contribution only begin to run when there is a sale of the property or a breakup of the relationship, on the theory that the implied agreement was that reimbursement would happen only at that time. If the claim is for payment of post-separation support, the clock would ordinarily start ticking only when the parties cease cohabiting or when the alleged promise was breached. For example, in the California case of Johnnie Cochran, the court of appeal concluded that the deadline clock would only begin to run when the boyfriend stopped making the postseparation payments (as otherwise someone could make payments for two years and then stop, thus running out the statute of limitations).[15] Unfortunately, because there is no formal process of a legal separation for unmarried couples, even determining the end of the cohabitation period can be difficult and subject to dispute.

Statute of Frauds

Most lawyers (and many nonlawyers) wrongly believe that the statute of frauds will preclude any claims regarding real estate unless there is a written agreement. While sometimes this defense can be useful, in fact many state courts have held that it would be unfair to impose this requirement on marriage-like or family relationships where such formality is not typical.[16] Other courts have focused on the claimant's reliance, holding that the defendant is estopped from asserting a statute of frauds defense. In any case, it is always prudent to raise this defense where a year or more has passed since the couple broke up, especially where there is some question about the closeness of the personal relationship; but you shouldn't expect to gain much traction from such a defense. Many states have specific rules for claims regarding a will contract, so those defenses are more likely to be valid in any post-death claim situation.

Lack of Consideration

Whenever the claimant did not invest money into the property or business, a lack of consideration should be raised as a defense. In some instances, you may be able to raise a defense of meretricious consideration. Such defenses seem to still have viability even though the moral opprobrium against nonmarital sexual relations has waned.[17] Promises of future gifts typically are not enforceable, and general allegations about love and support will not be sufficient consideration in most courts.

While this defense will seem unduly technical to most practitioners, it can serve as a justification by a court to deny a claim that otherwise seems weak; and thus, this defense should never be disregarded.

Choice of Law and Venue Issues

If the parties entered into the alleged contract in a state that doesn't honor such agreements, there may be a question as to the enforceability of the alleged agreement, even if it would be honored in the state in which they now live.[18] In most states the venue for any real estate claim is the county in which the property is located, which can create serious logistical problems for couples who own multiple properties in different states or counties. While no one wants to be forced into filing multiple actions in a variety of jurisdictions, raising that defense in advance could be a strong motivation for a claimant to settle a claim to a multiplicity of properties.

Breach by the Plaintiff / Failure of Consideration

Every response to a nonmarital claim should include an evaluation of the overall performance by the claimant, looking for evidence that the plaintiff did not perform his own obligations. One of the defenses to a claim for a partial interest in real estate would be that the claimant didn't contribute the required share of the property expenses. This is also true regarding any claim for a business interest.

Satisfaction and Accord

To the extent that the claimant has already received some benefit, either during the relationship or thereafter, a defense of satisfaction and accord should preclude a further claim. In some instances, this defense can be based upon the free housing and other benefits or on monetary payments received by the claimant during the course of the relationship. In other situations, you can point to specific actions, such as signing a deed or relinquishing possession of an asset, as proof of a prior oral or implied settlement agreement. As long as something has been paid to the claimant, it is always worth raising this defense.

Other Equitable Defenses

Because most of the claims that are raised by unmarried partners are equitable in nature, all of the standard equitable defenses (unclean hands, laches, etc.) can also be raised. As with the other defenses, it is not simply a matter of hoping that the court will strictly apply these doctrines to dismiss a case. Rather, an unsympathetic judge may be unpersuaded by the case for other reasons but then will invoke these defenses as justifications for the denial of the claim. If you are defending a nonmarital property or monetary claim, you always need to be mindful of telling the story in a way that blends the legal doctrines with the emotionally compelling truth rather than thinking of legal defenses merely as technicalities.

D. Dealing with the Typical Claims

It should not be a surprise that, for the most part, the lives of your clients are not neatly organized along the lines of the numerous legal doctrines that apply to their lives—and the same will be true about their disputes. Part of developing a client-centered practice is learning how to reframe those doctrines so that they are most readily applicable to the cases in front of you. As a guide for starting out on that path, here is a survey of the most frequently recurring areas of conflict and some suggestions on how to approach each of these territories.

Disputes Regarding Real Property

The Excess Contributor. Perhaps the single most frequently recurring dispute involving nonmarital breakups is that of the excess contributor (i.e., a claim by one of the partners that she invested more into a co-owned house without a clearly stated proportional ownership on the deed or a written co-ownership agreement). Most such claims relate to an excess (or solely funded) down payment, followed closely by claims over the payment for a renovation. Less frequently will claims be made for excess contributions to the ongoing monthly expenses, not because this doesn't happen very often, but simply because most partners are more willing to let go of those types of excess payments. It's also true that judges and juries are far less sympathetic to claims based upon ongoing excess contributions to regular expenses as compared to excess capital contributions.

In many states, joint tenancy deeds carry a stronger presumption of equal ownership than tenancy in common titling. But because most owners don't pay much attention to the vesting of the title (or if they do, it is solely with regard to the survivorship aspect of joint tenancy), it usually isn't helpful in settlement negotiations to focus solely on that factor as a technical legal matter. If it makes a difference in terms of likely court outcomes, by all means mention the vesting of title, but don't rely solely on the legal analysis to settle the matter. Also, be prepared to evaluate the broader range of financial and nonfinancial contributions because many couples trade off excess property contributions with greater payments for non-tax-deductible or later-arising obligations or for sweat equity or other labor contributions. It also is essential to pay attention to the actual value delivered by the contribution; an expensive interior painting job may not have actually raised the value of the property very much.

Any dispute over the allocation of the equity also should be integrated into the discussions about the fate of the house (i.e., whether it is going to be sold on the open market or kept by one of the owners). If there is uncertainty as to the equity allocation and neither party has a duty to sell to her partner, it may be possible to trade off a claim of greater equity percentage for a buyout opportunity. And if there is also uncertainty about the value of the property in a buyout scenario, it may be possible to strike a deal that combines the allocation issue with the overall valuation dispute. In other words, it is generally much simpler to reach an overall settlement that incorporates all of the issues rather than trying to reach a resolution for each particular legal issue.

In recent years, the tougher problem to resolve has been the insufficiency of the proceeds of sale (or equity in a buyout scenario) to reimburse either partner's down payment, let alone that of the excess contributor, or provide the equity or profit to distribute between the co-owners. If there was no enforceable legal agreement between the parties, it will be hard for the excess contributor to obtain a monetary judgment against a co-owner for a share of the loss. And, of course, collecting on such a judgment will probably be very difficult. Always encourage your clients to ask for some proportional share of the loss, but they should be prepared to recover very little, if anything at all.

The Off-Title Contributor. These are often the most painful cases. I once represented a man who had turned over his paycheck each month to his more sophisticated lover, who used the money (in combination with his own funds, of course) to pay the mortgage on the couple's residence.

After more than twenty years together, the property value had soared to nearly $1 million, and the mortgage loan had been entirely paid off. My client claimed that he always thought he was on the title, but he had entirely relied on his partner to handle the legal matters. Sadly, the judge denied our claim of a 50 percent ownership on the grounds that the amounts contributed by my client did not greatly exceed the rental value of his shared use of the residence and that there was no reasonable evidence to support his claim of equitable co-ownership.

Part of the problem here is that there is usually some reason, and not always a legally palatable one, for one of the partners being off the title. Sometimes it is to hide assets from an ex-partner or spouse, sometimes it is to avoid creditors or qualify for a public benefit, and other times it is because one party has been in bankruptcy or has bad credit. Sometimes one of the partners held sole title prior to the commencement of the relationship, and the partners never figured out exactly how to allocate the equity. In each of these situations, the owner can rightly proclaim that there wasn't a clear agreement to overcome the strong presumptions of title, and it is rare for a nonowner to be able to marshal clear and convincing evidence to prove any kind of ownership interest. In these cases, the best arguments are going to be the equitable ones, taking into account each partner's actual contributions, the value of housing that each one received, and the fundamental injustice that can result if nothing is shared with the nontitled contributor. But be realistic with your client: Proving an equitable interest does not mean that your client will suddenly become a 50 percent owner. Even after your client has been deemed an equitable co-owner, the equitable share of the proceeds or equity might only be 10 percent or 20 percent.

A key piece of your assignment if you represent the off-title contributor is to motivate your client to accept a reduced amount in settlement, knowing the risks of going to trial. I've witnessed the problems that result from not being able to do that; indeed, in one particularly painful case, the titled owner offered my client nearly 40 percent of the equity paid out over time, and my client rejected it as being less than an equal division—and went on to lose at trial altogether. You must be unvarnished in your warnings to your client about the steep hurdle of overcoming presumptions of title in these cases and urge your client to compromise her claims accordingly.

Property-Related Debts and Overpayments. It's quite typical that one of the parties will have paid a greater share of the property expenses over time without any clear agreement about how this imbalance would be adjusted at the time of sale or a buyout by one of the partners. Many partners have an informal arrangement that presumes that there will be a balancing over time, but then they break up before the adjustment has taken place. This is one area where there is a serious risk of a valid statute of limitations defense because courts are reluctant to go back too many years into the history of the relationship to reimburse an excess contributor to the monthly expenses. Also, from an outsider's perspective, a decade of delay before a demand for reimbursement will make the claim appear to be an after-the-fact claim, merely a part of the breakup drama. Most likely, the actual month-to-month arrangement will be deemed to be the agreed-upon allocation unless the excess contributor made a demand for reimbursement shortly after making any excess payment.

It's another story when the nonpayment is recent or when there has been an active effort to collect from the deadbeat co-owner, and in these situations it is entirely appropriate to present a claim for reimbursement. You will want to be sure that your client understands the doctrine of "whole from the whole, half from the half." If your client paid $1,000 to a third party for a property-related expense, then your client is entitled to a reimbursement of $1,000 out of the proceeds of sale—but only $500 if it is framed as reimbursement from a co-owner.

Another frequently recurring problem is where a portion of the mortgage loan proceeds (especially from a line of credit) has been used to fund one partner's separate obligation, or at least an obligation that one of the partners claims is personal. It is quite common for couples to take out a line of credit to pay off one partner's student loan or credit card debts in order to lower the interest rate and make the payments tax-deductible. However, if the couple breaks up before the loan is paid off, there may be a dispute over how the remaining portion of the mortgage loan should be paid. Hopefully, there will be enough equity on the part of the debtor to cover a personal share of the mortgage loan; and if the underlying debt was clearly personal, that share of the mortgage loan should be paid off entirely by that borrower. But if the debtor doesn't have the equity or any separate funds to cover the loan, chances are that the other co-owner will be stuck with the obligation (or will see his share of the equity reduced by this obligation).

Disputes over Money

Shared Account Claims. In most states there are specific legal presumptions mandating equal co-ownership of joint accounts, in contrast to a solely owned account with a right of survivorship or POD provision. In some states (such as California), there are appellate cases holding that *either* partner can withdraw the entirety of a joint account, under the doctrine that each owner owns 100 percent of a joint tenancy asset.[19] Rarely does this take place; rather, the most frequently recurring conflict is where the contributions to the joint account have been unequal or have been made entirely by one partner. In that situation, the excess (or sole) contributor has the legal burden of overcoming the presumption of equal ownership. It is rare that there was sufficient discussion or any sort of unambiguous action by the partners so as to provide clear and convincing evidence of an agreement rebutting the equal ownership presumption, and hence the excess or sole contributor is at serious risk of having to share the account with the lesser-contributing or noncontributing partner.

But even when you have taken stock of the legal rules, your primary focus should be on honoring the real understanding of the parties, to the extent that you can get them to be honest about their earlier assumptions and discussions. Think globally about all of the financial issues. Doctrines of fairness also should be on the table, though it can be difficult to reach a consensus on what is really fair in any particular situation. If the partners had an overall practice of keeping their assets separate, it seems only fair to allocate the joint account in proportion to contributions. But if they shared funds from time to time and were casual about how money flowed in and out of various accounts, it will seem artificial to suddenly allocate an account based upon a set of deposits that may not have reflected their true financial positions.

Solely Titled Accounts. This situation is usually easier to address. If both parties put their funds in an account titled in just one partner's name, it is only fair to assert that this was for the sake of convenience or management and was not intended as a gift of the funds to the account holder. True, there might be an inappropriate motivation behind the way that

One of the best features of marital dissolution procedures (in most states) is a duty of disclosure of all assets, whether shared or individual. No such rule applies to nonmarital dissolutions, and one of the most difficult professional issues is how to negotiate a settlement in the absence of full financial disclosure. You can always ask for information, and hopefully your client has been paying some attention to the other partner's financial dealings so as to be able to spot a serious concealment; but it isn't easy to be sure about any of these key facts. You can try to insist on a statement in a settlement agreement that all information has been disclosed, but that doesn't really satisfy the need for immediate disclosure—and it is hard to know in the future when you've been misled. Hopefully, you can engage in sufficient discussion and informal discovery to get a good sense of what assets exist since you don't want to have to file a lawsuit just to get the information when you are close to reaching a decent settlement.

When in doubt, it is always good to include a warranty of disclosure in the settlement agreement; at least you will have a legal basis to raise a new claim if something emerges later on that wasn't disclosed. But the best source of information is your own client, who hopefully can dig deep into his memory bank to uncover any undisclosed assets.

the accounts were handled (e.g., concealing funds from a creditor or former partner), but those legal impediments should not be used to take advantage of a former partner in a negotiation. There may be legitimate questions as to the allocation of the account, however, especially where money has gone in and out over time.

Debts to Each Other and to Others. Oftentimes, it is hard to know what is a debt as opposed to a gift. The paper documents are often misleading. For example, parents sign gift letters to enable their kids to get a loan even though everyone expects that the gift will be paid back; partners state on loan applications that they have no debts even though they've agreed to repay a loan from their partner; and car loans are taken out solely in the name of the partner with the better credit. As with the other issues, you should always start with a frank discussion of the real arrangements even if they are not legally enforceable. It rarely is productive, especially in an early or amicable negotiation or discussion, to focus solely on the legal barriers to court enforcement of a claim, especially when that is a door that in most instances can swing in both directions. Be prepared to raise the legal obstacles when the other party is being obstinate or greedy, but try to resolve the issues based upon the true understandings of the parties.

Claims for Postseparation Support. Given how difficult it is for any claimant to win a claim for postseparation support, even in a state like California that theoretically allows these claims, it may be a surprise to some lawyers when they are urged by their clients to present such claims. It should not be a surprise at all, however, to hear how outraged the responding partner will be when presented with a claim for support. "We weren't married!" is the first and most emphatic response, even by those who were registered in a marriage-equivalent registration. Those partners will be considered married if they are living in a recognition state, and so they will definitely have the same problems that all higher-earning spouses have to handle. Many same-sex married spouses will also object, either by asserting that they only got married to make a political statement or by claiming that somehow their marriage wasn't fully recognized and therefore should be exempt from these rules. Then there are those who simply feel that the alimony rules were designed to protect dependent wives and mothers, not underemployed ex-lovers who aren't willing to go work for living.

Where the partners are registered as civil union or domestic partners in a marriage-equivalent registrations, the claimant will have solid legal footing to claim support as a marriage-equivalent spouse. But the situation for those who are not covered by marital law will be quite different, both legally and emotionally.

First, it rarely makes sense for a lawyer to take such a claim on a contingency, and so most claimants simply won't be able to afford a protracted legal battle. From a defense perspective, the question will be how hard the responding party wants to defend the claim and how much money she is willing to spend on a legal defense. You might be confident that your client will prevail in defending such a claim; the trickier question is whether it is prudent to spend your client's money on a vigorous defense when a reasonable settlement might actually cost less in the end.

The emotional dynamics are harder to resolve. For some partners, it will be easy to reach an amicable settlement that addresses the real financial problems of the lower-earning partner, taking into account the understandings by which the parties lived during their time together.

Structure the settlement along the lines of the real financial needs, not on some theoretical alimony claim. In addition, the claimant should recognize that any such settlement is fundamentally voluntary on the part of the paying party, and so the settlement amounts are likely to be lower than what a married spouse would receive as alimony.

The legal unpredictability of these financial disputes, along with the wildly fluid and ambiguous personal histories of the parties' relationship, can lead to a delicate professional challenge for lawyers working in this field. It's easy to simply fall into the trap of being the zealous advocate for an angry and blaming client, but most likely that will quickly lead to conflicts with the client—not least because you probably won't be able to deliver a quick victory for your client. Over time, you will also begin to hear the other side's point of view, and thus you may starting having doubts about the legitimacy of your client's claim. You may even come to a point where you understand why your client got dumped.

Family law attorneys are accustomed to working with fixed rules for the most part, and they don't have to get so embroiled in the details of implied agreements or long-forgotten promises of support. The contract-based emphasis of the civil law claims for unmarried partners pushes the lawyer to inquire into the story of the relationship and to present equitable justifications for claims or defenses, and this can end up leading the lawyer (and the client) into emotionally treacherous territory.

You also may find yourself wondering what really is in the best interest of your client if the claims are legally weak and the client is spending more than he should on the legal process. If you've taken the case on a contingency basis, which is allowed in most states for nonmarital claims, you may also begin to regret having done so if the value of the case appears to be dropping and the stress and difficulty of the case dramatically increases. This can be a vicious circle: The client grows fatigued and runs out of money, the lawyer begins to have doubts about the viability of the case, and everyone's performances suffer as a result.

Be extremely cautious before you take on these cases, and always be open with your prospective clients about your attitude toward compromise and your concerns about the viability of a legal claim. Regularly assure your clients that you will be continually loyal to what you consider to be their best interest, even when they don't share that opinion. Counsel compromise when you think the case is weak, and always insist that your clients pay you in full for your work. Be careful to let your clients know in writing where you see the problems in their case; and if they choose to proceed with litigation, make sure that it is clear that they were doing so on their own initiative, at times over your objections.

These are situations that cry out for mediation or a collaborative negotiation approach, where the parties are part of the discussion at every juncture and where the overall issues of finances, fault, implied agreements, and true financial needs and capacities can be addressed. Trying to resolve the issues in any other fashion (as discussed in the next chapter) will be nearly impossible.

Disputes over Things

Computers, cars, artwork, furniture, and especially cats and dogs: The fights over these valuable things can be extremely painful for your client and are rarely subject to any easy legal resolution. Ownership is usually ambiguous as there aren't titles to most of these objects; and even where titles exist, the choice of the names on the document was often the result of a haphazard historical event. The partner who picked up the dog at the kennel got named as the owner, the one who gave his credit card number over the phone got listed as the computer owner, and the one with the better credit ended up as the legal owner of the car. Married couples don't live in such ambiguous worlds as generally their household items will be considered jointly owned regardless of names on the licenses and titles.

Making matters worse, the typical default legal rules (whoever paid for something or is listed on the title is the owner) rarely make sense either. Couples often share expenses by drawing from each partner's income in a variety of ways, sometimes trading off making payments or sometimes just using the account that is available at the time. One person may have paid for the painting bought in Santa Fe, but maybe her partner paid the entirety of the hotel bill. So is it fair to award the painting solely to the one who paid for it?

The simple answer is to tell your clients to resolve the issues by mediation, but that is not always productive, and many folks are reluctant to spend hundreds of dollars per hour arguing over the silverware. While mediation should definitely be considered, you should always encourage your clients to design their own distribution system and to try to work it out without the help of expensive professionals. Here are some specific suggestions for making this possible:

- Start by distributing the items that both parties agree are the personal belongings of each partner. No one should be allowed to hold onto someone else's things as hostage for negotiating over the disputed items.

- Gifts can't be taken back even if the recipient turns out to be an unfaithful jerk. Tell your clients that they need to be honest about what gifts were made, either by them or by their friends or family members. You can be sympathetic to their frustration, but you also want to keep asking them whether acting on that anger is really going to be helpful to them in the long run.
- If no one kept clear records of who paid for what portion of the joint items or if they are untitled (i.e., all items except for a car), the partners should consider them jointly owned in equal shares. There are various ways of dividing up the joint items, but a particularly fair and workable one is to create a list and then have each partner pick one item in turn. That way, they can each choose whether they prefer a sentimental object or one with greater monetary value. Anything that remains in dispute should be put in storage or left with one partner but with a written agreement that its ownership is still in dispute.
- For items that can't be allocated in this way (say, for example, a car), one partner should set its value and let the other one pick whether she is the buyer or the seller of the half-interest.
- For anything that still remains unresolved after these procedures are used, the partners should select a neutral person (who need not be an attorney or judge) to serve as arbitrator. Each of the parties should be given at most an hour or two to present her case to the arbitrator, whose decision should be final.
- Although some people can make it work, shared custody of pets just isn't practical in the long run. Rather, one person should have custody, and the other one can have visitation; and if the partners can't be relied upon to make such arrangements on their own, then probably neither one of them should be keeping the pet at all. The one who doesn't get the pet should get something else of significant emotional value, and there should be some other accommodation to reflect the seriousness of the sacrifice.

Disputes over Business Interests

The legal rules about business claims typically are the same as most other personal property assets: title presumes ownership, and joint title presumes equal ownership. The problems arise when couples have been casual about the titling of their business, such as putting it in one partner's name because that partner has better credit or adding someone who really didn't invest anything just to "feel right" or to gain an advantage (such as a minority ownership credit or a local business advantage). As with the other claims, you want to start with an open exploration of the truth so that the full story is out on the table. You may need to do this in a confidential mediation setting, especially if there are questionable legal nuances that you wouldn't want exposed to the world. This is also the case if there are outside interests at play, such as unrelated partners or investors who would be upset to learn about what has transpired.

The primary message you have to continually repeat to your client is that if he doesn't handle the business issues carefully and respectfully, chances are the value of the business will plummet. Customers don't want to be around nasty marital (or nonmarital) conflict, and employees and co-owners will likewise abandon ship if it looks like it is sinking in the morass of a lovers' quarrel. If there are significant business assets, it may be prudent to bring in an outside temporary manager of the company to insulate the business's operations from the relationship conflicts.

The other important message to convey is that access to information is not the same as taking control or ownership. Even if one of the partners is not a legal owner, chances are he could file a lawsuit alleging an equitable interest and thus get access to the company's financial records in discovery. You may want to suggest a confidentiality agreement and an inspection arrangement that precludes making copies of any documents. This will assuage fears about the misuse of the information, but you should also try to find a way to cooperate in providing access to information. There is no reason to force someone into litigation just to get the pertinent information. After dealing with the information concerns, you can then go forward to the harder job of negotiating true ownership.

You also will need to be realistic, and at times downright skeptical, when it comes to determining the value of a contested business. Appraising a business is not easy, and there are many subjective formulas for basing the value depending on the type of business. There may be unreported income or artificially inflated expenses that seriously warp the appraisal process. Again, you don't want to have to file litigation just to conduct discovery on the assets of the business, so try to work something out in a negotiation or mediation setting and then do your best to make a deal that is realistically tied to the real value of the business.

NOTES

1. *See* Appendix (chart of state rules).
2. As to parentage issues, the partners' marital status will be mostly irrelevant if they are both legal parents; if, however, one of the partners is not a legal parent, the substantive issues are as described in Chapter 10.
3. *See* Appendix (chart of relevant state rules).
4. *See, e.g.,* Metro. Water v. Marquardt, 59 Cal. 2d 159 (1963); Masterson v. Sine (1968), 68 Cal. 2d 222 (1968).
5. *See, e.g.,* Wilcox v. Trautz, 693 N.E.2d 141 (Mass. 1998).
6. *See, e.g.,* CAL. CIV. CODE § 1619. The jury instructions for an implied contract are most illustrative: "In deciding whether a contract was created, you should consider the conduct and relationship of the parties as well as all the circumstances of the case. Contracts can be created by the conduct of the parties, without spoken or written words. Contracts created by conduct are just as valid as contracts formed with words. Conduct will create a contract if the conduct of both parties is intentional and each knows, or has reason to know, that the other party will interpret the conduct as an agreement to enter into a contract." California Jury Instructions (CACI) 3.05 (2010); *see also* Gardner v. Charles Schwab & Co., 267 Cal. Rptr. 326 (1990); Connell v. Diehl, 938 A.2d 143 (2008 Pa.).
7. That was exactly what happened in the California case of Maglica v. Maglica, 66 Cal. App. 4th 442 (1998), where the girlfriend of the founder of the Maglite flashlight company won a significant percentage of the value of the company—about $28 million more than the amounts she had been paid over the course of their years working together. The case settled before the California Supreme Court ever had a chance to review the appellate court decision, but the reasoning of the lower courts is very instructive.
8. Padilla v. Padilla, 38 Cal. App. 2d 319 (1940).
9. *See, e.g.,* Small v. Harper, 638 S.W.2d 24 (Tex. Civ. App. 1982); Sullivan v. Rooney, 533 N.E.2d 1372 (Mass. 1989).
10. Kershman v. Kershman, 192 Cal. App. 2d 23 (1961).
11. Milian v. DeLeon, 188 Cal. App.3d 1185 (1986); Donnelly v. Wetzel, 37 Cal. App. 741 (1918).
12. Alderson v. Alderson, 180 Cal. App. 3d 450 (1986); Toney v. Nolder, 173 Cal. App. 3d 791 (1985).
13. Devaney v. L'Esperance, 949 A.2d 743 (N.J. 2008); Norton v. McOsker, 407 F.3d 501 (1st Cir. 2005); Bergen v. Wood, 14 Cal. App. 4th 854 (1993).
14. Cochran v. Cochran, 56 Cal. App. 4th 1115 (1997).
15. *Id.*
16. Cline v. Festerson, 128 Cal. App. 2d 380 (1954).
17. Taylor v. Fields, 178 Cal. App. 3d 653 (1986).
18. Henderson v. Superior Court, 77 Cal. App. 3d 583 (1978).
19. Lee v. Yang, 111 Cal. App. 4th 481 (2003).

CHAPTER FOURTEEN
THE NONMARITAL DISSOLUTION PROCESS

As cumbersome and oppressive as some of the marital dissolution rules may seem to married couples and their lawyers, at least there are rules. I have often experienced a related version of that previously described illness (family law envy): In this setting I refer to it as "divorce court envy," wishing that I had some semblance of a formal process and structure to manage messy breakups. Indeed, the absence of clear procedural rules or, what is sometimes worse, the application of inappropriate civil law rules for nonmarital dissolutions can make it especially tortuous to resolve these disputes. On the other hand, the very informality of the nonmarital dissolution process allows for a flexibility and creativity that can be helpful, if effectively managed.

A. IMMEDIATE DISSOLUTION CONCERNS

In many states, the mere filing of a marital dissolution petition sets in place a structured dissolution process, which typically includes automatic restraining orders prohibiting either spouse from taking any action with regard to the couple's financial interests without the consent of the other partner. In many states, there are mandatory requirements of financial disclosure as well as mandatory court-supervised mediation. Oftentimes, the family law bar is a close collegial group, which can help smooth some of the rockier bumps in the road. Even in the most contested of cases, the judges have been specially assigned to deal with the nastiness of family breakups; and so to some degree (based upon the local court budgets and arrangements), they are up for the job in front of them. In addition, family court rules allow reasonably ready access to a judge who can rule on particularly bad behavior. There's a reason why we have specially designed family courts and family judges: Our legislators know that warring spouses sometimes need to be controlled, and they've designed a system with those particular behaviors in mind.

There are no such statutory protections for the unmarried divorce, and this makes all the difference in the resolution of these disputes. You will have to be on active alert to these differences and be prepared to take action to protect your client. In some instances, your client may be the initiator of the breakup, and so he will have advance notice of what is about to transpire; however, if he is the noninitiator, he may have to act quickly, oftentimes when he is most vulnerable emotionally. The two main messages to deliver to your clients are that (1) they cannot rely on a mandatory and pre-established court process to protect their interests, and (2) the civil court rules that do apply to them were not designed for their particular variety of chaotic and rapid-fire conflicts.

Bank Accounts

Your client should immediately evaluate the status of all bank accounts in which he has any financial interest and verify who is the named owner of the account. If there are shared funds in a joint account, then the bank should be contacted and instructed to not release any funds without joint signatures. Your client should consider withdrawing 50 percent of the funds from any joint account. Even if the law (or bank rule) allows withdrawal of 100 percent of the funds, urge your client to take no more than their 50 percent out of the account: Withdrawing 50 percent leaves him fully protected and minimizes the risk of a parallel excessive grab from another account by his ex. If your client's partner has access to your client's individual funds through an electronic transfer program, the passwords should be changed or the electronic access should be cancelled. This can be particularly tricky for some couples as they may have electronically linked their separate accounts in ways that allow transfers between accounts by either partner. If segregating the accounts is not possible, your client should consider opening up new accounts and transferring all balances to the new account so that the partner cannot wrongly take any of your client's funds.

I once represented a man in a heated battle with his ex, with a lot of money at stake. They had deposited about $600,000 from a loan refinancing into a joint account, which was to be used for a renovation that had been stalled. We were in the middle of the mediation session when my client pulled me aside and revealed that he had just shifted all the funds from the joint account into his own account, fearing that his ex would suddenly withdraw the funds if the dispute didn't settle in mediation. He also instructed me not to reveal this to the other side, and I was feeling pretty uncomfortable about his actions.

A few hours later, his ex's lawyer came to me and said that we had a problem. Apparently, his client had just tried to make the very same withdrawal, only to discover that my client had beaten him to it by a few hours.

I certainly felt some relief upon hearing this news as at least we could have a laugh over the near-synchronicity of their respective aggressive acts. The matter eventually settled a few months later, and the allocation of these funds was finally resolved. However, this was a vivid reminder of how unpredictable the nonmarital dissolution process can be.

Credit Cards

No one wants to be held liable for someone else's debts, especially when that someone is the person who has just dumped you. A client of mine discovered that her ex-partner had posed as her (something that generally only a same-sex partner can do) to obtain an "authorized user" credit card and had run up a $10,000 bill on cash advances. When confronted with the wrongdoing, she blithely said, "You did what you needed to do to be happy [by having an affair], so I needed to be happy, too." Unfortunately, the credit card company didn't consider this action fraudulent since the wrongdoer had previously obtained my client's personal information by her consent, not by theft.

If your client has a shared card or has authorized a partner to use a sole credit card, your client should cancel it before any wrongful charges can be incurred. Most companies consider both partners jointly and severally liable, so it is no defense to state that the other partner incurred the charges. Sometimes it can be difficult to close down these accounts, and sometimes it may be necessary to transfer the balances to the client's own account in order to close down the accounts. Sorting out the accounts can be even trickier when one partner has allowed the other to use a joint account for strictly personal use. Again, the company will look to the borrower for repayment (or both of them jointly if they are co-borrowers on the card), and the fact that the other partner ran up the charges without approval of your client is not a valid legal defense to a demand by the card company for payment.

It may take some time for you and the couple to figure out who really owes what for the past charges, and that is okay since your immediate goal is to prevent any *subsequent* charges from being incurred. When necessary, you should be prepared to talk with a senior staff person at the credit card company. If the company utterly refuses to accommodate your request to limit the future charges, at a minimum you should document your request in writing so that you can later refer to this request if you are forced to challenge any subsequent claims for payment.

Real Estate Tasks

Whenever the partners are co-owners of a residence or other real estate, there are many high-priority tasks. In most instances the clients can tackle these chores on their own, but some of them might require legal assistance, especially for the less sophisticated and more emotionally distraught clients.

Deciding when to fight (i.e., litigate) and when to compromise is one of the most delicate professional dilemmas facing lawyers handling non-marital dissolutions. The absence of a mandatory court process opens up settlement options that marital divorces don't have, but it also injects a strategic complexity that can be very subtle and amorphous. Some options and issues to consider are as follows:

- Severing the joint tenancy is logical: Most clients would not want their share of the property to pass to the person who just dumped them. Advise your clients about the rule of joint tenancy rights of survivorship and give them the opportunity to sever the joint tenancy if that can be done unilaterally in your state. In some states there is a requirement of notifying the other partner of this change; but even where it's not required, it's only fair to do so.
- Where your client is off the title but has made significant monetary contributions to real property, you may need to file a lawsuit

Postseparation occupancy disputes between unmarried partners can be horribly dramatic, in the worst sort of ways. I've helped manage a wide variety of scenarios, and there is no simple strategy to avoid extreme complications. On one occasion, my client voluntarily moved out of his own home, and soon thereafter his ex moved his new boyfriend in. When my client tried to move back in a few months later, his ex refused; and, to my amazement, a judge refused to order him to let my client back in on the grounds that my client had voluntarily left and moving back would create a risk of harm. Even worse, when the property was later put up for sale, the new boyfriend claimed that he was a rent-controlled tenant! Needless to say, it took quite a chunk of court time to unravel this mess.

In another situation, my client was not the owner but had contributed cash to the expenses for more than a decade. Shortly after the breakup (but before he moved out), he went to visit his ailing mom; and when he returned home, his ex had locked him out. At my direction, my client called the cops. They not only told the owner that he had to let my client back in (and could only evict him using the legal process because he was a licensee) but also threatened to arrest the owner if he failed to cooperate with their demand. As I always tell my clients, a call to the police is a "toll-free" call.

Eviction lawsuits against a nonowning partner can be very messy given the vagueness of the owner-occupant relationship. They also can trigger a claim of equitable co-ownership by the partner, which in some jurisdictions will stall the eviction action until the much more protracted ownership dispute is resolved. This is just one more reason why a negotiated or mediated solution should be attempted whenever possible, even if it means paying some money to negotiate one of the partners moving out. If that doesn't work, a seasoned eviction attorney should be retained, and she should be forewarned of the unique emotional dynamics of the personal situation.

promptly in order to be able to record a Notice of Pending Action (lis pendens) to prevent the titled owner from borrowing against or selling the property. It is always worth trying to obtain the titled owner's agreement not to sell or encumber the property while the dispute is pending; and if a lot of money is at stake, you should consider recording the stipulation or a memorandum of agreement to block any backdoor refinancing or sale. If you can't get an agreement, a lawsuit seems inevitable. Your client may be reluctant to leap out of the box with a lawsuit, for good reason, but he should be told about the risks of delaying such action.

- In many breakups the major concern is who is going to live where; and if both of the partners are owners of their shared home, they both have the right to continue living there unless they've agreed otherwise in writing. Ousting a legal owner can be difficult and can result in serious legal problems for the ousting owner. In most states an owner who remains living in the residence owes an amount equal to the fair rental value, up to the actual monthly expenses of the property, with any excess costs above that split equally between the two owners. It may take some hands-on intervention at times to help your client sort through the occupancy issues, and often it means balancing the financial concerns (cheap housing) with the practical issues (a place to live) while at the same time addressing the legal problems of ownership. Moving out generally does not jeopardize anyone's ownership rights, but it can shift the dynamic and give leverage to the one who is living there. Try to take a practical approach, bearing in mind any potential legal consequences of your client moving out.

- Occupancy is even stickier where only one partner is the owner since the other one probably isn't a conventional tenant, nor is he a trespasser. In some cities, it is relatively easy to demand that a nonowning partner leave the premises, but in other places there's no alternative to an unlawful detainer action if the nonowner won't leave voluntarily (since the nonowner occupant is an invitee or lodger, not a trespasser). Oftentimes, a bit of gentle persuasion can be effective, and other times an offer of financial help to cover the first month's rent in a new apartment will do the trick. "Self-help" usually is risky, though many clients will try it for fear that a legal process will be too expensive or time-consuming. What counts here is that you explain to your client the local occupancy and eviction rules as best you can, allowing him to make the decisions that will hopefully avoid a nasty crisis.

- If your client elects to move out voluntarily, get some documentation (at least unilateral, but hopefully mutual) that confirms how the parties will pay expenses going forward and also addresses the issue of whether the change is permanent. One option is to put together a simple agreement whereby the occupancy is traded off, for a few months for each partner, until they can figure out what to do with the house or apartment in the long term.

Domestic violence happens just as often with unmarried couples (both gay and straight) as it does between husbands and wives, and dealing with its consequences can be especially problematic in the absence of a marital dissolution process. Civil restraining orders can be sought to get a violent co-occupant (and even co-owner) out of a residence, and sometimes this is what is needed. However, initiating a civil restraining order (or, in some jurisdictions, a criminal restraining order) process can result in a barrage of hostile reactions, and so it isn't always the most prudent course of action.

The most delicate situations are those that arise in connection with the occasional scuffle or shoving match. They seem to occur most often when the couple has remained living together for an extended time period after a breakup, often because they can't agree on what to do with their house or apartment. Ironically, the battles seem to be most explosive when one partner wants to have a serious talk about the dissolution, and the other one just wants to be left alone. Here we are not dealing with a long history of wrongful conduct but rather an isolated incident of uncontainable anger.

The partner who takes legal action to complain about an assault often ends up regretting having done so. It can trigger significant legal entanglements for the other partner, with very real financial and practical consequences, and that partner usually takes some kind of revenge. Hopefully, the revenge won't be an increased round of violence, but years of protracted litigation over the house or money or the costs of the legal defense can be a heavy burden.

The best course of action is to work closely with your clients as the pros and cons of legal action are evaluated. Make sure that they understand how the restraining order process works and how the police are likely to respond, and help them to understand the benefits and the risks of taking legal action. Most situations will be readily categorized as either too trivial to warrant further action or too serious to ignore; and for the fuzzier in-between situations, your goal should be to empower your clients to make the most reasoned decision, knowing that the outcomes are not entirely predictable.

B. Midterm Practical and Financial Issues

Once the more immediate housing and financial issues are resolved one way or another, you will be able to focus on the midterm issues. Midterm issues include any issues that don't need to be addressed in the first few weeks or months, but are still more urgent than the long-term or permanent resolutions that will need to be achieved eventually. For the most part, the parentage and custody issues are not all that different than those facing married spouses; but where there are children and if there are immediate issues of child scheduling (or, worse, situations like potential kidnapping), your client should immediately retain an experienced custody attorney who is prepared to go into court promptly.

The two major midterm sets of issues involve conflicts over housing and finances. As described above, there is no generic rule for occupancy of a co-owned residence, and an owner typically has the right to evict a nonowner. If both of the partners are renters, then the one who signed the lease probably has superior rights of continued occupancy; but if both are on the lease, then they each have equal occupancy rights. Your clients will need to understand that the judicial system does not offer much short-term help in these situations, both because of the cost and the time delay inherent in any formal litigation process. Thus, they will need to work with their attorneys, counselors, or mediators, or initiate some kind of a negotiation process to develop things to a stage where one of the partners is sufficiently motivated (by threats or dollars or a combination of the two) to move out voluntarily.

Unmarried partners won't have any statutorily imposed duties of financial support imposed after a separation, and so there probably aren't many ready-made legal solutions to the immediate financial conflicts either. Each partner owns his own stream of income and is responsible for his own expenses. A restraining order might be appropriate if there is a significant amount of money at stake and the accounts can't be shut down by a direct instruction to the bank. But any claim for post-separation support or for a share of an account titled in the other partner's name is going to have to await a trial, so there aren't any instant solutions for these problems either. Compounding the difficulties inherent in these sorts of disputes is the lack of an attorney fees clause or pendente lite attorney fees award similar to that of the family law rules. If the lower-asset or low-income partner doesn't have significant resources, he probably isn't going to be able to hire you to apply for a temporary order of any kind. Instead, you may need to use an array of practical tactics—and negotiated persuasion—to obtain interim relief.

You also want to be working in a calm and practical manner with your client to determine which bills really need to be paid and which can be deferred until a long-term solution is reached. For partners who co-own a home, be sure that the mortgage and the property insurance bills get paid, but local property tax bills probably can be deferred for a few months. If your client is dependent on the use of a car, you certainly don't want to let the car payments or automobile insurance payments lapse.

Allocation of savings and checking accounts should be done on a practical basis; when in doubt, split them in two and agree to work out the more refined allocation tasks later on. Strongly urge your clients to separate their incomes as soon as it is clear that a dissolution is happening, rather than continuing with a joint account. Some folks, however, prefer to use a marital model instead; and for them it can work just fine if they continue to pool their incomes and continue to share all expenses for a time, even while they are living in different residences. Keep track of the larger picture at all times; if the couple has a home with $500,000

Another difference between marital and nonmarital breakups is the degree of involvement of the lawyers. In most instances no one will file a lawsuit, so clients can, in theory, handle most of their disputes on their own. At the same time, there can be so much uncertainty, both legal and practical, and such strong emotions that relatively simple tasks (e.g., closing a bank account or dividing up furniture) can balloon into full-scale legal drama. Some lawyers will only participate if they can run the entire show, legitimately fearing that they will be called in to clean up messes that could have been avoided had they been in the game from the outset.

I am willing to take a more nuanced and more flexible approach. I charge by the hour; and if clients want to try to tackle something on their own, I will meet with them, coach them, and sometimes even vet the drafts of their letters. I recognize that many of my clients can't afford to use me in every situation, and I also believe in empowering clients to tackle their own disputes to the extent that they can do so. I've been told repeatedly by clients that they felt stronger and more effective when they wrote their own demand letter or handled a meeting with their ex, and certainly they are better off if they can resolve issues directly with their former partner.

Clear communication here is essential. Make sure that you document the limits of your engagement in writing, and check in frequently with your clients (email works perfectly for this task) to make sure that there isn't any confusion as to which of you is handling which tasks. And try your best to be patient and forgiving when they mishandle things or lose their temper inappropriately. Breaking up can be just horrible for some folks, and they certainly aren't at their best in these painful times.

in equity, it is okay if one of the partners racks up $5,000 in extra bills; this can always be resolved as part of the equity adjustments. If one of the parties is utterly broke, however, using joint funds to cover an excess payment for a nonshared bill may result in a valid claim, but one that is never reimbursed.

Whenever your client is paying more than she thinks she is, encourage her to document that in writing, even in just a simple email, so that the excess payment is not considered a gift or a completed agreement. Likewise, frequently warn your clients that accepting an excess payment by a partner doesn't preclude that partner from seeking a reimbursement when the overall financial settlement is reached unless he signed an agreement waiving such a claim.

Part of your job is to remind your clients that breakups are messy and that the lack of any formal dissolution process can enable the messiness to get even messier. It is possible that bills will go unpaid or be paid in unequal proportions, credit card charges will be racked up, and housing arrangements will be disrupted, often for months at a time. The goal is to stay focused on the major areas of dispute and try to prevent the minor skirmishes from throwing everyone into such a tizzy that they mishandle the resolution of the more significant disputes.

C. COURT JURISDICTION AND VENUE PROBLEMS

Always start out with the intention of resolving every nonmarital dispute through some form of alternative dispute resolution method, sticking with such approaches even when more trigger-happy lawyers would rush to the courthouse. Filing a lawsuit is an aggressive act in a dispute that does not require court involvement, and it usually triggers an equally intense reaction by the other partner. In many instances it results in the other party hiring a litigator who has no interest in reaching a negotiated resolution. Family lawyers usually understand how emotional these disputes are, and they often rein in their clients whenever possible; but many civil litigators don't take this approach, and they sometimes instinctively amplify the problems with a "take no prisoners" approach to the litigation.

But focusing on alternative approaches to resolution should not be done in a vacuum, and you should always be aware of the procedural nuances of the litigation option. In part, this sort of watchfulness is necessary to enable you to sprint into court if needed, but it is also important as you analyze your client's best options and educate your client. Access to a jury trial (or the inability to have a jury decide the dispute) can make a big difference in how you advise your client about a proposed settlement offer, and knowing who the likely judge will be for your case can help you steer your client away from a very unfortunate fate.

With very few exceptions, you can assume that your client's dispute will not be heard in family court. Of course, if the partners are married (under state law as a same-sex couple) or registered in a marriage-equivalent registration (either domestic partnership or civil union), then their disputes probably will be adjudicated in the family court system.[1] If your clients have entered into a same-sex marriage and now live in a nonrecognition state, it may be very difficult to get *any* court to hear their case—and may in the end require that one of the parties relocate to a recognition state to obtain a dissolution.[2] Furthermore, in nearly every state, any dispute between legal parents will be resolved in family court regardless of the marital status of the parents. The tricky question is what happens when the partners are unmarried and are both legal parents of children but also have money and financial problems that are not directly connected to any custody or child support issues.

Each jurisdiction has its own approach to this quandary. In some states the nonmarital financial issues can be joined or consolidated with the child support or custody issues in a single legal action in family court. This makes good sense because the underlying disputes are often related (e.g., child custody is directly tied to occupancy of the house, and child support disputes often are interrelated with the fights over postseparation support or ownership of a bank account). If they can be combined in this way, it usually is a good idea to cooperate with such a request, though there are limited situations in which it is strategically advantageous to keep the money and property disputes separate from any custody dispute. For example, if your client is the sole owner of record, you might not want a family court judge to rule on a claim by a nonowning partner since the "it's a family" bias of the family court judge could lead to a more sympathetic ruling for the nonowner. Combining the actions also allows a judge to form opinions of your client in one phase of the dispute, which then might shape the outcome of the legally unrelated matters.

In other jurisdictions, the two cases have to be filed separately; but in some instances they can then be consolidated or combined, at least for pretrial matters. There are no universal rules here, and oftentimes there are not even any local court rules that expressly cover these questions. There is an enormously wide variety of responses by individual judges, even in the same county. Sometimes the right to a jury trial for a palimony claim will keep it out of family court unless both parties are willing to waive their right to a jury trial. If there is a right to attorney fees for the lower-earning partner in a child support claim, you might want to pack as many of the other property issues into that battle so that more of your fees can be included in the fee demand; but for that very same reason, you may face trenchant opposition from the other side.

An equally complicated situation arises where the partners lived together as an unmarried couple and later married, but they have arguments over assets that were acquired prior to marriage. They certainly will need to process their marital dissolution through the family courts, but it is not as clear where or how they will adjudicate any disputes that involve nonmarital assets or claims that arose prior to their marriage. Some states have some rules on this issue, but many don't. California, for example, allows some claims regarding premarital assets to be raised in the family court action, but only regarding jointly titled property such as a co-owned home. Claims by one spouse to separately titled property based upon premarital promises or for financial support based upon the premarital cohabitation are typically relegated to a civil court action, which then may or may not be consolidated with the family court dissolution.

In most states a claim for palimony based upon premarital cohabitation typically cannot be raised in the marital action.[3] If a statute of limitations is about to run, it may be prudent to file a separate civil action to preserve the premarital claims; then, once the marital dissolution action is under way, you can make an effort to bring the nonmarital claims into the marital action or possibly consolidate the two actions in a coordinated proceeding.[4]

There also are looming issues of the timing of the conflicts and the scope of attorney competence. Many civil litigators have no experience in family court and thus won't take on the custody or support case, and yet they want to control the entire matter. On the other hand, very few family law attorneys feel comfortable stepping into a civil courtroom or handling a contract-based claim for support. Practically, it can be very expensive and cumbersome if your client has to hire two lawyers, one for each court battle, but in some instances that may be unavoidable. Ideally, you (or one of your colleagues) will have been sufficiently cross-trained in both areas of law and practice to handle both sides of the dispute, possibly with help from colleagues along the way.

The venue rules can also be a problem, especially if your client owns properties in multiple counties or even multiple states. Most states require that property lawsuits between unmarried partners be filed in the county where that property is located, which can result in having to file more than one lawsuit. However, you can often include all of the real property disputes in one lawsuit, filing it in the county where the parties live. Usually the other side won't object, and if neither side objects, the judge probably won't care—and it's far more efficient that way.

There also can be problems where there are a variety of financial or property conflicts, only one of which is covered by an arbitration clause. The partners may have signed a property co-ownership agreement that contains a binding arbitration clause, but they may also have a fight over a brokerage account that isn't covered by that agreement. In this situation, you will have to decide whether you want to lead with the arbitration or the court litigation, and then you will want to make an effort to bring the other set of disputes into the same forum. Rarely is it in your client's best interest to be fighting on two legal fronts.

Whenever you are considering litigating any kind of nonmarital dispute, you must scope out the likely cost, procedural obstacles, and time delays of a civil lawsuit. While on the surface they may appear to be the same as what occur in any type of civil lawsuit, the implications can be unique when it comes to a battle between unmarried partners:

- Access to a jury trial is a door that can swing both ways. Juries can be very unsympathetic to a nonmarital partner's claim, but they also can be swayed by a particularly poignant story. As unpredictable as jury trial outcomes are for any kind of case, they are particularly unpredictable for these disputes.
- Judge assignments can make a tremendous difference in pretrial proceedings, especially when the judge is the fact finder. You should have a clear understanding of which court is likely to hear your case and think about how the local judges are going to treat

your client. Many civil judges are really grumpy when they are confronted with these sorts of cases (and they are likely to remind you that they had lobbied hard to avoid ever having to do a divorce, which is why they steered clear of an assignment to family court), and this can be very detrimental to your client.

- If your client is unconventional in any way (i.e., an effeminate-acting gay man, a "butch" lesbian, transgender, or even a "free spirit" heterosexual), give some serious thought to the biases, both conscious and unconscious, that a judge might bring to your client's case.

- Discovery is an unpredictable business when it comes to a non-marital dispute. What documents are really available and what the judges will allow you to investigate are both wildly unpredictable. Some financial records may have been lost, other records may have been destroyed, and a judge who thinks that the claim as a whole is ridiculous may be very unresponsive when it comes to issuing discovery orders.

- Attorney fees awards are very rare, even in situations (such as with partition actions in some states) where they are technically available. Your client should be prepared to pay the entire freight of the bill and should not expect you or the ex partner to foot any of it. In most states you will be allowed to take palimony and property cases on a contingency basis or perhaps arrange for a partial payment (at a lower rate) with a contingency bonus, but you should not be shy about talking about the real cost of these cases and verifying in advance that your client can afford to go forward. There are cases in which the parties spent upwards of $100,000 per side fighting over barely $250,000 in home equity. Both of you should regularly evaluate the cost/benefit of any lawsuit.

- Decisions in these cases are wildly unpredictable, even more so than in any other kind of case. Judges and juries come to the disputes with their own opinions on what is right or wrong for unmarried couples, and the case law in most jurisdictions allows a wide range of decisions by the trial court or jury. You will win cases that you truly expect to lose, and you will lose ones that you are absolutely sure you can win. Everyone (including judges) has deeply ingrained beliefs about how personal relationships should be structured, and these beliefs will greatly affect the decisions by anyone who has been given the power to adjudicate the disputes. Clients should never assume that their point of view will be shared by others, and neither should you.

- Pursuing a litigation strategy can be incredibly costly to clients, in more than just the financial sense of the term. I watched as one client lost his job due to his boss's perception that the client's court case distracted him from his work, and one of my clients even got fired for serving a subpoena on his ex-boyfriend at the office where they both worked. The emotional strain on the clients can be enormous, and seemingly unrelated problems in their lives (tax issues, property issues, financial disputes with relatives) can be swept into the litigation with absolutely unpredictable results.

All of this leads to an obvious conclusion: Try to stay out of court whenever possible!

D. PARTICULAR PROBLEMS WITH PARENTAGE AND CUSTODY DISPUTES

If both partners are already established as the legal parents of any minor children, then in most states their disputes will be handled in the same manner as those of divorcing married spouses. The absence of a legal relationship between the parents is not supposed to matter when it comes to deciding issues of custody and child support, and most state courts abide by this principle. There may well be disputes about what is in the best interest of the child, what to do if one parent wants to move out of state, and how financial obligations should be allocated if there are disagreements between the parents—but those are the same disputes that arise when married couples with kids break up.

There are three areas of nonmarital parentage disputes that can be problematic, however:

- If the parents were not legally married and they also have financial disputes that are not related to their children (e.g., ownership of a house or allocation of a bank account), those disputes typically will not be handled in family court even if one exists in their jurisdiction. Instead, they will be sent to the general civil division of their state court. This results in a procedural nightmare, where parallel disputes about money are being adjudicated in different courts. Both cases can involve similar arguments about access to financial records, evaluation of a partner's work capacity, or responsibility for ongoing financial obligations regarding a house, and these battles affect both the child support and the broader property and financial disputes. In some courts, the two sets of disputes at least can be combined into one unified proceeding, so that should always be considered.

- In most states legal parentage can be established by a voluntary stipulation of parentage, but in some states (such as Ohio and Massachusetts, for example) only a court order will be legally sufficient. Contrary to what most nonlawyers think, just adding a second parent's name to the birth certificate is not enough to establish legal parentage. Furthermore, in many states a single mother can insist on sole legal and physical custody of the child until the father files a paternity action and is established as a legal parent. Thus, if the mother does not want to voluntarily share custody (and financial obligations) with the person believed to be the father of the child, formal court proceedings to establish legal parentage will need to be completed before the custody and support orders can be issued.

- For same-sex partners who have not completed a second-parent adoption by the nonlegal or nonbiological parent and have not obtained a pre-birth judgment of parentage under the UPA, the threshold question of parentage can be very difficult to resolve. In some states there are doctrines of intentional parentage or de facto parentage, allowing a nonlegal parent to establish legal parentage—but only after a family court trial. Couples who have married or state registered may be entitled to invoke a presumption of parentage if they are living in a registration or marriage-recognition state, but this presumption may not be of any use to them if they live or relocate to a nonrecognition state.

E. Alternative Dispute Resolution Methods

Mediation

Mediation is wonderful, especially for nonmarital disputes. The lack of clear legal procedures and the often-vague substantive rules combined

Jo Ann Citron, a family law attorney in Boston who specializes in helping unmarried partners resolve financial and custody disputes, summarizes the situation in Massachusetts as follows; used with permission, www .citronlaw.net.

In 2007, the last year for which statistics are available, 40 percent of all births were to unmarried women. New York Times, Mar. 19, 2009, at A14. It comes as no surprise, then, that custody disputes between unmarried parents are on the rise. While a few of these cases are initiated by a person claiming to be a de facto parent within a same-sex, nonmarital relationship, the majority fall into the category of what used to be called "paternity" cases but that are now more appropriately termed "disputes between never-married parents."

Even if a father has established paternity by being named on the child's birth certificate, or by filing a Stipulation for Voluntary Acknowledgment of Parentage, he lacks the automatic custodial rights that the law grants to a married father. The Massachusetts paternity statute vests sole legal and physical custody with the mother unless and until a court issues an order granting the father rights of access to his child. Thus, while some paternity actions are initiated by or on behalf of mothers seeking to establish paternity for the purpose of an award of child support, acknowledged fathers are initiating an increasing number, seeking rights of access. Treating legal fathers differently from legal mothers and nonmarital children differently from marital children is arguably unconstitutional; however, no court has been asked to rule on the constitutionality of this statutory provision.

In practice, our courts make little distinction between marital and nonmarital children. Custody disputes between never-married parents look much like custody disputes between divorcing parents. In ruling on a father's bid for access or on a mother's attempt to deny or limit access, a judge is unlikely to assess the child's best interest based on the legal relationship between the two adults. Divorcing parents have long been required to attend approved parent education classes for instruction on the special pressures that divorce creates for children and on strategies to shield the children from the effects of the adult conflict. In 2008, Massachusetts established a pilot program (in Suffolk, Essex, and Hampshire Counties) under which the parties to a paternity action are required to attend similar parent education classes that focus on the needs of their children.

with the intense emotional issues and practical complexities cry out for an informal conflict-resolution process. But designing the appropriate mediation arrangement is not at all simple, for the following reasons:

- *Timing.* Oftentimes, one partner is ready to resolve everything within a week of the breakup, usually because they've been planning it for months already. If the other partner is stunned by the news and doesn't want the relationship to end, he may not be ready to talk about money and property issues for several months. Most therapists say that it takes about six months for the noninitiator to reorient to the new reality psychologically, and so it probably won't be effective to try to schedule the mediation much earlier than that. In some instances, having a short mediation session early on can be helpful, however, especially when you need to focus on the immediate practical issues; and you can use that setting to get a process-oriented agreement in place to serve as a guide for the ensuing conflict-resolution process.
- *Discovery.* Because nonmarital dissolutions don't require any exchange of financial disclosures, one partner may be pretty much in the dark about the other's finances, or even about their family generally. It really doesn't make sense to try to negotiate a resolution of a complex dispute when only one partner has the relevant documents and knowledge about the finances. If you are going to try to avoid court litigation, then there should be some kind of agreed-upon exchange of information in advance of the mediation.
- *Pre-mediation Tasks.* In addition to exchanging financial documents, it often can be very helpful to assemble a list of the personal property that is in dispute. It is almost always useful to get a professional appraisal of real property (or an opinion of value from an experienced real estate agent) and maybe even a contractor's estimate for work that needs to be done. In many cases, both partners should meet with a financial adviser in advance so that they know what they can afford and what their ongoing expenses are going to be. For some clients, a meeting with a retirement counselor should take place as well.
- *Selecting the Mediator.* For some disputes a therapist mediator works best, and in other cases a lawyer mediator is preferred. Lawyer mediators seem preferable simply because the emphasis should be on the money and property matters rather than the emotional dynamics. Of course, if child custody or scheduling issues are involved, a social worker or therapist is by far the best. There are well-trained therapist mediators who are very familiar with the

legal process and are comfortable talking about financial affairs, and they should be considered. The lawyer mediator should definitely have experience in marital and in nonmarital disputes so that he doesn't approach the conflict as something that will unfold like a commercial real estate dispute.

- *Gender and Sexuality.* A lot of clients feel that the mediator must mirror them in terms of gender and sexuality, and for some clients this is true: They need to be working with someone with whom they are entirely comfortable in every dimension. This factor is less important than most clients think, and a skilled mediator should be able to cross any of these boundaries. But be sure to ask your clients whether they have any preferences. And if you are considering using someone who doesn't have extensive experience working with clients like yours, you will want to talk with them in advance to ascertain her fitness for this assignment.

- *The Role of the Lawyer.* There are three basic tasks for the lawyer advising a client in mediation: Educate the client about the applicable law, help the client evaluate what is a fair and acceptable settlement, and review the settlement documents to be sure that they protect the client adequately. You don't need to be in the room with the mediator as long as your client is calm and focused enough to be able to present his own position, but you should be mindful of when this is not the case. You will want to meet with your client in advance of the mediation to be sure that he is prepared to handle the sometimes intense dynamics of such a process, and then review any agreement that he is inclined to sign.

- *Mediation Process.* Most family law mediators prefer to meet over repeated sessions no more than two or three hours long, spread out over several weeks or months. This avoids the emotional overload that can happen in the sort of marathon session that often is used in commercial disputes, and it allows the parties to confer with their counsel and gather the necessary information in between the mediation sessions. Mediators will not usually allow parties to sign an agreement at the very mediation session where a tentative agreement is reached because they understand how pressured folks can get, and they recognize the need for the partners to review the agreement with counsel before signing it. This is especially true where large sums of money are involved, in which case a review by tax advisers might well be needed. Commercial mediations, by contrast, often last all day and end in a same-day signing of the agreement. The family law approach is optimal for the nonmarital disputes, except for highly sophisticated partners who have moved past the emotional dynamics and are able to address the financial and property issues in a businesslike manner.

- *The Role of the Law.* The law always plays a role in these mediations to some degree, but it should never be the only factor. Parties may have made all sorts of agreements outside of conventional legal parameters, and the mediator and the attorneys need to be open to evaluating the situation with an openness to these other dimensions. At the same time, at various points the parties (and, of course, their attorneys) will want to shift their focus onto the likely legal outcomes, and no one should pretend that these concerns are irrelevant.

Arbitration

Private binding arbitration is highly popular for resolving nonmarital disputes, for good reason. It is usually cheaper than litigation (although that may not be true if you have to hire an expensive retired judge or pay for a three-arbitrator panel), and it is usually quicker (but not if you have to file litigation to compel arbitration or enforce an arbitration award). It also allows for a broader approach to resolving the conflict, and usually an arbitrator is more willing to consider equitable arguments. If the parties have already signed a binding arbitration agreement (as part of a property agreement, for example), then your decision has been made—though sometimes it makes sense to re-evaluate the options now that you see what the real areas of conflict are likely to be. If no arbitration agreement exists, you will have to decide whether arbitration in this particular situation is best for your client.

Here are some of the factors to consider:

- If you are defending against claims that you believe lack merit, having a cheaper and faster process is not necessarily good for your client. The formality of litigation can be intimidating to some claimants (even though it might end up being faster and cheaper than arbitration in some instances), and so your refusal to arbitrate could result in the claim being abandoned.

- If your case has hypertechnical features (either in the nature of the claim or in the defenses), you might want the formality of a court process. That way you can seek to dismiss the claim before any trial (such as on a statute of limitations defense), and you can present technical arguments to the judge, who might be more familiar with such arguments and more willing to toss out an otherwise sympathetic claim based upon technical defenses.
- Discovery and compliance problems might be issues. If you are dealing with an angry ex who is not readily compliant with requests for documentation or for entering into reasonable stipulations, you may need the powers of a judge (and a sheriff) to accomplish your goals. In some of these situations, court action makes sense even when there is a binding arbitration clause in an agreement, simply to bring the other party to the table or to get the legal process started. This is especially true when one needs to enforce orders upon third parties (such as bank officers) or to obtain possession of property.
- If you feel that you need a jury to overcome the literal interpretations and reactions that a judge or arbitrator (usually a lawyer or retired judge) will bring to the table, you can't go with arbitration.
- Always avoid allowing the arbitrator to be selected at random or through a panel program (such as the American Bar Association or JAMS, for example). You should try to know the legal background of the arbitrator and get some sense of how he feels about same-sex or unmarried partners; you also want to know that he will approach the case in a way that feels right and fair to your clients.
- Make sure that you monitor costs. Sometimes you can customize the process in cost-efficient ways. If the dispute is mostly about the value of property, you should consider appointing a senior real estate appraiser as your arbitrator. Try to avoid using multiarbitrator panels, and consider appointing a less experienced arbitrator who is familiar with the rules of nonmarital law rather than defaulting to a retired judge who charges twice as much and may not know anything about this field of law.

Collaborative Law

Collaborative law involves two lawyers, each representing one partner and working together collaboratively to resolve the dispute. In formal collaborative practice, each lawyer pledges not to commence litigation (forcing the parties to start over with new lawyers if they want to litigate, thus slowing down the "I'm heading to court" reaction). The parties each commit to understanding the other's point of view, openly disclosing all information and legal arguments, and focusing on solutions rather than arguments. Oftentimes, experts (especially tax advisers for high-asset disputes or therapist coaches for high-conflict couples) get involved from the outset as joint neutral experts. In pure collaborative practice, all negotiations happen in the presence of the clients so that the lawyers don't get into battle mode and lose track of the client-centered purpose of the process.[5] This is pretty much what *all* lawyering should be about.

Collaborative practice can work great for these kinds of disputes, especially given the lack of formal disclosure requirements and the wide range of opinions about the legal rules. It motivates the parties to learn a new way of communicating, by working directly with lawyers who will likely be calmer and more rational, and flushes out the more extreme arguments or unreasonable positions. It is not cheap, but for high-asset couples it can be very efficient, especially if joint neutral tax accountants or property appraisers mitigate the need for costly dueling experts.

F. REAL ESTATE CONFLICT-RESOLUTION STRATEGIES

For many of your clients, the major arena of conflict will be their residence. Here is a summary of some of the most pertinent strategies that should be considered in resolving a real estate divorce.

First Dibs to Purchase

Unless the parties previously signed a co-ownership agreement, neither partner will have a first right to buy out the other's interest in the property. However, it often works best to arrange for some kind of buyout, for everyone's sake. It avoids a nasty market sale and leaves at least one person still in the house—and often willing to pay a bit more to the other partner in exchange for this privilege. The standard judicial partition rules use procedures that really aren't workable in most breakup situations, and the rules rarely cover the myriad of details in such a buyout, including the following:

- *Valuation.* You will need to find a way to estimate actual market value, which is not the same figure as what a loan appraiser would proffer. The market usually gives some value to illegal construction, for example, though less than when it is entirely legal, and a market appraisal is usually more thorough (and more expensive) than what a lender is willing to pay for. That is why you will want to use an appraiser who regularly does divorce appraisals. You may need to obtain contractor estimates if there is necessary work to be done so that those costs can be deducted from the appraised value. It is preferable to obtain a joint neutral appraisal rather than having each partner get her own appraisal, but the joint appraisal shouldn't be binding on the parties because otherwise the warring partners will just find something else to fight over. It's best to look to such appraisals as nonbinding (but highly valuable) information for the negotiation process, but you should also be open to each side getting an independent appraisal if the partners don't trust the joint appraiser's result. Real estate agents' opinions can be useful but rarely should be the only measure of value as they are often too general and too casually done to be persuasive.

- *Right of First Refusal.* I discourage the use of a right of first refusal, which is where an outside buyer makes an offer and one of the owners has the right to "refuse" it by matching it. In most markets, this right has to be disclosed to all potential buyers, and it depresses offering prices and also makes for a messy situation with an agent who is expecting a commission. Go with a first right of offer instead, based upon an appraisal; and then if neither one buys out his partner at that juncture, the property goes on the open market with any right of first refusal. As a further protection, you can agree that if the house doesn't sell at a decent price, you can revisit the buyout negotiations after the listing agreement has expired.

- *Anticipated Future Commissions.* Even though an agent rarely is involved in a partner buyout, the buying partner probably will eventually incur a commission whenever the property is sold in the future. A savvy buying partner, therefore, will want to deduct the amount of that anticipated future commission (typically 5 percent or 6 percent) from the amount to be paid to the selling party. This approach seems reasonable and makes economic sense, but the law in most parallel marital law contexts doesn't allow for this deduction (on the grounds that the future commission is too hypothetical and may never be incurred). Since there is no absolute right to a buyout, there certainly isn't any right to deduct the anticipated future commission. However, from a selling party's perspective, it is an expense that would be incurred if the property were sold on the open market, so some adjustment in price to reflect this factor only makes sense.

- *Negotiation of the Buyout Price.* The optimal approach to negotiation is the bottom line approach, where the parties focus on the net amount of cash to be paid to the selling party. Of course, many factors will go into that calculation, including the market value, the allocation of equity percentages, the anticipated commission deduction, and possibly some compensation for the selling party's loss of the residence, both emotionally and practically. But rather than trying to reach a resolution on each of these component parts, it is far more effective to focus on the amount of the net cash payment. It is quite possible that the parties will disagree on each individual component but agree on a net figure, so why get tangled up in all of the detailed elements? It is entirely fine to talk for the partners to talk about their opinions on each of the various factors as part of the negotiation process, but don't feel that you need to resolve every element in order to reach a global solution.

- *The Loan.* In many instances, the selling party can stay on the loan despite a due-on-sale clause since banks rarely even notice a change in ownership between partners. True enough, the selling partner may risk having her credit score dinged if her ex doesn't pay the mortgage on time and may face restrictions when she tries to buy another property, but sometimes it is worth taking on these risks to get a decent payment from a buying party who can't afford to take out a new loan in her own name. In other situations, it may be very unwise to stay on the loan as the selling party, especially if there is personal liability for the loan or if the property value is less than the total loan amount. This is one of the most delicate aspects of any buyout negotiation: Most clients find it fundamentally too dangerous to stay on a loan after they've ceased being an owner, though in many situations it is less risky than remaining an owner and being primarily liable for property expenses. If you are advising a buying partner's perspective, you should always point out that not refinancing at the time of a buyout could result in a burden of a later refinancing when interest rates are higher than the present time. If the property is already underwater, then it usually makes sense for the couple to simply abandon the property, unless one of them has enough confidence in the future real estate market and enough income to hold onto the property through the present dark economic times.

- *Costs of Transfer.* Most counties impose some form of deed registration or transfer tax, and in some cities the amount can be hefty. In the San Francisco Bay Area, for example, the transfer tax on a high-value home can be as high as $7,500 or more. As part of the "no fault" approach to these dissolutions, encourage your clients to split these fees equally, or just assume that the buyer partner is paying the entire tax and then reduce the buyout price accordingly. The refinancing costs of a new mortgage loan, however, are usually borne solely by the buying party as part of the costs of the buyout. If the sale triggers any increase in property taxes or mortgage loan rates, those also are borne by the buying party.

Joint Sale of the Property

If neither partner is going to keep the house and the parties are not open to keeping it (as a co-owned rental or for the use of one of them), then a market sale is the most likely option. The parties should have a shared goal at this point, which is to get the best price they can as soon as possible, but oftentimes the dueling partners aren't able to focus on the task in an effective manner. You should recommend a detailed settlement agreement that lays out the sales protocol, including the appointment of the agent, the marketing and listing decisions, and the financial arrangements. You also want to be clear that the sale won't be held up even if there are last-minute disputes about bills to be paid or the equity split or the personal belongings. If the owners haven't resolved their internal disputes about contributions or labor, then the proceeds of sale can be escrowed in a joint account, and these disputes can be resolved later on—the last thing you want to face is a lawsuit by a buyer because the sale didn't close.

A standard agreement should bestow a lot of control in the agent since he is the professional who knows what is best when it comes to selling a property. You might want to include a provision for an "instant arbitration" in case of any dispute (you usually don't have time for a conventional arbitration in the midst of a marketing effort), with a presumption that the agent's recommendation is correct. This can be especially useful if the parties are in dispute about the acceptable sales price. You should recommend against allowing each partner to have a separate agent: it is far better to have a single professional on board who is running the show, and you want to make sure that the agent has the interpersonal skills to be able to manage a warring couple throughout the sales process.

The Underwater Residence

A particularly unpleasant situation is a "foreclosure divorce," where the couple is in foreclosure and breaking up. It is hard enough for happy, intact couples to deal with the pressures and complexities of an under-valued and over-mortgaged property, but it is nearly impossible for an angry, depressed couple to deal with these problems. The partners frequently are distracted by arguments over how they got into this mess (e.g., who decided to buy the house at the top of the market or who insisted on taking out equity for a stupid investment or now-irrelevant renovation). Furthermore, they each may have very different concerns and feelings about the foreclosure options, with one wanting out at any cost and the other one hoping to salvage some equity or perhaps a decent credit rating. However, in most instances they have to work together because neither of them can take any definitive action unilaterally.

In these situations, it always is useful for the two partners to be working with a joint attorney, at least on loan-related issues. They need to get a clear understanding of the loan realities (which loans are recourse and which are not; how much is owed; and what, if any, sort of loan modification can be obtained) and their real estate options (short sale, loan modification, foreclosure or otherwise). They also should each have a good sense of the relative cost of each option, both in financial terms and with regard to future credit ratings. They should understand what the worst-case scenarios are and what will happen to both of them if they aren't able to work together in a strategic manner. You should lay out a best option for them jointly, taking both parties' concerns into consideration, explaining why it is better than doing nothing or continuing to argue. If either partner has separate counsel, explain these options to that partner, especially if she is working with a family law attorney who doesn't really understand real estate law. Motivate the partners to take reasonable steps to minimize the damage while at the same time acknowledging that in many instances their anger and resentment will preclude such solutions.

Occupancy disputes can be particularly heated in these sorts of situations: there is the prospect of an owner camping out in the residence without making payments for months while the loan foreclosure process plays out. Each owner has an equal right to occupy the property, and your client should not be too quick to move out only to have to pay rent somewhere while the other owner is living for free in the family residence.

G. THE TAX COMPLICATIONS

It should come as no surprise that many if not all of the tax problems discussed in the earlier chapters will come home to roost in a nonmarital breakup. The partners will be treated as unrelated parties under federal tax law and generally under state law as well, except for state-registered partners in a marriage-equivalent registration system or same-sex married spouses. Thus, any transfers of money or assets that occur as part of the dissolution will need to be analyzed in this unfavorable legal framework.

Property Transfers

If one partner is buying out the other's interest in their home, it will be considered the sale of a percentage interest in a personal residence. A selling partner who has owned and occupied the house for at least two of the past five years is eligible for the $250,000 residential exclusion; otherwise, gain will be subject to capital gains tax. Gain is not the same as proceeds of sale; for example, a return of down payment or improvement costs is not gain. But where equity has been withdrawn or the loan has been refinanced, there may be gain even if there is no cash paid to the selling party. Gain above $250,000 will be subject to capital gains taxes, both state and federal. Because the parties are not federally recognized spouses, they don't have the opposite-sex couple's right to extend the three-year sale deadline based upon a dissolution agreement (even if they are married or state-registered).

A selling partner who was not on title is presumed not to be an owner and generally isn't eligible for the residential exclusion. Some partners in this situation simply construe the payment as a gift or reimbursement of payments, which would not be taxable. But if neither of those options will work, there is one tax case that implies that an off-title contributor may be able to be construed as an equitable owner and thus eligible for the exclusion, but this is far from legally certain.[6]

If the property is not a personal residence, then a sale will follow the ordinary tax rules for investment properties, including the possible use of an I.R.C. § 1031 tax-deferred exchange. If the couple owns more than one investment property, an exchange between the partners can work very well. Because your clients will not be using a marital exemption from the capital gains burden, any payments made by either partner will increase that buying partner's basis, which will reduce the potential capital gains exposure upon a future sale by that buying partner. The central lesson to keep in mind is that each situation presents its own challenges; thus, if the sums involved are large and the situation is at all complicated, a tax expert with knowledge of nonmarital transfers definitely should be consulted.

The two thorniest tax problems with real property transfers are (1) allocating the basis between the partners and (2) determining the buyout price. If the two partners contributed jointly to the down payment and used funds from a variety of sources to pay for renovations, it can be challenging to determine who owns what share of the basis. And if one partner moved out some time ago and has lost the right to take the residential exclusion, the impact of the basis allocation can be different for each partner. Further complicating the situation, partners may be able to reach an agreement on a global buyout payment, which may also include the resolution of some nonproperty disputes, without being able to agree on a buyout amount for the particular item of real estate or otherwise sort out the tax-allocation issues. Ideally, a unified position on the tax issues can be documented in the settlement agreement; but in some instances you will only be able to reach an agreement on the net payment, and the tax allocations will remain unresolved. In that situation, each party will stake out his own tax position, for better or worse.

Asset Transfers and Postseparation Support

Bottom line: There is no clear law on the tax treatment of asset transfers or postseparation support for unmarried couples. Some experts contend that if one partner had an equitable interest in the asset being transferred or if there is a duty of support implied or imposed by the state's

The taxation of nonmarital partner settlements poses a sticky ethical and professional thicket for lawyers in two respects. One involves the question of how to deal with the fundamental uncertainty of the legal rules when it comes to structuring and documenting settlements, and the other involves the limits on the lawyers' role in the settlement drafting and the tax reporting process. Although the rules are uncertain, there are wiser and dumber choices. If one partner is willing to use up some of the gift exemption, frame the settlement in that way; and if there are legitimate claims for a real estate interest or reimbursement of a loan or advancement, suggest that option for a portion of the payment. Try to be flexible within the boundaries of the law, but also allow your client to take reasonable risks as long as he knows what he is risking. If you can't resolve the tax allocation of the settlement, guide your client toward a settlement, as it is better to have a settlement without a tax allocation than to have no settlement at all.

The lawyers' role in the reporting process needs to be carefully considered as well. Don't be part of an agreement that is fraudulent, and always encourage your clients to confer with their own tax advisers before finalizing a settlement agreement. For particularly complicated high-asset situations, you might want to ask an expert for an opinion letter (which will protect the client and the tax preparer from a penalty for submitting a return without a reasonable basis). You should also discuss with your clients the option of submitting an informational return that discloses a payment and declares the reason why it is not considered taxable. There is no absolute bright line here. You will have clients take positions that worry you from time to time—mostly in the area of real estate basis and the move-out date for the residential exclusion—but as long as they understand the risks and have credible grounds for the position you are describing in the settlement agreement, you won't need to independently investigate their financial records or refuse to draw up the agreement.

I don't prepare tax returns for clients and I don't offer tax opinions; and as long as they understand the limits of my role, I will try to help them develop a legal tax strategy that is realistic and most useful for them—without ever jeopardizing my own license to practice law.

appellate law on unmarried partners (such as in the *Marvin* decision in California or its progenies elsewhere), payment of that support or sharing of that asset is not a taxable event.[7] Others are of the opinion that unless there is clear statutory or case law on exemptions from taxation of a transfer or payment, it is a gift or it is income to the recipient, or both.

Given the recent increase in the gift tax exemption limit, it is tempting to treat the transfers of nonmarital assets or postseparation support payments as gifts, but in fact it is hard to conceptualize a settlement agreement in terms that reflect such an arrangement. If the payment is "in consideration" of a release of claims, then it really isn't a gift, and if the payments are being made over time, it is even harder to construe the agreed-upon future payments as a gift. One safe-harbor option is to have the higher-asset partner make the gift prior to any settlement agreement being signed; and then the parties can agree that in light of the *past* gifts, the lower-asset partner no longer has any financial needs and thus can waive any potential claims and agree not to press any claims.

H. Documentation of the Settlement Agreement

Another distinction between marital and nonmarital dissolutions is that there is no requirement of a written settlement agreement between unmarried partners. Even if a lawsuit was filed, it can simply be dismissed. Partners can sort out all of their affairs without ever signing even a simple agreement. They can transfer the title to their home, divide up their belongings, split up the bank accounts, and even pay something in postseparation support without a written agreement. In fact, most couples probably complete their nonmarital dissolution in just this manner, without any negative consequences.

Nonetheless, you should always recommend a written agreement for three simple reasons:

First, the agreement-formation process itself brings all of the issues to the surface and provides a structured method of addressing them. When you draft an agreement, you will undoubtedly be reminded about some issue that the parties neglected to discuss, such as a transfer fee or a car title to be assigned. There is a focus and linearity to the agreement-documentation process that helps avoid a missed or miscon-strued issue.

Second, most often a dissolution process is implemented over time, and it is very risky to start the process without a detailed road map in place from the outset. You don't want your clients to begin dividing up some of their accounts or personal belongings with one set of assumptions about other items, only to find out a few months later that they don't agree on some fundamental remaining detail of those other matters. Working out all the components in advance protects both parties from a last-minute surprise or belatedly arising conflict.

Third, part of any well-written settlement agreement is a mutual release, which prevents either partner from coming back a year or two later and asking her ex-partner for something more. Many lawyers have the experience of being contacted (either as a mediator or lawyer) regarding a claim by a party who signed over a quitclaim deed or trans-ferred a bank account to her partner but now claims that she is entitled to some further compensation. From a legal perspective, the absence of a signed release of claims can easily result in a messy battle with a lot of hurt feelings.

Having a written agreement isn't always possible; and if one of the parties adamantly refuses to sign any agreement, it is almost always bet-ter to get the deed signed without an agreement. But having an agree-ment is always better than not having one.

Settlement agreements don't have to be all that fancy in most non-marital dissolutions. The Nolo books for unmarried couples (both opposite-sex and same-sex versions) have simple, plain English forms that can work in many situations.[8] You should use a plain English sim-plified settlement agreement that most nonlawyers can understand. You want the agreement to be something that both partners can understand even if they don't meet with an attorney, and you will need to explain any of the legal terms using language they can understand. Focus on the practical aspects of the settlement, including buyout provisions, property transfers, and recovery of personal belongings, and be spe-cific about the timing and logistics of the implementation process. In addition, always include a further dispute resolution process, most likely mediation and binding arbitration, in case an argument arises about the interpretation or implementation of the agreement.

Here are the basic ingredients of the standard settlement agreement:

- A recital of the parties' identities and confirmation of their past relationship and nonmarital status;
- A description of the main assets at issue, with loan details for any residence;
- A summary of the basic terms of the agreement, including the allocation of bank accounts, payment of loans, or agreements for postseparation support;
- All of the details of the real estate resolution, either as a buyout or a sale, with timetables for implementation and allocation of tasks;
- A summary of the practical aspects of the separation process, such as vacating the residence, delivering the personal belongings, sorting out the furniture, and deciding about the pets;
- A statement of the agreements about any tax issues, including an allocation of the investment basis and the tax treatment for any transfers of assets or payments;
- Provisions for allocating the expenses of the dissolution, including the preparation of agreements and any other fees;
- A mutual release of all claims, including the release of any unknown claims to the extent that it is legally permissible to do so;
- A dispute resolution provision, including mediation, arbitration, and/or court proceedings, and an attorney fees clause for such adjudication.

I. STRATEGIES FOR HANDLING THE NONMARITAL TRIAL

Some cases just don't settle, despite your best efforts. Nonmarital disputes are particularly hard to settle simply because the law is so unclear. True, emotions can run high in marital disputes, and there can be unresolved matters even where the legal rules appear to be quite clear. But where the legal rules are so unclear, and especially in those states that allow implied and oral contract claims to be made, predicting the legal outcome is not at all simple. When you combine the legal uncertainty with the volatile emotions of a nasty breakup, reaching agreement is not always possible.

Every trial poses its own challenges, but there are a few salient points that are specific to nonmarital dissolution disputes, as follows:

- Your client's fundamental nature as a person is always going to be on trial, and you should be working diligently to coach your client as to how to best present his story. I've often repeated the maxim that all my clients tell the truth—it's just that some of them do a better job of it than others. Nothing is too small to be ignored: Pay attention to what your clients wear in court, be mindful of their demeanor at all times, and work with them to empower them to tell their narrative in a convincing manner that does not come across as bitter or resentful. In every one of these cases, there is a contest going on as to who is the biggest jerk, and you want to be sure that your client loses that contest.

- Be cautious and conservative in your interpretation of the law, and don't assume that the judge is going to see things your way. Judges are notoriously conservative when it comes to ruling on these cases, so they are likely to interpret the legal rules narrowly whenever possible. The same goes for evidentiary rulings: Don't assume that your client's stories are going to be fully admitted into evidence; and be mindful of the hearsay, best evidence, and parol evidence rules.

- Be forewarned: Juries do not like these cases, and they are likely to be as conservative as judges, even in liberal havens such as San Francisco. Most jurors assume that they would not be so stupid as to contribute money toward a house titled only in their partner's name or to leave a job to follow a lover cross-country without any assurances of financial security in writing. They may be very harsh in their judgments of your client as a result.

- Burdens of proof can be fatal to a seemingly sympathetic palimony or property claim. Repeatedly exhort your clients to be as "clear and convincing" as the deed that doesn't mention their name if they expect their oral testimony to justify their claim for an ownership interest in that asset. In most states the right to make a claim in derogation of title is accompanied by a very high burden of proof, defeating many an otherwise viable claim.

- Winning a claim doesn't always mean winning it in its entirety. A judge may find that your client has an ownership interest in the partner's property but then reduce the value of that claim by your client's accumulated share of the ongoing expenses or the value of the housing that your client received. Since it is very unlikely that either side will be awarded attorney fees, you need to watch out for the likely prospect of winning an award that is less than the amount of your accumulated fees.

- Do not ever count on an appeal to rescue your client from a dismal trial court verdict. In most states the legal rules are highly subjective, and an appellate court cannot overturn factual determinations. Plus, very few appellate judges want to reach out and change the law or remand a case to the trial court for something that they are likely to consider fairly trivial.

- It is crucial that you make it as clear as possible to your clients, in vivid language if needed, that a trial is a miserable endurance race in which most likely neither side wins. It requires taking time off of work and spending a lot of money on fees and experts and court costs, and it may be wildly unpredictable. My last court trial lasted only six days, but it took six months to complete because of the judge's schedule (and his evident dislike of our case). Hearings get postponed, trial settings get continued, and judges make all sorts of unpredictable rulings in these kinds of cases; your client will need to be prepared for the failings of the court system.

- Help your clients develop a vibrant support system if they are going through a trial. Make sure that your clients have a cheering squad in the courtroom (though they must never express their cheers aloud). It is important for your clients to know that there are friends and family who love and support them and who will help them organize their files, drive them to court, and take them out to dinner each night after court.

- Be sure that you have a solid understanding of who your client is, what his fears are, and what his primary goals are. Whenever I have a case that looks like it is going to trial, I typically will take my client out to dinner—at no charge—and invite him to bring his new partner along if he has one. I tell him in advance that we are not going to be talking about his case, but about him. I want to have a clear sense of his financial, medical, and emotional condition; and I want him to know that I care about him in all respects. We are going to have to work together under some fairly challenging conditions, and we need a solid foundation of communication and understanding to see us through the stormy days of trial.

• Remain open to settlement at all times, even after the trial has commenced. Listen objectively to how the evidence is being presented, and be honest with your client about the vulnerabilities of the case. Scorning a decent settlement offer when there is a serious risk of losing the case is not helpful to your client. You always want to do your best job in presenting your client's case, but you also want to be mindful at all times that there is a serious risk of loss.

DOCUMENTS FOR THE NONMARITAL DISSOLUTION PROCESS

(FORMS FOUND ON INCLUDED CD)

Form 18: Interim occupancy agreement
Form 19: Complaint for palimony et al.
Form 20: Complaint for palimony (longer version)
Form 21: Sales agreement re: property
Form 22: Settlement agreement for real estate buyout
Form 23: Financial settlement agreement (long)

NOTES

1. Even though Washington State courts apply family law as a presumptive equitable framework for adjudicating nonmarital disputes, there is no separate family court and so the disputes are handled in civil court. Most of the states that treat registrations as marriage-equivalent also extend the same rules to partners who registered in other states with equivalent registrations (such as a Vermont civil union), and those partners' disputes also will be handled in family court.
2. Courts in Oklahoma, Rhode Island, and Texas have refused to grant divorces to such couples on the grounds that granting a divorce is a form of recognition of the marriage. It may be possible in some jurisdictions to obtain a judicial decree of nullity even if a dissolution is not possible, but be careful as it is not entirely certain that this ruling will be binding on the state where the marriage took place. If your clients are not able to obtain such an order and they do not want to relocate, then the only option is to have them enter into a detailed separation agreement, which will at least isolate their finances pending a judicial dissolution.
3. While such claims do arise from time to time for opposite-sex couples, they are quite frequent in the dissolutions of long-term same-sex

relationships, where by definition the earlier phase of their relationship could not have been covered by marital law.

4. As with any kind of consolidation like this, you always want to be mindful of the risks of having a family court judge ruling on the nonmarital issues.

5. INTERNATIONAL ACADEMY OF COLLABORATIVE PROFESSIONALS, http://www .collaborativepractice.com.

6. Reynolds v. Comm'r, 77 T.C.M. 1479 (1999).

7. *See* Comm'r v. Duberstein, 363 U.S. 278 (1960); United States v. Davis, 370 U.S. 65 (1962); Gould v. Gould, 245 U.S. 151 (1917); Marilyn J. Baker v. Comm'r, 79 T.C.M. 2050 (2000).

8. *See* RALPH WARNER & TONI IHARA, LIVING TOGETHER: A LEGAL GUIDE FOR UNMARRIED COUPLES (Nolo Press 2008); FREDERICK HERTZ & EMILY DOSKOW, A LEGAL GUIDE FOR LESBIAN & GAY COUPLES (Nolo Press 1980); sample agreements available at http://www.nolo.com.

CONCLUSION

Counseling and representing unmarried partners, both gay and straight, is a fascinating and forever challenging area of the law. You will be working with a delightfully wide spectrum of clients, and they will bring you a correspondingly diverse array of legal questions and requests. Your legal mind will stay supple, you will understand the broader framework of the law in new and innovative ways, and you will never be bored by your cases. It is a wonderful line of work, whether it becomes the mainstay of your practice or makes up just one segment of your client population.

You will also find that serving the legal needs of unmarried partners is rarely simple. You will be asked a plethora of questions that truly have no certain answers, and so you will need to learn how to provide advice in the absence of absolute legal certainty. You will find yourself working with folks who may not have handled their financial or legal affairs in a tidy or organized manner, and some of them will be uncomfortable with the legal advice you are giving them. However, you will begin to understand that even where the legal system does not adequately protect marginalized members of society, you can create safety nets and viable pathways to protecting your client's families and their assets.

So embrace the challenges, make yourself available to those who need your assistance, and stay the course. Doing so will bring you both financial and personal rewards.

COMMON LAW MARRIAGE, MARRIAGE-EQUIVALENT REGISTRATION & CONTRACTUAL/EQUITABLE CLAIMS

A Summary of State Law Provisions

State	Common Law Marriage	Marriage Equivalent Registration	Contract/equitable Claims Permitted	Other Provisions
Alabama	yes	none	contract claims not allowed because common law marriage recognized	
Alaska	no	none	palimony claims precluded but property claims allowed	
Arizona	no	none	equitable and implied/oral property claims allowed	
Arkansas	no	none	equitable and property claims allowed	
Colorado	yes	none	equitable property claims allowed; support claims not allowed	designated beneficiary not marriage equivalent

State	Common Law Marriage	Marriage Equivalent Registration	Contract/equitable Claims Permitted	Other Provisions
Connecticut	no	prior civil union registry replaced by marriage for same-sex couples	written, oral & implied contracts honored but palimony claims not allowed	
Delaware	no	civil union (same-sex only)	written, oral & implied contracts honored but palimony claims not allowed	
D.C.	yes	civil union	contract claims allowed (same-sex & opposite-sex couples)	
Florida	no	none	implied contract/trust claims allowed; support claims allowed	
Georgia	yes, if created before 1/97	none	not permitted/public policy exception	
Hawaii	no	civil union (same-sex & opposite-sex)	equitable property claims allowed; implied and express claims allowed	

Idaho	yes, if created before 1/96	none	contract claims generally not allowed because common law marriage recognized
Illinois	no	civil union (same-sex & opposite-sex)	not permitted/public policy exception
Indiana	no	none	equitable property claims allowed
Iowa	yes	none	support claims not allowed
Kansas	yes	none	contract & equitable claims for property allowed but palimony claims not honored
Kentucky	no	none	palimony & contract claims generally not permitted
Louisiana	no	none	generally not permitted/public policy exception limited property claims allowed; support claims not allowed

State	Common Law Marriage	Marriage Equivalent Registration	Contract/equitable Claims Permitted	Other Provisions
Maine	no	none	palimony claims generally not permitted but some business claims allowed	domestic partnership not marriage equivalent
Maryland	no	none	written, oral & implied contract claims allowed	partial recognition of same-sex marriages
Massachusetts	no	none	written, oral & implied contract claims allowed; support claims not allowed	
Michigan	no	none	palimony claims not allowed	
Minnesota	no	none	written contracts only; support claims not allowed	
Mississippi	no	none	limited contract & property claims allowed but palimony claims precluded	

Missouri	no	none	constructive trust and equitable claims allowed
Montana	yes	none	property & contract claims allowed; palimony claims not allowed
Nebraska	no	none	equitable property claims allowed
Nevada	no	domestic partnership (same-sex & opposite-sex couples)	equitable property claims allowed; support claims not allowed
New Hampshire	yes (for inheritance only)	contract & property claims honored; palimony claims not allowed	domestic partnership replaced by same-sex marriage
New Jersey	no	civil union (same-sex, opposite-sex over age 62)	palimony claims based on written contracts only (as of 2010)
New Mexico	no	none	equitable property claims allowed; limited recognition of out-of-state-domestic partnerships

State	Common Law Marriage	Marriage Equivalent Registration	Contract/equitable Claims Permitted	Other Provisions
New York	no	none	oral & written claims allowed based upon express contracts, including support claims	partial recognition of same-sex marriages
N. Carolina	no	none	equitable property claims allowed	
N. Dakota	no	none	limited equitable property claims allowed	
Ohio	yes, if created before 10/91	none	support claims not allowed	
Oklahoma	yes, if created before 11/98	none	contract claims generally not allowed because common law marriage previously recognized; support claims not allowed	

State		domestic partnership (same-sex only)	
Oregon	no	none	oral and equitable property claims allowed
Pennsylvania	yes, if created before 1/05	none	equitable property claims and support claims allowed
Rhode Island	yes	none	equitable property claims allowed; support claims not allowed
S. Carolina	yes	none	no contract claims allowed because common law marriage recognized
S. Dakota	no	none	contract & property claims allowed but no palimony claims honored
Tennessee	no	none	no contractual claims allowed except for property or business claims

State	Common Law Marriage	Marriage Equivalent Registration	Contract/equitable Claims Permitted	Other Provisions
Texas	yes	none	written contracts only	
Utah	yes	none	no cohabitation contracts or palimony, because common law marriage recognized	
Vermont	no	none	limited property claims allowed	civil union replaced by same-sex marriage
Virginia	no	none	cohabitation illegal; nonbusiness or property contracts invalid	
Washington	no	domestic partnership (same-sex, opposite-sex over age 62)	marital law presumed equitable terms for cohabiting couples	
W. Virginia	no	none	contract & property claims honored but palimony claims not allowed	

Wisconsin	no	none	written, oral & implied contract claims allowed	domestic partnership not marriage equivalent
Wyoming	no	none	written, oral & implied contract claims allowed	

RESOURCES

Cynthia Bowman, Unmarried Couples, Law, and Public Policy (Oxford Univ. Press 2010).

Andrew Cherlin, The Marriage-Go-Round: The State of Marriage and the Family in America Today (Knopf 2009).

Continuing Educ. of the Bar: Cal., California Domestic Partnerships (2011).

Larry Elkin, Financial Self-Defense for Unmarried Couples: How to Gain Financial Protection Denied by Law (Doubleday 1994).

Sheryl Garrett & Debra Neiman, Money Without Matrimony: The Unmarried Couple's Guide to Financial Security (Dearborn Trade 2005).

Wendy S. Goffe, Marriage, Domestic Partnerships, Civil Union: The Developing Landscape, Advanced Estate Planning Techniques, ALI ABA, San Francisco, California (Mar. 24, 2011).

Frederick Hertz & Emily Doskow, A Legal Guide for Lesbian & Gay Couples (Nolo Press 2010).

Frederick Hertz & Emily Doskow, Making It Legal: A Guide to Same-Sex Marriage, Domestic Partnerships & Civil Unions (Nolo Press 2011).

Ill. Inst. for Continuing Legal Educ., Unmarried Partners: Estate Planning and Property and Parental Rights (2010).

Courtney Joslin & Shannon Minter, Lesbian, Gay, Bisexual and Transgender Family Law (West 2011).

CHARLES KINDREGAN JR. & MAUREEN MCBRIEN, Assisted Reproduction Technology: A Lawyer's Guide to Emerging Law and Science (ABA Publ'g 2011).

GORAN LIND, COMMON LAW MARRIAGE (Oxford Univ. Press 2008).

HAROLD LUSTIG, FOUR STEPS TO FINANCIAL SECURITY FOR LESBIAN & GAY COUPLES (Ballantine 1999).

APRIL MARTIN, THE LESBIAN AND GAY PARENTING HANDBOOK (Harper Collins 1993).

NANCY POLIKOFF, BEYOND (STRAIGHT AND GAY) MARRIAGE (Beacon 2008).

ELLIOT SAMUELSON, THE UNMARRIED COUPLE'S LEGAL SURVIVAL GUIDE: YOUR RIGHTS AND OBLIGATIONS (Citadel Press 1997).

DORIAN SOLOT & MARSHALL MILLER, UNMARRIED TO EACH OTHER: THE ESSENTIAL GUIDE TO LIVING TOGETHER AS AN UNMARRIED COUPLE (Marlowe & Co. 2002).

RALPH WARNER & TONI IHARA, LIVING TOGETHER: A LEGAL GUIDE FOR UNMARRIED COUPLES (Nolo Press 2008).

INDEX

ABOUT THE AUTHOR

Frederick Hertz practices real property and land use law in Oakland, California. He previously handled litigation involving the dissolution of real property co-tenancies, including tenants-in-common, family co-ownerships, and domestic partnership dissolutions, and the related aspects of property and financial disputes between unmarried couples, both same-sex and opposite-sex, as well as the purchase and sale and ownership of real property matters.

Mr. Hertz continues to serve clients in transaction matters, primarily in the areas of drafting real property co-ownership agreements, cohabitation agreements, and consultation with property owners on investment and ownership strategies. He also represents clients in co-ownership disputes that can be resolved through negotiation or mediation. Mr. Hertz also represents private and nonprofit clients in land use permitting and zoning matters in the East Bay area, with an emphasis on the representation of community groups and local developers in urban infill development and the rehabilitation of historic properties.

Mr. Hertz also works as a mediator and arbitrator, with a special emphasis on the mediation of co-ownership and other disputes between unmarried couples, business partners, tenants-in-common, co-owners, family members, and domestic partners.

A native of St. Paul, Minnesota, Frederick Hertz graduated from Boalt Hall (University of California, Berkeley School of Law, 1981), clerked with the Minnesota Supreme Court (1981-1982), and subsequently received a Master's Degree in Urban Geography from the University of California, Berkeley (1991). He has previously taught Real Property Law in the Paralegal/Legal Studies Program of St. Mary's University, and Small Firm and Solo Practice Management at Golden Gate Law School in San Francisco.

Mr. Hertz writes and speaks nationally on property issues facing unmarried partners. He is the author of *Legal Affairs: Essential Advice for Same-Sex Couples* (Henry Holt & Co./Owl Books, 1998) and co-author of two Nolo Press books: *Legal Guide for Lesbian and Gay Couples* and *Living Together: A Guide for Unmarried Couples*. He has been quoted in *The New York Times*, the *Advocate*, *American Demographics*, *Hero Magazine*, *Kiplingers Magazine*, and the *New York Observer*, and has appeared on NPR's *All Things Considered*, *Sound Money*, and on the *Oprah Winfrey Show* and the *Today Show*. Mr. Hertz's most recent book is *Making It Legal: A Guide to Same-Sex Marriage, Domestic Partnerships & Civil Unions*.

For more information on Mr. Hertz's practice involving lesbian and gay couples, check out his website, www.samesexlaw.com.